WRITING TELEVISION AND RADIO PROGRAMS

WRITING TELEVISION

Edgar E. Willis
The University of Michigan

AND RADIO PROGRAMS

HOLT, RINEHART AND WINSTON, INC.
New York / Chicago / San Francisco / Atlanta
Dallas / Montreal / Toronto / London

WRITING TELEVISION AND RADIO PROGRAMS

Library of Congress Catalog Card Number 67-26165

ISBN 0-03-056075-6

Printed in the United States of America

0 038 09

Acknowledgments

I express my appreciation to the following writers and copyright owners for granting me permission to quote their scripts and other materials in whole or in part:

Don Brinkley for "May God Have Mercy" from The Fugitive series, produced by Alan Armer for QM Productions.

Paddy Chayefsky for excerpts from Television Plays, published by Simon and Schuster, Inc., © 1955.

Norman Corwin for an excerpt from Thirteen by Corwin, published by Henry Holt and Company, © 1942.

James Costigan for "White Gloves," presented on the United States Steel Hour.

Paul Crabtree for "The Pilot," Michael Dyne for "A Tongue of Silver," and William Noble for "Snapfinger Creek," published in Best Television Plays, edited by Florence Britton, © 1957 by Ballantine Books, Inc.

J. P. Miller for "Rabbit Trap," Tad Mosel for "My Lost Saints," and Gore Vidal for "Visit to a Small Planet," published in Best Television Plays, edited by Gore Vidal, © 1956 by Ballantine Books, Inc.

Tad Mosel for excerpts from Other People's Houses, published by Simon and Schuster, Inc., © 1956, and for an excerpt from "The Out-of-Towners," published in Television Plays for Writers, edited by A. S. Burack, by The Writer, Inc., © 1957.

Horton Foote for excerpts from Harrison, Texas, published by Harcourt, Brace & World, Inc., © 1956.

Milton Geiger for "One Special for Doc," © by Milton Geiger, 9515 Vanalden Street, Northridge, California. No use of this material is permitted without arrangement with the author.

George Roy Hill and John Whedon for "A Night to Remember," published in The Prize Plays of Television and Radio 1956 by Random House, Inc. © 1957.

An excerpt from The Vintage Mencken, collected by Alistair Cooke, © 1956 by Alfred A. Knopf, Inc., excerpt quoted by Allan Sloane in his radio play, "Bring on the Angels," published in The Prize Plays of Television and Radio 1956 by Random House, Inc. © 1957.

Archibald MacLeish for "The States Talking," published in The Free Company, edited by James Boyd, by Dodd, Mead and Company, © 1941.

Arch Oboler for an excerpt from Oboler Omnibus, published by Duell, Sloan and Pearce, © 1945.

Carl Reiner for "Where Did I Come From?" from the Dick Van Dyke Show.

Reginald Rose for excerpts from Six Television Plays, published by Simon and Schuster, Inc., © 1956.

Rod Serling for excerpts from Patterns, published by Simon and Schuster, Inc., © 1957.

United Artists Television, Inc. for an excerpt from the Highway Patrol series.

Jack Webb and Sherry TV for an excerpt from the Dragnet series.

An excerpt from The Eternal Light by Morton Wishengrad, © 1947 by Morton Wishengrad. Reprinted by permission of Crown Publishers, Inc.

Excerpts from Humor: Its Theory and Technique by Stephen Leacock, published by Dodd, Mead and Company, © 1935.

Ogden Nash for "Everybody's Mind to Me a Kingdom Is or A Great Big Wonderful World It's." Reprinted by permission of the author. Copyright © 1950 by the Curtis Publishing Company, Inc.

Excerpts by Sherwood Schwartz and George Wells from Off Mike, edited by Jerome Lawrence, published by Duell, Sloan and Pearce, © 1944.

Will Glickman for "The Song and Dance Man," presented on the Bell Telephone Hour by Henry Jaffe Enterprises, Inc.

Ralph Johnson, Patricia Matusky, and Deborah Goodell for music continuities presented on WUOM, The University of Michigan Station in Ann Arbor.

Allan Jackson for a five-minute newscast presented by CBS News and for excerpts from "You Have to Write, Too."

James Benjamin and CBS News for "The Age of Anxiety—Part I," presented on the Twentieth Century.

Excerpts from Monitor—broadcast weekends on NBC Radio.

An excerpt from I've Got a Secret, presented by Telecast Enterprises, Inc.

Frank McGee for "Leg Watching," broadcast on Emphasis by NBC.

ScotTowel Storyboard, courtesy of Scott Paper Company and J. Walter Thompson Company.

Total Commercial, courtesy of General Mills, Inc.

Wyler Commercial, courtesy of Wyler & Company, a Division of the Borden Company, and Compton Advertising.

"Grapefruit Virtues," courtesy of Florida Citrus Commission and Campbell-Ewald Agency.

"Something Special," courtesy of Marathon Oil Company and Campbell-Ewald Agency.

"Number One," courtesy of Chevrolet Motor Division and Campbell-Ewald Agency.

Goodman Ace, Jack Benny, Sid Caesar, Peter DeVries, Phyllis Diller, George Gobel, Jean Kerr, Henry Morgan, and Portland Allen Rines for excerpts from comedy material.

Bill Flemming of ABC Television for material from a sports broadcast.

Eric Sevareid for a talk presented on CBS News.

Preface

The objective of *Writing Television and Radio Programs* is two-pronged: first, to provide practical instruction for those seeking a career in broadcasting; and second, to help guide students enrolled in writing courses for general education purposes toward the achievement of fruitful creative experiences. The principal program types in American radio and television writing are discussed and a chapter on the writing of commercials is also included.

After an opening chapter, which orients the student to the broadcasting industry and the place of the writer in it, the book continues with a consideration of the major forms of dramatic and nondramatic writing. Most chapters concentrate on one or the other, but where it is feasible to treat the creation of certain material in both dramatic and nondramatic forms, the two are considered together, as in the chapters on comedy and writing for children. A separate chapter provides the technical information a writer needs to prepare television and radio scripts. Each chapter ends with questions and projects designed to encourage a review of the main points.

Because the creation of drama is a more complex process than the creation of most nondramatic material, I have devoted a major share of this book to dramatic writing. Separate chapters take up the various aspects of this art as they occur in actual writing, beginning with the creation of the dramatic ideas and following with the techniques used to express these ideas in the pages of a script. After this over-all consideration, the characteristics and problems of special forms of drama are reviewed. The emphasis throughout is on television drama because of the virtual disappearance of the radio play from American commercial stations. Still, the writing of radio drama in college classes can be a valuable exercise and a satisfying creative experience; for this reason, some attention is given to the special techniques required by this form.

Script samples, analyses, and references are used throughout to illustrate principles and techniques of writing. For some of the shorter nondramatic forms, such as music continuities, newscasts, commercials, and feature talks, it has been possible to include complete scripts. The greater length of television plays and the space required to treat the theory and practice of dramatic writing have made it impossible to include complete programs from this field. For this reason I have relied for my illustrations mainly on published scripts. To permit students to read these plays in their entirety, I hope that teachers will be able to make the volumes in which they appear available on a reserve shelf. They are listed in a special section of the bibliography. Yet recognizing that not all students will have access to these volumes and that some of the scripts referred to have not been published, I have tried to make each of the script references and analyses sufficient in itself to establish the point being considered.

I should like to note two ways in which my editorial practices differ somewhat from the traditional. First, I have used italics to distinguish the titles of radio and television series from the titles of programs within series. Program titles appear in quotation marks. Second, to minimize the number of footnotes, I have documented most of my references only in the bibliography; I have used footnotes, however, when two or more references to the same source occur and, occasionally, for other reasons. A few quotations appear without documentation. Long before the writing of this book was contemplated, they were set down without proper bibliographic information in notes accumulated during the twenty years I have been teaching writing for broadcasting. I have included them believing that their substance is valuable even though their exact source is unknown.

In a separate section I have acknowledged the cooperation of those who have permitted me to use material from scripts and other works. Here I should like to take note of others who have contributed. For helping me to assemble some of the material for this book, I express my appreciation to three of my former students who are now pursuing successful careers in broadcasting and film making: Bonnie Buchanan, who has done production and research for NBC's *Monitor* and the *Smithsonian* series; John Rich, first director of the *Dick Van Dyke Show*, and Alan Armer, a producer of *The Fugitive* and *The Invaders* series. Others who have assisted me in a variety of ways are the late Inez Richardson, Stanley Donner, Garnet Garrison, Mary Duncan, Sister Mary Camille, and Elizabeth Wareham. I owe particular thanks to my colleagues Henry Austin, Ben Yablonky, Robert Davis, and Edward Stasheff for their careful reading of portions of this manuscript and for their many perceptive suggestions.

Most of all I am grateful to my wife, Zella, for typing the manuscript and for her helpful comments, which have led to many improvements in both form and content.

E. E. W.

Ann Arbor, Michigan
June 1967

Contents

1

The Writer and Broadcasting

Writing involves a craft that you have to learn and a talent that you must possess. Neither is common and both are essential.   Goethe

The writer who prepares scripts for television and radio programs, first of all, must have talent and training similar in many respects to that required of people who write for other media. In addition, he must respond to the demands that arise from the particular way in which television and radio reach their audiences. Finally, his work is deeply affected by the aims and standards of the industry for which he is writing. In this chapter we examine the art of writing in general and consider the nature of the broadcasting industry.

BROADCASTING'S DEMANDS ON THE WRITER

Must people who write television and radio programs possess special talents not required of writers in other fields? The evidence indicates that no singular capacities are required. Proof of this statement lies in the achievement of many people who have written successfully both for broadcasting and for other media. What matters is the ability to write well, not the medium for which one writes. The individual who can write effectively to begin with can easily learn to adapt his talents to the demands of television and radio. When Archibald MacLeish, already distinguished as a poet, turned to radio, his poetic dramas were almost immediately accepted as classics. Walter Cronkite and Harry Reasoner first established their reputations as newspapermen before going on to distinguished careers in broadcast journalism. Movement in the reverse direction also establishes the principle that what counts is writing ability per se. Robert Bolt was a successful radio dramatist before he wrote such works for the stage and screen as *A Man for All Seasons, Lawrence of Arabia,* and *Dr. Zhivago.*

These examples suggest, as a matter of fact, that television and radio, rather than being fields with special identities and demands of their own, actually encompass a number of different fields which do have separate identities and impose unique requirements. A person who can compose a satisfactory newscast cannot necessarily write an acceptable drama. This situation is true of writing in general. Ernest Hemingway was an outstanding novelist and short story writer, but he was not successful as a dramatist. To reverse the coin, George Bernard Shaw's novels are now forgotten; only when he turned to drama did he find the vehicle that made his name live. Persons skilled in a particular type of writing may apply that special skill in a number of media. Paddy Chayefsky and Frank D. Gilroy should be thought of primarily as dramatists who mastered their art in television and then applied it successfully to the stage and screen. Writers specializing in comedy may write it for television, the movies, the stage, night clubs, or even for a comedian's after-dinner speech. The television news analyst may also write a newspaper column. A copywriter may devise advertisements that can be adapted to both print and broadcast media. A person who studies the art of writing for broadcasting, then, is primarily engaged in studying the writing of a particular form—such as drama, advertising, documentaries, news, and comedy. Learning to adapt that form for television or radio presentation is an important part of his task, but it is no more important than the task of mastering the form itself.

INNATE TALENTS OF THE WRITER

It is commonly said that writers are born not made and that writing cannot be taught. This statement rests on the assumption that to be a writer one must have already within him certain innate talents. It does seem to be true that instruction cannot bring certain necessary talents into being, although it can nurture them if they do exist. Let us begin, then, by considering what capacities an aspiring writer must bring with him to his teacher. These capacities will differ, of course, according to the type of writing the student plans to do.

SOMETHING TO WRITE ABOUT.   An obvious necessity for a writer is material on which to base his work. The immediate inspiration for the beginner is usually his own experience, and an essential is the capacity to live deeply. He cannot afford to let experience merely wash over him. It must mark him with indelible imprints. But to provide all of the substance required for writing, his observation must reach beyond the bounds of immediate reality. The writer needs a native curiosity that will lead him to gain a sense of what Taine called "the moral temperature of his times" and an understanding of the world that existed before his own day. Only in this way can he gain the sensitivity to the present and the sense of the past that are necessary to measure the relevance of his own experiences. To put it another way, he must have the capacity to escape the limits of his own background, for one who relies entirely on his personal experience soon exhausts his resources and becomes shallow and monotonous. Moreover, even works that find their main inspiration in the life of the writer must reflect faithfully the personalities and experiences of others involved in the story, people whose passions and ways of life may be utterly alien to his own. For the dramatist, the ability to project into other lives is an essential.

LANGUAGE FACILITY.   A writer's tools are words and he must have a special way with them. Clarity and precision in word choice, for example, are essential for the news writer who must describe events accurately. This skill can be sharpened with instruction, but some innate feel for language is necessary. Another basic requirement for every writer is the ability to see on his own what hangs together and what does not and to recognize whether or not the material he writes at any given moment stems from what he has just written and leads directly into what he is about to write. Only if he has this capacity of self-criticism, will his work have unity and coherence, qualities especially important to the documentary writer, who must analyze a problem and handle its treatment with clarity and logic. The writer for broadcasting must be particularly sensitive to the sound of spoken language. "Word deafness" may be a handicap to a novelist, but in a television or radio writer it is a fatal flaw. If a person lacks this sensitivity, no teacher can give it to him.

THE ABILITY TO CREATE.   Experience and knowledge make a major contribution to a writer's work, but most forms require the writer to create something that never existed before. If he is to bring new ideas into being, he must be gifted with native inventiveness. The commercial writer needs it to find a new way of presenting an old appeal. The documentary writer needs it to devise a framework for presenting factual material in an interesting way. The dramatist needs it to work his way out of plotting cul-de-sacs which might prevent a story from flowing credibly and inevitably to its end. The task of bringing new characters into being requires, in addition, the gift of creative imagination. These characters may reflect real persons but if that is all they do, the dramatist has failed to move beyond the achievement of mere versimilitude. The most satisfying characters emerge when reality is enriched with imagination. The ability to recombine and modify familiar elements into something that never existed before cannot be created by instruction. It must be there when instruction begins.

THE CAPACITY TO RE-EXPERIENCE.   Writers must have good memories, and there are some who have displayed a gift of almost total recall, but the mere recollection of events is not enough. If a writer is to infuse his work with the vibrations of actual existence, he must be able to live through experiences again. Many people can recite accurately the facts of a past event, but only a few have the ability to bring back those facts clothed with the emotions and sensations they originally aroused. The writer of comedy must add to this talent the knack of seeing people and events from a unique point of view.

STORYTELLING.   The ability to tell a good story is of crucial importance in creating drama and some types of documentaries. The great dramatists seem to know instinctively how to grip the attention of an audience from the first moment and hold it to the end. Instruction can provide a writer with some knowledge of the techniques involved in the art of storytelling, but much of this understanding must come to him naturally.

SELF-EVALUATION.   The practice of writing is a lonely art and loneliness seems particularly to be the fate of the broadcast writer, one he shares with poets and novelists, who rarely see the reactions of the audience that receives their work. In most instances the radio-television writer has access only to the reactions of those who put on the program and their judgement, like his, may be warped by this participation. The broadcast writer needs a generous gift of self-criticism to be able independently to measure the reach of his accomplishment. The ability to maintain a fresh and objective eye for something as personal as a piece of writing, into which one may have poured his whole being, is not a common one. A person fired with dedication and commitment may easily confuse the high purpose he set out to achieve with what he has actually written.

ACQUIRED SKILLS OF THE WRITER

The argument that writing cannot be taught seems to imply that it is impossible to acquire any writing skills at all. It is axiomatic, of course, that a teacher cannot give a person the innate gifts we have just considered, but it seems equally clear that certain requirements can be acquired through instruction. A student cannot learn to be inventive, but he can learn how to apply what gift he does possess. He can learn the lore and disciplines of the medium; he can be taught how to adapt to broadcasting's demands; he can discover the ways in which a particular idea may be framed for presentation on radio or television. In this way the potentialities he possesses can be exploited and developed. Knowledge of the principles involved in such functions as designing plays, selecting items for a newscast, persuading people to buy products, or motivating laughter can also provide the student with criteria for evaluating his own work. The result may be that he flounders less in error and spends more time in rewarding trial. Most important of all, a teacher can be a writer's first audience, providing the feedback that lets him know that he is either on target or has completely missed the mark.

D. H. Lawrence's statement regarding the novel that "all rules of construction hold good only for novels which are copies of other novels," seems to be true only in part. There is need, at the very least, for criteria that give the various forms of writing their shape and identity. And while the writer's skill is still untested and unproved, it may be dangerous to disregard practices that experience has shown are effective. Some rules are made to be broken, perhaps, but not by beginners.

Still, the study of writing may have its dangers. Young writers desperately seeking guidance may assume that there are certain techniques and formulas that can be used in script after script. Such an assumption may carry them into prescribed channels which repress their imaginative powers and limit their capacity to find new ways of expressing ideas. Principles should not become frozen into detailed procedures which become so inflexible that they enclose and stultify. The beginning writer can use the patterns of the past as reference points, but in the end he must try, not to write like someone else, but to write in his own individual way.

THE NATURE OF THE INDUSTRY

A writer, no matter what his medium, must respond to requirements that have nothing to do with artistic achievement, requirements that may, in fact, prevent him from realizing his full creative potentialities. The major influence as far as broadcasting is concerned is that most of the scripts the writer turns out have only a secondary role: they exist merely for the purpose of attracting an audience so that the program can accomplish its primary goal of selling goods. Other conditions affecting his work are the regulation that stations must operate in the public's interest and the fact that programs are heard in people's homes, often entering unbidden on the heels of other programs. The audience, moreover, is very diverse, containing people of widely different ages, classes, occupations, and races.

RESTRICTIONS ON WRITERS

The conditions under which programs are received give television and radio a unique intimacy, and dictate a certain reserve in the material that can be presented. Another inescapable condition is that broadcasting, dominated as it is by the advertiser, will usually seek the largest possible audience. This means that the audience's preferences for programs, as they are made explicit in ratings, will largely determine the life and death of programs. In addition to the restrictions that are inherent in these conditions, there are a number of specific restrictions that control the work of the writer.

OFFENSIVE MATERIAL. It is obvious that material offensive to public decency and morals cannot be presented. The Federal Communications Act and the codes created by the industry contain specific prohibitions against broadcasting material that is indecent, profane, or obscene. Unfortunately, these words, although they seem to be specific in tone, are actually vague terms subject to varying interpretations. The expression "Holy Cow" was once cut from a radio script and a broadcaster even went so far as to eliminate the line "Out damned spot" from a radio production of *Macbeth*. The climate is now somewhat more liberal to the extent that the words "damn" and "hell" may be used occasionally if their use can be justified by the dramatic demands of the script. There is still great concern about shocking the public, however, particularly on the part of the advertiser, for he feels that an offended viewer is less likely to become a purchaser than one who is happy and satisfied with a program.

Another type of material the writer must avoid is that which reflects unfavorably on certain people or products. News writers must be careful to avoid libelous material. Writers of commercials cannot directly disparage competing products. People are particularly sensitive about humor directed at their race, their occupation, or their social class. It is a fact of human psychology, which writers must accept, that people enjoy jokes on other people, but not jokes on themselves. Another point of exceptionally tender sensitivity is the identity of the character who has the villain's role in a drama, especially if he is a member of a minority group. It has become almost an axiom in American television that the villain, if he is identified at all, must be a white, native-born, Protestant American, who belongs to no particular occupational class.

CONTROVERSIAL ISSUES. Because a program exists primarily to sell goods, its capacity to enrich the hearts and minds of its viewers tends to be a secondary consideration. If a play incorporates an honest statement about life that in the advertiser's view may inhibit the sale of his products, the honest statement must usually be sacrificed. The result is that plays dealing with controversial public issues are likely to be banned or modified because of their potentialities for offending certain members of an audience. The sponsor of Reginald Rose's script, "Thunder on Sycamore Street," written originally to dramatize a case of discrimination against a Negro, forced the writer to transform the Negro into a white exconvict. Advertisers are somewhat more willing to sponsor documentaries dealing with controversial issues because the aim of a documentary is to present the truth of a situation objectively, but the dramatist colors the presentation of events with emotion and imagination, and sponsors are reluctant to risk the arousal of passion entailed by such treatment.

PRODUCT SENSITIVITIES. Sponsors sometimes exercise taboos that have no relationship to audience values or standards but concern rather the sensitivities of the sponsor himself. Most of these taboos are related to the product he sells. Sponsors, in the first place, are anxious to avoid giving any free advertising to products competing with their own. This policy seems reasonable enough, but its execution has occasionally reached the point of absurdity. The TV dramatist, Rod Serling, said that he was asked to replace the words "American" and "lucky" in a script with the words "United States" and "fortunate" because the program was being sponsored by a cigarette company that did not wish to remind its audience of either the American Tobacco Company or its cigarette, Lucky Strike.

Sponsors also censor material that will reflect in any way on the product being advertised. The classic example of sponsor interference for this reason took place in the *Playhouse 90* production of "Judgment at Nuremberg" when the reference to a gas chamber as a means of liquidating Jews was cut from the script because one of the sponsors, the American Gas Company, feared the possible mental association with its product. Another example of sponsor sensitivity regarding its product occurred when the Westinghouse Company, one of the nation's leading manufacturers of light bulbs, in producing an adaptation of Rudyard Kipling's *The Light that Failed*, changed the title to "The Gathering Night." In another program the line "She eats too much anyway" was cut because the sponsor, a manufacturer of breakfast food, took the attitude that nobody eats too much.

THE TV AND RADIO CODES.   The broadcasting industry has drawn up codes that govern the practices of those program producers who express their willingness to abide by them. A review of these codes reveals, however, that they are limited in the guidance they provide a writer regarding what is acceptable program material.[1] Most of the regulations are worded in general terms that permit varying interpretations. An example is the prohibition in the TV code against "the use of horror for its own sake." A writer seeking to observe this restriction must first decide what "horror" is and then determine whether he is using it "for its own sake."

What the codes do is to reflect in a general way what society as a whole considers to be acceptable program material. A normally alert individual should know what these standards are, but a perusal of the codes will remind him of the danger areas. In addition networks and many stations have formulated their own codes of permissible practices, which, though generally compatible with the National Association of Broadcasters' code, often go further in spelling out policy in specific situations.

THE EFFECTS OF RESTRICTIONS

Of all writers, these restrictions are most likely to affect the work of the dramatist. It is easy to let such limitations make one angry and frustrated, but before letting his temper flare, the writer should consider for a moment the side of the sponsors. Many spend millions of dollars a year to pay for television programs, and their prime object is to foster sales. Is it unreasonable that a sponsor would try to eliminate from

---

[1] The Complete TV code is printed in Giraud Chester, Garnet R. Garrison, and Edgar E. Willis, *Television and Radio*, 3rd ed. (New York: Appleton-Century-Crofts, 1963), pp. 138–150.

his program anything that might drive viewers from buying his product?

A writer cannot escape, either, the fact that television and radio are mass media paid for mainly by advertisers who want the largest possible audience to hear their commercials. Only a change in the method of support can alter this situation, and no such change is imminent. A writer who cannot accept the fact that his material must attract mass audiences should seek another medium. Finally, it should be recognized that with many stations on the air eighteen hours a day, mediocrity in some instances is inevitable. Much of television serves, as Jack Paar has said, simply "to provide chewing gum for eyeballs."

These generalizations aside, it is still important to consider whether the restrictions of broadcasting permit the production of significant work. The writer who has complained most loudly and most continually about the restrictions imposed by sponsors is Rod Serling. Paddy Chayefsky has expressed similar views. In an interview he said, "Everyone of us before we sit down and write a television show, makes that initial compromise of what we're going to write. We don't . . . conceive a television idea that we know is going to be thrown out the window. That's the compromise. I have never, never, written down in television in my life, but I never aimed very high."[2]

Does this mean that television must be a medium in which, as someone has said, the bland leads the bland in an endless parade across the television screen. Perhaps the best refutation of this depressing view is the work of Serling and Chayefsky. It is generally recognized that, despite the restrictions under which they chafe, they have produced profoundly significant work. Chayefsky's "Marty" is now regarded as a classic. Serling complained specifically about the changes that sponsorship interference forced in his script "Noon on Doomsday," planned originally as a dramatic case study of a southern lynching. The sponsor demanded that he convert the southern setting into a vague New England environment and he was even forbidden to have any character drink Coca-Cola for fear that it might suggest the south. There is no doubt that these restrictions would be deeply disturbing to a writer, particularly the one regarding Coca-Cola because it is so patently ridiculous, yet in spite of them Serling in "Noon on Doomsday" created a striking human document about a senseless killing.

That the effect of restrictions may be overemphasized is indicated by a statement of Reginald Rose, writer and editor of *The Defenders* series. He conceded that petty restrictions annoy him as an artist, but added that "in a larger sense they are completely unimportant. When a major character in a drama is making a crucial decision between

[2] Quoted in Marya Mannes, "The Captive Writer," *The Reporter*, Vol. 21 (August 20, 1959), p. 32.

good or evil, the fact that he's drinking tea (instead of coffee because the sponsor sells tea) makes no difference to me." Rose even refused to complain that being forced by the sponsor to turn a Negro into an exconvict in his drama on the discrimination issue, "Thunder on Sycamore Street," made a fundamental difference to his play, saying: "The moral issue was identical. I did not compromise on the principle in the least."[3]

It should be noted also that delicate subjects are not entirely banned from the television scene even in dramas. "The Days of Wine and Roses," a searing study of alcoholism, was first produced as a television play. Reginald Rose wrote a two-part dramatization of the Sacco-Vanzetti case, one of the most controversial in American annals, and the series he edited, *The Defenders*, once presented a defense of an abortionist. It would be difficult to be more controversial than that. Even the long-standing taboo against the use of suicide to extricate a character from a dilemma was breached without arousing audience protests by TV adaptations of Arthur Miller's *Death of a Salesman* and Katherine Anne Porter's short story, "Noon Wine."

Occasionally, a resourceful writer may contrive a way of obeying a restriction without significantly changing that part of his work which conflicts with it. One of the strictest requirements in broadcasting is that people must be punished for their crimes, yet a number of the stories on the *Alfred Hitchcock* series revolved entirely around the way a criminal cleverly avoided detection. Hitchcock nodded in the direction of the taboo by appearing after the play was over to let the audience know that eventually the criminal was caught and punished. Devices that provide escape hatches from other restrictions may occur to ingenious writers.

A further point to remember is that restrictions existing during one year may vanish in another. The trade journal, *Television Age*, pointed out that "a writer who for years went around with a brief case full of westerns that no one would buy got rich overnight with the advent of *Gunsmoke*." For a long time sponsors believed that TV scripts involving medical problems would be offensive to the public and there was a special restriction against dramas involving mental illness. Then *Ben Casey* and *Dr. Kildare* appeared triumphantly on the scene followed soon after by *The Eleventh Hour*, a series that dealt specifically with mental health problems. The lesson is that scripts violating present taboos should not be angrily burned but should be put away for possible future use. As *Television Age* said, "Yesterday's anathema may be tomorrow's plethora."

---

[3] Quoted in Edith Efron, "Can a TV Writer Keep His Integrity?," *TV Guide*, Vol. 10 (April 21, 1962), p. 9.

THE EMPLOYMENT OF WRITERS

The writing of scripts for television and radio involves more than a challenge to the creative faculties. There are some practical considerations which must be taken into account, such matters as the nature of employment, pay, and the perplexing problem of getting started as a writer.

CLASSES OF EMPLOYMENT

Writers who are permanently attached to the staff of a broadcasting organization and are paid on a regular weekly or monthly basis instead of being paid per script are known as *staff writers*. They are the ones who turn out most of the newscasts, commercials, and general continuities broadcast by networks and stations. At the other end of the spectrum is the *free-lance writer*, who has no connection with a broadcasting organization and no assurance that a script on which he may have spent many hours of work will find a market. He is paid only if the script he submits to a station, network, production organization, or advertising agency is accepted. Free-lance writers often work at other occupations because the sale of scripts is too irregular to earn them a living and, for some, writing is merely a hobby.

A writer who secures a contract to do a particular piece of writing is known as a *commissioned writer*. Like the free-lance writer, he is paid by the script but, like the staff writer, he is assured that once designated to do a particular piece of writing, he will be paid for his work even if it is never broadcast. Most writers of this type receive their commissions on the basis of story ideas or outlines submitted to a script editor. The producers of a regular series try to assemble a stable of five or six dependable writers who turn out all the scripts for the series. Occasionally a free-lance writer may submit a script for use in a regular series, but the rate of acceptance is very low. Commissioned writers, like free-lance writers, may create scripts as a side line. One of the regular contributors to the *Dr. Kildare* and *The Man from U.N.C.L.E.* series, Jerry McNeely, pursued a full-time career as a professor at the University of Wisconsin.

THE PAY OF WRITERS

A topic of absorbing interest to young writers is the amount of money that can be earned in broadcasting, and yet it is one of the most difficult subjects on which to make generalizations. Of the three classes of writers just discussed, the staff writer is likely to receive the least amount of money per page but he has the advantage of being on a regular salary. The size of this salary is related to the size of the market area in which he works. A news or continuity writer in a small community may earn less than a hundred dollars a week whereas in a major city his salary may be several times that amount. Staff writers for networks and national advertising and production agencies usually earn the highest incomes. The annual earnings of a skilled advertising copywriter who works for a national agency may even approach the six-figure mark. The commissioned writer, by virtue of the reputation that caused him to be commissioned, is likely to receive the most money per page of script. The free-lance writer will not receive as much money per page as the commissioned writer, but he may receive more than the staff writer. In total income from writing, however, he may fall below the staff writer because he may sell only an occasional script.

The Writers' Guild of America, in contracts arranged with national broadcasting organizations, has established minimum fees which vary with the length and nature of the script. Established writers, of course, are paid more than the minimum; a few have received as much as $25,000 for a single script. The current going rate for an hour script for a series is generally between $3500 and $5000. Going rates tend to be two to three times minimum and reflect the bargaining strength of an established writer.

The income from a given script, of course, may not be restricted to that received for a single broadcast. If the program is repeated, the writer receives additional payment according to terms established by the Writers' Guild. A further source of income may be the adaptation of an original script into a movie or stage version. Success in writing may also be a stepping stone toward other positions in broadcasting which pay even better than writing. Rod Serling's income rose perceptibly when he became the producer and narrator of his own series, the *Twilight Zone,* and Reginald Rose markedly improved his financial position when he created and edited *The Defenders* series. In addition, TV writers frequently move on to lucrative careers writing for the stage or movies.

PROTECTING THE WRITER'S INTERESTS

Writers have sometimes been exploited by unscrupulous producers, the violations of rights having ranged from the outright theft of ideas or scripts to inadequate compensation for scripts or no payment at all for their reuse. The Writers' Guild of America was organized to establish a set of rules for protecting writers' interests, and it now has contracts with the major radio and television networks, film companies, and production agencies. Membership in the Guild is open to those who have written one TV script or have a commission to do so, and writers are expected to join the Guild within thirty days after their employment begins.

The Writers' Guild has numerous contracts for newswriters, writers of commercials, and so on. Each varies in clauses and resulting length. For instance the current contract for narrative scripts, made up of 100 single-spaced pages, is much too bulky a document to cover in detail, but a listing of some of its major points will indicate the types of conditions it treats. Reference has already been made to the regulations that establish minimum fees for scripts and payment for their reuse. Among other matters, the Guild contract prohibits employers from inviting writers to submit scripts on speculation, a system under which the writer is paid only if the script turns out to be satisfactory in the employer's eyes. A commissioned script for live or taped production must be used within a specified time after its delivery or the writer is free to sell it elsewhere even though he has been paid for the script by the producer who commissioned it. The Guild contract also contains references to the nature of the writer's credits, the requirements for rewriting the original submission, the payment of traveling expenses, the writer's privilege of attending rehearsals, the conditions affecting collaboration, and the rights of the producer and the writer in the sale of the script for subsidiary uses.

GETTING STARTED AS A WRITER

If the first question of an aspiring writer is: "How much do writers get paid for scripts?" the second is: "How do I get started as a writer?" Both questions are equally difficult to answer. There is, in fact, no well-defined route to a career as a writer for broadcasting. In a sense the individual who seeks a position as a staff writer has the easiest task. As in the news field, the potential staff writer applies to the head of the script department or to a director of the specific programs for which he wishes to write. Usually, he must call or write for an appointment, send or bring a résumé of his work, and be prepared to audition. This audition generally involves a five-minute on-the-spot writing of a given type of material—news, dialogue, commercial, and so on. A potential staff-writer, of course, would come prepared to present samples of his work. The route to employment for the free-lance or commissioned writer is not quite so obvious, however.

SUBMITTING SCRIPTS BY MAIL

An obvious means for a writer to reach the producer of programs would seem to be by mail, but gaining access in this way has now become virtually impossible. The problem is that producers usually refuse to open envelopes containing scripts from unknown writers. They fear that even if they find the script completely unacceptable and return it, they will be sued later for filching the idea and using it in a script prepared by another writer. It is true that ideas and even scripts actually have been appropriated by producers in the past, and on occasion the courts have awarded the injured writer substantial damages. It is equally true, however, that two people may think of similar ideas at the same time, and the appearance of two scripts with the same basic premise does not necessarily indicate that one writer has stolen his idea from the other. Establishing the ownership and originality of ideas is one of the most difficult of legal problems, and most producers try to avoid becoming caught in courtroom tangles by simply refusing to look at scripts submitted by strangers.

Does this mean that you would be completely wasting your time to send an unsolicited script through the mail? Usually you would be, but there are still occasions when producers will look at a free-lance offering. Despite the difficulties of breaking through the producer's barriers, some forty to fifty writers succeed every year in having a script accepted for the first time, and some of these acceptances are gained through mailed submissions. If you do decide to mail a script to a producer, there are two things you should do. First, include a summary or outline of its contents, about ten pages in length for an hour show, to permit the producer to evaluate your work without having to read the entire script. Second, request a release form from the organization to which you plan to make your submission, sign it, and send it with your script. By signing this form you certify that the script is your own original work and you acknowledge that two or more people may get the same idea at the same time and that the appearance of a script at a later date embodying your idea does not necessarily indicate that the idea has been stolen from you. The submission of a release does not grant the producer permission to use ideas without compensation; however, if you become convinced that your idea has been appropriated, you still have recourse through the courts.

PERSONAL SUBMISSIONS

Most new writers gain access to a producer through some form of personal contact which is possible because they are working in the production organization. First scripts are often brought to a producer's desk by the boy in the mailroom, by the extra who is appearing in the productions, or by the stenographer who types someone else's scripts. Occasionally, contact can be made through an intermediary who works in the organization; cousins, uncles, and brothers have paved the way to production for relatives outside the organization. An agent may help but he is likely to be interested in working only for writers who have already proved that they possess professional skill. But the best way for an aspiring writer to get his scripts considered is to find employment with a network, a film company, or a production agency.

In addition to making contact with script editors and producers easier, employment in a production organization is important to a writer for two other reasons. First of all, it gives him the opportunity to gain general knowledge of broadcasting and to learn specifically about the particular needs and idiosyncrasies of the company he works for. Second, if his script is accepted, he will be available, as writers are often expected to be, to participate in the rewriting process that goes on during rehearsal.

MARKETS OUTSIDE THE UNITED STATES

Most people are likely to consider that the United States offers the only outlet for a broadcast writer's work, but the other English-speaking countries of the world also offer markets. Radio drama is still produced in Canada and Great Britain and Americans sometimes write for these programs. Americans also write for Canadian and for British television. One British TV series, *Armchair Theatre,* during a single year featured the work of twenty American writers.

GETTING DOWN TO WRITING

If you are going to have scripts to submit, you must first write them. This is a process that includes more than the time you spend at your desk putting words on paper. The initial step is the moment of inspiration followed by a period of reflection and research. Next must come the specific planning of the script. The writing follows and after that comes a period of rewriting when you polish your work to the finest sheen of which you are capable.

GETTING STARTED

One of the most difficult challenges a writer faces is reaching that point when he actually starts to put words on paper. It is said that Ernest Hemingway postponed the awful moment by sharpening as many as twenty pencils before finally taking one in hand to write. By constantly putting off the act of writing, it is possible to imagine for a whole lifetime that one is a writer without ever putting down a word. How can you get started? Most professional writers emphasize that one of the best ways of warming up the creative machinery is to apply yourself regularly to the task of writing. Do not wait for inspiration. As Guy de Maupassant said: "Get black on white—get down to work." Sitting down in front of a typewriter is the act that for some people starts their imagination working.

Once started it is important to keep writing for a certain period each day and to keep at a given writing project until it is completed. The warm-up period you need to get words flowing will be wasted if you do not continue writing for a considerable period of time. How long you spend writing at any one time is a matter to be decided, of course, by your individual bent. The important thing is to write regularly and for sustained periods of time.

METHODS OF WRITING

Writers differ so greatly in the way they write that it is impossible to draw conclusions about the best practices. Some compose at great speed and turn out a prodigious amount of work in a short time. The novelist Georges Simonen has completed a novel in as little as eleven days, and he revises very slightly.

Other writers, in contrast, find that rapid composition is impossible for them, and they must perfect each sentence and then each page before they proceed. The constant revisers are those who tend to hate what they write because it falls so short of their expectations; for them every word constitutes a drop of their life's blood. James Thurber sometimes spent 2,000 hours perfecting a single short story and he once poured out a total of 240,000 words in various drafts for a story that in its final form totaled no more than 20,000 words.[4] Some writers find that the best approach is to get something on paper as quickly as possible and then polish the result through cutting and revision.

Writing is hard, hard work. The act of putting words on paper is arduous in itself, but a writer does not finish working simply because he leaves his desk. He may continue to wrestle for hours with a problem in plotting; he is constantly alert to soak up the impressions that can enrich his work; he is always watching for the idea or event that may be the root of a new script. The glazed look one frequently sees in the eyes of writers involved in social situations reveals that they have

[4] Malcolm Cowley, "How Writers Write," *Saturday Review,* Vol. 40 (November 17, 1957), pp. 12–13.

deserted the immediate world of cocktails, chatter, and laughter for a world of their own creation. What is the reward for all this hard work? For a few it brings some fortune and a little fame, but the majority who aspire to a writing career are doomed to insecurity, frustration, and anonymity. Yet many make the try year after year. Rod Serling in his book of plays, *Patterns*, explains how this can happen: "Writing is a demanding profession and a selfish one. And because it is selfish and demanding, because it is compulsive and exciting, I didn't embrace it. I succumbed to it."[5]

QUESTIONS AND PROJECTS

1. Does drama need to reflect the social and political issues of the day to be pertinent and vigorous?

2. Do the restrictions that characterize television and the desires of advertisers to reach mass audiences constitute severe limitations on your creative achievement as a writer?

3. Compare and contrast the innate talents needed by a news, commercial, or continuity writer with those needed by a dramatic writer. Evaluate your own potentialities in these terms.

4. List the specific proficiencies you hope to gain as a result of taking a course in television and radio writing.

5. Examine your practices as a writer. Devise procedures for planning, getting started at writing, maintaining progress, revision, and evaluation that will lead to your optimum achievement as a writer.

6. John O'Hara once said that it would be better for a person who hoped to be a writer to go to sea for four years than to spend that amount of time in college. What is your reaction to that statement?

[5] Rod Serling, *Patterns* (New York: Simon and Schuster, Inc., 1957), p. 2.

2

The Nature of Drama

Two things can lick a play. One is that the audience doesn't believe it, and the other is that they don't care. Howard Lindsay

Drama is similar in some ways to other literary forms that tell a story, but in certain other respects it is quite different. There are also variations in the nature of drama depending on the medium in which it is presented. These characteristics and distinctions, particularly as they apply to broadcast drama, are the main concern of this chapter. Some suggestions for the would-be dramatist who needs guidance in finding, developing, and evaluating ideas for plays are also included.

DRAMA AS A STORYTELLING FORM

When a writer sets out to tell a story, there are certain requirements he must fulfill if he is to be successful. These requirements apply whether his medium is the short story, the novel, the drama, or some other form. Let us consider these requirements now with special reference to the drama.

AUDIENCE INTEREST

Kenneth Tynan, in his collection of critical pieces, *Curtains,* said that a play "is basically a means of spending two hours in the dark without being bored." This statement suggests that one of the inescapable requirements of a drama is that it interest some kind of audience. It is not always necessary to attract the multitudes, for there is the *succès d'estime* that wins the plaudits of a small but perceptive group of people, but a play must reach to some degree beyond the dramatist's own peculiar concerns. Audience interest has played a major role in establishing the enduring place of works that we now accept as classics. The great plays of writers like Sophocles, Molière, and Shakespeare have attained their particular distinction because, having won audiences in their own day, they have continued to win them down through the centuries. They became classics simply because people keep wanting to see them.

The arousal and maintenance of audience interest is as important to the television writer as it is to any other dramatist, but admittedly it is much more difficult to measure than in a theatre where box-office receipts and the responses of a visible audience provide immediately accessible evidence of interest. Because the audience for a broadcast drama is broken up into small units that are widely separated, we have to depend on the crude measure of an audience rating to estimate interest, and even this inadequate measure usually reflects the popularity of an entire series rather than the attraction of a specific program, which may be what we are particularly interested in. The reaction of critics can provide an index to the success of those plays that are actually reviewed, but they are only a small proportion of the total number broadcast.

There have been occasions, of course, when audience approval of a play has been reflected in a flood of letters. This type of response to Rod Serling's "Patterns" propelled that playwright overnight into the front rank of TV dramatists. Such striking evidence of public interest is unfortunately rare. The success of a television play is usually evaluated by the small group of people who work on the production, but their involvement is likely to deprive them of the essential grace of objectivity. The reactions of those who really count, the people sitting in their homes who may have been absorbed throughout the play or have disgustedly switched it off, are unfortunately unknown.

APPEAL TO THE EMOTIONS

Some people have a tendency to equate dialogue with drama, but not everything written in dialogue is drama as an examination of Plato's

Dialogues will reveal. There are a number of differences between his works and those we identify as drama, but the principal one is that Plato made his primary appeal to the intellect and the dramatist makes his primary appeal to the emotions. He may present ideas, of course, but his basic emphasis must be on the arousal of feeling. A number of writers have stressed this point. The play and screen writer, John Osborne, said in reference to his own work: "I want to make people feel. They can think afterwards." Paddy Chayefsky expressed a similar view when he said; "Don't ever make the basic line the social comment of your script. Drama is concerned only with emotions."[1]

INTEREST AND EMOTIONS.   Not only is the arousal of emotion the heart of drama, but it can also contribute to gaining and holding the interest of the audience. The power of emotion to generate interest can be seen when we look into avenues of life other than the drama. People flock in large numbers to see a circus. Why? There is spectacle, of course— colorful parades, a constant change and flow of events—and there are feats of endurance and accomplishments that seem to defy natural laws. All of these have the power to hold attention. When, however, do the viewers grow most silent and expectant? It is when the animal trainer enters a cage of snarling beasts or the tightrope walker defies death as he treads a precarious path far above the heads of the crowd. Now the viewers are not merely attentive, they are enthralled. To their interest in the circus as a spectacle has been added something else: *concern.* They see a human being apparently facing death. Anxiety stirs within them. They are worried about the outcome. Their interest has reached its apex because now their emotions are involved. In the same way the dramatist's best means of breaking down a viewer's detachment is to stir his emotions as soon as possible and keep them stirred through- out the play.

TYPES OF EMOTIONAL RESPONSE.   The emotions aroused by drama can be of various kinds. Sometimes a viewer may share the feelings that overwhelm a character in a play. A mother loses her child. We experi- ence in some measure the shock of her bereavement. We may shake with the anger that convulses a character, tremble with him as danger approaches, or share his exultation in victory. This direct, personal identi- fication with the emotion of a character is called *empathy.* A dramatist who can arouse this response in his viewers has found the most powerful means of exciting and sustaining interest.

Sometimes a dramatist cannot cause an audience to feel what his

[1] Paddy Chayefsky, *Television Plays* (New York: Simon and Schuster, Inc., 1955), p. 83.

characters feel but he can create concern for them. This is called *sympathy*. To make the members of an audience anxious about a character's welfare is a guarantee of interest. Kenneth MacGowan argued that, the chief purpose of drama, so far as technique is concerned, is to make an audience worry.[2]

Creating a character for the audience to detest can also arouse interest. In this case the emotion the dramatist arouses is not sympathy at all but hostility. The pioneer screen villain, Eric Von Stroheim, described as "the man you love to hate," entranced audiences with the prospect and hope of his eventual downfall. Scorn for a character can also induce interest as, for example, the distaste we experience for the weakling who, under the stress of fear, turns and runs from his duty. Sometimes our emotional response is simply one of laughter. Characters in comedies frequently endure the most agonizing experiences, but their problems are presented in such a way that what results is merely ludicrous. We cannot empathize with their feelings or even sympathize with them, but our laughter is the evidence of our interest.

THE PLACE OF CONFLICT.   The one best way for a dramatist to arouse an emotional response is to present people torn by problems and twisted by conflict. We might wish for a real world in which all problems are solved, but such a world can never be the province of the dramatist. Untroubled people have no power to arouse the emotion of an audience.

The essential role of conflict in drama seems self-evident and yet a number of authorities have questioned whether it is absolutely necessary. One of these is William Archer who said in his book, *Play-Making*, "Conflict is one of the most dramatic elements in life . . . but it is clearly an error to make conflict indispensable to drama."[3] To support this view, he cited the balcony scene in *Romeo and Juliet*, which he said presents "not a clash, but an ecstatic concordance, of wills." It is true that this particular scene lacks conflict, but few would argue that conflict must be present in every scene of a drama. It is sufficient that it exist in the pattern of the play as a whole. This condition is met by *Romeo and Juliet*, for as an entire work it is replete with conflict. Is it not, in fact, the knowledge of the bitter feud between the respective families of the young lovers that gives the balcony scene its special poignancy? The whole meeting is shadowed by conflict and actual conflict follows soon.

Instead of accepting conflict as an indispensable element, Archer put

---

[2] Kenneth MacGowan, *A Primer of Playwriting* (New York: Random House, Inc., 1951), p. 116.

[3] William Archer, *Play-Making* (Boston: Small, Maynard and Company, 1912). The discussion on this point occurs on pp. 31–36.

his emphasis on another quality. "The essence of drama is crisis," he said. It is difficult to conceive of a crisis developing, however, without some kind of conflict in the background. Perhaps it is fruitless to worry this point further considering that even those who deny the absolute necessity of conflict in drama still recognize that it pervades most drama. Even Archer pointed out that certain plays would have been stronger if there had been a greater obstacle between the characters and the realization of their will. Was he not saying, in effect, that these plays would have been better if there had been more conflict?

It is difficult to visualize a drama completely devoid of conflict. It need not occur in every scene but it must have a significant place in the structure of the play as a whole. It is even possible to conceive of a play that begins after all of the actual conflict is over, but even though existing only in retrospect, it remains a vital element in arousing the emotions of the audience. The conflict in a drama may vary greatly in intensity and it may appear in many different forms, but it must always be there.

TYPES OF CONFLICT. What are the various types of conflicts? It is conventional to categorize them as conflicts of man against man, man against a group, a group against a group, and a man or a group against a natural force or obstacle. This list neglects the type of conflict that is most likely to move an audience—the spectacle of a man confronted by two or more courses of action who tries to make a decision under the stress of conflicting drives, recognizing that he must endure the consequences of his decisions. This is internal conflict, the struggle of a man with himself, the most dramatic conflict of all. Even in cases where external obstacles create the conflict situation, the struggle within the man as he seeks ways of overcoming the obstacle is often more important than the clash with the obstacle itself.

It should be noted, however, that not all types of conflict are dramatic. An example is the conflict that arises when characters in a play do nothing more than argue over an issue. The advancement of the various points of view may have some attraction as an intellectual exercise, but it lacks the element so essential to drama—the capacity to move an audience to feel deeply. Yet some student writers in their eagerness to be profound mistakenly concentrate on this intellectual type of confrontation. Drama should not be permitted to degenerate into mere debate or it soon ceases to be dramatic.

THE ISSUES OF CONFLICT. The objective of a dramatist is to elicit from his audience the maximum possible emotional response. The development of conflict will arouse emotions, but the extent of the response will depend on the significance of the issues at stake. Conflict over minor matters has little power to stir feelings. The conflict must focus on issues that are crucial, on such subjects as life or death, success or defeat, faith or unfaithfulness, health or illness, freedom or captivity, honor or degradation. John Steinbeck said that "people are more interested in violence than in guilt, in murder and accidents than in uneventfulness, in divorce than in marriage." This does not mean that drama must always focus on unusual people and extraordinary actions. Characters like the boy across the street or the woman in the next block may be proper subjects of drama provided that the situations into which we plunge them provoke conflicts involving issues of fundamental importance. It would be difficult, for example, to interest an audience in an individual whose basic problem is trying to decide whether to go to a movie or stay home and read a book. A child, however, with a penny clutched in his hand trying to decide which piece of candy to buy may be a completely satisfactory subject for drama. The decision he faces at that moment of his life is one of transcendent importance.

Fortunately for the playwright there are moments of extreme crisis in the experiences of almost all of us. Because they produce consequences that color life in a vital way, they are the stuff of which drama can be made. Paddy Chayefsky is frequently cited as a TV dramatist who wrote successfully about little people doing ordinary things. The title character in his famous play, "Marty," was an ordinary fellow and his predicament was a familiar one, but it gripped audience interest because it was a matter of such supreme importance. At stake in this moving drama was Marty's acceptance by society and his prestige as a person. The very usualness of this problem, in fact, added a universal quality which enhanced the dramatic effect.

THE PLACE OF VIOLENCE. One of the perennial issues in American broadcasting is the amount of violence purveyed on television. There is naturally much public anxiety about the effect it may have on viewers, particularly on children in the audience. This issue is a matter of great concern to the television writer because drama by its very nature involves violence. That may be a shocking statement to those who share public dismay at the amount of violence on TV but it is true, nevertheless. The essence of drama is conflict and conflict breeds violence. Without violence of some type or other there can be no drama. What are you as a writer to do in this situation?

First of all, you must accept the fact that the violence issue exists. You should realize also that there is no final answer yet to the question of how it actually affects those who view it. Finally, you should recognize that insisting that drama must involve violence does not mean that all criticism of it on TV is without foundation. Violence presented for its own sake is properly to be condemned, although drawing the line between the violence that is necessary to the story and that which is indiscriminately piled on sometimes requires a fine exercise of discrimination. The presentation of sheer brutality, however, not only is unacceptable, but it may also blunt the attainment of the dramatist's goal by blurring the essential issues with excess.

Violence, moreover, need not necessarily be physical or obvious. Words that slash and tear are violent; a man walking tensely out of a house leaving his weeping wife behind him is indulging in a violent act. Even when violence does take place, it need not occur before the viewer's eyes; it is often most effective when it is imagined rather than seen. Sometimes the conflict may not provoke an actual outburst, but if violence boils below the surface threatening to explode, it is an implicit element in the drama.

To understand the necessity for violence, one has only to consider the popularity of westerns, detective stories, adventure tales, and crime dramas in which it is a natural ingredient. Even the comedy dramas that top the rating charts make frequent use of violence, turned inside-out, to provoke laughter. The early 1960s saw the rise to popularity of the medical series exemplified by *Ben Casey* and *Dr. Kildare*. They regularly presented violence in one of its most hideous forms, the spectacle of disease ravaging the human body.

The would-be dramatist who abhors violence completely had better put away his typewriter and turn to other activities. He cannot be successful if he restricts himself to writing what one sponsor is supposed to have requested, "happy plays about happy people with happy problems." To write effective drama you must engulf people in difficulties, you must arouse their passions, you must incite them to conflict. If you do these things, you will provoke violence. If you fail to do them, you will have no drama.

CHANGES AND DEVELOPMENT

To create drama it is not enough merely to entangle a character in a predicament. The people involved in that problem must strive to free themselves or the emotional response of the audience will soon subside. Drama comes from struggle, not from capitulation. Moreover, that struggle must bring changes and developments or, again, the attention of the audience will wander. The experience can be compared to watching a truck stuck in the mud. The sight of spinning wheels arouses our interest at first, but if the wheels continue to spin without visible results, we soon turn to more diverting activities. In the same way, the struggle of the character must advance him toward his goal or shove him farther back, or he must make decisions that envelop him in new complications.

INTERPRETATION OF LIFE

Is it enough that a drama should merely hold the attention of an audience until the last scene is over? In the narrowest sense perhaps we can say that a dramatist who succeeds in doing this has accomplished all that we should expect of him. It is certainly true that much of TV drama diverts while it is on the screen, but with the final fade-out immediately passes into oblivion. To write a truly significant drama, however, one that accomplishes more than temporary diversion, we must meet the challenge that George Bernard Shaw laid down: "The function of a playwright is to select incidents from the chaos of everyday living and arrange them in a pattern so that the spectator might leave the theater an enlightened man."

The reference of significant drama, then, is life. Its proper subjects are real people doing things for reasons that can be discovered by an audience. It gives a vision of the real by adhering to the surface of life as people live it. Achieving fidelity to human truth does not mean, of course, that life in all of its detail and ramifications must be presented. As we have noted previously, a normal life is dramatic only in its moments of crisis. Alfred Hitchcock said, "A story needs to be true to life but never banal . . . Drama is life from which we have wiped out the stains of boredom." The dramatist selects a vital moment of life and then intensifies it. By placing a magnifying glass over one human event, he provides enlightenment about human existence in general.

THE SPECIAL CHARACTERISTICS OF DRAMA

To this point we have been considering some general requirements for effective storytelling that apply with particular emphasis to the dramatic form. But drama has some characteristics of its own, which set it apart from other types of stories such as the novel and the short story.

THE CONVENTIONS OF DRAMA

A dramatic presentation seems to conform to reality, at least in some respects, but it is never actually real. It becomes real only in the imagination of the viewer, who, in Coleridge's famous phrase, undertakes "the willing suspension of disbelief." The presentation may vary from one that provides only the barest clues to reality, from which the viewer erects his own vision of the situation, to one that offers a virtually complete representation of reality. The radio drama, limited as it is to sound stimuli, presents the greatest challenge to the imagination of the audience. The stage drama employing a complete and realistic set presents a lesser imaginative challenge, but even in this case the viewer must accept certain nonrealistic conventions. The room he sees, for example, has only three walls and he observes characters who are perfectly willing to carry on the most intimate conversations before a crowd of people.

There are conventions also in language. The play that employs naturalistic dialogue makes little demand on the credulity of the viewer, but the audience to the poetic dramas of a William Shakespeare, a Maxwell Anderson, or a Christopher Fry must be willing to believe in human beings who habitually and extemporaneously express themselves in soaring iambic verse. To cite another convention that applies particularly to television, the hands of the people who inhabit the world of the TV cartoon have only three fingers.

THE GROUP EFFORT OF DRAMA

The work of a novelist flows directly from the writer to the consumer by means of the printed word. A play, on the other hand, does not consist merely of the script that records it; it achieves its true existence only in the production that intervenes between the work of the dramatist and the ultimate consumer. The success of the play depends to a great extent on the nature of the collaboration provided by the director, performers, designers, and production crew. If they are skilled, they can transmit with complete integrity what the dramatist has put into his play, and, in some instances, they may even reveal meanings richer than he thought were there. If they are clumsy or lacking in perceptiveness, they may distort or even destroy what he sought to accomplish.

THE PRESENT TENSE OF DRAMA

The playwright presents his story through the actions of characters living through situations that are actually experienced by the audience as they happen. The novelist merely tells his audience what has happened. The immediacy of the play contrasted with the retrospective quality of the novel constitutes one of the basic differences between the two forms. Because drama presents what is happening, it follows that all of its action occurs in the present. In a play it is perpetually now. Time within a play can change, of course, it can return to a past event or thrust forward into future time, but whatever takes place in a specific time period is produced as if it were happening in the present tense. This means that in any given scene the dramatist is bound to a large extent by what can actually happen in the real time devoted to the playing of that scene. Another aspect of this situation is that drama proceeds at an inflexible pace. The viewer cannot pause and seek clarification by going back and re-examining the previous action as the reader of a novel can; the audience of a play is irresistibly drawn forward at whatever rate the dramatist sets.

RESTRICTIONS ON COMMENT

In addition to using dialogue—the main resource of the dramatist—the novelist has an unlimited opportunity to narrate, describe, analyze, and qualify. In so doing, he can present his own views as an observer of the scene. The dramatist, unless he resorts to the unusual device of using narration as a vehicle for presenting his own views, is denied the privilege of presenting his own comment directly to the audience. As George Pierce Baker, the teacher of writing, said, "In most novels the reader is, so to speak, personally conducted, the author is our guide. In the drama, as far as the dramatist is concerned, we must travel alone."[4]

THE PLACE OF IMPLICATION

Because the dramatist lacks a direct route to the viewer, he must communicate with his audience largely through skillful use of the technique of implication. This technique is employed, of course, in other forms of fiction, but in the drama its use is crucial. Unless a viewer is permitted to gain most of his knowledge through his interpretation of implications, he cannot react to drama as something experienced and the form will lose most of its special force and unique quality. Thorton Wilder, who is both a novelist and dramatist, emphasized this point when he said, "A dramatist is one who believes that the pure event, an action involving human beings, is more arresting than any comment on it."

DRAMA'S EMPHASIS ON THE HIGH POINTS

One of the most perceptive distinctions between novel and play writing was made by William Archer when he said that drama is "the art

[4] George Pierce Baker, *Dramatic Technique* (Boston: Houghton Mifflin Company, 1919), p. 7.

of crisis, as fiction is the art of gradual developments."[5] The dramatist presents only the culminating events in the lives of his characters, the action that involves them at or near their moments of crisis. In addition to retaining only those details that have the maximum vividness and significance, drama presents changes in swift and startling succession. The audience has little time to wonder or reflect. The long slow build-up in which the novelist may indulge is denied the dramatist, for he simply has no time for such development and could not hold an audience with it anyway. The dramatist must begin when the situation is coming to a boil, not when the fire is first lighted. It follows that the writer's choice of events to be dramatized is a matter of transcendent importance in the construction of a play. He must select only those events that contribute directly to the achievement of his purpose, rigidly excluding everything else. What actually occurs in his play, of course, can only be part of the complete story; the rest takes place outside of the action, between the scenes, or before the play begins, but these events are merely suggested by what is actually presented. Drama telescopes, focuses, and intensifies.

DRAMA ON TELEVISION AND RADIO

Should drama written specifically for the TV screen or radio loud-speaker have characteristics that distinguish it from drama written for other media? In trying to answer this question, one must recognize that television and radio drama have not remained static. In the comparatively short period of time that has gone by since I first began teaching writing for broadcasting, in 1946, a number of changes have occurred, some of which may challenge previously held assumptions about the nature of broadcast drama. Before trying to define that nature, then, let us examine the most important of these changes and consider their impact.

One thing that has happened is that both television and radio have been transformed from live media, which presented programs while they were actually being produced, to media which usually present recorded material. Yet "liveness" was once considered to be an essential attribute of broadcasting. Gilbert Seldes writing in 1950 said that "everything in the movies exists in the past tense; in . . . television everything is in the present." With almost all television drama now being produced on film, that distinction has become completely meaningless. Let us take a moment to review the reasons for the shift from live to recorded television. Mainly it reflects a reaction to practical considerations rather

[5] William Archer, *Play-Making*, p. 7.

than to artistic demands. (1) Recorded material does not vanish as it is produced but can be replayed for further profit, known as *residual* income. (2) Recording permits greater flexibility in the production of programs. Performers and facilities are not bound by an inexorable broadcast date, and the filming method of recording permits production of greater physical scope than is possible in a TV studio. (3) Recording insures a presentation free from error. Most advertisers, remembering the dog that spurned the sponsor's dog-food, the razor that refused to budge just after the announcer had told how easily it operated, "click-click," the soft drink bottle that exploded in the actor's face, the announcer who coughed hoarsely after inhaling his sponsor's cigarette, and the refrigerator door that refused to open, have fled to the security of film or tape, which can be reshot or edited into perfection. Live drama was also often marred by faults that could not be corrected. Lloyd Bridges committed one of the most memorable errors when, apparently losing himself in the role he was playing on a live drama, he suddenly burst into ad-libbed profanity. Perhaps that is why he spent a good deal of time thereafter playing not only on film but also under water in the long-running syndicated series, *Sea Hunt*.

Has the shift to filmed and taped drama transformed the dramatist's task? It is true that it has affected some of his script techniques, but it has not brought about any fundamental changes in his approach to writing scripts. In some ways the shift to recorded techniques has made the dramatist's task easier by permitting him to widen his scope and by relieving him of the onerous task of writing for sustained production.

There have been other changes. Radio drama in the United States has been supplanted almost entirely by its television counterpart, but this development has not altered any basic scripting principles. The radio drama that remains is still bound by the limitations that existed before and it still benefits from the same advantages. In television drama there have been varying trends in subject matter. As this is written, the psychological stories of "little people," which predominated in the early days of television, have largely given way to action dramas featuring spies and Western heroes. Another change is the virtual replacement of the anthology series, which featured dramas involving new characters and subject matter each week, with series in which the same characters appear regularly in dramas dealing with the same type of subject matter. Yet even these changes, marked as they are, do not alter basic principles of drama nor the writer's adaptation of that drama to the television medium. These basic principles remain constant and so, too, does the intrinsic nature of television and radio. This means, then, that the live television drama of yesterday can be used to illustrate fundamental principles for the dramatist who is writing the recorded drama of today.

Even if it could be argued that certain types of dramatic subject matter involve unique principles it would still be unwise to concentrate only on the types that are popular at the moment. The student who did so would be unprepared for the possible return of yesterday's favorites or for the unknown trends of tomorrow.

THE NATURE OF TELEVISION DRAMA

The scope of drama presented on television is as wide as the scope of drama itself. Masterpieces of the great Greeks, works of Shakespeare, Broadway successes of every variety, confined "kitchen-sink" dramas which immerse us in the problems of little people, and their very antithesis, sagas of the wide-open West which celebrate the exploits of heroic figures—all have been produced on television, apparently with success. Even when the form was still live, there seemed no absolute limit on what could be done. The *Kraft Theatre* in its dramatization of Walter Lord's *A Night to Remember* even accomplished the remarkable feat of sinking the *Titanic* in a TV studio. It is obvious that television permits the writer to deal with every kind of subject matter, yet the question remains whether certain types of drama are more adapted to presentation through this medium than are others. Tom Prideaux, a critic writing in *Life* said, for example, that "epic Greek dramas, which need the illusion of outdoors and Godlike grandeur, look preposterously dinky on TV." To determine what types of drama television can best present, let us consider some of the ways in which TV plays reach their audiences.

A VISUAL MEDIUM. Television drama is more visual in its nature than the drama presented from the stage of a theatre. One reason for this is that the person viewing a TV screen can see the action better than a person who is watching a stage performance. This close-up view, as we shall note shortly, makes television a much more intimate medium than the stage. A second reason for the visual emphasis in TV is that the audience's view of the scene can be constantly varied. The TV drama, unlike the stage play, does not present a whole picture that is on display for long periods of time. Instead it presents bits and pieces of a picture, the specific image selected from the entire panorama of the action being the one that will best advance the purpose of the drama at the given moment. The power to change the picture means that the TV dramatist does not, like the stage dramatist, have to spend time arranging exits for people whose function is completed and who are merely cluttering up the scene. In most cases he eliminates unwanted people simply by cutting away from them and taking his audience elsewhere. Moreover, he has the privilege of entering a scene to eavesdrop for a moment before moving to another scene. He can also develop parallel actions in widely separated locations, cutting back and forth between them, a method that is almost impossible on the stage. What has been said about TV drama, incidentally, applies equally to movie drama.

THE PLACE OF DIALOGUE.   The quality of the dialogue has a crucial effect on the success of a dramatist's work no matter what his medium, but in television, dialogue is not the whole play as it so often is in the theatre. With the probing eye of the camera available, the TV writer does not need to depend on words to convey most of his meaning. A single close-up, imaginatively selected and skillfully produced, may create a stronger dramatic climax than a whole sequence of dialogue. This means that the TV dramatist will usually contrive relatively more action and less dialogue than his stage counterpart, and the dialogue he writes will be linked more directly with action. Moreover, it is likely to be sharper and tauter than the dialogue of a stage play. The movie drama, because it is presented on a larger screen, goes even further in its emphasis on action and in its submergence of the word.

THE INTIMACY OF TELEVISION.   The relative smallness of the screen and the fact that programs are received in homes under informal conditions, usually by an audience of no more than two or three people per set, both contribute to making television an intimate medium. This is the major way in which the movie differs from television. The basic principle that derives from this intimacy is the oft-repeated dictum that television is a close-up medium. A principle that follows from it is that television is more often concerned with people than it is with scenery, and with people in small groups engaged in sharply restricted activity. The large movie screen can present gross movements effectively—the tumult at sea, the mob assaulting the castle, the ebb and flow of a battle scene. The activity presented on television is usually of a different order, intense, and rigidly contained. When battle erupts it usually involves two people rather than thousands.

In view of this difference it may well be asked why so many movies originally made for theatrical exhibition are shown on television. One reason is that many movies in their use of close-ups and in the nature of their action are well-adapted to the TV screen. Those that are not gain large TV audiences for other reasons: they may have become well-known through their theatrical release; perhaps they have the high quality that sometimes comes from large budgets; and they often feature major stars. It should be remembered also that many movies are shown on television simply because no other programs are available. Their use does not necessarily prove their appropriateness to the TV screen but signifies rather the creative limitations of the TV industry.

Another characteristic that derives from television's intimacy is that the broad movements needed on the stage are out of place and so, too, is the declamatory speech addressed to an auditorium full of people. Instead there should be direct, personal dialogue suited to the audience of two or three people who are watching the drama on any given TV set.

Television's limitation to a close-up technique does not necessarily operate to the disadvantage of the writer. In contrast to the stage, where slight reactions cannot be seen, the close-up camera can transmit a delicate change of expression or a tiny gesture which can often communicate a wealth of meaning. Because television can focus on inflections, on nuances of feeling, and on faces it can provide a closer texture and richer insights than are possible with a stage presentation.

TV DRAMA AND LITTLE PEOPLE. The intimacy of television gave rise to the idea that the peculiar province of TV drama is the domain of little people. In the middle 1950s many dramas were concerned almost entirely with the problems of ordinary human beings. Paddy Chayefsky, one of the writers of that period, explained this choice of subject by saying that TV finds its special function in telling "a small story about a familiar character and pursues this small story with relentless literalness to one small synthesized moment of crisis."[6] Tad Mosel expressed the same viewpoint when he said, "Never before has there been a medium so suited to what I call the 'personal' drama."[7] It cannot be denied that drama with this focus dominated American television for awhile, but it cannot be denied either that it faded in the later 1950s to be replaced by dramas dealing with other kinds of subjects. This is not to say that such dramas have no place on television, but it does seem unreasonable to contend that most television drama should concern the problems of little people.

THE TIME RESTRICTIONS OF TELEVISION. Time restricts the television dramatist in two ways. The first is that in American television he is required to fill a specific time period with his play whether or not his dramatic idea fits comfortably into that particular time slot. He cannot, like the stage or screen playwright, write a script that will be as short or as long as the idea itself dictates. Selecting ideas that fit the time periods assigned to a drama involves one of the writer's most critical decisions. There are fifteen-minute ideas, half-hour ideas, hour ideas.

[6] Paddy Chayefsky, *Television Plays*, p. 177.
[7] Tad Mosel, *Other People's Houses* (New York: Simon and Schuster, Inc., 1956), p. IX.

The dramatist who decides to deal with a half-hour idea in an hour's time, or the reverse, is taking the first step toward trouble.

A second aspect of television's time restrictions is that whatever time may be available, it is usually shorter than the time at the disposal of the stage or screen dramatist. The TV play longer than an hour is the exception; most are of the hour or half-hour variety. This means that the panoramic approach, in which a drama wanders leisurely through many years and involves a multitude of characters, is out of place on television, although it may be appropriate for stage or screen presentations. The TV drama must be sharply focused in its approach. Even though the short time periods of television tend to be restricting in their effect, they do provide an opportunity for the treatment of ideas that lack sufficient substance for the longer periods of the stage and screen. The critic, Marya Mannes, pointed out that television can "open the door on one life in one room for one moment and . . . record one small shift in human relations . . . one half turn in a situation."[8]

THE NATURE OF RADIO DRAMA

It is regrettable that radio drama, as far as commercial broadcasting is concerned, has reached a state of near extinction, for it has certain qualities that establish it as a unique art form. More than any other dramatic medium it demands the active collaboration of the audience, for the listener's imagination is the stage of radio. Sound, moreover, has unusual power to arouse an emotional response and radio, because it concentrates the listener's attention on sound, makes maximum use of this power. Of all the dramatic media, radio is most untrammeled in the form it can take. The radio dramatist can switch backwards and forwards in time without limit; through the use of the listener's imagination he can place the drama in one setting for an instant and then snatch it suddenly away to another. Finally, radio can be produced quickly and inexpensively. If the young dramatist has production facilities and performers available to him, such as he might find in a college workshop, the radio script provides him with the best opportunity he is likely to have to test his dramatic ideas in actual production.

THE SOURCES OF DRAMA

One problem facing aspiring dramatists is that, bursting with the urge to write, they sometimes experience difficulty in finding things to write

[8] Marya Mannes, "Time for a Story," *The Reporter*, Vol. 21 (July 9, 1959), p. 34.

about. Whether the desire to express oneself can exist separately from ideas one wishes to express is questionable, but it does seem that unchanneled creative energies occasionally need firm direction.

THE ORIGIN OF DRAMATIC IDEAS

The experience of writers demonstrates that ideas for novels, short stories, and plays spring from every avenue of life, sometimes so insidiously that an author may be unable to explain how a specific idea came into his mind. The root of a story may be something seen, heard, told, or read. It can be one of the dramas we sometimes see in everyday life: a girl in a railroad station holding a uniformed man tightly to her as though she can never let him go; a dazed motorist staring stupidly down at a body crushed beneath the wheels of his car; the adoring look in a girl's face as she looks down at the ring on her finger; the teen-ager trying to tell his father that he has just smashed a fender; a lonely mother on a beach watching her deformed child play in the sand; the look of relief in a woman's eyes as she comes from the confessional. Or it may be as slight a happening as a chance remark heard in a subway, a cry of pain in the night, or the sound of a laugh with no mirth in it.

Katherine Anne Porter tells us that the process of creation that resulted in her masterful short story "Flowering Judas" began in Mexico when she saw a grossly fat man serenading a beautiful girl. Her story became an explanation for this situation. Jessamyn West's chilling story "Horace Chooney M.D." had an even slighter beginning. This eerie tale of a murderous physician, whose treatment was designed to kill rather than cure, had its beginning in the mere sight of a doctor's shingle hanging broken and weather-beaten in unkempt weeds along the side of a country road.

THE WRITER'S DIRECT KNOWLEDGE

The work of a great many writers suggests that the best writing often finds its inspiration in what the writer knows from direct, personal experience. The writing career of Ernest Hemingway provides a striking demonstration of the relationship between personal experience and effective writing. His books reflect his life as an expatriate in Europe, his experiences in World War I and the Spanish Civil War, and his life in the Caribbean area. William Faulkner was another writer whose work was based on personal experience and his own words indicate that he found no need for going beyond it: "I discovered that my own little

postage stamp of native soil was worth writing about and that I would
never live long enough to exhaust it."[9]

THE LITERAL TRANSCRIPTION OF LIFE

Life, then, can be the inspiration for dramatic writing, but the dramatist who tries to present life exactly as he experiences it will usually
fail to write effective drama. One reason for this, oddly enough, is that
actual happenings, even though unquestionably authentic, are sometimes
so bizarre as to be utterly unbelievable when presented in a play. The
novelist and dramatist, Somerset Maugham said that "life is full of im-
probabilities that fiction does not admit of."[10] There is the added difficulty that people in real life are often so capricious and unpredictable
that they do completely unexpected things. A dramatic character must
act in terms of the drives and values that have been established for
him. He must be consistent. Above all, he must be believable.

A second problem with real life as dramatic material is that it is
often routine and monotonous. The conflicts that exist, although they
may be of sufficient urgency to arouse interest, generally fail to sustain
interest because they remain constant and unresolved. Drama must have
crises that gradually rise in pitch until they reach a climax, and these
are infrequent in real life. The form and arrangement that drama demands is also missing in most real-life happenings.

We can conclude then that although events in one's own experience
must usually be the inspiration for a dramatic idea, the writer who
attempts a literal transcription of these events is in danger of being
either absurd or dull. On the foundation that life has provided, he must
erect his own edifice of dramatic truth. The absurd and improbable
must be rearranged and justified; the tediousness that is everyday life
must be telescoped and heightened into a form that has order and development. In the words of George Bernard Shaw, "The dramatist picks
out the significant incidents from the chaos of daily happenings and
arranges them so that their relationship to one another becomes significant." It must be remembered also that life is dramatic only in its moments of greatest intensity, and only these moments should be selected
for dramatic treatment. Whether the completed script reflects accurately
the true event is quite immaterial. Katherine Anne Porter, commenting
on the inspiration of her story, "Flowering Judas," said that as soon
as she saw the beautiful girl being serenaded by the fat man she "knew
a story; perhaps not her true story, not even the real story of the whole

---

[9] Quoted in Malcolm Cowley, "How Writers Write," p. 36.

[10] Somerset Maugham. "The Vagrant Mood," *The Decline and Fall of the Detective
Story* (New York: Doubleday & Company, Inc., 1953), p. 109.

situation, but all the same a story that seemed symbolic truth to me."
The important question about a drama is not—is it true?—but rather—
does it seem to be true? Will an audience accept and believe it?

GOING BEYOND DIRECT EXPERIENCE

Is a writer ever justified in going beyond what he knows from direct
experience for dramatic material? It can be said, to begin with, that
some people discount sharply the importance of personal knowledge
in a dramatist's work. The playwright, Moss Hart, scoffed at the dictum
that a writer should deal only with what he knows best, calling it "a
preposterous piece of dramatic wisdom (that discounts) the vital and
immeasurable quality that imagination gives to all writing." Hart's own
first major work tended to prove his point: it was the play, *Once in
a Lifetime,* written about a Hollywood he had never seen, which, with
the later collaboration of George Kauffman, became a smashing Broadway success. George Pierce Baker struck a note similar to Hart's when
he said, "A common fallacy of young dramatists is that what has happened is better dramatic material than what is imagined."[11] Perhaps
the outstanding example of imaginative accomplishment was *The Red
Badge of Courage* in which Stephen Crane, who had never been to
war, composed some of the most vivid descriptions of battles ever
written.

Writing what one knows about directly would seem to be a means
of ensuring authenticity and relevance to life, but carried to the extreme
it can be unduly restricting. It denies the power of the imagination
to project a writer into unknown realms and overlooks his capacity to
gain new understandings through vicarious means. It would restrict him
to his own times, his own place, and his own acquaintances. Moreover,
even in writing plays based on direct knowledge, there come moments
when this knowledge alone will not suffice. Most writers must break
beyond these bounds, and some, the truly venturesome, may escape
them almost entirely, using personal experience merely as a reference
point from which imagination may soar.

QUESTIONS AND PROJECTS

1. Many authorities have described what they consider a "play" to be
and have attempted to define the qualities inherent in the word, "dramatic." How would you define these terms?

---

[11] George Pierce Baker, *Dramatic Technique,* p. 67.

2. Watch three TV dramas during a week with the following objectives:

    a) Note the conflicts they involve and classify them as struggles involving man against man, man against a group, a group against a group, a man or a group against a natural force or obstacle, or internal conflict. Do any of the dramas seem to lack a readily identifiable conflict situation?

    b) Be alert to the elements of violence the dramas contain; determine whether these elements are explicit, implicit, lacking in force, or too obvious.

    c) Decide whether the dramas concentrate on the high points by summarizing the story as a whole and then differentiating between the action actually shown in the play and that which is merely described or implied or which takes place between the scenes.

3. Do you believe that live television drama, performed as the audience is watching, provides any values or experiences not communicated by filmed drama?

4. List three incidents from your own experience that might be the starting points for dramas.

3

Inventing the Plot

There are three kinds of audiences: thinkers who demand characterization; women who demand passion; and the mob who demand action. Victor Hugo

Inventing an intriguing plot and creating unique, full-bodied characters are two of the most important tasks involved in writing a play. These two functions can be identified as separate processes in play construction, but the writer does not necessarily carry them out separately. What he does with one so directly affects the other that he often invents his plot and creates his characters in one simultaneous operation. It is impossible to discuss these two functions at the same time, however, so we shall give most of our attention to plotting in this chapter and consider the creation of characters in the next.

PLOT AND CHARACTER

Critics have long debated the relative importance of plot and character without arriving at any final answer. One conclusion does seem certain:

a weakness in either plotting or characterization can seriously damage the total effect. It also seems clear that strength or weakness in these two elements affects a play in quite different ways.

A play that was strong in characterization but weak in plot was Horton Foote's "A Member of the Family," produced on the *Studio One* series. It presented an arresting character portrayal of a childless man who tried and failed to make sons of two of his nephews in succession. Presented in rich and significant detail, this character became a unique individual whose problems could elicit emotional response from an audience. The plot that involved him, however, lacked the needed tension. Too many scenes were static, and there was no inevitable and progressive development toward a final climactic scene. This plotting weakness made the play somewhat dull to watch, but the incisive characterization of the lonely uncle desperately clutching for family ties stayed vividly in the memory long after the final fade-out.

A play that reversed these qualities, being strong in plot but weak in characterization, was "One More Mile to Go," presented on the *Alfred Hitchcock* series. The play centered on the struggle of a killer to dispose of his wife's body, which he had hidden in the trunk of his car. Fate in the guise of a defective tail-light kept intervening to defeat his plans. Tension developed rapidly as the killer met one problem after another, each provoked by the defective tail-light and each more critical than the last until in the climactic scene, it finally defeated him. The plot had excellent unity and an ingenious pattern of development; the peaks of tension grew steadily higher, and there were frequent surprise twists to intrigue the viewer; the excitement and suspense it generated were undeniable. The weakness of the story was that we knew almost nothing about the killer and his motives. Because he was a puppet set in motion to achieve a plot purpose, who never came to life as a real person, he could win neither sympathy nor understanding. The result was that with the final fade-out he passed immediately into limbo.

Plotting and characterization, then, make two different contributions to the success of a play. A good plot is the most important factor in keeping an audience absorbed while the play is actually going on. Characterization can also help to keep viewers interested as they watch a play, but its most important contribution is to make the play memorable.

THE ELEMENTS OF A PLOT

A number of people have tried to develop a technique for plotting that would simplify the writer's task of inventing stories capable of holding an audience's attention throughout the performance of a play.

Some have even tried to reduce the process to a mathematical formula, but, unfortunately, there is no such easy route to the production of good plots. No formula can substitute for ingenuity and inventiveness. Moreover, the problems of devising plots vary so much that it is difficult to lay down principles that have universal application. As you look back on your efforts to invent plots, you will probably say with Maxwell Anderson, "Every new play was a new problem and the old rules were inapplicable," All of this does not mean, however, that a dramatist is completely on his own in developing plots. Even though there are no devices that can produce good plots automatically, there are some guidelines that can direct a writer as he starts down the road of invention. The first step is to consider the elements that make up a plot.

DECISIONS BY A CHARACTER

One element of great importance in the plotting structure of many plays is the sequence of decisions a character makes as he confronts a problem. Let us suppose that a poverty-stricken accountant whose wife desperately needs expensive medical attention considers the possibility of embezzling money to pay for her treatment. The decisions he makes as he is pushed first in one direction by his need and then in the other by his desire to remain honest constitute basic steps in the development of the plot. This movement, plus the intense internal conflict experienced by the character, engage the attention of the audience. The impact is heightened because the issues at stake, as they should be in all plots, are of vital importance to the character.

A CHARACTER'S STRUGGLE TO REACH A GOAL

A second element of major importance in plot construction is the struggle that follows a character's decision to accomplish a certain goal. This element would enter if the accountant came to the conclusion that he could solve his problem only by embezzling money. The basic plot would then chronicle his struggle to do so without being detected.

In some instances the decision-making element may be of no importance because the goal is self-evident. An example is a situation in which a character in danger struggles to save his life. The average person in such circumstances would not ponder the goal itself, for the urge to survive is instinctive, but would be entirely engrossed with accomplishing it. Decision-making might be an element in the plot, however, as he considers the various means of attaining his goal, but such decisions are usually of secondary importance to the struggle itself.

DRAMATIC ACTION AND PLOTTING

A criticism frequently made of a play that fails to sustain interest is that it lacks action. There is scarcely any fault more grievous than writing a play in which not enough happens. The need for action is implicit in the statement of a *Time* theatre critic who said, "Drama is really a verb masquerading as a noun."[1] If this action is missing, or is deficient in quantity or intensity, the play may be worse than unsatisfactory; it may not be a play at all. The first step in avoiding this fault is to understand what action is.

THE NATURE OF ACTION. Perhaps the most common mistake is to equate action entirely with activity. This is not completely an error, for activity is one of the principal ways of indicating action, but activity alone does not comprise all the action of a play and it may not even include the action that is most important. In a sense action can be defined in two different ways depending on whether it is connected with a decision or with a goal.

The conflict a character experiences as he considers a choice and the decision he finally makes constitute the vital action in many plays. The changes in equilibrium that take place as the balance alternates from favorable to unfavorable during a character's struggle to reach a goal plus the events leading to these changes and the consequences that follow make up the other major type of action.

If action is to be equated with anything, it can best be equated with change. There is action in a play when changes are constantly taking place. These changes, of course, must be in those matters that affect the vital issues of the play. It is through changes that a play develops and moves steadily forward to the final change that is the climax. Movement created by changes catches an audience's interest and holds it until the last scene is over.

ACTIVITY AND ACTION. What is the role of purely physical movement or activity? It has an important function to perform, quite aside from its part in revealing action. Some movement on the television screen is necessary merely as a means of providing exercise for the viewer's eyeballs, for a completely static picture would in itself soon become an interest killer. Fortunately, the dramatic action of most plays must be expressed to some extent in physical activity. This is usually sufficient to provide the amount of movement necessary to keep the audience awake. Where it is not sufficient, the director introduces incidental ac-

---

[1] "The Theater," *Time*, Vol. 85 (April 23, 1965), p. 59.

tivity or business—such as lighting cigarettes, rises, or movements around the set—to keep the screen active.

The most important activity, however, is not this incidental business, but the activity springing directly from a situation that reveals the vital action. An excellent example of the function of activity in disclosing action occurred in *Violent Saturday,* a movie that portrayed an Amish father who, throughout his life, had abhorred violence. One day he sees an intruder enter his barn and attack his family. For a few moments, this gentle father undergoes an agonizing conflict. Then, in a wild burst, he seizes a pitchfork and destroys the intruder. This scene struck with staggering effect, but it was not the mere act of violence that provided this overwhelming power. What filled the viewer with awe was the picture of a man in a situation of great stress making a decision that flew directly in the face of everything he had been taught to believe. This decision was the vital action of this scene, not the activity that expressed it.

Physical activity alone, however, is not a certain sign that a scene contains sufficient dramatic action. There may be frantic movement as people dash hither and thither about the set, but the story may still fail to progress. If movement does not in some way lead from one development to another, if it does not bring about changes in the minds or fortunes of the characters, then, despite all the bustle, the scene lacks action.

Scenes with little physical activity, on the other hand, may be replete with action. There was a scene in a television play that showed just one man sitting at a desk, speaking quietly to a TV camera. A minimum of activity was involved. No other person was even visible on the set. Yet the scene vibrated with action. Why was this? It was simply that in talking to the camera, the man disclosed to the TV audience that he had made what was probably his most critical decision. The play called, by the way, "Fearful Decision," starred Ralph Bellamy in the role of a man whose son had been kidnapped. In this scene he revealed that he had decided not to pay the ransom demanded by the kidnappers because he has discovered from a study of previous kidnappings that paying ransom had little or nothing to do with saving the life of the victim, and the payment of ransom might encourage this type of crime. It was the implication of this decision and its possible effect on the life of his son that gave the scene its dramatic power. A later scene showed people of the town throwing stones through his front window to express their disapproval of what they thought was a callous disregard for his son's life. But this violent incident did not generate nearly the tension precipitated by the quiet scene in the TV studio. The revelation of a critical decision has far greater power to engage the emotion of an audience than the elementary spectacle of people merely threshing about.

SPEECH AND ACTION.   The most important method of revealing action to the audience is through the kind of activity that we call speech. Does a scene showing two people sitting across a table from each other quietly talking contain enough action to hold the interest of an audience? We cannot answer this question until we know what the two are saying and its relationship to the vital issues of the play. Does the dialogue grow from a decision made by one of these characters or from a change in equilibrium between them which is leading inevitably to another change? If the answer is "yes" then this scene contains dramatic action. Its power, of course, depends on the importance of the issue at stake.

If, on the other hand, the talk between these two deals with general matters that are not directly relevant to the basic issues of the play, the scene lacks action. The plot has stopped its forward movement; no change is taking place or is being prepared for; the play has become sluggish and static. A scene may also come to a standstill if characters merely argue a matter without settling it one way or another, for action occurs only when there are developments in the story. If the characters' speeches help to reveal and develop the action of the play, they can be equated with action. If, on the other hand, speeches go on while the action of the play comes to a standstill, they no longer reveal action. The play has become "talky."

THE PLOTTING STRUCTURE

Before discussing the structure of a plot, it may be well to explain what a plot is. The plot is the basic pattern of events that constitute the essential action of the play. It is the fundamental development through which the rise, progress, and resolution of the conflict are revealed to the audience. To put it another way, the plot is the exposition of the conflict. It may be one raging within an individual as he struggles to reach a decision or one between an individual and external forces that obstruct his way to a goal. A main objective in designing a plot is to reveal how one event influenced another and why people acted as they did. Always the overriding aim is to stimulate the maximum emotional response in the audience.

Is there any difference between the "plot" and "story" of a play? Distinguishing these terms is difficult, and many use them interchangeably, but some think of the story as the sequence of events told in chronological order, whereas the plot is the arrangement of these events into a pattern that accomplishes the writer's dramatic purposes.

TWO TYPES OF PLAYS

We have noted that a plot usually revolves around a conflict in which the significant elements are decisions and a struggle to reach a goal. In many instances a given play concentrates on one type of conflict or the other, particularly the shorter ones which are common in television, and this concentration often helps to provide a desirable unifying quality. A play that is plotted around the choices made by the leading character is *decision-centered*. A play that focuses mainly on a struggle by the leading character to achieve a goal is *goal-centered*.[2] Not all plays fit into these two categories, of course; some deal equally with decisions and a goal and there are plotting patterns that are only remotely connected with these two elements.

BASIC PLOTTING DESIGN

A general plotting pattern that fits most plays, whatever their forms may be, does exist although the nature of the complications differs from one type of play to the other. In this pattern four main steps can be discerned.

OPENING SITUATION.   Plays should begin with a character enmeshed, or about to be enmeshed, in a problem situation, which involves the conflict that is to be at the center of the play's action. A beginning scene must meet two requirements. First, it must be clear. Above all, the viewer must understand what is happening. If he becomes confused about who is who or what is going on, if facts and reasons get mixed up in his mind and the complications start before he gets matters unraveled, the play is lost. This does not mean that the significance of every happening must be immediately obvious, for events often take place in the beginning that are not fully explained until later in the play. This was particularly true of the *Perry Mason* series, for example. The basic development of these programs, however, was clear, as it should be with all dramas. The viewer might not completely understand the significance of every event at the moment presented, but he could follow the action without becoming confused.

The second requisite for the opening scene is that it seize attention immediately. This requirement sometimes presents the writer with a

[2] For an application of this classification to the short story see: John Gallishaw, *The Only Two Ways to Write a Story* (New York: G. P. Putnam Sons, 1928).

dilemma. He must begin with a conflict and yet, to achieve clarity, he may need some time to explain the nature of the conflict. To start a play with a long exposition, however, as some playwrights for the stage used to do, would be deadly. The conflict already developed is the best hook for the viewer's attention. The explanation of the conflict must be inserted skillfully into the scene so that it seems to be part of the dramatic action. Techniques for introducing exposition unobtrusively are described in the chapter on Dialogue and Narration.

COMPLICATIONS.   The next step is to sharpen and deepen the conflicts until the final crisis is reached. The developments that intensify the conflict and make it more critical are called the complications. In the decision-centered play, they arise as the character is catapulted into a succession of circumstances all of which force him to make a choice involving the same values. The accountant with the sick wife, referred to earlier, must be confronted with a series of events that force him to keep choosing between his wife's health and his desire to lead an honest life. As one decision follows another, he discovers that instead of solving his problem, he becomes even more deeply involved. The conflict within the character becomes more intense, his decisions more difficult, and the potential consequences more ominous.

The goal-centered play is structured in the same general way, but the nature of the complications is somewhat different. Instead of designing a series of developments requiring decisions, the writer must invent a series of situations in which there is a change in the balance of power involving the character and the force that is threatening him. The best design presents situations in which the character first loses ground against his adversary and then gains it, and the maximum tension is likely to develop if, in balance, the hostile force constantly becomes more powerful and threatening. It is possible to write successful plays of this type, however, in which the focal character steadily gains on his antagonist. The constant shift in equilibrium gives the play its forward movement. *The Lone Ranger* radio and TV series exemplify on a somewhat elementary level the manner in which these changes can take place.

1. *The balance can be shifted by the entrance of another character into a scene.* In a typical situation the Lone Ranger comes on the villain and gets the drop on him. Then an accomplice of the villain sneaks up behind the Lone Ranger and the balance of power shifts back to his adversary. The villain and his accomplice proceed to tie up the Lone Ranger, but while they are thus engaged, Tonto, the faithful Indian friend of the hero, slips up behind them and once more the Lone Ranger forges ahead.

2. *A new act can accomplish a shift in the balance of power.* Let us assume that the Lone Ranger finds himself staring into the muzzle of a gun held by the villain and hears the villain order him to drop his own gun to the ground. The Lone Ranger obeys, but as he drops his gun he reverses the balance by kneeling suddenly and sweeping a handful of dust into his opponent's eyes.

3. *New information can change the equilibrium.* The villain wrests the gun from the Lone Ranger's hands. This action seems to put him ahead except that the Lone Ranger tells him calmly that his gun isn't loaded thus putting matters right back where they were before.

The examples just cited may seem too simple for actual use, yet they are actual incidents from programs in *The Lone Ranger* series, and similar devices continue to be used in plot construction. Many plays feature devices more subtle than these, of course, but any developments, whether simple or elaborate, that move a struggle first in one direction and then in another serve as complications.

THE FINAL CRISIS. The point in the story where the conflict reaches its greatest height is the final crisis. In the decision-centered play it is the instant when the character makes the choice that will irrevocably take him down one road or the other. In the goal-centered play it is the time of the final decisive struggle in which the character achieves a victory or goes down to defeat. The term, "climax," is often used to describe this part of the play and, suggesting as it does the point where the action rises to the highest point, it is a singularly appropriate word. If there is to be an explosion, this is where it takes place.

THE RESOLUTION. The part of the play in which the writer describes what happens as a result of the character's final climactic decision or struggle is the resolution. In some cases no explanation is necessary; the nature of the climax itself may be sufficient to indicate the consequences; at other times a brief explanation may be required. An extended resolution is undesirable, however, because the tension of the story has been dissipated with the climax. All that remains to hold attention is the curiosity of the audience regarding the eventual outcome. The writer should indicate what that outcome is and then get out of the way to make room for the final credits. If it is obvious that viewers will want to know whether the villain went to jail, they should be told but further details are unnecessary. These days, for example, the audience to a love story does not need to be told in so many words that "they lived happily ever after."

Some of the most satisfying plays are those that do not really come to an end with the final scene. This is particularly true of television drama, where the shortage of time may force a writer into presenting a small portion of a longer story, which the viewer is invited to consider as going on long after the final fade-out. The "slice of life" suggests the whole. As a matter of fact, this is a realistic approach. Major problems are not solved completely in most cases and even when they are, new problems rise to take their place. A sharper impact may be gained if the viewer can visualize life and its problems going on even after the play is over.

ANALYSIS OF A DECISION-CENTERED PLAY

To make the general principles of plot construction more meaningful, we shall consider specific plays to show these principles in action. The first is a decision-centered play which gained immediate critical approval when it was presented on the *Philco-Goodyear Television Playhouse*. Translated into a movie, it won further acclaim and an Academy Award for its star, Ernest Borgnine, and it was a resounding commercial success as well. The play is Paddy Chayefsky's moving drama, "Marty."

THE OPENING SITUATION.   In the first scene of the play we are made aware at once of the focal character's basic problem. He is a man already past the age when most people are married and he is subjected constantly to the pressure and taunts of a society which always seems to resent a bachelor. The question facing him is immediately clear. What will he decide to do about getting married? What steps will he take toward or away from matrimony?

THE COMPLICATIONS.   In the next scene Marty's problem becomes intensified. We discover that because he is a short, homely man, his desire to get married is constantly blocked by the fact that girls "don't go for him." We also become aware of the emptiness of his present existence. His pal, Angie, urges him to call up a girl they had met at a movie. In deciding not to call the girl, he makes the first significant decision of the play. Later he changes his mind and does call her. He is met with a sharp and cruel rebuff. The scene ends on a strangely ironic note. Marty, quivering with the pain of rejection by the girl, is asked by the bartender as he leaves the phone booth, "When you gonna get married?"

The next scene introduces the subplot. It concerns Marty's Aunt Catherine who continues to live with her son after his marriage. Her daughter-in-law, finding this situation intolerable, tries to find some other way of caring for her mother-in-law. The mother discovers her daughter-in-law's attitude and immediately experiences the agony of the rejected.

This subplot performs two functions. First of all, it reinforces the theme of the play, which is concerned with the unhappiness of the unwanted. Secondly, and more importantly, it intensifies Marty's problem of deciding what to do about his bachelor state by showing that marriage is not without its difficulties.

The pressure to solve his problem is renewed in the next scene when Marty's mother persuades him against his better judgment to go to a dance hall in the hope that he will meet some nice girl. Soon after arriving he endures heartache again when a girl refuses to dance with him because she says she doesn't feel like dancing, yet immediately accepts another man's invitation. Then comes a turning point in the play. Marty sees a girl, who like himself is homely and unwanted, suffer the grinding humiliation of being passed off to another man by the man who had met her there on a blind date. She refuses to go along and ends up on the fire escape weeping in despair. On impulse, Marty asks her to dance with him. At first she collapses sobbing into his arms, but soon the two are dancing and it becomes apparent that Marty's final critical decision will be made in terms of this girl.

He takes her to his home, attempts to kiss her, is resisted, but soon they are talking about other dates, and then she does permit him to kiss her. Marty's mother comes home and he introduces her to the girl. It is clear that Martys' interest is not only deep, but that it is also reciprocated by the girl.

It would seem that Marty's problem is now near solution. Surely this girl will provide an escape from his empty, bachelor life. New complications are immediately introduced, however, to prevent this easy solution. The mother who had seemed so anxious to get her son married immediately becomes full of narrow objections when a girl appears who may actually steal him from her. She criticizes the girl's looks, suggests that she is too old for him, implies that her morals may be weak, and even objects because the girl is not Italian. Part of the mother's attitude can probably be explained by her knowledge of the rejection her sister experienced after her son married. Again we see the subplot working to reinforce the main action of the play.

THE FINAL CRISIS. Even more critical than his mother's attitude is the attitude of Marty's pals when they discover his new attachment. They profess amazement that he could possibly be interested in such a "dog" and in heartless and vulgar terms they rip her to pieces. Instead of his calling her, they recommend that he spend a night with the boys. Marty's dilemma has now reached its height. Shall he turn his back on the girl and face a continuation of the same arid life that has been his before? Or, enduring the objections of his mother and the taunts of his pals, shall he grasp what is likely to be his last chance for normal, married life? He decides finally for the girl. His finger dialing her number symbolizes this final, critical decision.

THE RESOLUTION.   No time is spent in this play with a resolution and no time needs to be spent. The play ends with the climax and properly so. It is not necessary to tell whether Marty actually succeeded in making the date nor whether he eventually married the girl. These are questions that can well be left to the audience's speculation. The author does provide a strong hint about Marty's new attitude by having him say to his pal just before entering the telephone booth, "When you gonna get married, Angie?" but he provides no final answer. It is a sign of Chayefsky's skill that he knew his play was over when the telephone call began.

A SUMMARY OF THE PLOTTING.   There is much about the play "Marty" that is worthy of discussion. The characters are sympathetic and believable; the dialogue has an authentic ring; the theme, which is analyzed at greater length in a later chapter, is developed with richness and power. All of these qualities would not have been enough, however, to make this a completely satisfying play. Fortunately, Chayefsky also provided a plot that proceeds with sureness and direction from the opening scene to the final fade-out. Without this sound basic structure, the play's other virtues would have been dissipated. Let us review the plot briefly with particular attention to the decisions and their consequences, showing how the action of the play rises on a constantly accelerating plane to the climax.

1. Marty's bachelor existence and his unattractiveness to girls is explained.

2. Marty rejects Angie's suggestion that he call a girl. He experiences loneliness.

3. He finally calls the girl but experiences rejection.

4. Under the urgings of his mother he decides to go to the ballroom. He anticipates rejection.

5. He asks a girl to dance and again experiences rejection.

6. He asks the second girl to dance, is accepted, and there follows a series of decisions which move him steadily toward a deeper and more meaningful relationship with this girl.

7. The conflict reaches its height when Marty is caught between his desire to call the girl again and the objections of his mother and friends.

8. He decides to call the girl—and does so.

Point one in this outline covers the opening situation of the play. Points two through seven describe the complications which cause the action to rise steadily toward the climax. Point eight details the final crisis and the character's climactic decisions. The resolution, as we have noted, is left to the audience's imagination.

AN ANALYSIS OF A GOAL-CENTERED PLAY

Scripts in the ABC-TV Network presentation, *The Fugitive,* which won an Emmy award as the best dramatic series of the 1965–66 season, exemplify the principles to be followed in plotting the play that revolves around a struggle by a character to accomplish a previously determined goal. The leading character is Dr. Richard Kimble, a pediatrician, who escaped in a train wreck on his way to the death house after being unjustly convicted of the murder of his wife. Unlike Marty, he does not need to ponder what his goal should be. That goal is clear—to avoid being captured until the real murderer is found. As he strives for this objective, he must make some decisions about how to attain it, and decisions are also made by other characters. What seizes our attention, however, is not the decisions, but the desperate efforts of the leading character to reach his goal. The particular play to be analyzed, entitled "May God Have Mercy," was written by Don Brinkley.

THE OPENING SITUATION.   Kimble, who is serving as an orderly in a Michigan hospital under an assumed name, discovers from some lab reports that there is a patient in the hospital who knows his true identity. In a parallel scene the patient, a man named Victor Leonetti, is told by his doctor that he has only ten months more to live, but the nature of his illness will permit him to lead a relatively normal life. He decides not to tell Anne, his wife, because they have recently endured the loss of their daughter Jeanie from a heart ailment.

THE COMPLICATIONS.   Anne Leonetti, walking through the hospital on the way to her husband's room, sees Kimble, who had been their doctor during Jeanie's fatal illness. Thinking that her husband must also have seen Kimble at one time or another, she mentions the incident to him. Leonetti had not seen him, it turns out, and Anne immediately regrets her impetuosity, for it is clear that her husband's hostility toward the doctor has not diminished. He blames Kimble for taking a vacation at a critical moment in their daughter's illness and he accepts the judgment of the court that Kimble is a wife murderer. When Anne drops her husband at his office, it is obvious that the first thing he intends to do is call the police and inform them of Kimble's whereabouts. On an impulse, Anne, who believes Kimble to be innocent of his wife's murder and holds him blameless in Jeanie's death, drives back to the hospital to warn him. A few moments later she picks him up at the back of the hospital and drives away as the police pull up in front. While Anne and Kimble talk, it is revealed that Jeanie died because Leonetti had refused to approve open-heart surgery. As Anne says: "Once he stops blaming you for Jeanie's death, he'll have to blame himself." Kimble also tells Anne that he was not on vacation when Jeanie had her fatal heart attack but was in New York trying to obtain the services of a specialist. The police arrive just as Kimble gets out of the car; Anne watches horror-stricken as they shoot him down.

In the opening of Act II Anne tells her husband what has happened and reveals what she has learned about Kimble's "vacation," information that is confirmed by a phone call to the specialist. At the hospital where Kimble is receiving treatment for a serious shoulder wound, Leonetti joins a crowd around a police officer, then quietly trudges away, showing obvious remorse at what he has done. In the hospital Kimble, knowing that he has a much better chance to escape from the x-ray room than from a barred hospital room, is crushed to discover that no x-rays are scheduled. Act II ends as Leonetti comes into the police station to confess that he is the real murderer of Kimble's wife.

As Act III opens Anne tells the police that her husband could not possibly have killed Kimble's wife because he was with her the evening of the murder, but the fact that Leonetti seems to know every detail of the killing throws doubt on her story. The local police, now joined by Lt. Gerard, the Indiana police officer who has been conducting a relentless search for Kimble, attempt to break Leonetti's confession, but he has obviously done his homework well. In the hospital room, Kimble, left alone for a moment, hits his wounded shoulder with a heavy bottle in an effort to make an x-ray necessary. The attempt succeeds; an intern orders x-rays. Soon after Lt. Gerard comes to tell Kimble that Leonetti has confessed, but Gerard says, as he leaves the room, that he doesn't believe him.

In the opening of Act IV as Anne talks with Kimble about Leonetti's confession, Kimble realizes that she has never been told of the terminal nature of her husband's illness. Now armed with the truth, Anne convinces her husband that he is wrong and foolish to throw away even ten months of his life. As a result, Leonetti informs the police that his confession is false. Meanwhile Kimble has been taken to the x-ray room where he finds Toby, an orderly, and Gloria, the x-ray technician, more interested in each other than they are in him.

THE FINAL CRISIS.   Taking them off guard, Kimble knocks Toby unconscious with a judo chop and locks Gloria in a supply closet. He then dresses in Toby's trousers and a top coat he finds on a rack and eludes the guard at the door by going into the corridor through the dark room.

Outside the hospital, he climbs into the back of a laundry truck parked at the dock just as the driver, who had failed to close the doors properly, pulls away. Their flapping attracts the attention of the driver who stops to shut them just as the police come rushing out of the hospital looking for the fugitive. The driver shuts the doors without seeing Kimble. Questioned by the police, he says that he has seen no one and then drives off.

THE RESOLUTION.   In the epilogue Anne and Victor Leonetti thank a frustrated Lt. Gerard for permitting her to see Kimble, and Leonetti says that if Kimble is captured he will pay all of his legal fees. "I'll tell him about it. . .when I find him," Gerard replies sharply. In the final scene of the play Kimble leaves the laundry truck while the driver is making a delivery and heads toward the sound of a distant train.

A SUMMARY OF THE PLOTTING.   Characterization and the development of a theme receive less emphasis in this play than they do in "Marty," and in this respect scripts in The Fugitive series are typical of plays of the goal-centered type. The accent is mainly on action. Most of the efforts at characterization are expended on the people in individual scripts who play principal roles in a given adventure—in this case Anne and Victor Leonetti. The running characters—Kimble and Lt. Gerard— emerge as complete and vivid characters only through the series as a whole. The main way in which "Marty" differs from this script, however, is in the nature of the complications that make up the plot. In "Marty" the writer created a series of situations that forced the main character to make decisions about a basic value in life. In The Fugitive script the complications consist of turns in the situation that affect favorably or unfavorably Kimble's struggle to maintain his freedom. In designing them the writer has created a story that is marked by sureness and direction, an accelerating pace, and a constantly increasing tension. Sometimes unfavorable developments pile up so ominously that the attainment of the goal seems impossible, but the balance does swing back and forth until finally it ends in the fugitive's favor. To indicate these shifts in balance, the complications of the plot are now listed in the order of their appearance in the script with each complication being described as favorable or unfavorable to the attainment of the character's goal.

1. Kimble discovers that Leonetti, a man who knows his real identity, is a patient in the hospital—unfavorable.

2. Anne Leonetti sees Kimble in the hospital and recognizes him— unfavorable.

3. Anne tells her husband that she has seen Kimble—unfavorable.

4. Leonetti reports Kimble's whereabouts to the police—unfavorable.

5. Anne warns Kimble of her husband's action—favorable.

6. Kimble escapes from the back of the hospital and is driven away by Anne—favorable.

7. The police set up a network throughout the area—unfavorable.

8. As Kimble gets out of Anne's car, the police drive up and shoot him down—unfavorable.

9. Leonetti discovers that Kimble was not on vacation during Jeanie's last attack but was seeking the services of a heart specialist—favorable.

10. Leonetti demonstrates his deep remorse—favorable.

11. Lt. Gerard, informed of Kimble's capture, comes for him—unfavorable.

12. Kimble discovers that he is not scheduled to have x-rays—unfavorable.

13. Leonetti confesses that he killed Kimble's wife—favorable.

14. Anne tells the police that her husband was with her on the night of the murder—unfavorable.

15. The police officer replies that her husband knows every detail of the murder—favorable.

16. Kimble manages to exacerbate his wound thus increasing his chance of having x-rays ordered—favorable.

17. Leonetti evades the traps Lt. Gerard sets for him during questioning and shows his knowledge of the crime—favorable.

18. X-rays for Kimble's shoulder are ordered—favorable.

19. Lt. Gerard tells Kimble that he does not believe Leonetti's confession—unfavorable.

20. Leonetti withdraws his confession—unfavorable.

21. Kimble escapes from the x-ray room—favorable.

22. He finds a hiding place in the laundry truck—favorable.

23. The driver, hearing the door flapping, stops his truck as the police come out—unfavorable.

24. He shuts the door and drives off without seeing Kimble—favorable.

25. Gerard recognizes that once more Kimble has escaped him—favorable.

Point one in this outline describes the opening situation. Points two through twenty list the complications which turn the situation first one way and then the other as Kimble's struggle moves to its climax. Points twenty-one through twenty-four cover the final crisis. Until the real murderer is finally captured, no script in this series can have a final resolution. What resolution there is, detailed in points twenty-five and twenty-six, lies in Lt. Gerard's realization that once again his quarry has slipped through his net as one more adventure for the fugitive doctor comes to an end.

OTHER PLOTTING PATTERNS

It should not be assumed that a given body of material must fit inevitably into a decision-centered or goal-centered framework. Written
from another viewpoint, *The Fugitive* script we have just reviewed might
well have become a decision-centered play in which Victor Leonetti,
as he tried to decide what to do about Richard Kimble, would have
played the leading role. Such a script, of course, would not have met
the prescription for *The Fugitive* series, which requires that attention
be focused on Dr. Kimble as he struggles for a goal in a shifting pattern
of hostile and friendly forces. Some plays do not fit into either framework
but deal about equally with factors of decision and accomplishment,
particularly the longer dramas presented on the stage or in the movies.
Because of their length, they can often dramatize a struggle to reach
a decision and then treat the struggle to reach the goal selected by
the decision. A dramatist writing such a play would use a combination
of the plotting techniques just reviewed. Before deciding on this combination approach, however, it may be well to consider whether you can
simplify your plotting problems and, incidentally, gain greater unity
of effect, by revising your plot so that it centers on either decision
or a struggle to reach a goal. The relatively short time periods of the
broadcast media often require the concentration that is gained when
one or the other type of struggle is emphasized.

One other common plotting pattern can be discerned in many of the
plays broadcast on television. The type of play that finally answers a
question presented at the beginning of the script or that provides an
explanation for a series of mysterious happenings might be called *revela-
tion-centered*. The script "Tatia" written by Robert Lewin for the *I
Spy* series is an example. The two heroes wonder at the beginning of
the play whether a beautiful free-lance writer who seeks them out is
really interested in their story or whether she has been commissioned
to kill them as the agent of an enemy spy syndicate. Events lead the
two heroes and the audience first toward one theory and then toward
the other.

Charles Beaumont's "In His Image," broadcast on the *Twilight Zone*,
provides a further illustration of this type of play. A young man returns
to his home town to discover that the buildings and general atmosphere
are utterly different from what they were the week before. When his
arm is injured in an automobile accident, he discovers that it is made
up of springs, resistors, and wires instead of being composed of human
tissues. The explanation finally revealed is that the man is not a man
at all but a robot whose recollection of events provided by his creator
is entirely synthetic and has little relation to reality. Plotting effectiveness

for this type of play depends on piquing the audience's curiosity, using a technique of gradual revelation, and ending with a solution that answers satisfactorily the questions posed at the beginning of the script.

IMPROVING THE PLOT

An experience common to many writers is the discovery that a plot which seemed to be developing smoothly has suddenly hit a snag and come to a dead stop. What does the writer do in such a situation? To answer this question without reference to a specific story is somewhat difficult, but perhaps some general suggestions may be helpful. First of all, do not give up in despair. Very few stories have suddenly sprung into being full blown in a writer's brain. The construction of almost every plot demands its moments of agony, and unfortunately there are no sure-fire formulas whose use is guaranteed to produce a satisfactory plot. There are certain basic procedures, however, which experience has shown to be effective. As an addition to the principles already discussed, let us consider a few more that may help the writer who is having plotting difficulties.

TROUBLE AND PLOTTING

An old French proverb has this counsel for the playwright: "Get your character into a tree. Throw stones at him. Get him out." Exactly the same advice was offered by the American playwright and actor Frank Craven when he said, "Get your character into a pot. Light a fire. Get him out." These admonitions sum up succinctly the fundamental responsibility of the dramatist in plotting his play. Start with a person in trouble. Intensify that trouble. Resolve it. The resolution, by the way, despite the admonitions just quoted, does not always free the character from his trouble. As the play ends he may still be in the tree, perhaps with a storm coming up. Or if the pot is his fate, the fade-out may come with the water just coming to a boil. But whatever its precise nature, the playwright must be making some kind of trouble for somebody at least until the resolution of the play is reached.

Yes, the aspiring playwright must be a trouble maker! Make as much trouble for your characters as you possibly can. Perhaps a guide to the most effective procedure is to combine the two pieces of advice with which this section began. Get your character into a tree. Throw stones at him. Get him out of the tree. But do not let him escape safely to the ground just yet. Instead, let him drop from the tree right into Frank Craven's pot of boiling water!

Assume that you have designed a plot that makes trouble for a character and yet still seems to lack sufficient impact to win sustained attention. What can you do to infuse such a pallid plot with a greater charge of excitement and power? One of the first questions you should ask yourself is— have I made the trouble for my characters serious enough?

Remember that your primary challenge in writing a play is to make an audience react emotionally. One of the ways already noted for doing this is to portray a character twisted with indecision as he tries to make a choice between two clashing values. To gain the maximum emotional response, those values must be as important to the character as you can possibly make them. Moreover, they must involve a problem that has meaning and reality for the average listener.

Suppose that you are writing a play about a man who has lost his faith in God. This theme will probably strike a responsive cord as far as the audience is concerned, for most people believe in the existence of a God and, at the same time, most people occasionally experience doubt. You can therefore expect sympathy and understanding from your audience. Is this enough? Perhaps, but there is at least one way in which this particular problem can be made more serious. Suppose that the individual suffering the loss of faith is not an ordinary layman, but the representative of an organized religion. It is his responsibility not just to believe in God—that would be taken for granted—but to enhance and sow that faith in other people. A loss of faith for such a person cannot be kept a secret. This complication of the problem will make his emotional response that much more intense and it will have a similar effect on the emotional response of the audience.

Up to now we have been looking at this man's trouble only in terms of his personal involvement. What if the problem reaches out to affect other people? Suppose, for example, that he has a niece, a mature person who has already passed the age when most women are married. Now, however, there is a prospect in the offing, not a man she is in love with yet, but certainly one with whom a happy married life is a possibility. Suppose, furthermore, that this prospect is a devout believer who is attracted to the niece, at least at first, because of the position her uncle holds as a propagator of the faith. We have succeeded in making the main character's trouble even worse, for more than his own happiness is now at stake. If his loss of faith becomes known, it is likely to smash what may be his niece's last chance for a normal life as a married woman.

You may have suspected that this example is not a hypothetical one. It is the plot development of a television play so successful that it was repeated a number of times—Paddy Chayefsky's "Holiday Song," the story of a Jewish cantor who temporarily lost his faith.

The principle that intensification of trouble amplifies the emotional response applies just as much to the goal-centered play as it does to the decision-centered play. One effective technique is to make the audience think that the hero has surmounted the last obstacle only to discover that he is in deeper trouble than he ever was before. This particular device was used effectively in the drama "Into the Night" by Mel Dinelli, broadcast on the *G. E. Theatre.* The play told the story of a young couple who fell into the clutches of a criminal fleeing the law. The group stopped at a farmhouse and the young man managed to get close enough to the old farmer to whisper to him the story of their predicament. With the farmer instructed to call the police at his first opportunity, the solution to the young couple's problem seemed near at hand. Their whole edifice of hope came crashing down, however, when the old farmer turned out to be deaf. Even more disturbing, it turned out that the criminal had overheard the whispered conversation and had made preparations to eliminate these hostages, who had all at once become a threat to him. This sudden turn for the worse, just when a solution seemed so near, had a powerful emotional impact. The initiative, however, did not remain with the criminal. Just as he was aiming his gun to kill his young hostages, the old farmer came up unexpectedly from behind holding a leveled shotgun. He revealed that he was not deaf after all, but had feigned deafness when he noticed the criminal listening to the young man's whispered words.

SURPRISE AS AN ELEMENT IN PLOTTING

This play also illustrates another effective technique for heightening emotional response. The revelation that the old farmer had actually heard the young man's plea for help came as a stunning surprise—to the criminal, to the young couple, and, most important of all, to the viewers. Surprise is one of the plot constructor's most important tools. It is probably not too much to say that some elements of surprise should be built into every plot. Some types of stories, of course, depend almost entirely for their impact on an unexpected plot twist. The type of detective fiction that makes the culprit the least likely suspect is an example. To make surprise the only objective of a story, of course, may be a mistake, for it can lead to an over-all result that is thin and unsatisfying. T. S. Eliot struck the proper note of moderation when he said, "The audience should be kept in constant expectation that something is going to happen; and that, when it does happen, it should be different, but not too different, from what the audience had been led to expect."

How can you introduce the unexpected into your scripts? One means is to take an audience down a road and then suddenly push it farther down that road than it expected to go. William Faulkner's story "A Rose for Emily" provides an example of this technique. Readers are prepared for the revelation that Emily has murdered her lover, but they are unprepared for the grisly disclosure that the corpse had been laid away in her bed.

The most common device for surprising an audience is to lead them to expect one thing and then suddenly reveal that the reverse is true. Hans Christian Andersen's "The Ugly Duckling" is a classic example of the reversal technique. A more modern example is provided by the TV play "Mock Trial" by Edith and Samuel Grafton, which was presented on *Kraft Theatre*. In this play a group of law students conduct a practice investigation of town officials, one of whom is the mayor. One of the students finds that while the mayor was the county tax collector, there was a discrepancy between the deposits of tax money and the amount supposed to have been collected. Armed with this evidence, the student attacks the mayor with a series of relentless questions. At this stage the student appears to be cast in the role of the heroic investigator, and the mayor seems to have been a cheap, grasping crook. The reversal comes when it is disclosed that the discrepancy resulted because the mayor delayed the due date of certain taxes to prevent farms from being taken over during the depression. Suddenly the mayor becomes the hero and the student is exposed as a headstrong, foolish young man. The same story might have been told without this surprise effect, but its emotional impact would have been greatly reduced.

BELIEVABILITY AND PLOTTING

No matter what kind of plotting problem faces a writer, he must always be concerned about attaining believability. The various segments of the plot must fit together in a reasonable, natural way. The resolution must be one that can be justified in terms of what has gone before. This test must also be applied to each development as it occurs. Does it grow naturally from the situation that just preceded it? Do the plot complications arise from factors that are inherent in the story? Solutions should not be thrust in suddenly from the outside.

One of the most important rules is that coincidence or fortuitous acts of fate should not be used to extricate a writer from a plotting dilemma. A coincidence may be employed to create a problem, but it should never be used to solve it. In other words, we can no longer use the easy way out of a plotting cul-de-sac sometimes employed by the Greek dramatists when their characters became entangled in such complicated circumstances that only the gods could bring order out of chaos. Down they came from their Olympian heights, lowered to the stage by a great crane, to straighten matters out. This kind of a solution, *deus ex machina,* is no longer acceptable. For example, in the play in which a criminal held two young people as hostages, the writer might have extricated the young people from their threatening situation by having the criminal fall dead of a heart attack just before he pulled the trigger of his gun. Such a solution would have destroyed the impact of the play. The use of coincidence or an act of fate to solve a problem, unless it develops inevitably from what has gone before, is always a sign of plotting weakness. In the chapter on Designing the Script we shall consider other problems of maintaining plausibility that arise while the script is being planned and written.

ORIGINALITY IN PLOTTING

To the young writer who aspires to create a plot that is completely original the best admonition is: quit trying. At least as far as the basic elements are concerned, no new plots have been developed for thousands of years. Even when people first began to write dramas, there were not many plots to go around. Some authorities say that no more than seven completely different plots have ever existed.

Actually, concern with creating original stories is a relatively modern development. In Greek times the playwright felt himself limited to the dramatization of one of a few well-known legends. His contribution was to promote new understandings of the characters and problems involved. Shakespeare's habit of borrowing plots or combining several of them to make a new story, as he did in *Macbeth,* is well known. Only two of his plots have not been traced to other sources. What made his plays creative triumphs was not the plot but the sharp probing into human motives and the glorious dialogue through which plot and characters were revealed.

The impossibility of creating a new plot, at least as far as its fundamental structure is concerned, should not be taken, however, as minimizing the importance of designing a satisfactory plot. Perhaps no fault is more common in the beginner's scripts than plotting weakness. If the plot cannot be new, at least it should live up to the criteria that have been described in this chapter. This means that it must meet the tests of credibility, of structural soundness, and of interest value. Great ingenuity and inventiveness are necessary to design a plot that will have these qualities.

And even though the basic elements of a plot cannot be new, the manner in which that plot is embodied in a script can be original with the writer. The use of new subject matter, for instance, can invest a familiar pattern of entanglements with qualities of freshness and distinction. The writer uses a standard design when he constantly shifts the balance of power in a goal-centered play, but the devices he uses to cause that shifting can be his own creation. He cannot invent new values for use in a play of decision, but he can originate new circumstances in which old values can be tested. So far as these factors are concerned, almost every story confronts a writer at times with a new frontier through which he must break the first path. In this strange territory he is pretty much on his own. For the unique problems he is likely to meet he must find solutions equally unique. His only resource in meeting this challenge is his own capacity for imaginative and creative thinking.

Perhaps the writer's best chance for originality is in the characters he creates to inhabit his plot. The pattern of entanglements can affect people who are uniquely his. It is with the problem of creating characters that we are next concerned.

QUESTIONS AND PROJECTS

1. Recall some of the plays, movies, or television dramas you have seen. Do your most vivid recollections seem to stem from effectively created characters or from ingeniously contrived plots?

2. Watch a TV drama with particular attention to the activity of the characters (speech, physical activity, and so on) and decide whether it is effective in revealing the action of the play.

3. Diagram the plotting line of a play to determine whether it can be categorized as decision-centered or goal-centered. If it is the first, list the crucial decisions of the leading character; if it is the second, describe the turns in the situation and indicate whether they are favorable or unfavorable to the attainment of the character's goal.

4. Isolate the surprise elements in a number of TV plays and decide whether they added to the dramatic experience.

5. In several TV dramas describe the nature of the trouble facing the leading characters. Could this trouble have been intensified to enhance the emotional impact in any instances?

4

Creating the Characters

The world will forgive a great deal if only a writer can create people. Norman Cousins

Of the many challenges facing a dramatist, the most important of all is the challenge of bringing to life characters who have flesh and blood reality, who, because of their vitality and individuality, seize the attention of an audience and achieve existence as absorbing, believable human beings. The works that have won an enduring place in literature have done so primarily because of their characters. The brooding, hesitant Hamlet sticks more vividly in our memory than the precise series of events that entrapped him. The picture of a proud Oedipus propelling himself to doom in a relentless search for truth comes first to our mind rather than the specific complications that brought about his destruction.

The process of characterization involves two steps. First, the dramatist must bring into being in his own mind the characters of his play, determining for himself precisely what kind of people they are. Second, through such means as dialogue, setting, action, and reaction, he must reveal his creations to his audience. In this chapter we are concerned with the first of these steps: the creation of characters. In a later chapter we shall review the techniques of character revelation used in the actual writing of scripts.

A DEFINITION OF CHARACTER

The task of defining a person's character may be approached in a number of different ways. We may describe a certain individual as a selfish person who in a crisis is likely to seek a solution that will be of benefit primarily to himself. We may characterize a person of the opposite stripe as kind and generous. We may say of someone else that he always puts his work first even at the expense of denying his family a much-needed vacation. Looking at character from still another viewpoint, we may attach the tag of "cold fish" to the individual who is difficult to know. When we think of a certain person, a tie that is always askew may come first to mind. These details are all reflections of general qualities that add up to the complex concept we know as character. Let us examine the nature of these qualities.

CHARACTER VALUES

The ultimate test of a person's character is the way he behaves, particularly in a critical situation. More important than anything else in determining how he behaves are the values or drives that dominate his life. They determine the choices he makes as he faces critical decisions, and these choices, in turn, reveal what kind of man he is. Thus, a man's character is determined directly by his system of values. It follows that the most crucial step in the creation of a character is to decide the values that control his behavior.

What are some of the values that motivate our lives? A few men have an insatiable lust for power and are willing to sacrifice all else to gain it. Others give up everything for the love of a woman. Javert in Victor Hugo's *Les Misérables* finally destroyed himself because of his insensate dedication to what he considered duty. The artist Van Gogh had such an overwhelming desire to paint that it crowded all other values out of his life. Some men crave fame and attention; others deliberately avoid it. Albert Schweitzer fled from the world that would honor him to minister to suffering human beings in a remote African village.

Most people, of course, are motivated by a number of different values, many of which never come into conflict. A man may desire to get to the top of his profession and, at the same time, want to take good care of his family. By attaining the first goal, he can help gain the second. But desires sometimes crash into each other head-on, a desirable happening in drama, for it is clash that creates a dramatic situation. In "Marty," for example, the focal character had to decide whether he was willing to endure the scorn of his pals for the privilege of continuing his association with the girl who had attracted him. His decision to dial her number told us that one value had triumphed over the other. Characterization in the goal-centered play is similarly based on values. The choice of the goal reflects the character's basic desires, and the tenacity with which he struggles to reach that goal reveals to what degree those desires influence his life.

People are not always aware of the desires that motivate their behavior. Extremely powerful drives, those controlling the individual's most vital decisions, may exist on a subconscious level, and, in fact, some people might actually be horrified if they understood the real nature of their drives. A citizen, for example, may gain a reputation for outstanding community contributions because of his willingness to head various campaigns. Is this an indication of his desire to help other people? It may be. On the other hand, his eagerness to assume these responsibilities may merely reflect a hunger for fame and praise or a lust for power—the desire to control people and things. Another example of the influence of hidden values is provided by the letter a young swain once wrote to his sweetheart: "I would go through fire and water or climb the highest mountain to be with you." Then he concluded with a P.S. "If it rains tonight, I won't be over."

The fact that an individual is unaware of what motivates his conduct does not in any way lessen its impact upon his behavior. Some hidden desires have tremendous influence and they are legitimate material for the dramatist's use. In fact, some of the most satisfying plays are those portraying characters motivated by drives whose existence they either fail to recognize or would deny, but which the dramatist makes crystal clear to the audience. One reason such characters are particularly satisfying, perhaps, is simply that we know why each character acts a certain way even if he does not. We enjoy the pleasure of superior knowledge.

CHARACTER TRAITS

Another way of approaching the process of characterization is to identify the traits that describe a person. A trait is defined as a distinguishing quality or characteristic. Traits are related, of course, to a character's system of values, but identifying specific traits adds another dimension to characterization. The overwhelming desire of Richard Kimble in *The Fugitive* series is to maintain his freedom, but his struggle to achieve that goal is marked by great personal bravery, resourcefulness, and sometimes a concern for others that brings him very close to capture. The revelation of these character traits, which are separate from his dominating desire to remain free, adds immensely to the richness of his characterization; without these traits, in fact, he would be little more than a shadow.

To enumerate all of the traits that can identify characters would require a very long list. Almost everything we say about a person relates in some way to his traits. Creating characters involves the defining of character traits that will enhance and amplify the basic characterization achieved through the establishment of character values.

One of the most important steps in establishing the traits of an individual is to decide his characteristic way of reacting to a situation. If in the face of crises he retains full control of his faculties, he exemplifies the trait of coolness or self-possession. If he scarcely reacts at all, he is phlegmatic; if he responds chaotically, he is hot-headed or impulsive. Some people, characteristically, view matters with optimism; others always see the dark side. This type of trait is often referred to as the temperament or disposition of a character. Another aspect of temperament is the way a person behaves in dealing with other people. He may conduct himself in a kindly, understanding, cruel, or thoughtless way. He may be blunt in his relations with other people or he may be smooth and diplomatic.

CHARACTER MANNERISMS

A mannerism is any characteristic mode or peculiarity of speaking, dress, or behavior. It is less basic a quality than a trait but it also contributes to the establishment of a character. The addiction of some men to wearing bow ties is a form of mannerism. The peculiar way in which a cowboy rolls his own cigarettes or his habit of wearing a match behind his ear are other examples.

In many cases, mannerisms are directly related to basic character values. In the movie *Executive Suite*, the story of the struggle for control of a large corporation, the man who most wanted to be elected to the top position was shown over and over again nervously wiping his hands with a handkerchief, a mannerism that helped to reveal his desperate desire for the top job. But sometimes mannerisms, at least on the surface, may appear to be in direct conflict with the character of the individual. Some of the gangster movies of the 1930s, for instance, featured savage killers whose utter ruthlessness was hidden behind a façade of apparent gentleness and consideration. This kind of contrast may have a shock value that serves to heighten the impact of the basic character traits. The mannerism, however, should not be confused with the trait, which is the reflection of the elemental character of each individual. An individual's peculiar way of doing things may be characteristic of him but, in the true sense of the word, it may not actually characterize. Mannerisms, however, can make a character more interesting, and, as Kenneth MacGowan pointed out, they can sometimes make a character more palatable.[1] A hero who is a poet, artist, or musician—and therefore suspect to the average audience—can be made more acceptable if he is shown doing what average people do—reading comic strips, quarreling with his mother-in-law, or making model planes.

BUILDING THE CHARACTERS

Characters, we have seen, are an amalgam of various values, traits, and mannerisms. With these general qualities in mind, how does one go about building a specific character? The first step in characterization is to develop in your mind as complete a picture of the character as you can. Eugene O'Neill, it is said, wrote out the life stories of his characters before he began writing a single line of dialogue. Ibsen once said about his character, Nora, in *A Doll's House:* "The things I know about that young woman that aren't in the play would surprise you." Without question the dramatist should know a great deal more about his characters than he can reveal to his audience.

SELECTING CHARACTER QUALITIES

With a complete character in mind, the next step is to decide what facets of that character are to be emphasized in the play. You cannot hope, of course, to establish the whole character. For one thing, the time limitations of most radio and TV dramas make that impossible. Further, broadcast drama requires the focused rather than the panoramic approach; it centers on a limited area and you must concentrate on those aspects of character that serve to illuminate your specific play idea. Finally, you should leave some character development for your audience. As Tennessee Williams said in discussing his play *Cat on a Hot Tin Roof,* "Some mystery should be left in the revelation of character in a play, just as a great deal of mystery is always left in the revelation of character in life."

As far as values are concerned, you will select those values that are related to the basic conflict of your play. In the decision-centered play, for example, you will concentrate on the clashing values that pull the

[1] Kenneth MacGowan, *A Primer of Playwriting* (New York: Random House, Inc., 1951), p. 73.

main character first one way and then another. In other characters you will look for those values that represent one side or the other of the major conflict. This selection of values will be complemented by the addition of those traits and mannerisms that are pertinent and can be treated in the time available. Selectivity, then, is essential in building characters.

ACHIEVING RICHNESS OF CHARACTERIZATION

If only a portion of a complete character can be presented in a play, how can a dramatist give the impression that he has created a real person, an individual, who, as the expression goes, is three dimensional? The answer is that he must approach the problem of creating characters by selecting a few characteristics that he can treat in depth rather than by trying to achieve breadth of characterization. If a writer probes deeply enough into a character, even though what he reveals remains relatively narrow, he does achieve a characterization that seems to be full and rich. Thinking about even the great characters of drama, we realize that we know relatively little about them; what we do know, however, is so deep and satisfying that we feel we have become acquainted with a real and complete person.

The principal means of achieving in-depth characterizations is to use a technique that Martin Maloney called *tagging*.[2] This process involves deciding on one or two pertinent characteristics and then creating scene after scene in which these characteristics are revealed in different ways. If you create a character whose dominating trait is selfishness, you may show that trait operating in his family relations, as he works with his business associates, and as he socializes among his friends. An outstanding example of character tagging is the person the radio and television audience knew as Jack Benny. Down through the years one over-riding trait was tagged again and again—his deep concern for money or, to put it more simply—his stinginess.

Concentrating on the few character qualities that are directly related to the point of the play does not mean that you must ignore other character qualities completely. You can suggest the existence of these qualities through hints and implications which are not fully developed. The viewer may take a mere incidental reference and with his own imagination fill in the details for himself. Remember that audiences will work for you if you give them the opportunity. Being able to provide useable suggestions, however, depends on your complete acquaintance with the character in question. You must be so full of him that hints about him flow inevitably into your script.

[2] Martin Maloney, *The Radio Play* (Evanston: The Student Book Exchange, 1949), p. 107.

Character richness can be attained, finally, by the skillful development of traits and mannerisms. They add interest and color and, by filling in the picture, contribute materially to an impression of depth.

CREATING ORIGINAL CHARACTERS

Another problem in characterization is to create people who become original and distinct personalities for the audience. In a sense this problem is related to the one we have just considered, for as a character becomes rich and complete, so is he likely to become an individual who is different from other people. What makes him different? It is difficult to think of creating a distinctive character by conceiving some entirely new human desire or creating a brand new human trait. The fundamental aims of mankind have existed since the beginning of drama, as have the various human traits. It is probably safe to say that no new goal can possibly be invented that would constitute a basic addition to man's aspirations. What can be done, however, is to devise ways for arranging the various elements of character into combinations that are new and different.

THE PROBLEM OF THE STEREOTYPE

The opposite of the original character is the stereotype, the character who is copied directly from the arrangement and invention of some other writer, who may in turn have copied it from some writer before him. Even as early as the nineteenth century the playwright Anton Chekhov identified newspaper reporters who drink, starving authors, and good-natured nurses as types to be avoided because they had been done over and over again. Despite Chekhov's stricture, these types persisted into the twentieth century, and stereotypes like them abound in television drama. The tremendous volume of material necessary to keep TV screens alight is one reason for the prevalence of stereotypes. The creation of new and original characters is a time-consuming process. Moreover, there are limits to a writer's creative resources; he cannot keep inventing new characters indefinitely and yet he must keep writing in order to turn out his required quota of scripts. Under such conditions it is only natural, indeed inevitable, that many of the characters he puts into his plays will be imitations of his own previous creations or copies of characters by other writers.

Another reason for the longevity of many stereotypes is that when first created they were original and arresting characters. In this sense, they resemble clichés, which because of their very color and vividness, tend to be perpetuated until ceaseless repetition dulls our reaction to them. A stereotype in point is the hard-boiled spy character who flourishes in the movies and in such television programs as *The Man from U.N.C.L.E.* The prototype is the Ian Fleming creation, James Bond, whose exploits were recounted in a series of novels. James Bond is succinct and direct in speech. He is tough. Physical punishment that would mash ordinary citizens into permanent insensibility causes him only momentary discomfort. He can administer violent punishment himself, crushing skulls and breaking arms with the verve and abandon of a man who truly loves his work. He likes blondes but is supremely successful in eluding permanent entanglements. The same applies to brunettes and red heads. He is quick, intelligent, and capable of infinite adaptations to critical situations. James Bond is an interesting and original character creation. The very effectiveness of the portrayal inspires imitation.

The 1961–62 TV season saw two television hits featuring young doctors who struggled with medical problems under the guidance and harassment of two older, experienced physicians. The success of *Ben Casey* and *Dr. Kildare* prompted the creation of *The Nurses,* a series that featured a student nurse guided by an older and wiser senior nurse. These two characters, the nurses, were essentially the same as those developed in the two doctor series. Only the sex had been changed.

What is the writer to do about character stereotypes? We cannot say that he is certain to fail if he uses them, for most of the examples just cited have had resounding commercial success. What we can say, however, is that the constant employment of stereotypes will soon make writing sterile and routine; it will deprive the play of that quality which is most likely to make it memorable—the arresting character who seizes our interest because of its individuality. Stereotypes inhabit the program fillers; they may develop some temporary interest for audiences if the characters they are based on were sufficiently intriguing to begin with, but they do not linger in people's minds. It is the original creation that audiences remember, not the pale imitations. It is only through individual characterization that plays gain lasting memorability.

Another objection to the stereotype is that it often perpetuates false ideas about people, particularly the idea that certain characteristics, occupations, or human failings are associated with certain races or nationalities. Thus we are led to believe that policemen are always Irish, that the Oriental is undeviatingly wise and inscrutable, that Scotsmen are always inordinately concerned about money. The television program *The Untouchables* provoked great resentment among Italian-Americans through its consistent identification of members of that national group with the criminal elements in our society. The writer must be constantly on guard against adopting and transmitting stereotypes of this nature. He must recognize that most general statements about classes of people are untrue, at least in part, and he must realize that any given member of a national, racial, occupational, or educational group is a unique human being. The highest achievement in characterization is to establish the individuality and complexity of a person—to show, in other words, how he differs from other people rather than to show how much he resembles them. Creating a unique character is obviously much more difficult than using a stereotype, whose characteristics may be quickly recognized and understood by the audience. Only writers who have ample reserves of insight and originality and who are not limited by what has been done before can bring new and individual people into being.

Despite all this, we must accept the fact that, for the reasons already given, character stereotypes will continue to inhabit television dramas in large numbers. And it must be acknowledged that, in some instances, they can serve the television writer, whose time for characterization is always severely limited, by permitting him to identify quickly the characteristics of minor or incidental characters. He must refrain, of course, from employing any objectionable stereotypes. But the use of characters who can be quickly established because their qualities are immediately recognizable permits him to spend most of his time portraying the major characters of his play, whom he makes the original and unique creations of his script.

THE RELATIONSHIP OF CHARACTER AND PLOT

It is obvious that there is a direct relationship between the characters of a play and the development of its plot since the plot usually arises either from the decisions a character makes as a series of choices confronts him, or from changes in balance for or against him as he strives to reach an objective. The decisions made or the willingness to continue or quit the struggle reflect in turn the character's basic values. If his values were different, his decisions would be different also, and the design of the plot would change. Or, to look at it from the opposite point of view, if the plot takes a certain turn, calling for a decision that is out of keeping with the character's previously held values, then either the character must be changed or that particular plot development must be abandoned.

Lajos Egri in his book *The Art of Dramatic Writing* commented on what would have happened to Shakespeare's plays *Hamlet* and *Romeo and Juliet* if the characters of Hamlet and Romeo had been interchanged. The young, impetuous Romeo, confronted by the terrible secret of his father's death, would have acted instantly instead of brooding and hesitating as Hamlet did. Hamlet in Romeo's shoes would scarcely have been guilty of the rash acts that made Romeo's meeting with Juliet possible or of the disregard of consequences that permitted him to court her. With Hamlet in the lover's role, Juliet would have been safely married to another man before Hamlet had done anything at all. The character of Hamlet dictated the particular kind of play in which he appeared; or to look at it the other way, the plot Shakespeare used demanded the particular kind of character that Hamlet was.

This gives rise to the question: which comes first, plot or character? If this is taken to mean which arises first in the writer's mind, there is no absolute answer. Either character or plot may be the starting point for a play. If it is the concept of a character that sparks the creative drive, then the writer must devise a series of situations, gradually developing in their intensity, in which that character acts. The way he acts will reveal to the audience what kind of man he is, for in the words of Walter Kerr, "Character is best revealed by the response it makes to circumstance."[3] The character's inner nature is revealed because he takes one road, having had the chance to take another. In constructing plots this way, the writer follows his characters, permitting them to create the complications. There is nothing wrong with this approach. In fact, a number of writers, among them John Galsworthy and Georges Simonen, have said that every plot must inevitably grow from character, for the situations are inherent in it.

It may happen, on the other hand, that the initial idea for a play is a plot twist, or perhaps an exciting climactic scene. Now the problem of the writer is to create characters who will make the development of that scene believable. They must be imbued with the kind of drives that lead directly to the situation the writer conceived as his beginning idea. In this instance plot has given rise to character.

Both plot-to-character and character-to-plot approaches can be used. While the process of play construction is going on, it is probably wise for you to remain flexible as far as both elements are concerned. Be ready to make changes if they seem to be necessary. You may have to change a preconceived character somewhat to satisfy the demands of the story. Or character values may dictate modifications in the plot. Do not cling unreasonably to your original ideas. Be ready to modify and adapt them to bring about the strongest possible result as far as both character and plot are concerned.

If a play depends for its interest primarily on plot action and gives little attention to character development, it is included in the class of plays called melodrama. The goal-centered play is more likely to fall into this category than the decision-centered play because the struggle

---

[3] Walter Kerr, *How Not to Write a Play* (New York: Simon and Schuster, Inc., 1955), p. 128.

to achieve a goal takes place primarily outside the chief character, and the focus of attention is on the activity that arises from his effort to overcome obstacles. The decision-centered play, on the other hand, spotlights an inner conflict; the emphasis is on the character values that will survive when this conflict is resolved.

CLASSES OF CHARACTERS

There are a number of ways in which characters in a drama might be classified, and various terms have been developed to denote the different characters in terms of their importance in the story.

THE FOCAL CHARACTER

In most plays there is one character on whom the interest of the audience centers—the focal character. In the decision-centered play, he is the character who makes the decisions that constitute the vital action of the drama. In the goal-centered play, he is the character who struggles to overcome obstacles in order to reach his goal. We might call this person the hero or protagonist except that both these terms denote a person who wins the sympathy of the audience, and the audience may be chiefly interested in a villainous individual whose struggle to achieve an evil purpose elicits neither sympathy nor hope for his success. If this is the case, he qualifies as the focal character even though he is far from being a hero.

Do all plays need a focal character? Most absolutes are wrong and to say that to be successful all plays must have a focal character is probably wrong also. Kenneth MacGowan pointed out that modern plays sometimes make a group the hero instead of one individual, and in other plays two or more characters make equal demands on the interest of the audience.[4] Such plays, however, should be thought of as exceptions to the general rule that a drama should be built around the struggles or decisions of a focal character. Although two or even three characters may play pivotal roles in the play, almost approaching equality in their interest to the audience, the best effect is likely to result if the main attention is directed toward one character to whom the other characters are subordinated. For one thing, concentrating interest on a single person provides the writer with a valuable means of attaining unity. This is especially important in the TV drama which, being shorter than the average stage presentation, needs a focus of interest. Secondly,

[4] Kenneth MacGowan, *A Primer of Playwriting*, p. 81.

the emotions of the viewers are most likely to be engaged when their attention is centered on the struggles of one individual.

OTHER PRINCIPAL CHARACTERS

The focal character is obviously a principal character in a play, but other people in the play often have such vital roles in the action that they, too, qualify as principal characters. In "Marty" the title character's mother and the girl he meets at the dance hall are principal characters. In *The Fugitive* script, analyzed in the previous chapter, Richard Kimble is the focal character and Victor and Anne Leonetti and Lt. Gerard are other principal characters. In plays that feature a continuing conflict between persons, as this one does, the focal character's antagonist would always be a principal character.

SECONDARY CHARACTERS

Less important than the principal characters, yet still playing significant functions, are the characters we label as secondary. In most cases they are not vital to the basic conflict but are used to carry out some special function. A good example is Angie, the main pal of the focal character, in Paddy Chayefsky's play "Marty." Their conversation helps to make clear the nature of Marty's problem.

The function performed by Angie is a very important one in the writing of drama. In serving as Marty's *confidant*, he makes it possible for the playwright to transmit Marty's thoughts to the audience in a natural, acceptable way. Since the dramatist should avoid long, introspective speeches and cannot actually describe a character's thoughts the way a novelist or short story writer can, he must rely on dialogue between a character and his confidant to make these thoughts clear to the audience. In another of Chayefsky's plays, "Holiday Song," a man named Zucker becomes the confidant of the cantor who has lost his faith. It is through their conversation that we discover just what problem is agitating the cantor. A common example of the confidant is the secretary of a private detective.

In the decision-centered play there is another service that can be performed by secondary characters—namely, to represent the choices facing the focal character. Marty has to choose between marriage and the bachelor life. His buddy, Angie, not only functions as a confidant but also represents the man who seems deliberately to have chosen the unmarried state. The opposite choice of marriage is represented by Marty's cousin Thomas.

Rod Serling's play "The Strike" provides an excellent example of secondary characters serving to spotlight the two choices confronting the focal character. This play, set in Korea during the war there, finds a Major Gaylord in command of what is left of a division. Across the river overwhelming numbers of Chinese soldiers threaten the remnants of his forces. He has sent a patrol of twenty men into the enemy lines to reconnoiter. Then he receives word that the Chinese artillery has been located and he is ordered to call for an air strike to destroy it. The tragic irony is that his patrol is operating in the very area where this artillery is located. An air strike means almost certain death for the patrol, yet the artillery endangers the lives of the 500 men in his division. Two of his officers, Captain Franks and Captain Chick, who serve as his confidants, urge him to make the difficult choice of destroying the smaller number of men in order to protect the larger group. The other choice is represented by Lieutenant Jones, the officer under whose command the men on the patrol had operated. He begs Major Gaylord not to give the order that will destroy them; when he fails to dissuade him, he makes a futile attempt to cross the river to warn his men. A hail of Chinese bullets kills him. These characters are secondary, yet their illumination of the choices implicit in the Major's dilemma contributes enormously to the effect of the play.

INCIDENTAL CHARACTERS

The characters who are needed to fill out a play or a scene are called incidental characters. Usually they appear in a service function and, in many cases, they are not even identified by name. A nurse in *The Fugitive* script is an example of an incidental character. Others who fall into this category are taxi-drivers, maids, gas station attendants, and hotel clerks.

Generally, the writer spends very little time in building up the incidental characters in a play. Even if he had time to develop them, he would be unwise to do so, for they would divert attention from the people in the play who are really important. Roger Busfield points out that J. P. Miller in his TV play, "The Rabbit Trap," inserts an old man merely to deliver a message, but makes him so interesting that the audience expects the old man to return to play a vital role. He never does return and thus the audience's expectation is deceived.[5] Incidental characters should be kept to their proper function. To make them too vivid will confuse and mislead the audience.

[5] Roger Busfield, *The Playwright's Art* (New York: Harper & Row Publishers, 1958), p. 100.

THE NUMBER OF CHARACTERS

How many characters are necessary for a play? The answer is the fewest number needed to tell the story. Paddy Chayefsky emphasized this point when he said, "There shouldn't be a character in the script who doesn't have to be there to answer the demands of the main character's story."[6] Generally, television drama requires fewer characters than do stage plays or movies. One reason for this is that TV drama has no time for the extended subplots that are often included in a theatre drama. Another reason is that the small TV screen is an inappropriate vehicle for transmitting the mass effects that the stage or movie screen can handle satisfactorily. Restricting the number of characters in radio drama is even more important for an audience that must distinguish between them on the basis of voice alone. If you do not absolutely need a character, have no compunctions about erasing him immediately.

CHANGES IN CHARACTERS

In the introduction to the printed version of his TV play "The Lawn Party," Tad Mosel says of his leading character, "She doesn't change throughout the entire play." Apparently feeling defensive about this, he adds, "If someone cares to tell me I shouldn't write a play wherein the protagonist doesn't change, I have no answer."[7] The implication of this statement is that there is something wrong with a play in which characters do not change. Is this actually the case?

First of all, we should consider what we mean by character change. By change we do not mean an incidental alteration in a person's behavior but a fundamental transformation of his basic nature. His system of values must change. What was important to him before must no longer be important and new values must rise to replace the discarded ones. The selfish, self-centered person who becomes thoughtful and altruistic is an example of a character changing. Is it possible to make this kind of shift in an individual's personality believable?

One approach to answering this question is to ask whether people who have reached mature development ever change in real life? To say that changes never take place would be unduly cynical, but when such changes do occur they generally develop over a long period of time. It is not the impact of a single catastrophic event that usually accomplishes the transformation but the repeated effect of many similar incidents.

[6] Paddy Chayefsky, *Television Plays* (New York: Simon and Schuster, Inc., 1955), p. 86.

[7] Tad Mosel, *Other People's Houses* (New York: Simon and Schuster, Inc., 1956), p. 115.

It can be seen immediately that a television playwright faces almost insuperable difficulties in trying to duplicate this sort of real-life situation. The relative brevity of TV drama makes it difficult to record, or even to suggest, the gradual development needed to make fundamental character changes believable. Most TV dramas, furthermore, are designed to present a single, intense crisis in the life of an individual. Basic changes under this kind of a plotting design must either be catastrophic, or they cannot take place at all.

Are catastrophic character reversals always to be ruled out? You may be able to cite examples of individuals you have known who seem to have undergone sudden personality transformations. In some instances we accept such overnight shifts as genuine simply because we see them and they appear to be real. They are always difficult to understand, however. There lies the nub of the problem for the playwright. He must not only present the change but he must also make it believable. In life we accept many things that we do not understand. Not so with a play. Audiences must understand what is going on or they will refuse to accept it. A character who changes traits suddenly in mid-play usually becomes inconsistent and unbelievable. The playwright has failed to comply with the inescapable requirement that what he presents must be credible.

Despite the difficulties, however, it is sometimes possible to write a TV play in which a character does actually change. A case in point was "Give Us Barrabas" by Henry Denker, a play so well received in its first presentation on the *Hallmark Hall of Fame* series that it was repeated. The whole point of this play was that the character, Barrabas, did change. Without this change there would have been no play. The opening scenes showed Barrabas being released to the mob in place of Jesus. At that point Barrabas was a depraved criminal, a coarse, violent man who lived completely for himself, with no thought of others. He was supremely confident of his ability to make his way in the world by using his wits. Then the invisible presence of the man who had been crucified in his place began to work on him. Subtly the play recorded the changes that took place. His utter self-reliance was gradually replaced with the realization that he needed someone outside of himself. He began to search for a meaning to life and in this search came to recognize that he had a responsibility for more than himself. The gentle, concerned, unselfish Barrabas of the end of the play was a completely different person from the snarling animal who had opened it. This was a case in which character transformation was made believable. To repeat, it was the point of the play and it provided a moving and satisfying experience for the viewer.

The type of play in which a character actually changes must be considered a rare exception, however. There is some question whether even

Nora in Ibsen's *A Doll's House* actually undergoes any basic transformation, even though she is often cited as an example of a character who changes. It is true that at the beginning of the play she appears to be a flighty, improvident child who contrasts sharply with the mature, assured woman who slams the door at the end. Yet the exposition of the events that took place before the play begins—particularly the forging of the note—reveals that even in those early years Nora was a person of courage and resourcefulness. It seems clear that she assumed the doll-wife pose to please her vain and foolish husband and her willingness to play this role is a further reflection of her adaptiveness. Nora did not change. The events of the play merely revealed her true nature.

Does this mean that the TV dramatist cannot usually do what many critics of drama have considered essential—namely, to portray characters who develop? Obviously this is so if development is thought of as character transformation. But there is another sense in which this word can be applied. Development can be looked on as the process through which the playwright reveals the character to the audience. It is the unveiling or disclosure of the person's values and traits by showing him reacting to a series of crucial problems. Through this gradual revelation the audience, which knows nothing about the character at the beginning of the play, comes to understand him. This is the sense in which Ibsen developed the character of Nora. William Archer compared the process to that taking place when a photographer develops a picture.[8] Through the application of chemicals, the forms inherent in the negative are gradually made clear to the viewer. Exactly the same process occurs in playwriting. The character does not change; his traits are merely brought out. This type of character development must take place in a play, and, as we have noted before, it is usually the only kind of "development" that can be satisfactorily accomplished.

SOURCES OF CHARACTERS

What is the single most important source of characters? Martin Maloney said of the writer, "The referent for his characters is himself; it is his perception of humanity which he publishes, in his characters, to the world."[9] The implication of this statement is that in creating characters the writer cannot escape himself; even if he does not project his own person, his characters cannot transcend his innate capacity to observe, to understand, and to interpret human behavior. His indelible

[8] William Archer, *Play-Making* (Boston: Small, Maynard and Company, 1912), p. 373.
[9] Martin Maloney, *The Radio Play*, p. 84.

personal imprint will be on all of them. There cannot be more in a character than a writer can see in life or put there through the workings of his imagination.

REFLECTIONS OF THE WRITER

Many writers do, as a matter of fact, create characters who are representations of themselves. An outstanding example of this practice was Thomas Wolfe who, despite his vehement denials that he was doing so, wrote a series of novels that were mainly autobiographical in nature. *David Copperfield* is largely the story of Charles Dickens' early life. The plays of George Bernard Shaw frequently present characters whose personality, wit, and general attitude toward life have proved to be indistinguishable from that of the writer himself. There is nothing wrong with this practice, by the way, if the resulting character is unique and impelling.

OTHER PEOPLE

Most characters, of course, must come from outside the writer, for as Chekhov said, "A play will be worthless if all the characters resemble you." The most likely source of ideas is the experience you have with people in real life. Probably nine-tenths of the characters you create will have their inspiration in a person who actually lived. This does not mean that this person will be translated into a dramatic character without any change. You may have to make modifications to fit the demands of your plot or to point your theme more tellingly. Furthermore, it is impossible for you to depict a character in totality. As we have noted previously, you are limited to a consideration of those values and traits that are directly related to the play's basic issue. Finally, no matter how well you may think you know a person, your knowledge, like the part of the iceberg you see above the water, is an inadequate representation of the depths that are unseen.

FICTION AND HISTORY

Your vicarious experience can furnish information about people you have never met who may provide the foundation for excellent characters. Your reading is an example. You cannot copy other writers' characters directly, but a character in fiction or in a play may start your mind to working until you end up, not with the character you read about, but with one that is your own original, unique creation. The people of history may be another source of ideas. Sometimes they can be used in plays that are biographical or semibiographical in nature, in which case you attempt to portray a historical personage with as much fidelity to his known character as you can. In other cases the actual person will merely serve to trigger your creative impulses; the final creation may bear no resemblance to its inspiration. Finally, you should not overlook the experiences of your relatives and friends in seeking characters. Their stories about people they have known can be a fruitful source of character ideas.

CONFLICTING VALUES

Since drama depends for its existence on conflict, the people you know or have read or heard about are likely to be helpful as character inspirations to the degree that you can see in them the kind of conflicts in values that result in exciting drama. Robespierre, a leader of the French Revolution, is a good example of a historical personage who could serve as the focus of drama. He was a finicky, almost prudish man who disliked violence and bloodshed. In his early life he opposed the practice of capital punishment and yet during his period of power as a revolutionary leader, France endured its most violent bloodbath. The guillotine became the solution to every problem until in the end it took even Robespierre's life. What happened to his original scruples? Did he accept the guillotine and capital punishment because he felt there was no other way to save the Revolution? Was he torn by internal conflict? We do not know, of course, but the dramatist does not need to know in order to make this type of character play the leading role in a compelling drama. He cannot, naturally, twist historical facts to suit his purpose, particularly if he claims that his play is biographical, but he can use his imagination to a certain extent to invent details that will point and intensify the conflict as long as those details are consonant with what is known. Of course, he may decide not to write about Robespierre at all but about a character of his own creation who is torn by the same type of conflict—a district attorney, for example, who, although personally opposed to capital punishment, must prosecute a man for murder in a state where the electric chair is the penalty for that crime. In that case the writer's imagination can have free rein.

STEPS IN CREATING CHARACTERS

Let us review briefly the steps you should follow in developing a character for your plays.

1. Seek a beginning idea for the character first. If the idea for your play has its origin in a plot twist, the basic nature of your character

may be dictated to you. But the filling out of the character will depend to a large degree on your personal experience and recollections of real or fictional people.

2. Establish the basic motivations of the character. This means that you must decide the values that are to affect his choice of goals or determine his decisions. As you do this, you must keep in mind the plot line and the theme of the play. The values of your characters must be related to and reinforce these elements of the play.

3. Devise the other aspects of personality that will give depth and individuality to the character. This involves the development of traits and mannerisms which complement the basic values. Remember, too, that to present an effective characterization, you must see the person you are representing in far more detail than you can possibly reveal to the audience. This richness in your conception will help you to provide the touches and implications that will aid the audience to amplify and round out the character.

QUESTIONS AND PROJECTS

1. Design a complete profile for a potential character in a drama, creating a full complement of values, traits, and mannerisms. Decide which of these characteristics you will emphasize in a drama through the process of tagging.

2. Observe a number of TV dramas with special attention to the use of stereotyped characters. Decide in each instance whether the use of the stereotype is justified.

3. Speculate on what might have happened to the plots of some familiar plays if qualities of certain characters were reversed. What would happen to Shakespeare's *Macbeth*, for example, if Lady Macbeth were cautious, kindly, and good?

4. In a number of TV plays place the characters in the following categories: focal, principal, secondary, and incidental.

5. Describe a person you know whose conflicting values would provide satisfactory material for dramatic treatment.

5

Finding the Theme

A good way to destroy a play is to force it to prove something.
Walter Kerr

Most authorities agree that to create drama you need at least one character, some kind of setting, and, if not a plot, at least a situation on which the action can turn. Whether you need a theme, however, is a disputed matter. Some consider it an essential element in a play, whereas others decry its importance and may even argue that too strong a theme obstructs the attainment of dramatic objectives. In this chapter we review the place of a theme in play construction, examine its nature, and consider its contributions and possible dangers to effective drama.

A DEFINITION OF THEME

One reason that authorities disagree on whether a theme is necessary is that the term means different things to different people.

THEME AS BASIC SUBJECT MATTER

The term "theme" is often used to denote the basic subject matter of a play. In this sense we can say that the theme of *Macbeth* is ambition; of *Othello*, jealousy; of *Hamlet*, revenge; of *Julius Caesar*, political power; and of *Romeo and Juliet*, young love. In this sense, the theme of the television series, *The FBI*, was the fight against crime and of *Dr. Kildare*, the practice of medicine in a large hospital. The individual episodes in these series dealt with specific themes that fell within the larger subject matter, with kidnapping in *The FBI* series, for instance, or with the challenge posed by a suicidal patient in *Dr. Kildare*. The dramatic material of Rod Serling's TV play "Requiem for a Heavyweight" is the boxing game, particularly as it is represented by a pitiful fighter used callously by other people for their own ends.

THEME AS A STATEMENT

A second way in which "theme" may be defined is to describe it as a statement about life that is implicit in the action of the play. Shakespeare's *Macbeth* is not only about ambition, but it also tells us that excessive ambition destroys. Rod Serling said that his play about boxing projected the following proposition: "Every man can and must search for his own personal dignity."[1] Turning to other TV plays, we find that Gore Vidal's "Visit to a Small Planet" argues that war is the avocation of adolescents and that "Thunder on Sycamore Street" by Reginald Rose conveys the idea that courage can defeat prejudice.

Some people, although recognizing that dramas often make statements like these, do not refer to them as themes. The drama critic, Walter Kerr, uses the word "theme" to refer only to the subject or topic of discourse that becomes a basis for variation and development in the play. The proposition a writer seeks to establish by the argument of the play he calls the "thesis."[2] Other writers have used the terms "premise" and "root-idea" to describe this statement, and the word "moral," which is frequently used with reference to the lesson advanced by children's stories, is a commonly used term.

Sometimes a theme of this type may be worded as a question to which the action of the play provides an answer. The producers of the radio daytime serials, usually known as soap operas, had a special fondness for this approach. Many of them permanently imbedded in the opening continuity of each broadcast a question that spotlighted

---

[1] Rod Serling, *Patterns* (New York: Simon and Schuster, Inc., 1957), p. 243.

[2] Walter Kerr, *How Not to Write a Play* (New York: Simon and Schuster, Inc., 1955), p. 60.

the theme of the entire series. Thus, the announcer introducing the daily episodes in *The Life of Helen Trent* always asked the question: Can a woman find romance after thirty-five?

THE NECESSITY OF A THEME

In considering whether a theme is an essential element in a play, it is obvious that we must first decide how we are using the word, for the meaning we attach to it is of critical importance in determining our answer. If we equate theme with subject matter, the problem disappears. All plays must treat some kind of dramatic material. There may be disagreement about what this material is, but none that it exists. We have a problem only if we define theme as a proposition advanced by the play which can be readily identified and expressed in a single sentence. For the balance of this chapter, then, theme will be taken to mean the proposition or thesis of the play, since it is only when theme is defined this way that any question regarding its necessity arises.

One way to decide whether a theme as we are defining it is an essential element in play construction is to examine plays, usually considered to be successful, to determine whether they reflect a single-sentence statement about life on which everyone will agree. What do we find? We discover that the themes of some plays are readily identified by most people, even though the precise language in which they are stated may vary slightly from one person to another, but the themes of other plays are obscure, and, if identified at all, will be stated by different people in widely varying ways.

Most people will agree that Shakespeare's *Macbeth* projects the theme that excessive ambition destroys, even though individual wordings of this idea might differ. To use a television example, it seems clear that the theme of Paddy Chayefsky's "Marty" is that everyone needs to be accepted by certain other people to attain a full and satisfying life. This idea is reflected both by the experience of the focal character, Marty, and by that of the lonely and rejected girl whom he meets at the dance. It is also implicit in the experience of Marty's aunt, who seeks acceptance by her son and daughter-in-law.

Among the plays that seem to defy attempts to condense their basic messages into single declarative sentences is Shakespeare's *Hamlet*. Expressions of its theme have been evolved, of course, but it is difficult to find even two people who will accept a given statement as a reflection of the play's fundamental meaning. *Julius Caesar* and *Oedipus the King* are other plays in which it is difficult to isolate a single underlying idea. The contemporary playwright, Arthur Miller, has written a number of plays with easily identifiable themes, but the play that many consider to be his greatest work, *Death of a Salesman,* if it reflects any basic idea at all, seems to mean something different to everyone who sees it.

It is apparent, then, that a single clearly identifiable theme is not an absolute requirement in play construction. Notable plays have succeeded without one. This is not to argue that these plays fail to project important ideas. Just the opposite is true. One problem, in fact, of isolating a dominating theme in some great works is an embarrassment of riches. The observations about life and people they reflect are so many-faceted that to encompass all of the meanings in a single statement is impossible. To argue that the major message of *Hamlet* is—he who hesitates is lost—as some have done, is to sink to a superficial interpretation which ignores most of the significant ideas in the play.

Even plays that have one strong underlying idea may also express other ideas. Most people would agree that the major theme of "Marty" can be stated in a sentence that expresses man's need for acceptance, but there are other meanings in this drama. When Marty's finger dialing the girl's number at the end of the play indicates that he has decided not to succumb to his friend's taunts about the girl but is burying his pride to do what he really wants to do, we may gather the message: A man's own reaction to a girl is more important than his pride or his friend's opinions. Still other ideas may be reflected by the action. The play's author, Paddy Chayefsky, for example, says that "there is a distinct homosexual relationship between Marty and his best pal, Angie."[3] Another aspect of the play is Marty's response to his mother and some may draw significant meanings from this relationship, although Chayefsky emphasizes that the tie between them is not of the silver cord variety.

What seems to be a common characteristic of great plays is richness of meaning, whether or not this meaning can be communicated in a single statement. Different people, in so far as each individual experience has elements that are unique, may respond to this meaning in different ways. That we all agree on the meaning of a play is not important. What is important, if a play is to be accorded the highest rank, is that we find some meaning there.

THE CONTRIBUTIONS OF A THEME

Even though we have discovered that a single dominant theme is not an essential element in a play, we must still recognize that there are many dramas in which the enunciation of a clearly defined proposi-

[3] Paddy Chayefsky, *Television Plays* (New York: Simon and Schuster, Inc., 1955), p. 176.

tion or thesis does add materially to the effectiveness of the work. Let us consider the ways in which a theme of this nature may contribute to a play.

THEME AND SUBSTANCE

One contribution a theme can make is to assure the dramatist that his play contains at least one statement about life for the audience to ponder. The enrichment of substance that results will give his play more fiber and make it more satisfying. A long-running series on television was the one produced by Alfred Hitchcock, first in a half-hour format and then in an hour version. Most of the scripts, particularly those running half an hour, depended for their effect on a surprise twist or "gimmick," and it is difficult to find in many of them any particular theme or philosophical point. Occasionally, however, a clearly identifiable theme was projected. Such was the case with the adaptation of John Collier's short story "Back for Christmas." It tells of an Englishman who murders his wife and buries her in the cellar just before sailing to the United States on a vacation trip. Supposedly, they are to be back for Christmas. It is the husband's plan, however, to pretend that once in America, they will decide to remain there. His scheme appears to have worked perfectly until one day, safely in America, he receives a bill addressed to his wife. It seems that to surprise him when they returned to England at Christmas, she had arranged to have a winecellar dug in the very place where he had buried her body. The twist is ingenious, and the theme it expresses, that "murder will out," adds substance to the story.

In another play in the Hitchcock series a young wife is attacked by an intruder while her husband is at work. When the wife points out the man, the husband chases him into an apartment and kills him. His grim satisfaction is abruptly turned into chill dismay when his now obviously unbalanced wife identifies another man as her assailant almost as soon as they drive away from the apartment. Not only is this sudden turn unexpected and horrifying, but it also brings out the point that revenge and murder are innately senseless.

The reason these two dramas made a greater impression than some of the other shows on this series was that both projected strong themes. Many others which existed only for the revelation of a twist at the end seemed flimsy and insubstantial by comparison. The short stories of O'Henry can be cited as further examples of this point. Most are now forgotten, and justly so, having been formulated for just one reason—to support a tag at the end that would surprise the reader. One of his stories, however, has become a classic, "The Gift of the Magi."

It is true that this story contains one of O'Henry's best and most ironic twists, but that does not explain the story's staying power. "The Gift of the Magi" has survived because it has something important to say about the human heart.

Another "gimmick" story, one of the most famous in literary history, Frank Stockton's "The Lady or the Tiger," provides a further example of the way a theme can enhance an audience's experience. The twist in this story—namely, that Stockton left his story unfinished, inviting his readers to supply their own version of the concluding events, was original enough to make this work memorable, but the question the reader faces in deciding how he would end the story adds tremendously to its impact. Would a savage princess prefer to see the man she loved in the arms of another woman or would she rather see him die? It is the existence of this question that provides the main substance of this story.

It must be admitted that many plays seemingly devoid of significant ideas do reach the air waves. Their purpose is to divert an audience for the few moments they flicker on the television screen, but they do not pretend to provide any substance for contemplation. Most comedy scripts achieve their purpose if they succeed in provoking laughter. Even when they do reflect statements about life, the message is not particularly important nor is it meant to be taken seriously. Comedy dramas about family situations frequently feature plots in which a man is brought face to face with a problem which, through naïveté, ignorance, or stupidity he promptly complicates. In the end he is rescued from the web in which he has entangled himself by a wife who seems infinitely more capable and adaptable than he is. The theme inherent in these plots—that men as a group cannot be trusted to cope effectively with even life's simplest problems—is an example of what appears to be a satisfactory idea for a comedy show.

Most scripts with messages as slight as this, whether they are comedies or dramas, fade quickly from our minds, but it must be admitted that a few, because of the sheer ingenuity of their plot or twist, linger with us even though they make no significant philosophical point. Such a drama was the TV adaptation of John Collier's short story "De Mortuis." A man is discovered in the basement of his home by two neighbors who immediately jump to the conclusion that he has murdered his wife and buried her beneath the cement. During the conversation that follows, the neighbors reveal their sympathy for the husband, let him know that they feel the deed is fully justified by his wife's unfaithfulness, and promise to keep the matter completely secret. The facts are, however, that the husband has committed no murder. His wife is away on an errand and his neighbor's words have provided him with his first knowledge of her infidelity. The neighbors leave as he stands stunned by the revelation. Then we hear the wife's footsteps on the floor above. She calls for him and he asks her to come downstairs so that he can show her something. It is difficult to discern in this story any particular thesis, but the contemplation of what followed those final words provided a memorable dramatic experience.

THEME AND UNITY

The theme of Paddy Chayefsky's "Marty" is mainly reflected in the actions of the title character as he seeks acceptance, but one of the strengths of the play is the reinforcement of this theme in the actions of other characters. Marty's need is balanced by the need of the girl he meets at the dance who, also, has endured the bitterness of constant rejection. The plight of Marty's Aunt Catherine, who is about to be evicted by her son and daughter-in-law, provides another variation on the theme. Still another variation is inherent in the action of Marty's mother who, discovering that her son may be developing a serious relationship with a girl, reacts sharply to protect herself from the loneliness that will inevitably follow his marriage. Marty's problem alone might have been enough to sustain this play, but its echo in other lives unifies the story and reinforces the theme, enhancing the emotional impact of the one and the vital meaning of the other.

A further example of how variations on a theme may work to the advantage of both theme and story is provided by another Chayefsky play, "The Mother." It tells how an old woman refuses to accept support from her daughter and insists on going out to find work despite the fact that she is not well. Her desperate struggle to maintain her independence is duplicated in the action of a minor character, the Boss, for there is an implication that he hired the old woman against his better judgment to prove to himself that he still has freedom of action. Reginald Rose in "Thunder on Sycamore Street" intensified the problem of prejudice by making two characters endure the agony of deciding whether to resist prejudice or succumb to it.

THEME AND DIRECTION

Another contribution of a theme is that it may guide a writer toward the development of a story in its most effective form by helping him to make decisions about his plot. A certain theme may take a story in one direction, another will guide it down a different road. Not dominating but serving, a theme may lead a writer to those decisions that will best focus and crystallize his story.

The impact of theme on story and its role in determining story decisions can be illustrated by a script written by one of my students at
the Stanford-NBC Radio and Television Institute. The play, "Chester
Swivel Gets His" by Alfred Wilkinson, was essentially one of the "gimmick" variety. At the beginning, a being identified as Fate tells the
audience how an insignificant little man named Chester Swivel is that
afternoon going to meet his end under the wheels of a truck—destined
to come roaring down a certain street at the precise instant that Chester
Swivel steps into that street from a drug store. So that the audience
will not grieve too deeply, it is demonstrated that Chester's existence
under the thumb of a shrewish wife and a tyrannical boss is incredibly
miserable; his imminent translation into the other world can be interpreted as nothing but a boon.

Events then occur exactly as Fate has planned them. The truck proceeds on schedule through the streets of the city toward its rendevous
with the insignificant Mr. Swivel. Chester enters the drug store just
as planned; he purchases a paper; he starts for the door as the truck
turns into the street a block away. And then the phone rings. The call
is for Chester Swivel. He turns back to answer as the truck goes roaring
by outside the door—leaving Chester Swivel unscathed. Overwhelmed
at this incredible disruption of his plans, Fate storms at the audience,
unable to believe that anything could have interfered. Then suddenly
he knows what has happened. *A member of the audience had placed
that telephone call to Chester Swivel to save him from his doom!*

That was the climax of the play and the "gimmick." How should
the play end? Important decisions regarding both theme and story are
involved. Should Fate merely summon another truck and send Chester
to his reward as previously ordained? That ending suggests the theme:
"You cannot avoid fate." Or should the audience member's intervention
be permitted to succeed with the result that Chester is doomed to spend
thirty more miserable years oppressed by both wife and boss? The theme
suggested by that ending is: "Beware of interfering with fate." Which
is the better theme and which is the more satisfactory ending to the
story? How would you finish this script?

THE NATURE OF THEMES

The meanings that plays project are so diverse that it would seem
impossible to establish a catalogue of criteria that can apply. Yet an
examination of a number of themes reveals that there are some general
observations that can be made about them.

IMPORTANCE, UNIVERSALITY, AND ENDURANCE

If a theme is to help invest a script with significance, three attributes are necessary. First, the statement the theme makes about life should be an important one. Second, this statement should be one that is meaningful to as many people as possible; it should have the quality of universality. Third, the theme should concern one of the eternal questions of life and death that everlastingly face mankind.

NOT ORIGINAL

Originality is a quality to be sought by the dramatist in all aspects of his writing except in his choice of themes. Clearly, if he is to deal with the enduring questions of the ages, he cannot expect to say anything strikingly new. As Alan Downer put it in *The Art of the Play*, you will generally find the writer "affirming one of the Ten Commandments or the Bill of Rights, or condemning one of the Seven Deadly Sins." What marks a writer as original and creative is not what his play says but how it says it.

REPETITION

Just as a writer should not avoid a theme simply because it has been dealt with by other writers, he should not avoid it either because he has previously dealt with it himself. That some problems have an unusual appeal to certain writers is demonstrated by the plays of three writers who have won distinction in television. Horton Foote in the preface to his collection of plays, *Harrison, Texas*, said that all of the plays in this book "share, besides the same locale, one of two common themes: an acceptance of life or a preparation for death."[4] Three of the six plays in Tad Mosel's collection, *Other People's Houses*, deal with the problems of older people who have outlived their usefulness. Paddy Chayefsky seems to be particularly concerned with probing the roles that acceptance, prestige, or recognition play in people's lives. His scripts, "Marty," "The Big Deal," and "The Catered Affair" suggest his interest in these subjects. A given theme may be repeated many times as long as the means used to reveal it are new and arresting. A writer's deep concern with a problem is perhaps his best reason for dealing with it again and again.

[4] Horton Foote, *Harrison, Texas* (New York: Harcourt, Brace & World, Inc., 1956), p. VIII.

NOT NECESSARILY TRUE

Must a theme make a true statement about life? Many times it does and often the truth of the theme is so obvious that a play is scarcely necessary to establish it. The average individual going to see *Macbeth* does not need to be convinced that excessive ambition can be an evil thing. What this play does, however, is to overwhelm him with the truth of this observation. It projects its thought so forcibly that acceptance passes beyond mere understanding. A passive truth has been made vivid and alive.

A theme need not necessarily be true, however, and just as some themes are obviously true, so some are obviously false, at least as far as universal application is concerned. Reginald Rose's "Thunder on Sycamore Street" says that courage defeats prejudice. Only an incurable optimist would maintain that this is always true. Fortunately, inevitable truth is not required. A theme need be true only in terms of specific characters involved in certain actions against a particular setting.

EMOTIONAL POWER

Because a drama exists primarily to arouse the emotions of an audience, it seems clear that the choice of theme should be related to attaining this objective. The best themes are those that have potentialities for appealing to the deepest feelings of an audience. A theme whose point is dry and intellectual is a barrier to the achievement of a play's maximum emotional power.

THE THEME IN PLAY CONSTRUCTION

Although we have discovered that the theme as a statement of a proposition or thesis is not an essential element in a play, we have also noted that such themes, when they do exist, often make definite contributions. In view of these somewhat contrary ideas, it may be well to consider the way a dramatist deals with a theme in constructing a play.

Plays are written for various reasons. A dramatist may be motivated primarily by the desire to project a vivid character. Another may be inspired by a novel plot idea. Some set out merely to tell a good story in which character and plot ideas are of equal importance. Then there are some dramatists who devise plays with the express purpose of communicating a social message or enunciating a pronouncement about life. Should a theme of this nature ever be the main inspiration of a play?

In answering this question we must recognize that some authorities maintain that the motivation for writing a play should always be the desire to communicate a theme. Albert Crews in his book *Professional Radio Writing* argued that "the theme amounts to your reason for writing the play." John Galsworthy emphasized the importance of the theme when he said that "a drama must be shaped so as to have a spire of meaning." An analysis of many of the works of Henrik Ibsen and Arthur Miller reveals that they were inspired mainly by a desire to communicate a message about life or society.

THE DANGERS OF A DOMINATING THEME

Some dramatists whose goal in writing a play is to establish a theme may produce a satisfactory piece of work, but there is danger in this objective, particularly for the beginner. A play written expressly to prove a point may fail to become an effective dramatic work. One reason for this is that a theme usually makes its appeal to the mind, whereas the success of a play depends primarily on its power to arouse the emotions. The writer who makes his characters and plot serve the theme rather than in making the theme serve them, will probably fail to move his viewers, for he is concentrating on making people think rather than on making them feel. His play has become an argument. Many of the plays that are most satisfying, as a matter of fact, do not set out to prove a point at all but to ask a question.

Another damaging result of concentration on a theme is that it subordinates characterization to the making of a social pronouncement or the proclaiming of a text. When this happens, the people of the play never become living, breathing humans at all but remain mere puppets being manipulated to express an intellectual idea. If the play is to succeed, its characters must become more than mere fleshless symbols whose sole function is to perform a role in developing a pattern of thought leading to a logical conclusion. They must become, instead, creatures of flesh and blood capable in themselves of arousing the passions of the audience. "It is better to make a man than to make a point," advises Walter Kerr.[5]

If you must write a propaganda play, as the playwright Howard Lindsay said, at least avoid letting "any character in the play know what the propaganda is . . . The minute you let one of your characters know what the propaganda is . . . that character will start talking, you can't stop him, and your play will become self-conscious." But, Lindsay added, "A play doesn't have to have a moral. Human nature is a good enough

---

[5] Walter Kerr, *How Not to Write a Play*, p. 58.

theme . . . It is enough to see human beings acting in the circumstances of life."[6]

The danger of letting the theme dominate is illustrated by Tad Mosel's "The Lawn Party," a play that the author himself said "was not as popular as some of my other plays."[7] Mosel said he wrote this play because of his interest in a theme—the search for beauty. It is true that his chief character, India Price, is skillfully established as a person with an instinctive revulsion for anything ugly, but the characteristic that strikes with greatest force is her almost incredible selfishness. Driven by a desire to give a party that will satisfy a senseless whim, she seems oblivious to the agony to which she subjects her husband, ignores completely the wishes of her daughter, and treats a helpful and thoughtful neighbor with callous insensitivity. In the first two acts the characters and plot carry this play away from the theme that the author had in mind. In the third act, seeming suddenly to remember his theme, the author wrenched the characters and plot out of their natural course to serve the theme's purpose. The end result was unsatisfactory, for the theme remained vague and the story lacked unity. It is a mistake to force a story into the service of a previously conceived theme. In the case of "The Lawn Party," the writer should either have developed a story that would more effectively reflect this theme, or, having been taken up and carried off by his plot and characters, he should have abandoned his previously chosen theme and sought another.

DEVELOPING A THEME

If, as a matter of fact, you succeed in depicting characters "acting in the circumstances of life," the enunciation of the theme will take care of itself. The playwright Clifford Odets argued that it is enough to give birth to the material and let it say what it has to say. Paddy Chayefsky's "Marty" was obviously written with the development of character uppermost in the dramatist's mind. He created a moving portrayal of a human being but he was successful also in projecting a compelling theme. Because his theme did not dominate or distort, his characters lost none of their human values in a story that remained natural and convincing, and yet the theme was illuminated with impressive power. Tad Mosel in "The Lawn Party," on the other hand, thinking primarily about his theme, ended with a play in which both characters

---

[6] Quoted in A. S. Burack, *The Writer's Handbook* (Boston: The Writer, Inc., 1949), p. 370.

[7] Tad Mosel, *Other People's Houses* (New York: Simon and Schuster, Inc., 1956), p. 114.

and story were distorted and which did not manage to project even the theme satisfactorily.

In most of your dramatic writing the problem of deciding upon a theme will be of minor importance in the beginning. You will be absorbed in creating characters and filling them out; you will be concerned with developing the basic narrative line. Then perhaps you will ask yourself about the theme. Must you then proceed to find or invent one? Probably not. As we have noted before, your play does not need to project a clearly identifiable statement about life to be a success. Even if it ends with such a statement, it will probably not be because you sought it out and put it there. In most cases you will see your theme implicit in the characters and action you have already created. The theme will be a by-product which comes into existence as your audience sees the play. You do not need to find a theme. The theme will have found you.

QUESTIONS AND PROJECTS

1. When asked to define the message he was trying to communicate in his play *The Hostage*, Brendon Behan responded: "Message? What do you think I am, a postman?" Consider this reply in a general discussion of the playwright's responsibility for enunciating a theme.

2. Join with your classmates in defining the theme of a common dramatic experience—a play, movie, TV production, or a dramatic script. Discuss the significance of your agreement or lack of agreement.

3. Analyze a script obviously designed to give strong emphasis to a theme by describing how this theme is resonated in the lives of a number of characters.

4. Observe a number of plays or play scripts to determine the relationship of themes to plot. Speculate on the effect a change in theme might have had on the plot in some of these plays.

6

Designing the Script

The question is how to apply glue to the seat of the audience's trousers. Alfred Hitchcock

Thus far we have been considering the creative decisions a dramatist makes before he begins writing the actual script. He may have jotted down a few things that will become part of the final draft—some lines of dialogue, for example, which may escape him if he fails to record them—but the main task of putting his ideas into script form is still ahead. We now review some of the points to be kept in mind during the composition of the first draft—such matters as arousing and sustaining interest, achieving clarity, and attaining believability.

GAINING ATTENTION

The TV viewer is often a chance wanderer through the channels who tunes in tentatively to find out what is in store for him. If you fail to engage his interest at once, he will turn restlessly to another channel or switch off the set entirely. Even fairly regular viewers of a series

93

may measure the appeal of the opening stages of a particular episode before they decide to listen all the way through. Gaining the immediate attention of the viewer is the most important responsibility you face at the beginning of the script.

A PROBLEM ALREADY IN MOTION

The single best way to arouse interest is to confront the audience immediately with a character who is already enmeshed in a critical problem. Arrange your material so that your play begins with a character who has reached a turning point in his life. He may have just made a decision that will precipitate a conflict or have taken the first step toward a highly desired goal. You should start your play at a place in the story that will provide you with the action you need to seize the attention of the audience. This entering moment is called the *point of attack*. You will not ordinarily begin your play when the story itself actually starts, for to do so would probably make it necessary for you to precede the exciting events with a long, slow development which would lose most of your audience. Instead you visualize the action as actually under way before the program begins. The opening fade-in suddenly illuminates this on-going story at a moment of crisis. To extract the ultimate effect from this late point of attack, many writers begin their dramas without even the preamble of a program title or an opening format. Not until a basic problem or conflict is established do credits or a commercial interrupt the story, and in many cases the story continues as the credits are superimposed over the action. You then develop the background the audience needs to understand the situation as the play proceeds. The process of providing this information, called exposition, is explained in the chapter on Dialogue and Narration.

THE PROMISE OF A PROBLEM

Sometimes the nature of a particular story makes it impossible for a writer to introduce decisive action immediately. It may be that some preliminary exposition is needed before the audience can be plunged into the middle of the conflict. In such cases the writer may be able to seize the attention of his audience by the promise of a problem to come.

CONVENTIONAL METHODS. The usual way to let an audience know that a crisis is in the offing is to make some reference to it in the early lines of the play. The TV writer Rod Serling is adept at arousing the interest of the audience in this way. In his "Patterns," a drama of conflict among those who occupy the upper-echelon positions in a big business, he foreshadows the clash to come by inserting into a scene, designed primarily to establish a big-business setting, this comment by a stenographer: "Today's the day, and boy oh boy, it should be some day!" In another of his plays, "The Rack," the story of an army officer on trial for collaboration with the enemy, Serling emphasized the seriousness of the problem by having another officer refer to the charge as follows: "But it's close to treason and we can ask the limit."

In addition to dialogue, the promise of a problem to come can also be made in the opening narration. The syndicated series *Highway Patrol* always made use of this devise. One program began with this statement: "One of the most deadly types of criminals is the amateur who acts on impulse . . . He is a man afraid—and this makes him deadly." An MGM movie, *House of Numbers,* broadcast on one of the network movie nights, aroused interest by showing views of San Quentin prison while a narrator spoke these words: "Authorities used to believe there were only two ways out. The main gate, after you'd served your time . . . or the side gate, when you died. Then two men and a girl found a third way out."[1]

THE TEASER.   Another means of promising excitement to an audience is to take a scene of exciting action from the body of the script and place it at the beginning of the play ahead of the titles and before the regular development of the story begins. With the interest of the audience thus stimulated, the writer can then concentrate on providing a foundation for his story. *The Fugitive* series consistently used this teaser technique.

It cannot be disputed that teasers do have power to pique curiosity, but they have the fault of artificiality. They are so obviously devices for arousing interest that their power may be muted by that very obviousness. Another objection is that audiences may be disoriented by a scene that is presented completely out of context and without proper foundation. Children particularly are likely to be confused about where the teaser ends and the regular story begins. For these reasons, teasers, although they do have a place, should be used sparingly and with circumspection.

THE APPEAL OF THE UNFAMILIAR

An excellent way to arouse the interest of a viewer is to confront him immediately with novel or unusual experiences. Plays of the sci-

[1] With the permission of MGM from its motion picture, *House of Numbers,* copyright © MCMLVII in U.S.A. by Loew's Incorporated.

ence-fiction or horror types often catch attention by generating a powerful atmosphere through the accenting of the bizarre and the macabre. Conventional plays can also use this means to seize attention.

AN UNUSUAL SETTING. A setting unfamiliar to most people can help to arouse interest, for most of us are curious about places we have never seen. Rod Serling made deft use of setting to seize attention in his "Requiem for a Heavyweight" by showing something most people never see—what Serling called the "underbelly" of a fight arena—where fighters retreat after their appearances in the ring. This setting also contributed to the establishment of a powerful atmosphere.

One of the more unusual settings—the workshop of a maker of gravestone monuments—appeared in the opening of Howard Rodman's "The Explorer." Not only was this setting intriguing, but it also helped to establish the motif that dominated the action, for the play concerned the losing fight of an old man against the advance of death. The opening scene showed the inscription on his gravestone partially carved, and as the camera returned to this scene at regular intervals during the play to show further steps toward the completion of the inscription, the old man's losing fight with death was graphically suggested.

AN UNUSUAL EVENT. A certain way to arouse audience interest is to depict an unusual or mysterious event for which the play promises an explanation. The opening of Michael Dyne's "A Tongue of Silver" focused on a series of mysterious events: a great fireball that "burst out of the heavens and crashed like doom into the sea," the birth of a two-headed calf, and the appearance of the "Lord of the Nether Regions astriding down the road, ten feet tall with eyes like living coals and flame coming out of him." The opening of *Hamlet* with its references to the appearance of an unearthly being is another example of this technique.

THE APPEAL OF THE FAMILIAR

Sometimes an opening that projects a feeling of the familiar is as effective in arousing interest as novelty is. People are attracted by stories that provide echoes of their own experiences. One of the great attractions of Thorton Wilder's *Our Town* was its evocation of nostalgic memories of life in an American small town before World War I. A difficulty in using this appeal, however, is that what is familiar to one viewer may be totally unfamiliar to another. Still this need not always preclude the use of a given event or setting. What appeals to one person because of its familiarity may appeal to another because of its novelty.

A STRIKING CHARACTERIZATION

A powerful means of gaining attention is to bring a striking character into the action at the very beginning of the play. A good example of this power was the character of Lennie in John Steinbeck's *Of Mice and Men*, which was broadcast as a radio drama before it became well known as a book or received its stage and movie presentations. The great oaf Lennie, stroking a dead mouse in his pocket while he made plaintive excuses to his comrade George about killing it unintentionally, was a person who immediately riveted audience attention. Moreover, the potentialities for tragedy inherent in Lennie's combination of simple-minded gentleness and his capacity for outbursts of unintended violence held the promise of enthralling dramatic conflict.

AN INTRIGUING TITLE

The selection of a title for a TV series is a critical matter, for it can play a significant role in attracting audiences and thus be an important factor in determining whether the series will be successful. The appeal inherent in such titles as *Gunsmoke, The Fugitive, Bewitched, Run for Your Life*, and *Beverly Hillbillies* is obvious. The choice of a title for an individual program in a series is not quite so crucial, however, even though it may be listed in the program information. One suspects, in fact, that some program titles are created to provide an outlet for an extravagance of expression that most TV writing does not permit. Consider the following: In the *Naked City* series: "Give the Old Cat a Tender Mouse" and "Beyond this Place There May Be Dragons;" in *Ben Casey:* "In the Name of Love a Small Corruption," "Saturday, Surgery, and Stanley Schultz," and "Odyssey of a Proud Suitcase;" in *Sam Benedict:* "Life Is a Lie—Life Is a Cheat" and "A Split Week at San Quentin;" and in *Route 66:* "Five Cranks for Winter—Ten Cranks for Spring," "Robin Hood and Clarence Darrow, They Went Out with Bow and Arrow," and "A Horse Has a Big Head—Let Him Worry."

SUSTAINING INTEREST

It is not enough merely to excite the interest of an audience at the beginning of a play. To be successful you must sustain that interest as long as the play is on the screen. Your principal means for meeting this challenge is to develop a strong, accelerating plot involving striking characters caught in vital conflicts, but there are also other techniques that can be used.

SUSPENSE

The best way for a dramatist to hold the attention of an audience is to develop an atmosphere of constantly increasing suspense. The writer creates suspense, in the first place, by arousing his audience's curiosity about the way things are going to turn out. This may involve a suspense question about the eventual result of the action, or if the nature of the outcome is fairly obvious—that the young lovers will live happily ever after, for example—the suspense question asks how this happy conclusion is to be reached in view of all the apparent obstacles. The writer develops suspense, in the second place, by creating characters who engage the interest and sympathy of the viewers. As these viewers begin to worry about whether these characters will find a way out of the troubles enveloping them, the feeling of suspense initiated by curiosity begins to mount. The playwright accentuates this process by multiplying both uncertainty and anxiety until the tension reaches a fever pitch at the climax of the play. Suspense, then, is composed of two ingredients: curiosity and concern.

MINOR SUSPENSE.   Two types of suspense can be distinguished. Minor suspense is that created to catch the interest of the viewer and persuade him to go on looking from minute to minute until the playwright has time to develop the problem that will produce the major suspense of the story. It is obtained primarily by piquing curiosity. Some of the techniques used to catch attention are devices for creating minor suspense. The teaser, for example, makes a viewer curious about the background and explanation of the exciting event that precedes the regular beginning of the story. Minor suspense may involve a number of suspense questions which follow one another in quick succession until the major suspense question takes over.

MAJOR SUSPENSE.   The most important suspense developed by a play is that related to the goal or decision on which the action focuses. In the goal-centered play the dramatist develops suspense by making the audience both wonder and worry about whether the focal character will achieve his object. In the decision-centered play he creates curiosity and anxiety about the way the focal character will decide between the difficult choices confronting him. As the play progresses, suspense about the major question of the play intensifies and gradually displaces the suspense generated by the minor questions projected by the action.

The pilot play for the TV series *Run for Your Life,* "Rapture at 240" written by Luther Davis, provides a good example of the difference between minor and major suspense. The play tells how a lawyer named Paul Bryant, informed by his doctor that he will die in a year or two from an incurable but not a disabling disease, meets a young woman Leslie Thurston, who also seems headed for an early death but an unnecessary one. Under the influence of a father who argues that life is dangerous and dying just one more adventure, and trying to emulate a brother killed in a sports-car race, she risks her life in a series of daring but senseless adventures. In her mad plunge toward oblivion she spurns the values that motivate ordinary lives. Bryant resolves to salvage the worthwhile person hidden in Leslie Thurston by persuading her that one does not have to live dangerously to lead a full life. The question whether he can rescue her from her catapult to nowhere and direct her toward a normal life creates the major suspense of the play. Many minutes elapse, however, before the writer can develop this question and arouse the interest of the audience in its answer; thus he must hold attention temporarily by creating interest in other questions. This play provides a natural means of doing so in the dangerous escapades the girl attempts. Bryant must join and surpass her in these adventures if he is to have any chance of reaching her. At the beginning of the play, for example, he wagers that he can dive more deeply than she can. To win his bet and make an impression on her, he ventures down 240 feet where the rapture of the deep threatens his life. The audience at this point is held spellbound by the simple question of his survival. The arousal of this minor suspense therefore is immediate and short range in nature; the major suspense, on the other hand, once it has taken over, rises in intensity and lasts for the duration of the play.

EXPECTANCY

Reinforcing the effect of suspense in holding the interest of an audience is the development of expectancy. The two are closely related in that both involve the arousal of audience anxiety, but they are different in that suspense is created when an audience wonders what will happen, whereas expectancy develops when an audience is led to believe that a certain something will happen. At times a situation develops suspense and expectancy in equal measure, a combination that has great power to hold the attention of the audience. A spectator seeing a swimmer being drawn remorselessly to a falls expects to see him go crashing over the brink to his death, but at the same time the spectator wonders whether some unexpected development will intervene to save the swimmer's life. Prodded by expectation, curiosity, and anxiety he is certain to keep his eyes glued to the event.

A CLASSIC EXAMPLE OF EXPECTANCY.   A classic play that has held the interest of audiences through the centuries primarily through the development of expectancy is the Greek drama *Oedipus the King*. When the play begins, the audience, knowing the terrible facts of his past, realizes that Oedipus, trying to discover the cause of the plague that is decimating the country, is himself responsible for it. The spectators sit in expectant horror as Oedipus plunges recklessly on with the investigation that will unfold the horrible truth about his own life. As he writhes under the impact of one terrible discovery after another, they look forward in fascination knowing what the next revelation will be. Thus does Sophocles, in Archer's felicitous phrase, "keep anticipation on the alert."[2]

OBLIGATORY SCENES.   The development of expectancy sometimes leads to an obligation on the part of a dramatist to include a particular scene in his play. Archer, in fact, called such scenes "obligatory scenes,"[3] and the dramatist's success in developing them measures to a very great extent his skill in producing expectancy in the audience. A good example of an obligatory scene can be found in Rod Serling's "Patterns." Serling develops so much conflict between the president of the firm and an ailing executive that the audience expects to witness a confrontation between the two men. He whets anticipation for it by having a character refer prophetically to it as follows: "Tomorrow morning, in that meeting, in that conference room, he's going to whip Andy to death." Serling does not disappoint his audience and the promised scene is one of the high points of the play.

A writer who sharpens his audience's expectancy for a certain scene and then neglects to include it, on the other hand, is failing to deliver the goods which he himself promised. A movie of a few years back featured a department store owner who took a position incognito as a clerk in the shoe department to test for himself the character of the manager, whose handling of employees was reported to be brutal. The worst, it soon appeared, was true; the owner in his role as a clerk was immediately subjected to sadistic treatment. The scene the audience expected to see, in fact yearned for, was the moment when the owner revealed his true identity and provided his malevolent persecutor with his come-uppance. That scene never appeared and the audience was let down. This should not be taken to mean, however, that all expectancy must be satisfied with a scene. Occasionally, the dramatist can attain a better effect by suggesting to his viewers what is going to happen and letting them complete the development in their imaginations. Sometimes also expectancy is developed only to be reversed by an unexpected twist. As was pointed out in a previous chapter, surprise is one of the most powerful means for intriguing and satisfying an audience.

[2] William Archer, *Play-Making* (Boston: Small, Maynard and Company, 1912), p. 204.
[3] William Archer, *Play-Making*, pp. 225–259.

EXPERIENCING THE DRAMA

One of the major differences between drama and fiction is that drama reveals what is happening, whereas fiction tells what has happened. The dramatist may not be successful in holding the attention of his audience unless he takes full advantage of the power of drama to give his audience the feeling that they are experiencing an event as it is actually taking place. The mastery of a number of techniques is required if this impression is to be transmitted with the fullest possible effect.

GRADUAL REVELATION. The technique of gradual revelation has a role in all forms of storytelling but it is particularly important to the dramatist. It consists of the ability to unfold the story by degrees, a method that provides viewers with the excitement of telling disclosures at regular intervals but denies them full knowledge of the events until the play is almost over. This technique encourages the participation of viewers by inviting them to stretch forward from one revelation to the next. Gradual revelation also contributes to the effective pacing of a drama, for the movement of the play tends to accelerate when significant information is being revealed and to relax and slow down between disclosures.

A number of television plays provide excellent examples of the use of gradual revelation. In the opening moments of Rod Serling's "Requiem for a Heavyweight" it is revealed that the boxer's manager Maish owes money to an apparently unsavory character. Having aroused the audience's curiosity, the writer makes no further reference to the matter for several minutes. Then Maish divulges that the amount he owes is $3,000. Again the subject is dropped until Maish admits a short time later that he lost the money betting against his own boxer. This sordid revelation, delayed through almost half the play, strikes with far greater force than it would have had Serling told the whole story immediately.

Another of Serling's scripts "The Rack" provides a further illustration of the effectiveness of gradual revelation. The principal question in the mind of the viewer as this play gets under way is: How is it possible for an apparently honorable army officer to sink to collaborating with the enemy? Serling skillfully delays the full explanation until the play is almost over. The first disclosure is that an infantry captain is accused of collaboration. There are no further details until near the end of the first act when the fact that the captain had signed surrender leaflets and given lectures for the enemy is brought to light. There is a suggestion that he had done something even worse, but the revelation of what it was is delayed until much later in the show. The audience strains forward in curiosity, but even by the end of the act there is only the briefest explanation of the reason for the collaboration. "I sold my soul for a dirty blanket that smelled of fish," says the army officer. A little later he makes reference to the rack on which he was stretched, but it is not until Act III during the trial scene that the captain describes the treatment that had brought about his psychological collapse.

In planning your play, no task is more crucial than that of deciding how you are going to make the disclosures that are fundamental to your plot and characterization. You should plan carefully what you are going to reveal at various points in your play and how you are going to reveal it. A certain sign of amateur writing is the disclosure that comes too early and too completely. To keep anticipation at a fever pitch, you must dole out information in driblets, enough to keep the story moving, but not so much that the curiosity of the audience is muted because it is satisfied.

IMPLICATION.   Another primary tool in leading an audience to experience a play rather than merely observe it is the technique of implication. Through the use of this technique the viewer gains information, not through direct statements, but by making inferences on the basis of indirect evidence and suggestion. Thus the audience becomes a partner in creating the action and the characterization. This process compares with the one that goes on in real life. On the basis of facts and observation we draw conclusions about people and events.

The motion picture *Giant* told how a young lady, born and raised in a lush, green section of Maryland, is brought by her new husband to live on a bare and treeless Texas plain. Then one day she sees a tree and impulsively throws her arms around it and caresses it. Because the audience is permitted to see for itself how deeply she yearns for the trees of her native Maryland, rather than being informed of it directly in narration or dialogue, the power of the revelation is magnified.

William Noble in "Snapfinger Creek" portrayed a sacrificing mother, who in an impulsive moment, bets her husband that she can pick more cotton before sundown than his farm hand if he promises to pay for more schooling for their daughter Randy. When the day is almost over, Randy goes out into the fields to reason with her mother, who since morning has been picking cotton in the hot sun. In the following excerpt, by implication the writer reveals what this desperate effort is costing.

```
                      RANDY

        Ma, you gone clean out o' your senses?

        This bet is the silliest thing I ever did

        hear.
```

                    MA

I got no breath nor time to spare talkin'.

Sundown's not but a hour off.

                    RANDY

(HOLDING HER ARM) Ma, wait! What's that

there, showing on the cotton?

                    MA

 Leave me be, I said!

                    RANDY

(LOOKING AT SOME OF THE COTTON) It's blood

ain't it...Let me see your hands!

In "Patterns" Rod Serling, with an incident that contains not a word of dialogue, tells a great deal about the pitiful deterioration of Andy Sloane, the corporation executive, who is under fire from his boss. At the end of Act I Andy leaves his office, observed by a secretary. The act concludes with these directions.

                    MARGE

(TURNS SLOWLY TOWARD ANDY'S OFFICE, RISES,

GOES INTO IT. SHE SEES A BOTTLE OPEN ON

THE DESK, LOOKS AROUND, THEN CLOSES IT, PUTS

IT AWAY. SHE SLOWLY SHAKES HER HEAD--

PITYINGLY, SORROWFULLY, KNOWINGLY.) FADE

OUT.

In "Requiem for a Heavyweight," one of Serling's purposes is to reveal that fighters are often mere pawns in their managers' hands, used while they can perform, but callously discarded when their fighting days are over. The relationship between managers and fighters is brilliantly implied in a scene involving two managers and a fighter. The managers discuss the fighter in his presence in the most personal terms; when the fighter tries to speak they silence him. It is clear that he has the status a prize bull would have among farmers. In another scene Serling uses implication to permit the audience to leap ahead of the action when it becomes clear that McClintock's days as a boxer are almost over. On the way out of the prize fight arena his manager sees a poster advertising a wrestling match. He takes a few steps closer to the poster, stares at it, and then taps it thoughtfully with his finger. Immediately the audience knows what is in store for McClintock.

In addition to carrying the audience forward, implication can also reinforce a previous impression or action. In a science-fiction drama the point was made that telephone users could see as well as hear each other. In one scene a wife, who is away on a visit, calls her husband. As soon as he picks up the phone she remonstrates: "Fred, why are you wearing that tie?"

The dramatist, of course, must provide enough information to permit impressions to arise and conclusions to be drawn. Audiences must be told who people are and where they are. They must discover what actions or events in the past caused the present situation. If a viewer becomes confused about these points, he will lose interest. But he does not need to know all of the facts, only those necessary to follow the action. A writer who overexplains seriously diminishes the effect of his work by depriving it of the power of implication. "When explanations are necessary they are useless," said Robert Louis Stevenson. The writer walks a narrow line between excess explanation, which spoils the effect, and insufficient explanation, which permits no effect at all. The great artist includes only what is necessary to establish the point; the rest he leaves to the audience.

SHOWING THE ACTION. Another technique akin in its effect to the use of implication is to show the critical action to the audience rather than merely talk about it. One of the unique strengths of drama is its power to show events as they actually happen, yet writers often dissipate this strength by permitting their characters to talk about vital happenings instead of showing them happening. The audience does not want to hear what has happened. It wants to see it happen before its eyes. There is not enough time to dramatize all of the events, of course, so some of the incidental action must be communicated through exposition. But the audience must be a witness to the basic conflicts; it must see the major crises and the climax; it must agonize through the making of the vital decisions.

In the same way the audience should not be told that characters are experiencing certain emotions but should be permitted to witness those emotions in action. This can be done by letting the audience see what produces the emotions and the characters' reactions. Naming an emotion is a sure sign that an amateur is at work. The drama critic Sydney Harris said: "A drama should illustrate life, not talk about it."

MAINTAINING PLAUSIBILITY

In addition to keeping his audience interested in his play throughout its presentation, the dramatist has the further duty of maintaining his viewers' belief in it. Once they begin to disbelieve, to question the plausibility of an action or motivation, to think, "I don't believe the character would act that way," the writer is beginning to lose his viewers. Even if they continue to watch, they are no longer completely absorbed by the action of the play, for they have moved outside to look on instead of remaining inside and involved. Becoming objective and intellectual rather than remaining subjective and emotional, they can no longer experience the optimum dramatic impact.

In the chapter on plotting it was pointed out that overuse of coincidence is the principal way of damaging the plausibility of a play, but there are other factors that can keep an audience from accepting the action.

THE PROBLEM OF PREPARATION

One way to invite the audience's rejection of a situation is to fail to prepare for it. Preparation means to provide those details in advance that are necessary to get an audience ready for some later step in the action. If one character is going to snatch a knife from a table and attack another character, it is not enough that the knife merely be lying there ready to be used. Before the critical moment, the audience must be made specifically aware of the knife's availability. If a character is to die suddenly, the audience must have been given facts that make his death believable. It is true that people in real life frequently die suddenly and unexpectedly, but the writer who eliminates a character in this way reveals himself as an amateur. The TV play "Patterns" provides a good example of proper preparation preceding a sudden death. Near the end of the play the persecuted executive Andy Sloane dies suddenly, a tragedy that underscores the jungle aspects of the business world. But the viewer has been amply prepared for this event by frequent references to Sloane's poor health. These references, in fact, develop audience expectancy for his death.

In addition to leading an audience to believe a coming event, preparation is often necessary to clarify a future situation. There is a good example of this type of preparation in William Noble's "Snapfinger Creek." This play, it will be remembered, features a mother's bet with her husband that she can pick more cotton in a day than a farm hand can. At stake is the future education of their daughter. Actually the mother fails to pick sufficient cotton, but she wins her bet because her husband surreptitiously takes cotton from the farm hand's bag and puts it in his wife's bag. This action would have been unclear had not the writer earlier in the play specifically drawn the attention of the audience to the cotton picked by the farm hand. The role of preparation has been aptly described by the playwright John Van Druten in these words: "Playwriting, apart from being like a lot of other things, is also very like chess where a whole series of moves must be made to lead up to the one you want."

OTHER PROBLEMS OF PLAUSIBILITY

The playwright is faced with a number of other knotty problems that affect the plausibility of the action. The necessity of getting people out of a scene is a frequent cause of trouble. This problem arose in a *Dick Van Dyke Show*. The comedy derived from the fact that Laura Petrie had innocently used a deck of cards marked by her husband Rob to aid him in doing some card tricks. The discovery of the marked deck when, coincidentally, the Petries were big winners, provided the comedy climax. The point was that the pack could not have been introduced while Rob Petrie was present because he would have recognized the cards. To permit Laura to find the cards in the drawer and deal then while Rob was out of the room, the writer had him suffer suddenly from pinching shoes, which necessitated a trip to the bedroom for slippers. Comedy can withstand so obvious a device but serious drama might suffer greatly from it. Another questionable resort is using the hoary old dodge of having water boil over in the kitchen to lure the wife out of the living room. Arranging for one character to forget his glasses so that another can be asked to read a letter aloud for the audience's benefit is a further example of conspicuous contrivance.

Other problems of plausibility are matters of what might be called sheer reasonableness. In Frank D. Gilroy's "A Matter of Pride" an unemployed father who cannot afford to buy his son a suit for his high school graduation ceremony still seems to have enough money to spend his nights drinking in bars. Realizing the problem, the writer points out later that his friends buy him the liquor. This simply raises another problem: Is it reasonable for the man's friends to keep buying him liquor night after night?

In an episode in the *Sea Hunt* series, Mike Nelson travels to a Russian ship in a midget submarine to rescue a German scientist. He boards the ship, crosses the deck and reaches the scientist's room without being observed. Is it reasonable that a Russian ship at sea would have no watch posted?

In "Requiem for a Heavyweight" one of the poignant scenes features a meeting in a bar between McClintock, the boxer, and a social worker whose help he had previously sought. There is just one nagging question: Why would a social worker, who had met McClintock in what appeared to have been a routine interview similar to many she had every day, seek him out in a rundown bar frequented by prize fighters? Serling admitted this weakness, saying the "audience should be told more explicitly why she felt a compulsion to go to the saloon to help a broken-down fighter."[4]

One of the interesting points about reasonableness is that audiences are more likely to accept implausible events in the past than they are those that take place before their eyes. One of the most implausible events in all drama is the marriage of Oedipus to his mother. Considering the prophecy made about him, would he not have conducted an investigation that would have revealed the true situation before he married a woman older than himself? What saves this action is that it took place before the play begins. The situation on the stage is so absorbing that the audience does not question the events that caused it. But viewers can be counted on to evaluate everything they see happening directly before them.

Another problem which frequently arises is providing enough time in the play for off-scene action. A dramatist cannot send a character on a ten-mile errand and have him back in the scene in five minutes. One way to solve this type of problem, of course, is to break the action with a transition, but other factors may prevent using this solution. There are no general rules for solving problems of the kind we have been considering. The dramatist must simply exercise his ingenuity to find a solution that will fit a specific situation without making his play shriek of contrivance.

ACHIEVING CLARITY

In addition to being interesting and plausible, a play must also be clear if it is to hold the attention of an audience. A viewer does not have to understand the significance of every event as it happens, but by the time the play is over, all of the parts should have fallen into place and he should have answers to his questions. At no time should he become so confused that he loses touch with the development of events.

[4] Rod Serling, *Patterns* (New York: Simon and Schuster, Inc., 1957), p. 245.

One of the critical points as far as clarity is concerned is the beginning of a play. As the play opens, astutely designed visualization can function in a major way to provide needed information about the characters and situation. Narration and dialogue can, of course, aid in establishing this background. There are two main approaches to providing information through visualization at this point. By far the more common is to use an establishing approach, moving from the larger view down to smaller details. A much less used but sometimes effective approach is to begin with a close-up on a detail before pulling back to reveal the larger picture.

THE ESTABLISHING APPROACH.   One of the traditional establishing approaches is to move from the exterior of a building or a room in which the action of a play begins into the room itself. Rod Serling used this technique in "Patterns," his play of intrigue in a big-business operation. The show opened with a filmed shot of Park Avenue traffic followed by a pan to the clock on Grand Central Station showing 8:30 A.M. Serling then dissolved to a bank of elevators in the lobby of a New York office building and dollied in on the huge board listing the firms in the building. This close-up provided the audience with the information that in a building in which most firms had only a single office, Ramsey and Company occupied a full fifteen floors. Having established the size of the enterprise and the general atmosphere of the play, Serling began the action by dissolving to the desk of a secretary who had been seen entering an elevator in the lobby.

Other establishing approaches may begin further back from the initial action or closer to it. A play about Mark Twain, for example, might begin as far back as a map of Missouri, dissolve to a picture of the city of Hannibal, move to the street on which Twain lived, and dissolve to a picture of his house before beginning the action in a set representing the interior of this house. A play about life in a high school might begin with a teacher standing at the door of the principal's office just before entering it to begin the action.

In many instances a play skips the establishing shot and opens immediately on the set in which the initial action of the play takes place. Rod Serling's "Requiem for a Heavyweight" begins in the long corridor under a fight arena. Fight posters and the roar of an off-stage crowd identify the setting. Then a fighter, accompanied by his handler, walks painfully down the corridor and pauses under a light. The glare reveals a face and body covered with cuts and abrasions. We know immediately that here is a fighter who has just taken a very bad beating. With these opening shots, Serling, without a word being spoken, has skillfully introduced his main character and revealed the problem on which the play centers.

The effectiveness of visual means in revealing information about a character is also illustrated by the opening shot of Robert Alan Aurthur's play "Man on the Mountain Top." The scene is a cold-water flat in Greenwich Village, bare and almost unfurnished, in which a battered table stands with three books on it—the works of Einstein, the collected writings of Freud, and the Bible. Immediately we have learned a great deal about the main character of the play, an intellectual whose life is going to waste.

Sometimes a writer may use direct visualization to communicate essential information. We have noted the clock on Grand Central Station establishing the time in Serling's "Patterns." Paul Crabtree used a similar device when he opened his play "The Pilot" on a clock showing 4:45 P.M. and then tilted down to show a changeable calendar reading "Today is May 15th, 1930." Gore Vidal in a "Visit to a Small Planet" needed to establish that the action of the play was at some future date when interplanetary travel had developed. He communicated this information using the most direct visual means possible. On a shot of the night sky with a luminous object arcing across it he superimposed a title reading "The Time: Day After Tomorrow."

BEGINNING WITH A DETAIL. The reverse of the establishing approach is to begin with a detail and then pull back to reveal the relationship of that detail to the scene as a whole. Thus, a play may begin with a close-up of a knife, its blade darkened by blood. When the camera pulls back to reveal the knife on a table with a group of people looking down on it, the audience may assume that it is the lethal weapon in a murder mystery. William Noble in a play of quite a different nature, "Snapfinger Creek," used a similar technique. He began his drama by showing the reflection of two young faces in a stream. Then the camera pulled back to show a fourteen-year-old boy and girl standing on a tiny wooden bridge looking down at their reflections in the water. With this opening, Noble established the mood and milieu of his play in an artistic and at the same time efficient way.

TRANSITIONS

It would be an unusual play, indeed, which during its action did not involve some transitions in time or place. A significant element in maintaining clarity is the skill with which the writer indicates the nature of these transitions.

TYPES OF TRANSITIONS. Transitions can be classified into a number of categories depending on the nature of the change; it can be a change in place or time or in both. In one type of transition a scene is followed by another in which both the time and place have changed. The time of the second scene may be after that of the first, or it may be a flashback to a previous incident. A series of transitions that shows several incidents in the same general development is called a *montage* effect. In a television version of "Cinderella," this technique was employed to show the prince trying unsuccessfully to fit the glass slipper on the feet of several maidens in the kingdom before he finally found Cinderella.

A second type of transition shows the relationship between actions going on simultaneously in time but in different locations. A play of a man and woman about to be married might alternate between the bride and groom, showing their preparations for the wedding ceremony. A "chase" drama may show scenes of a detective pursuing a criminal intercut with scenes of the man he is pursuing.

A third type of transition shows the time relationships between actions occurring in the same location. In most instances the time of the following scene is later than of the preceding one, but this type of transition may also involve a flashback journey to a previous day or hour. Techniques that have been used to indicate this type of transition are such old reliables as the clock that shows the advance of time, the pages dropping from a calendar, the matched dissolve from an empty ash tray to a full one, and the trees in full leaf replaced by barren trees.

CLARITY IN TRANSITIONS. One good way to distinguish professional from amateur writing is to examine the nature of transitions. If they jump wildly in time and place without revealing clearly what changes are occurring, the audience can be quite sure that it is listening to the work of an amateur.

In radio drama, of course, transition devices must be entirely auditory in nature. Narration and dialogue are the most obvious means of informing an audience what kind of change is taking place. Sound effects may also be used to give information about place and time, but the sound must be subject to immediate identification. The introduction of boat whistles or foghorns can tell an audience that the action has shifted to the water front, a large clock chiming a particular hour can indicate the time, and the chirp of crickets at the beginning of a scene can inform the audience that night has fallen. If the action in a scene shifts from one part of a room to another, footsteps can indicate the movement. The intervals between scenes may be composed of music, sound effects, or speech, or various combinations of these elements, or it may consist of nothing but a pause. One of the common faults is to write fade lines containing essential information. When a line is faded, the writer must assume that the audience will not be able to hear the line; he must therefore make certain that the information the audience needs to follow the story is in the lines that preceded the faded ones.

There are a number of visual techniques for indicating transitions in television. These techniques and their relationship to the nature of the transition are described in the chapter on Technical Elements and Script Formats. Dialogue or narration can reinforce the visual techniques. A line at the end of the scene may foreshadow the location or time of the next scene. Dialogue may serve to illuminate the situation not only at the end of a scene but also at the beginning of the new one. A character who begins a scene with the line, "It's ten years since I've seen you, yet you haven't changed at all," has told the audience exactly how much time has gone by. Sound effects in television can sometimes communicate information about transitions, but music, which is often employed as part of a transition, usually can do no more than reinforce the emotional quality of the effect unless it can be given some kind of symbolic value. An example of this might be the use of the familiar "Take me out to the Ball Game" as part of a transition to a baseball diamond.

A beginning writer often becomes so fascinated with contriving complicated transition effects that he neglects to make essential facts clear. Ingenious transitions are not wrong in themselves, but if their complications defeat clarity, then ingenuity has been misused. The first objective in developing a transition sequence is to achieve clearness; artistic sheen and mere inventiveness must take second place to this objective. Some degree of consistency in the transition devices used in a particular script also helps the audience to follow the changes in time and place.

PLANNING, WRITING, AND EVALUATION

Some writers plunge directly into writing without making specific story plans and without knowing for sure just where their writing will take them. That method may work with the novelist, whose medium is much looser than the play, but for the dramatist, who must maintain the finest control of his materials and employ the strictest economy of means, writing without a plan can be a futile exercise. He may discover after all the trouble of writing a script, that he really had no story at all. In a letter to me on this point, Alan Armer, producer of *The Fugitive* and a number of other television series, said this: "Most scripts fail or succeed in the outline stage. If you build a strong foundation from a carefully detailed blueprint, your house cannot topple over.

If the dialogue is corny, it can be fixed. If a character emerges colorlessly, he can be dressed up. But if the story is essentially wrong, it is headed for disaster."

THE SCRIPT PLAN

There is no generally accepted term for the plan you prepare before you begin writing your script. Variously it is called a treatment, an outline, a scenario, or a script plan. There is no agreement either on the precise form it should take. It may be written as an outline, as a complete narrative, in an expository manner, or in combination of these approaches. The particular form you use can be one that best fits your individual needs and preferences. There are certain indispensable functions it should accomplish, however. Obviously, it should make clear your plotting development, the nature of the characters, and the thematic message. It should indicate how the script is to be arranged into acts and scenes and the main devices you plan to use. These points should be clear not only to you as the writer but also to others, for scripts are frequently commissioned on the basis of plans or outlines.

By preparing a plan ahead of time, you will have a guide that can provide your script with the direction it needs to reach your goals. You will have tested the strength of your play ideas. It is likely that the act of committing those ideas to paper has revealed weaknesses which you can correct before beginning to write the script. Moreover, the writing of a plan is a creative process in itself which can stimulate you to think of ideas for your play that never occurred to you before. It is worth emphasizing at this point that throughout the entire process of preparing a script you should be alert to make improvements whenever they suggest themselves. At no time do you need to take the irrevocable step that will congeal your play idea into a final, inflexible mold. Plays are rewritten right up to the moment of broadcast.

VISUALIZATION.   Once a stage dramatist has described the setting and action of a play, which the audience sees from one unchanging point of view, he can concentrate on creating the lines for his characters. Your responsibility as a television dramatist for controlling the visual elements, whether your play is to be performed in a TV or film studio, is much greater. In addition to writing the best lines you are capable of creating, you must be alert at all times to control the constantly shifting view of the action which is being presented to the audience. Your responsibility as a film writer for indicating the specific nature of a given picture is greater than when you are writing for television, but you must be concerned in both instances with what is on the screen.

One of your main tasks in preparing your plan is to design the visual portion of your script.

VIEWPOINT.   One of the decisions you may have to make in preparing your script plan is to choose a viewpoint. Viewpoint is to the writer about what it is to the painter. It determines what is to be seen and the angle from which the observation takes place. In the end it decides what is to be revealed to the audience. In this sense of the word, incidentally, viewpoint does not refer to the author's views or opinions, which he expresses through the script. That is another use of the word entirely.

The choice of a viewpoint from which the events are to be related is often not a significant matter unless you are using narration as an element in the script design. In that case we can distinguish three different viewpoints: 1) that of a narrator who sees all and knows all—the omniscient viewpoint; 2) that of the narrator who is the focal character in the story; and 3) that of a narrator, not the focal character, who may be a major or minor character in the story. There is a definite relationship, of course, between these viewpoints and the "person" in which the narration is given, as we shall note in the chapter on Dialogue and Narration.

Of these viewpoints the easiest to use is the omniscient, for a writer whose narrator knows everything can reveal whatever item of information is needed to advance the plot. The writer who tells his story from the point of view of a character is always restricted by that character's view of the events. Sometimes, however, this restriction may actually work to the writer's advantage. A good example is the detective story in which relating the events from the viewpoint of a minor character provides a natural way of keeping the audience in the dark about what is going on in the great detective's mind and paves the way for the surprising revelation of the means through which he solved the case.

Generally you should not switch the viewpoint from one character to another or you may damage the unity of the play. In some cases, however, a switch of viewpoint is justified if it adds an extra dimension to the story. There are some instances in which a switch of this nature is the major tool for achieving the effect the writer seeks. A case in point was the Japanese drama *Rashamon*, which related a single event as it was seen from the viewpoint of four different characters.

DIVIDING THE PLAY IN ACTS.   Because a television play does not proceed in one unbroken sequence as a movie does but comes to a stop at regular intervals to provide for the insertion of commercials and, in the case of longer works, for station breaks, the equivalent of a curtain must come every ten or fifteen minutes. These curtains need to be carefully planned. One of the first steps in preparing your script plan, then, is to divide your material into acts and to decide how each of these acts is to end.

DIVIDING THE ACTS INTO SCENES. The next step is to determine the content of individual scenes. A scene is defined as any sequence of action that continues in one place without a break in time. There may be only one scene between the television curtains that divide the play into acts or there may be several, separated from one another by transitions in time, in place, or in both. In describing these scenes in your plan, you should include the following items of information:

1. The way in which each scene begins and ends.
2. The transition devices that will link one scene with another.
3. The nature of the sets.
4. The characters involved in each scene, how they appear, and how they are removed.
5. The way the action develops and what you intend to accomplish with each scene.
6. Key lines of dialogue if they occur to you.
7. Major technical devices.

Some writers use a rather elaborate form that sets up the plan in three columns. One lists the characters in each scene; the second summarizes what they do or say; the third indicates what is to be accomplished in each scene in terms of character revelation, attention-getting devices, development of suspense and expectancy, exposition, preparation, complication, climax, and resolution.

THE FIRST DRAFT AND AFTER

With the scenario completed, you are now ready to put your play into the script from which it will be performed. One of the clichés of dramatic composition is that plays are not written, but rewritten. The Writers' Guild contract for narrative scripts, in fact, requires that for his fee the writer must prepare (1) a plot or idea synopsis, (2) a first draft of the teleplay which can be subject to reworking based on the client's suggestions, (3) a final draft on which either the client or director has the right to require one last revision. It is possible to revise too much, of course. Developing a state of continuing dissatisfaction with what one has written may cause the discarding of existing values without substituting anything better for them. It is the rare writer, however, who can overdo rewriting or produce a first draft that needs no revision at all.

The basic guide for the composition of the first draft is, of course, the script plan. Again it should be emphasized that you should not consider that everything has now frozen into a final form which cannot be modified, for the thought and reflection required by writing may stimulate you to think of ideas that will improve your play. You may decide to reverse the order of two scenes, for example, or think of a better way to accomplish a transition. You should make such minor departures from the plan freely and without hesitation. If you find, however, that the writing of the play is pulling you away from the plan in a radical way, you should stop and evaluate the entire situation. The new track may, in the end, turn out to be the better one, but it may lead you to write a play quite different from the one outlined in your script plan. If you decide to write that new and different play, you should revise your plan accordingly or otherwise you will be venturing into the task of composition without a design to guide you.

EVALUATING THE RESULTS

After completing each step in the process of script construction—plan, first draft, second draft, and so on—you must conduct a critical evaluation of what you have done. Many people find it difficult to attain the cold objectivity necessary to carry out this task. They tend to fall in love with what they have written, looking on it as they would on their own child—above and beyond criticism. Even those people who do not quite become infatuated with their work, once they have put dialogue on paper, often develop an inflexibility that prevents them from driving on to make the necessary changes. These are unfortunate attitudes. You need to examine your work with searching questions in mind.

CHARACTERS   Your scenario and script should throw into sharp relief the characters you have created. Do they seem to have potentialities for becoming real people with depth and dimension? Does the development of your action provide you with opportunities to reveal their true nature to the audience? Do your characters act with a consistency that makes what they do believable to an audience? Are their motives clear?

CONSTRUCTION.   The term, construction, refers both to the development of the plot and to its exposition in the scenes and acts you have devised. Some of the questions to ask about construction are: Will the interest of the audience be aroused at the very beginning of the script? Does each act have a high point? Is the basic problem of the script established early? Is there a steady progression in the development of the story or do certain scenes go round and round in one place instead of furthering the action? Do you have enough complications to insure a steady rise in the emotional tension of the story? Do the acts end with major developments that create suspense and expectancy sufficient to carry audience interest through the commercials? Does your story reach a satisfactory climax?

UNITY. Much has been written about unity in playwriting—particularly about the unities of action, time, and place—requirements that supposedly originated with Aristotle. An examination of Aristotle's works reveals, however, that the only unity he really stressed was unity of action. If this is taken to mean that the plot should develop in an organized, relevant way, we must agree with Aristotle's principle, for it seems obvious that a plot should contain no extraneous or unnecessary elements. But there seems to be no reason why a script should have unity of time or place. It need not be restricted to a period of a day, one of the implications in Aristotle's writings, but it can occur through whatever period of time is inherent in the plot and it can involve as many places as are significant to the story.

There is one other unity worth mentioning, however—the unity of mood. You should read your scenario to determine whether one general mood will prevail or whether there will be radical changes from one mood to another. This does not mean that you are permitted no variations in mood at all, for writers often use comic interludes to lighten scripts in which the dominant atmosphere is one of tragedy or despair (the porter's scene in *Macbeth* is a good example), but there should be an over-all unity of mood. Comedies should not suddenly become tragedies.

CLARITY. An audience that becomes confused about what is going on in a play soon loses interest. You should evaluate your scenario to see whether your plan proceeds clearly from beginning to end. Is all of the action understandable? Most particularly, you should make certain that your audience will understand what changes in time and location take place as the play moves from one scene to another.

EVALUATION BY OTHERS. You may be helped at this stage by the discerning criticism of other people who can express their reactions to a piece of dramatic writing in a meaningful way. The chief advantage of a course in writing, as has been mentioned, is that it provides an opportunity for the writer to find an audience outside of himself before turning his script into its final form. The teacher and other students bring a fresh point of view which may provide new ideas and insights.

You must be on guard, however, against following too slavishly the suggestions of others. For one thing, suggestions often conflict. For another, you must remember that it is your script and what others say must always be measured against the touchstone of your own purpose and inspiration. Of course, if the suggestions for revision come from a script editor or a sponsor, you may find that you have little choice in the matter. Some of the greatest collisions in broadcasting arise when irresistible sponsors meet immovable writers.

QUESTIONS AND PROJECTS

1. Observe and analyze a number of TV plays with special attention to the following factors:
   a) the techniques employed to gain attention
   b) the minor and major suspense questions
   c) the devices used to develop expectancy

2. Develop an item of information that might be revealed during the progress of a dramatic production. Indicate specifically how you would reveal this information at intervals through the play, delaying the final revelation until the action is almost over.

3. In watching TV plays, movies, and stage productions, be alert to note excellent uses of the techniques of implication. Describe these uses to your class.

4. Observe TV plays with particular attention to their plausibility. Are there any instances in which your credulity is strained? Are there examples of faulty or excellent preparation?

5. Analyze the visualization employed in a TV play, citing the information communicated by the visualization and the specific means used to convey it.

6. Examine the transitions in a TV dramatization. Define the nature of the transitions and the devices used to accomplish them.

7. Devise a narrative plan for your TV play similar to those used in Chapter Three to describe the plotting development of "Marty" and the script from *The Fugitive* series "May God Have Mercy."

7

Revealing the Characters

> *Good characters are so actual, so individual, so human that it is impossible not to feel that if one of them were pricked, real, warm human blood would flow.*   W. Somerset Maugham

In Chapter 4 we considered the first step in the process of characterization, the stage in which the writer creates the characters, bringing them into being in his own mind, deciding the fundamental values that will dominate their lives, and devising the combination of traits and mannerisms that will distinguish them. The second step in characterization is to reveal to the audience the characters who have been created. If these characters do not take form for the audience, the dramatist actually accomplishes nothing so far as characterization is concerned, no matter how vividly they may exist in his mind. Ultimate success in characterization depends on how well the writer carries over his character concepts to the pages of a script. Character creation must be followed by character revelation.

DESCRIBING A CHARACTER DIRECTLY

It would seem that one means of revealing a character is to tell the audience directly just what kind of person he is. If a given individual

118

is a vain, selfish person, whose concern with his own welfare is the dominating value of his life, why not tell an audience just that in so many words? There are at least two reasons why the technique of direct description should not be used.

First, the dramatist has no way of communicating directly with an audience unless he employs a narrator. Second, even though this technique is available, it should seldom, if ever, be used, for to do so violates the principle that the viewer of a play should be permitted to make inferences rather than being told things directly. What you should do as a dramatist is to provide your viewers with opportunities to observe a character's behavior in a situation and then let them decide what kind of person he is. In following this procedure, you are permitting an audience to arrive at judgments about a character's true nature in exactly the way we make up our minds about people in everyday life. Letting the audience draw its own conclusions is more important in characterization than it is in any other phase of dramatic writing.

Let us consider an example of this process in action. Some time ago I had the opportunity to observe the work of a young lady who served as a physiotherapist in a hospital treatment room. After watching her practice her profession for a period of four months, I came to the conclusion that she was a conscientious, dedicated, sensitive person and a highly skilled practitioner of her art.

How effective are these words in making a character of this individual? It is true that they communicate some information about her, but they fall far short of making her come to life as a person. Because the audience has been given no opportunity to see the character acting in a situation, that element so necessary to drama—an emotional response— cannot arise. Generalized, descriptive expressions make little impression. They carry some meaning but they do not succeed in creating a character.

What the writer should do is forget about the descriptive words and concentrate on recreating the situation and the behavior that brought these words to his mind. The same principle applies to other creative writers. John Ciardi said, for example, that "A good novelist does not tell us that a given character is good or bad . . . He shows us the character in action and then, watching him, we know."

What was the nature of the situation and the physiotherapist's behavior that gave rise to the character description above? The major case confronting her during this period was a quadriplegic, a nineteen-year-old boy whose neck had been broken in a diving accident. When she first saw him, his body was a pitiful, inert mass of flesh, paralyzed from the neck down, and his mind was filled with despair and anger at a world that had played so malign a trick on him. The use of routine measures in these circumstances would have been entirely understandable. Some hospital authorities, in fact, consider the destruction of the body's defenses and powers so complete in such cases that they are inclined to write them off as lost causes. Not this physiotherapist. It was clear from the beginning that she was resolved to make nerve impulses flow once again in tissues that his condition indicated were damaged beyond repair and she was determined to develop in the victim of the accident the will to live and to help himself.

A key measure in handling a case of this kind is to raise the patient on a special table, a little more each day, until a vertical position is achieved. The treatment causes pain and nausea and, carried too far, can bring on unconsciousness. This physiotherapist was not content merely to turn on the motor that would raise the table. Even though it was so heavy that she could scarcely move it, she dragged it across the floor to a window, hoping that a glimpse of the world outside might divert her patient's attention from the pain and discomfort of the treatment. His reaction was unappreciative, even hostile. In seconds he angrily shouted that he was bored with what he saw. She did not give up. Instead, she dragged the ponderous table to a second window to give him another view.

Despite her willingness to take these measures, her administration of the treatment itself did not lack firmness. Even though the young man demanded that he be let down as soon as the table started to rise, she carried out the process resolutely, increasing the angle of elevation and the length of the period day by day. She responded to his protests with jokes and cajolery, but never for a moment did she permit herself to be distracted from observing him. Being alert to every nuance of his condition, she could obtain the maximum benefit from every elevation and yet end each treatment before anything damaging could happen. And when the ordeal was over, she always patted him reassuringly on the shoulder.

There were other evidences of her sympathy and understanding. She brought some of the world outside into his hospital room by making a trip to buy him a hamburger. She took note of his birthday. As soon as her patient's condition and the weather permitted, she took the time to bundle him up on a stretcher and wheel him into the grounds around the hospital where he might realize that the world his accident seemed to have denied him was still his to enjoy.

At the end of four months two miracles had happened. The young man pushed himself down the hospital corridor in a wheel chair using arms that were no longer completely paralyzed. More importantly, the flicker of interest in life, first nursed into being, perhaps, when the physiotherapist gave him a glimpse of the world outside his hospital window, had become an intense desire to achieve some kind of usefulness. What-ever might happen to him, and no one could deny the cloudiness of his future, she had helped to give his present existence meaning and purpose.

Without question the words "conscientious," "sensitive," and "skilled" apply to this young lady, but a writer does not reveal her character effectively by using them. He does that by portraying her behavior in a situation. When he has done so, the descriptive words are no longer necessary, for the audience has been given the opportunity to create the character for itself. Each person can arrive at his own descriptive words. They may be different from the ones the writer would use, but that is unimportant. What is important is that the audience has seen a person.

There are a number of aspects in a situation and in the behavior of a person that can reveal his character. Further insights are provided by the reactions this behavior arouses in other people. Let us now con-sider the specific techniques that can be used for revealing character. Examples from TV plays and other dramas are used to illustrate these techniques.

WHAT A CHARACTER DOES

Of all the actions of a character, the most revealing are the decisions he makes. In the goal-centered play, the things he decides to do to reach his goal tell the audience how important its attainment is to him. As the focal character in the decision-centered play chooses among the conflicting values in his life, he reveals what kind of person he really is.

DECISIONS AS A CLUE TO CHARACTER

A number of published plays provide excellent examples of decisions that serve as clues to character. Paddy Chayefsky's script "The Mother" presents a recently widowed old woman who must choose between try-ing to support herself or accepting dependence on her daughter and son-in-law. Early in the script we discover that the mother has made her first decision: even though her daughter has offered to take care of her, she has decided to look for a job. She persists in this decision even though rain is pelting outside and despite a near-fainting spell on the subway the day before. The anguished pleadings of her daughter fail to turn her aside. Almost immediately a striking character takes form, the figure of a fiercely determined old woman for whom personal independence is more important than anything else—even life itself. Other qualities emerge also; we detect a considerable degree of obstinacy in this person as well as courage of a high order.

The major decisions that follow, particularly the last one recorded in the script, serve to confirm this first impression. Overcoming many obstacles, the old lady finally gets a job sewing sleeves in a children's-wear shop. At first she is successful, but then the inexcusable mistake of sewing all the sleeves for the left arm causes her to be discharged in disgrace. At first, this reversal overwhelms her; in momentary weakness, she calls her daughter and goes to spend the night with her. Her acceptance of defeat is only temporary, however. In a moving, yet simply written scene that concludes the script, the old lady the next morning puts on her coat and goes out to look for a job knowing, as she herself says, "that everything's against me." We see her as we saw her at the beginning—determined to be independent in spite of the formidable obstacles confronting her.

In this play the decisions of the mother make clear very early what kind of person she is, and the subsequent action merely serves to reinforce this characterization. Sometimes, however, a dramatist may leave the audience in doubt about a character for almost the duration of the play. In essence he confronts viewers with this question: What kind of person will the leading character turn out to be? It is not answered until the final climactic decision. J. P. Miller's "The Rabbit Trap" provides an example of this approach. The question is whether Eddie Colt, the focal character, will turn out to be a brave man or a coward. The distinction will be established by the choice he makes at the end of the play. The dramatist skillfully piles up evidence on both sides, showing Eddie veering first in one direction and then in the other.

Early in the play it develops that Eddie is the victim of an insensitive and domineering employer. Eddie's responsibilities to his wife and son beyond that of earning them a living have been constantly interfered with by the outrageous demands of his boss. For one thing, his vacation time has been cut short again and again. There is no great need for Eddie's services, but he is recalled each time because his employer, oblivious to the damage his imperious demands are doing to Eddie and his family, finds this the simplest way to solve a problem.

It soon becomes clear that in the face of this kind of treatment, Eddie has been too subservient, too willing to comply, too eager to please. In his entire relations with his boss he has lacked aggressiveness, but he believes that he must submit to his unreasonable demands in order to hold his job. It is this realization that gives Eddie's problem its special poignancy. To keep his family from being hurt, he must risk an even greater danger—the possibility that he will lose the means for earning them a living.

The play opens with Eddie and his family some distance from their home on a vacation. With his son, eight years old, he sets a trap designed to catch a rabbit alive and unhurt. Shortly, the usual imperious call to return to work comes from his boss. Eddie hurries back, forgetting the rabbit trap until he is almost home. The trap is too far away to get back to it and still report for work in the morning. Any rabbit unlucky enough to be snared faces a lingering but inevitable death. That is all Eddie's son can think about.

Eddie's dilemma is clear. By failing to go back to the trap and save whatever rabbit may have been caught, he will lose the respect of both his wife and son. Yet to leave his job means almost certain dismissal.

Eddie's struggle with himself is a desperate one. He makes several attempts to explain the situation to his boss, but this obtuse and insensitive individual, who can see only that he needs this man to get out a rush job, can make no sense out of Eddie's concern for a rabbit. He utterly fails to see that it is not the rabbit's life that is at stake, but what a boy thinks of his father.

In the end, Eddie walks out on his job. By taking this road, Eddie establishes himself finally as a strong and courageous man rather than the weak and subservient person he has often seemed to be. His boss fires him, of course, but even as he does so, he cannot restrain a grunt of admiration for this once-pliable fellow who now, for some inexplicable reason, is standing up to him. His wife sees Eddie in a new light, even though his decision, at least temporarily, has destroyed their security. For the son, Eddie has become everything a father should be.

These two plays illustrate how basic character is revealed to the audience by the critical decisions of the play. In the case of the mother, they establish that the prevailing value in her life is a desire to maintain her independence. As far as Eddie is concerned, his final decision reveals that his own self respect and the respect of his wife and son are more important to him than job security. Of course, other evidences of these values are needed in order to fill out the characterizations. One of the best means for accomplishing this is to provide incidental action that reinforces the character revelation achieved by the major action of the play.

INCIDENTAL ACTION AS A CLUE TO CHARACTER

Again we turn to Chayefsky's "The Mother" to find examples of character revelation through small but telling incidents. In an early scene, the daughter visits her mother to try to persuade her not to go out looking for a job. During the exchange she offers to make her mother a cup of coffee. The old lady refuses, insisting instead that she make the coffee for her daughter. She even refuses to let her daughter get the saccharin for her. This small incident effectively strengthens our impression of an old woman who is determined to be independent in the little as well as the big things.

Exactly the reverse of this action is used by Chayefsky to portray the mother's feeling of defeat just after she loses her job and goes to stay with her daughter. Again the daughter offers to get the saccharin for her coffee, and this time the old lady meekly accepts being waited on. This incident parallels and reinforces the main current of action. We can feel certain that the next morning when the mother recovers her courage and goes job-hunting, she will be getting her own saccharin once again.

Incidental action serves to reinforce the revelation of Eddie's character in "The Rabbit Trap." In a scene in the second act, Eddie reviews with his wife the frustrating interview in which he completely failed to make clear to his boss why he thought it necessary to return to the rabbit trap. Then he sees on the wall an award he has received for five years of faithful service to the company, an award dedicated to "Ever Ready Steady Eddie." In a burst of rage, he takes it from the wall and smashes it to the floor. In addition to showing his resentment against the injustices he is suffering, this impulsive act also foreshadows his final decision.

Another play of Chayefsky's, "The Big Deal," provides a further example of the power of a well-conceived incident to reveal character. In the first scene of the play, we see Joe Manx meet his daughter in a restaurant. Within the first thirty seconds, he borrows fifteen dollars from her on the pretext that he has come across an interesting proposition and needs the money to take a man out for a couple of drinks. The daughter loans him the money and then leaves. Joe fingers the money, straightens, and then lifts an imperious hand. "Waiter, Check!" he calls sharply.

This one incident tells us almost all we need to know about Joe Manx. We gather that here is a man who is kidding himself about "big propositions." We surmise that, but for the fortunate appearance of his daughter, he might have had trouble paying the check. We sense that there were past glories of accomplishment in this man's life. We know that more than anything else, he covets the role of "the big shot." The character qualities so clearly and yet so economically revealed by this one brief scene are all confirmed by later developments in the play.

Yes, the best clue to character is what an individual does. The playwright Percival Wilde put it this way: "A significant deed characterizes more positively, more economically, and more impressively in a few seconds than half an hour devoted to talk." In "My Lost Saints" Tad Mosel tells the story of an old woman who is determined to persuade her daughter to leave her position as a maid in the home of the Hallet's so that the daughter can live with her. The old woman comes to the Hallet's, then falls while washing windows and is injured. They generously provide her with a room and attend to her needs until she recovers; her hostile attitude toward this thoughtfulness is vividly demonstrated when she deliberately breaks the little china bell they loan her. Again words could never have carried the impact generated by this one revelatory act.

In Arthur Hailey's television play, "No Deadly Medicine," an old doctor conducting an autopsy permits the ashes from his cigar to fall carelessly on the corpse. He continues without even bothering to brush the ashes away. This incident is a telling indication of the old doctor's callousness. The obvious horror of a young doctor at this unthinking desecration of a dead human body shows, in turn, how different his attitude is from that of the older man.

The significance of these examples for the dramatist is obvious. It is clear that the most effective means for drawing a character is to devise revealing behavior. Much of this behavior may already have been invented by the time the character has been conceived and the plot constructed. Certainly the writer will have determined the actions of the focal character as they relate to his major decisions. What is still needed, however, are the supporting actions, the small incidents that amplify and develop the basic character structure.

WHAT A CHARACTER SAYS

A second important means of revealing a character to an audience is through what he says. In a sense this is also part of what he does, but speech is such an important aspect of behavior that it deserves separate treatment. Speech is the primary means through which the audience finds out about past actions and learns about those contemplated. It provides the main clues to the values dominating a character's life and thus reveals his true nature. When a decision is reached, again it is almost always speech that makes this decision clear to the audience. Most of the actions just described were made clear to the audience through dialogue or were illuminated through a combination of speech with some other form of activity.

The revelation accomplished through a character's speeches is generally indirect. They lead us to make inferences about the kind of person he is. When Torvald in Ibsen's *A Doll's House*, on finding out that Krogstad no longer planned to press the charge of forgery against his wife, shouted, "Nora, I am saved" instead of "We are saved," he revealed his innate egocentricity far better than any direct statement could have done. In the preface to the published version of his TV play, "Twelve Angry Men," Reginald Rose describes the jurors who make up the characters.[1] He says that Juror 3 has a streak of sadism in him. This quality is revealed in two significant lines, once when he says of the accused, "He's got to burn! We're letting him slip through our fingers here" and then again near the end of the play when, facing defeat, he screams, "He's got to die." The bigotry of Juror 10 comes through when he says of the boy on trial, "You know what you're dealing with."

Sometimes a dramatist may characterize by actually having a character make statements about himself that describe his true nature. Marty, the title character in Paddy Chayefsky's play, admits that he is a short, fat fellow "that girls don't go for." In another of Chayefsky's plays, "The Big Deal," the leading character, reflecting the opinion of other people, at one point refers to himself as "a big talker without a nickel to his name, who thinks he's a big shot." In Tad Mosel's play "My Lost Saints," Mrs. Hallet describes herself as a "foolish," useless woman." These are as appropriate descriptions of these particular characters as could be devised.

What a person says about himself, of course, cannot always be accepted at face value, for it is virtually impossible to view oneself objectively. The dramatist takes this fact into account in deciding what he will have a character say about himself. If he were presenting a character whom he wished to portray as vain and conceited, those are probably the last terms he would have the character use with respect to himself. Rather, he might have the character describe himself as humble and self-effacing. What a character says about himself may suggest the exact reverse of what he actually is.

HOW A CHARACTER SPEAKS

The manner of speaking is also an important factor in revealing character. Just as the choice of subject matter provides clues to an individual's basic nature, so does the way in which that subject matter is expressed. Among the significant characteristics of language are the vocabulary a person uses, the length and structure of his sentences, and their basic rhythm. Grammatical usage, pronunciation, and the particular epithets

[1] Reginald Rose, "Twelve Angry Men," *Six Television Plays* (New York: Simon and Schuster, Inc., 1956), pp. 113–115.

and idioms employed are other important speech factors that help to reveal character. In "Twelve Angry Men," Rose distinguished brilliantly among his characters by providing the most important jurors with distinctive word choices, language styles, and sentence structures.

The basic characteristic of Juror 7, a loud, wisecracking, gladhanded salesman type, is effectively suggested by such lines as "How do you like him? It's like talking into a dead phone," "Stories this guy made up!! He oughta write for *Amazing Detective Monthly*," "Why don't we have them run the trial over . . ."

Juror 4 is described as a man of wealth and position, a practiced speaker who expresses himself well at all times. Note the vocabulary that Rose provides him: "Potential menaces to society," "I can recount it accurately," "unshakable testimony," "exhibits in evidence," "insignificant details," "incredible coincidence." His use of language makes his breeding evident.

Juror 10's lack of breeding, on the other hand, is just as evident in the words and sentences he uses. "It don't mean anything," and "he's a common, ignorant, slob. He don't even speak good English." are examples.

The portrayal of unique individuals demands dialogue that reflects that individuality. When characters in a play all express themselves in the same way, the dramatist has obviously failed to project people who are distinctive and different. Yet this kind of failure is often observed in the beginning writer's scripts. One of the dramatist's most critical challenges is to write dialogue that is appropriate only to the particular character who utters it. We consider this problem in greater detail in the next chapter on Dialogue and Narration.

WHAT OTHERS SAY

Another means of revealing a character is to have people in the play describe him. In an early scene in Chayefsky's "The Big Deal," Joe's wife and daughter discuss him and in so doing present a relatively complete character analysis. We find out that Joe has become interested in "propositions" almost to the point of foolishness. We discover that, once "a big shot," he still craves the ego-satisfaction provided by that status; we find out that he was a big spender who liked to show off. The scalpel wielded by these two women is sharp; it exposes Joe for what he is as accurately and as scathingly as anything else in the play. Their analysis is direct and objective.

Chayefsky's play "The Mother" also uses other people's descriptions as a technique for communicating information about character to the audience. In his preface to the play, Chayefsky states that the daughter, who keeps offering to take care of her mother, is motivated by unconscious guilts and resentments. He says that she was an unwanted child who generally came in last in the race for the mother's attention. Now she is trying to buy that love by sacrifice, hoping to be recognized as the favorite instead of her sister. Under the surface, says Chayefsky, she almost hates her mother, and her desire to make the old lady dependent on her represents a subconscious desire to hurt her. Chayefsky in this preface provides a clear description of the daughter's character as he created it in his mind.[2] He transmits this concept to the audience primarily by having two other characters in the play—the daughter's husband and her sister—express their opinions of the daughter's underlying motivation.

The scene in which this exposition occurs takes place after one in which the daughter has berated her sister for neglecting their mother, behavior, she points out, that is in sharp contrast with her own self-sacrifices. After the daughter leaves, her husband and sister discuss the circumstances and emotions that have motivated her outburst. We learn that the mother has always been frightened of this particular daughter because her birth endangered her life. We discover that a son was actually the mother's favorite, a situation that made the daughter jealous and caused her to fight bitterly for acceptance. We also learn that, in the sister's opinion, the daughter's efforts to take over her mother is the worst possible way to deal with the old lady.

The technique of transmitting the concept of one character by describing him in the lines of other characters is an effective means for achieving characterization when it is employed skillfully. The most common fault is being too obvious. The discussion of a character by other characters in the play must occur in a natural way; it must be motivated by what is taking place in the play, rather than being forced in merely because something about a character needs to be told. The example just cited demonstrates effective motivation. The daughter's angry and unexpected outburst, revealing her hidden resentments and frustrations, is perfect justification for the discussion of her behavior which follows.

In many instances, of course, what one individual says about another is not necessarily a correct description of that person's character; rather, it is a means of revealing the characteristics of the person who makes the statement. How we describe other people furnishes one of the best clues to our own peculiarities and personality twists. A line from Horton Foote's "The Trip to Bountiful" provides a good example of this "reverse" characterization. It is the story of an old lady, Mrs. Watts, who manages

[2] Paddy Chayefsky, *Television Plays* (New York: Simon and Schuster, Inc., 1955), p. 177.

to visit her childhood home in Bountiful, despite the obstacles set in her way by Jessie Mae, her selfish daughter-in-law. Jessie Mae says of the mother-in-law she is exploiting, "She's just spoiled rotten." This line does not accurately describe the mother-in-law Mrs. Watts, but it does help us to see Jessie Mae as the selfish, vulgar, insensitive person she is. A little later in this scene, Jessie Mae says, "I've got Ludie and Mother Watts. That's all the children I need." In this case, the line contains both truth and falsehood. To call Jessie Mae's husband Ludie a child is essentially accurate, for the rest of the play amply demonstrates that he is a weak-willed, dependent person. But can Mrs. Watts be correctly called a child? Despite illness and the resolute opposition of her daughter-in-law, she manages to reach her childhood home in Bountiful, an achievement that demonstrates a resourcefulness and determination far beyond that possessed by the usual child. This is another example of an observation by Jessie Mae about her mother-in-law that tells far more about Jessie Mae than it does about the old lady.

OTHER PEOPLE'S REACTIONS

Another means of revealing a character is to show how people act in his presence. The portrayal of Mrs. Hallet in Tad Mosel's "My Lost Saints" as a childlike person who must be watched and cared for is accomplished primarily by showing how other people treat her. In one scene, for example, Mrs. Hallet comes downstairs dressed for church. The maid Kate immediately objects to the dress she is wearing and sends her marching upstairs to put on another one. The meek way in which Mrs. Hallet accepts this treatment provides a telling insight into her character.

That Ludie in "The Trip to Bountiful" is a weak-willed person completely dominated by his wife Jessie Mae is shown by the way Jessie Mae treats him. She calls him a goose and ignores his suggestions and objections, doing what she wants to do without regard for his wishes. Even though he violently objects to Jessie Mae's attempts to control his mother, he becomes her tool in carrying them out. Ludie's immaturity is further demonstrated in a scene with his mother later in the play. The entire flavor of this scene is that of a mother talking not to a grown-up son, but to one who is still a child. It is clear that when Ludie left his mother's home to marry Jessie Mae, he exchanged one dominating woman for another.

In addition to demonstrating fundamental qualities of character, the way in which people are addressed can also serve to add the minor touches that fill out a characterization. J. P. Miller's play "The Rabbit

Trap" provides a good example. Spellman, the boss in this play, absorbed completely in the work his company must accomplish, cannot see why Eddie wants to return to Vermont just to let a rabbit out of a trap. That he is not completely one sided, however, is shown by the relationship between him and his secretary Judy, who in one scene addresses him as "Sweetie." What his willingness to be addressed in this way tells us about Mr. Spellman is not particularly important, but it does help to make him more human and individual.

SETTING, COSTUME, AND PHYSICAL APPEARANCE

When we see a person sprawled on a sidewalk in a skid-row section, we immediately gain some insight into the sort of person he is. We can make inferences about the general nature of the values ruling him and we can make guesses about the actions that have brought him to this situation. The alcoholic white man in a south seas island background tells us by his mere presence in that setting a good deal of what we need to know about him. Consider Laura in Tennessee Williams' play *The Glass Menagerie*. Her constant preoccupation with her collection of little glass animals becomes a symbol of her basic characteristic—her withdrawal from the world of reality. The setting in which we place a person and the objects with which we surround him can supply significant information about his character.

Physical appearance and dress can perform the same function. Grooming, for example, or the lack of grooming can be a definitive clue to character. Setting and appearance may reveal a man's basic traits and values. The fact that an individual is dominated by selfishness or, in contrast, is inspired by concern for his fellow human beings can be communicated in part by his appearance, by the way he dresses, and by the kind of environment in which he lives. These elements can also illustrate an interesting mannerism. A personality quirk can be expressed in the clothes a man wears or the way he trims his moustache. Disclosure of personality characteristics through setting, dress, and appearance can be extremely telling, for by permitting the audience to make inferences, it reveals character in a natural way.

REPEATING CHARACTER QUALITIES

In an earlier chapter it was pointed out that characters in a drama, although they may appear to be full, well-rounded individuals, are actually people about whom we know very little. The impression of completeness is achieved in a number of ways, but certainly one of the most important devices is to concentrate on one or two basic characteristics which are emphasized in scene after scene. If your intention is to portray a person whose dominant quality is selfishness, you should show that person being selfish over and over again until the characteristic is impressed on the audience with an indelible imprint. Obviously, the traits selected for this kind of repetitive treatment should be the traits that are at the core of the play. It should be emphasized also that only the traits are repeated; the situations that reveal them must be different from one another or the play would soon sink to a deadly, monotonous level. Repetition of a trait in a number of situations and in different ways builds a powerful characterization, and the play gains color, depth, and variety. Let us see this principle at work in several television plays.

In the production directions for his play "The Trip to Bountiful," Horton Foote describes Jessie Mae as an obviously vain woman who is hard, self-centered, and domineering.[3] How are these characteristics communicated to the audience? As far as vanity is concerned, we discover that Jessie Mae is addicted to the reading of movie magazines and she even fancies that she might be successful in Hollywood. The impression of her vanity is further developed by the revelation that she spends long hours in beauty parlors.

Her dominant characteristics, however, are innate selfishness and complete insensitivity to the needs and wants of others. These aspects of her personality are portrayed again and again as the play progresses. That she expects to be waited on hand and foot is revealed when she asks her mother-in-law Mrs. Watts to go into the kitchen and get her a coke. Later it develops that Mrs. Watts prepares all the meals in the house.

It becomes very clear early in the play that whatever concern Jessie Mae has for her mother-in-law is motivated entirely by the realization that if anything happens to Mrs. Watts, it will automatically cut off her pension check. She expresses the fear that her mother-in-law may get to Bountiful and die of excitement, but the true nature of her regard is shown when she bemoans in the next breath the amount of money it would cost to bring her body back to Houston. And when she finally comes face-to-face with her mother-in-law at Bountiful, the first thing she does is grab for the pension check.

Her lack of refinement and insensitivity to other people's feelings are also illustrated many times throughout the play. In the opening scene, she brutally squelches Mrs. Watt's singing because, as she says,

[3] Horton Foote, *Harrison, Texas* (New York: Harcourt, Brace and World, Inc., 1956), p. 221.

"It gets on my nerves." To a complete stranger, she describes her mother-in-law as "crazy" and "spoiled rotten." She insists on bringing the police into the situation despite her husband's objections. Even though she knows what Bountiful means to her mother-in-law, she deliberately characterizes it to her face as an ugly swamp. She even denies her mother-in-law a few moments of peace on the front porch of her old home in Bountiful by honking her car horn loudly and impatiently.

Jessie Mae does and says different things as the play progresses, but each action confirms over and over again her basic traits of selfishness and callous unconcern for other people's feelings. The range of the character is actually fairly limited, as it must be in a play that has to deal with one problem at a time, but the repeated revelation of these two basic traits gives an impression of character depth and richness.

Tad Mosel is another television writer who is particularly skillful in reinforcing a given character trait by revealing it in a variety of situations. In his play "The Lawn Party," the action revolves around a character India Price, whose basic motivation is a dedication to the search for beauty. Many times through the play, Mosel shows her reacting favorably toward beautiful things and recoiling from ugly and unattractive things. Let us note some of the different ways in which this basic trait is echoed and reechoed.

India insists that her husband put his shoes on because feet are ugly. She comments on the fact that a neighbor Miss Mudd has an ugly name. We discover that she changed her own name from Clara to India because Clara sounded like glass breaking. The next-door lot owned by Miss Mudd has become overgrown and rock strewn; India abominates it. She recalls a lawn party she once saw as a child; her recollection centers primarily on its beauty—the green lawn, the colorful decorations, the white suits of the men, and the flowered crepe-de-Chine dresses of the women. A young man comes over with a shelf he has just finished for the kitchen. She caresses it, saying she likes smooth things, but as soon as he goes inside, she deprecates his awful blue jeans. She objects to her daughter shortening her name Beatrice to Beatey or Bea because the nickname sounds like a bug. Objecting to "okay" being used in place of "yes," she emphasizes that pretty words should always be used instead of ugly ones. She is overwhelmed when she discovers that her daughter wants a "hideous tool box" for her birthday instead of a pretty new dress. She objects to beer with such intensity that we know she considers beer-drinking to be vulgar. When she decides to give a lawn party, she talks constantly about how beautiful it will be. The stationery she buys for invitations is smooth and tastefully decorated; she takes hours to write these invitations, spacing the lines carefully and forming each letter perfectly. She is repulsed by a musty dress which has been stored in an attic. She reacts unfavorably to the name Doatsy Borden. She refuses to invite Miss Mudd to the party because she's afraid she will come in a grimy old black dress and go about perspiring and talking about hair and dirt and smells.

This repeated reflection through many incidents of India's almost obsessive attraction for beautiful things and her equally abnormal revulsion for ugliness builds a characterization that has both dimension and individuality. Moreover, the concentration on these aspects of her personality helps to bring out an even more important fact about her character— namely, that India Price in her search for beauty is a basically selfish person who tramples on the feelings and rights of her neighbor, her husband, and her daughter.

Another of Tad Mosel's plays, "The Haven," demonstrates how the technique of repetition or character tagging can establish a character who is the opposite of India Price, a person named Eunice, a good hearted, yet vulgar individual whose gaucheries and general lack of refinement are offensive to her husband Howard. He, in contrast to the sloppy Eunice, is always meticulously dressed and he has an interest in the finer things of life that Eunice can neither understand nor appreciate. Some of the incidents that Mosel uses to establish Eunice's vulgarity and sloppiness are these:

In applying nail polish, she smears almost as much on her fingers as she does on her nails; her lipstick, moreover, is almost purple in color. Her things are spread around her in confusion. She chews gum incessantly. She shortens her daughter's name from Germaine to Germy. She eats a popsicle very audibly and then licks her fingers and rubs them on the upholstery. She caresses her husband and gets nail polish in his hair. She tells risqué stories in mixed company. Her voice is loud and raucous. She opens a can of warm beer and it spurts all over her. She hums while a classical record is playing. She calls herself a "dumb slug" and suggests in other ways that she recognizes her deficiencies as a "lady."

Mosel does much more than establish Eunice as a person who lacks refinement; as a matter of fact, it is not Eunice's vulgarity that one finally remembers best, but rather her unselfish heart, her good nature, her willingness to forgive even though terribly wronged. But projecting her lack of manners and grace is of vital importance, particularly in the earlier portions of the play, for we must be aware of this characteristic in order to understand the genesis of the problem on which the play centers.

This listing of the specific devices through which writers of TV plays have communicated character traits suggests a method through which you can plan the ways for establishing a character in a play you plan to write. Let us assume that the concept of a character has crystallized clearly in your mind; you know what kind of person this character is and you can describe his basic qualities in detail. Your next step is to take one of his traits and list as many ways as you can think of through which that trait might be illustrated for an audience. Before you begin writing, you should subject the devices in your list to certain tests: they must be consistent with the rest of the characterization; they must meet the demands of the plot development; they must be devices that fit smoothly and naturally with everything else that happens. When actual composition begins, other ideas will undoubtedly come to your mind. Your original list can spark your inspiration and it can also help to assure complete and consistent character revelation by guiding the actual writing.

QUESTIONS AND PROJECTS

1. In viewing television dramas be on the watch for devices that reveal character. Note a use of each one of the devices described in this chapter as follows:

    a) What a character does
        1) his decisions
        2) his incidental action
    b) What a character says
    c) How a character speaks
    d) What others say about a character
    e) Other people's reactions to a character
    f) Setting, costume, and physical appearance

2. Create a trait for a character, then tag that trait through the use of each of the devices listed above.

3. Use as many as possible of the devices listed above to reveal the following traits or characteristics:

    a) A mother's inordinate fear for her child's health
    b) Deep religious belief
    c) Excessive pride in one's work

8

Dialogue and Narration

Certain ways of speaking suggest certain shapes of flesh. Henry Green

In the creation of a play nothing contributes more to the dramatist's success than his ability to write effective dialogue. It is the main channel through which the mind of the writer comes into contact with the mind of his audience. The playwright may have created vivid, individual characters whose conflicts are woven into an emotional, meaningful story, but if his dialogue fails to transmit these qualities, his previous creative effort is completely nullified.

THE FUNCTIONS OF DIALOGUE

Since most plays are made up primarily of dialogue, it follows that dialogue must accomplish almost everything that the play itself sets out to accomplish. It provides the most important of all clues to character values and traits and is the primary means of advancing the story and revealing the theme. In addition to accomplishing these major functions, dialogue may also be used to solve a technical problem or to create a special effect. A laugh or a gasp of horror in response to a line is an example of a special effect. One technical problem which frequently arises is the necessity of getting a character out of a scene to permit action that cannot involve him to be presented.

In writing dialogue to accomplish these last two purposes, a special word of warning is in order. When technical problems arise, they must be solved, and a special effect like a laugh is often desirable. But dialogue can be justified only if it is in harmony with character, plot, and theme. Even though a given dialogue section may have been motivated originally by the need to make a character exit, it must seem to come naturally from the characters who speak it and it must flow out of the situation in which they are involved. The line designed to provoke laughter must pass this same test.

THE CHARACTERISTICS OF GOOD DIALOGUE

At first thought it might seem that the best way to evaluate the effectiveness of dialogue would be to determine how faithfully it reproduces the attributes of everyday conversation. Before adopting that as our measure, however, let us consider what some of these attributes are.

Much conversation is undeniably interesting for its participants, but when we examine it as potential dramatic material, we discover that it has serious faults. It is replete with awkward phrases, poor word choices, and boring repetitions; only occasionally is there an authentic bon mot. The conversation of everyday life, moreover, rarely goes anywhere even in those situations that are filled with emotion. People in conflict may repeat the same arguments over and over again, sometimes for years, without ever doing anything to change the situation. Drama, in contrast, demands changes and development, and dialogue must be purposeful language which accomplishes and reflects those changes. A further reason why real life dialogue may fail to satisfy the demands of drama is that the right language does not spring automatically even to the lips of the most eloquent. After an emotional exchange how often have you been satisfied with the way in which you gave vent to your ideas and feelings? More likely, the retort that demolishes occurred to you on your way home. Only by a painful process of rejection and selection can the writer finally settle on just the words that suit his purpose.

We must conclude that conversation often stimulates not because of its brilliance but because it is part of a social situation which is stimulating in itself. Most of what is said is too dull and static to be suitable for complete reproduction in a dramatic script. Does this mean that everyday conversation as a guide to writing dialogue must be totally rejected?

THE SOUND OF NORMAL SPEECH

Even though the dramatist does not seek complete verisimilitude, there is one respect in which he does strive to reflect the quality of everyday speech. He wants his characters to sound like real people talking. What this means is that he must write dialogue whose *content* rises above what people usually say, but whose *form* is that of everyday speech. There are variations, of course, in the way this criterion is met. The writer of a naturalistic play may approximate the content as well as the form of ordinary conversation, and some playwrights may go in the opposite direction, composing dialogue that in its opulence departs even from the form of normal speech, as Oscar Wilde did in *The Importance of Being Earnest*. The usual objective, however, is to capture the illusion of everyday speech while surpassing it in direction, purpose, and diction. Let us therefore review the characteristics that give conversation its particular form.

INFORMAL WORDS.   Everyday speech abounds in short, informal, colloquial words. There are times, of course, when genteelisms do have a place in dialogue, and elegant words may be deliberately chosen in place of simple ones to reflect an ornate personality. Formal words are helpful also in flavoring the speech of a foreign-born person who, being unsure of himself and having learned the language from books rather than from life, is likely to be more studied in his utterance than a native-born person. But these are the exceptions. Even the most educated people tend to use short, simple words when they are engaged in conversation. If you could listen to a group of college professors around a luncheon table, you would note the prevalence of simple words and colloquialisms—even slang expressions. They usually restrict the use of long, complicated, specialized terms to their textbooks and scholarly monographs.

CONTRACTIONS.   The use of contractions is an absolute requirement for the dialogue writer. In ordinary conversation we do not say, "I am going," "I will be there," or "I could not do that," but rather "I'm going," "I'll be there," and "I couldn't do that." If you fail to write these expressions as they are ordinarily spoken, the director must laboriously instruct his actors to turn the compound verbs into contractions. Of course, there are occasions when you deliberately avoid using the contracted form, when you want emphasis, for example. "I do not!" is much more forceful than "I don't!" The noncontracted form, in addition, may be used to characterize the affected or pedantic person or to introduce a special quality into the dialogue. The writers of the TV series *I Dream of Jeannie* invested the 2000-year-old genie's dialogue with an archaic flavor by having her speak consistently without contractions. The foreign-born person, lacking the certainty and intimate feel for the language that the use of contractions demands, may also use formal compound verbs.

SIMPLE SENTENCES.   Short, simply constructed sentences are the rule when people talk. Consider the following line which appeared in a student-written script: "While helping me in the barn, Toby, who is too little to be much help anyway, backed into the pail of milk and kicked it over." The inverted order, the use of the relative clause, the length and complication of the sentence all help to disqualify it as effective dialogue. In real life these thoughts would probably be expressed somewhat as follows: "What do you think Toby did? Kicked over my pail of milk. Backed right into it, he did. And the little guy was trying to help me. He's too little to be much help anyway." When talking, most people take the direct route from subject to verb. They rarely use inversions. They qualify ideas in separate sentences rather than in relative clauses.

INCOMPLETE SENTENCES.   People often start a sentence, forget what they were going to say, and break off in the middle. Or what is more likely, they are interrupted by someone else. The device of the broken sentence or the interrupted line can help immensely to give conversational quality to dialogue. Often a single word, or even a grunt, is sufficient to express an idea.

SHORT SPEECHES.   In real life people seldom speak in paragraphs. For this reason, good dialogue is generally made up of a swift alternation among the various characters of words, parts of sentences, sentences, or at most short paragraphs. A quick leafing through of a script can reveal whether this requirement is being met. If the script appears to be a succession of great chunks of dialogue, one can conclude that the character's speeches are too long. Without reading a single word, it is safe to tell this writer: "Break it up. Shorten the speeches. Develop more interchange among the characters." An occasional long speech is sometimes appropriate, of course, but a script made up entirely of alternated paragraphs is likely to be stodgy, stilted, and slow-paced.

SOUNDS RIGHT WHEN SPOKEN.   The final test used by a good cook is to taste what he has made. The same kind of test for the playwright is to read his dialogue aloud. Only by doing this can he tell how it will strike the ear of the listener. If he has done an effective job, what is he likely to hear? He will have avoided, first of all, the articulatory stumbling blocks that invite embarrassing spoonerisms or awkward stutters. Tongue twisters of the "rubber baby-buggy-bumpers' variety have no place in dialogue. Neither do words like "inimitable" or "inestimable," which are likely to ensnare even the most wary. Other defects to watch for as dialogue is read aloud are too many alliterations and accidental rhymes, which may turn serious lines into absurd ones.

To summarize, when the writer reads his dialogue aloud, he should hear language whose content and general quality is infinitely superior to that of ordinary conversation. The ideas should be arresting and stimulating; in most cases they should be expressed with clarity, precision, and emotional power; there should be purpose and direction in everything that is said. These ideas, however, should be cast in the idiom of everyday speech. The carefully constructed, obviously premeditated tone of written English should be nowhere evident. There should be instead the simplicity, colloquial quality, and informality that characterizes what is spoken.

DIALOGUE APPROPRIATE TO THE CHARACTER AND MOOD

Dialogue is the writer's most important tool for leading the audience into an awareness of the character he has created. This is primarily a positive process of finding the right words and phrases. But there is also a negative phase to the process—namely, to avoid putting anything into the lines that will be inconsistent with the character who says them. When a particularly neat phrase or witty line occurs to you during the process of composition, the temptation to use it is difficult to resist. Before you put it into the mouth of a character, however, you must ask yourself whether he is the type of person who would be likely to say such a line. Remember that dialogue has no virtue in and of itself. It is an instrument for accomplishing the purpose of the script. To include a brilliant line that is incompatible with the character of the person uttering it exhibits your wit at the expense of characterization. No line, no matter how scintillating it may be, is worth that sacrifice.

Another requirement for writing dialogue appropriate to character is to give the various people of your play speeches that establish them as unique individuals. If the lines you write do not reflect the differences that separate people, your dialogue is defective. A good way to test your success is to switch lines from one character to another. If this transposition seems to make no difference, you have probably failed to write dialogue that really distinguishes.

CONTENT.   What are some of the ways in which differences among characters become evident in dialogue? The most revealing element undoubtedly is the content of the line. What a character says is largely determined by the drives and values that dominate him. As your characters vary, so should the content of their lines vary.

WORD CHOICE.   How a character says a line also serves to set him apart. Word choice is one of the most important factors. The words a person uses suggest many things about him. They reflect his educational and cultural background and give us clues to his personality. Caught in a difficult situation, will he use harsh, brutal words to smash his way out, or will he use words that reveal his sensitivity to the feelings of other people? Will his words reflect a frank, open personality or will they suggest cunning and deviousness?

In his play "Noon on Doomsday," Rod Serling created two diametrically different characters. One is John Kattell, a young man who, in a blind rage, senselessly kills an old man. The people of the town, sharing his prejudices and resenting the demands coming from outside that he be harshly punished, rally to his defense and acquit him. The other character is Frank Grinstead, lawyer and former state supreme court justice, who returns to the town to become its conscience.

Kattell's limitations are revealed through his constant use of meaningless clichés and empty phrases. He often stops to search for words and, in many instances, repeats one he has just used. The reiteration of expressions like "I'm mighty pleased," "No kidding, it's just wonderful," "It's a real blessing" betray his insensitivity to what he has done. Such colloquialisms as "friends like I got," "the guy who done it" and "that there" expose his lack of education.

The justice's superior culture and his contrasting attitude toward the situation are reflected by such words as "commemorate," "hanging crepe," "building a wailing wall," "petulance," "constitutionally unfit," "attitudes cemented along with the sidewalks." It is impossible to think of the murderer using this kind of language, or, on the other hand, to think of the Justice employing the hackneyed expressions of the murderer.

STRUCTURE.   Differences in sentence structure help further to distinguish the two men. Kattell's speeches are made up of exceptionally short sentences and parts of sentences which are delivered haltingly and repetitively. His inarticulateness helps to reflect his primitive mentality.

The justice's sentences are longer than Kattell's, although they still retain the relative simplicity that is the mark of spoken language. He selects words with precision. His ideas progress and develop as he arranges these words into sentences, and there is a flow of meaning from one sentence to the other. The speeches given to these characters are so different that not even one sentence can be switched from one to the other without the mismatch of line to character being obvious.

Since Kattell and Justice Grinstead are so completely different, writing dialogue that distinguishes them is not too difficult. In the same play, however, Serling achieved the more difficult feat of suggesting distinctions between two essentially similar people—Justice Grinstead and the trial judge, two lawyers who had much the same background—through the dialogue he gave them. The content of their lines reveals that they have contrasting attitudes toward the crime. Justice Grinstead's word choices are more exact and colorful; his thoughts march in a firmer order than do those of the judge. The judge's language tends to be more colloquial, and his use of clichés suggests fuzziness of thought. Both men express themselves forcefully, but the judge's language tends to be blunt and naïve in comparison with the sophistication and polish that characterize Justice Grinstead's speech.

RHYTHM.   One other general quality helps to make dialogue distinctive. Usually called rhythm, it is a product of the other factors, being the underlying cadence of speech that comes from a person's choice of words and the length and structure of his sentences. Short words in very short sentences give a staccato rhythm, the kind that might characterize a restless, energetic person. The boss in J. P. Miller's "The Rabbit Trap," for example, has his mind focused entirely on business and cannot understand how his employee Eddie can permit concern for a rabbit caught in a trap to stand in the way of getting a job done. Mr. Spellman's attitude, impatience, and nervous energy are effectively communicated by the staccato rhythm of the following passage:

```
                    SPELLMAN

Eddie, I know how kids are.  I've got two

of my own don't forget.  They drain a man

dry.  But rabbits are a dime a dozen.  A

dime a dozen?  They're a nickel a million
```

> ...But if your kid wants a rabbit you don't
> have to trap one. I'll buy him a rabbit.
> I'll buy him two rabbits. I'll put him in
> the rabbit business. Tell him that when
> you go home tonight, and see how fast he
> brightens up. I know kids.

Contrast this with a speech from Horton Foote's play "The Midnight Caller":

MISS ROWEN

> Dear ones, forgive me for comin' to supper
> this way, but I have to dress for tonight
> and I just thought I'd take my bath before
> supper and put on somethin' rather informal.
> Dear Mrs. Crawford tells me this is my last
> opportunity to dress so informally with the
> gentleman comin' tomorrow to live in our
> midst...

The smoothly flowing cadence of this passage, the even, regular rhythm give us a picture of a person who is forbearing and philosophical in attitude, an individual resigned to accepting things as they come. Appropriate rhythms can do much to evoke sharp and distinctive character attributes.

CONVEYING A CHARACTER'S VARYING MOODS. Thus far, we have been primarily concerned with the need for lines that distinguish one character from another. We must also remember that a given character does not remain a static individual throughout the play but reacts in different ways to what happens. Dialogue is defective if it does not convey his different emotional states to the audience. The dramatist must try to earn the accolade a reviewer gave to John P. Marquand: "His characters not only always speak as if they were themselves and nobody else, but as if they were themselves at a particular time and place and will never be quite the same again."[1]

In some ways the playwright faces a much sterner challenge in writing dialogue than a short story or novel writer does. The fiction writer can say: "He won her with charming words." The dramatist has no such easy escape. He must contrive those charming words.

PURPOSIVE AND ECONOMICAL DIALOGUE

As we have noted, much of the conversation of everyday life rambles without direction, accomplishing no other purpose than that of filling an empty space with sound. The dramatist may include some small talk of this nature to promote the illusion of normal speech, but most of the dialogue he writes should be big talk, the talk that deals with matters vital to the story. Most dialogue should be purposefully designed to reveal character, advance the story, or illuminate the theme. If it does none of these things and cannot be justified as small-talk dressing which provides an echo of reality, then it should be resolutely eliminated.

Another important attribute of dialogue is economy. Drama does not reflect life in its entirety, but distills its essence. The dramatist must condense conflicts to their essentials, sometimes capturing the illusion of years, without belaboring the audience with all the verbiage. Compression, concentration, and selection are vital necessities. Morton Wishengrad, writer of many scripts for the distinguished radio series *Eternal Light* emphasized this need when he said, "Good dialogue should sound like a pair of boxers trading blows, short, swift, muscular, monosyllabic."[2]

NATURAL AND UNOBTRUSIVE EXPOSITION

Since a dramatist can present directly only part of the crisis that is the play's main concern, a major problem is to provide the audience with the rest of the information it needs to understand the story. Dialogue is the main tool for providing this exposition, although narration, titles, movement, and business may also be used.

THE NEED FOR EXPOSITION.   Introducing needed information into dialogue naturally and unobtrusively is a difficult task, yet the dramatist

---

[1] Goronwy Rees, Review of "Women and Thomas Harrow," *The Listener,* Vol. 61 (January 22, 1959), p. 180.

[2] Morton Wishengrad, *The Eternal Light* (New York: Crown Publishers, Inc., 1947), p. XXVII.

should be glad that expository devices are at his disposal. Through their use he can concentrate his primary attention on the high points of a crisis, thus making his play as a whole more vivid and compelling. Moreover, by encompassing a larger segment of human experience than that actually presented in the play, exposition helps to give the dramatized events greater significance and breadth.

The necessity for gaining attention in television demands that plays begin with a crisis already in motion, but the dramatist cannot make the audience wait too long for the information it needs to understand the people and the action. These are some of the questions that need answering: Who are the characters? What kind of people are they? What is the place, the time, and the period? What in the past and the present is causing this crisis?

Exposition plays a particularly vital role in the opening scenes, but its function does not end there. Developments that must be explained take place outside of the immediate dramatic action throughout the play. Furthermore, all background information is not necessarily revealed at the beginning. Exposition must be provided at regular intervals.

In the past audiences were sometimes informed about the situation by an actor who addressed the audience directly or delivered a soliloquy. At other times dramatists wrote frankly expository scenes at the beginning of their plays. The commonest variation was the familiar conversation between two servants which brought out the essential facts. We discover, for example, that the master is returning after a year's foreign duty to find that his wife has run off with the butler. There is no drama or conflict in this scene; it is all explanation.

Narration can sometimes be used to provide background information. The scene that is obviously written just to present facts, however, is not acceptable. To begin with, it is not artful; presenting an obvious recital of information is a clumsy way to begin a play. The skilled writer will weave essential facts into his dramatic scenes in such a way that the listener absorbs them without realizing it. A second reason for avoiding expository scenes is that they are a poor means of seizing attention. Clash, not facts, arouses interest. As Erik Barnouw so aptly stated in his *Handbook of Radio Writing*, "The intriguing or arresting start, the quick plunge into essential conflict, have forever supplanted the two maids with the dusters."

RULES FOR EXPOSITION.   Implanting exposition in dialogue so that it reaches the audience naturally and unobtrusively requires adherence to certain rules.

1. *Motivate the presentation of facts.*   One of the commonest techniques for bringing out essential information is to create a character

who draws out the facts the audience needs to know. This person, of course, must be one who fits naturally into the action. If he has been obviously invented just to ask a question or two before vanishing into limbo, the writer must plead guilty to the crime of clumsiness.

An excellent example of a character who motivates exposition appears in Horton Foote's play "The Trip to Bountiful." The character is the girl Thelma, whom Mrs. Watts, trying to escape her selfish daughter-in-law to return to the home of her childhood, meets in the bus station. The conversation that takes place between the two is a completely natural one. Utter strangers are constantly meeting and talking in bus stations, and the fact that Thelma is a stranger means that she does not know what is going on. As she finds out what is happening, so does the eavesdropping audience. It is also completely natural for Mrs. Watts to pour out her heart to Thelma during the bus ride, for we often find it easier to talk to strangers about intimate matters than we do to close friends. By means of this scene Foote lets us know the intensity of Mrs. Watts' desire to return to Bountiful, a feeling we must understand to appreciate her desperate struggle to reach it.

In addition to using a confidant, information can be communicated to an audience by having characters give messages to servants, make telephone calls, send telegrams, or dictate letters. Again the writer must avoid the impression of contrivance by integrating these devices into the action in a reasonable and natural way. The common device of having a character read a letter out loud for himself is one that frequently seems obvious and artificial.

A mistake often made in providing exposition is to have one character give information to another character who, it is logical to suppose, already knows this information. An error of this nature makes the exposition distressingly obvious and it helps to destroy realism. Generally speaking, if one character gives information to another, the person giving the information must have a reason for unburdening himself and the receiver should not already know the facts.

Sometimes, however, information can be given by one character to another even though both know it, as long as the emotional situation motivates the exchange. Chayefsky's "The Mother" provides a good example of such motivation. The particular fact the audience needs to know is that the mother became ill in the subway the previous day while she was looking for work. This information actually reaches the audience when, via the telephone, the daughter is trying to persuade her mother to stay home. Being concerned about her mother's health, it is perfectly reasonable for the daughter to refer to the fainting spell. A little later in the scene she mentions it to her husband, even though they had probably discussed it the day before. But the repetition of this fact is completely understandable, for the matter is preying on the daughter's mind. Emotional motivation for exposition is the best motivation there is, which leads us directly to our second rule.

2. *Color the presentation of information with emotion.* One of the difficulties with exposition is that it frequently interrupts the dramatic action; the perfect solution is to make the presentation of necessary facts part of the mounting drama. In William Archer's phrase, information should be "wrung out, in the stress of the action."[3]

You will recall that Rod Serling's "The Strike" dramatizes the agonizing dilemma faced by a major in the Korean War who must consider endangering a 20-man patrol in order to safeguard the lives of 500 other men. If the audience is to appreciate the difficult decision facing the major, it must have a complete understanding of the military situation. To reveal these facts, Serling created a scene in which the principal focus is on the major's emotional reaction to the situation. The viewers gain the information they need while they are absorbed in the drama of the scene.

Another example of this technique can be found in Chayefsky's "Marty." During dinner, Marty's mother urges him to go to the local ballroom in the hope that he will meet a nice girl. Marty responds with a speech that graphically depicts his arid bachelor life. We see in sharp detail the lonely, unattractive little man who cannot bear the hurt of being brushed off by another girl. This information, which is vitally important in filling out Marty's character and indicating the precise nature of his problem, is brought out in one of the most poignant scenes of the entire script. Marty does not seem to be describing anything; rather he is expressing his feelings. There is no better way of keeping exposition inconspicuous than by imbedding it in scenes of high emotional power.

3. *Make the audience want the information.* Tad Mosel's "My Lost Saints" opens with the arrival at the Hallet household of an old lady, the mother of the maid Kate. She has lost her farm and yet she seems to be a fiercely independent person whose manner suggests unusual resourcefulness. It is natural, therefore, for Mrs. Hallet to ask her questions about her misfortune. The writer, however, was not content to have the old lady answer these questions with a straightforward explanation. Before providing the information, he brings audience curiosity to a fever pitch with the following exchange:

MRS. HALLET

How did you lose your farm?

---

[3] William Archer, *Play-Making* (Boston: Small, Maynard and Company, 1912), p. 119.

```
                    MAMA

        (FLATLY)  A man died on it.

                 MRS. HALLET

        (STARTLED)  How?

                    MAMA

        In court they said I killed him.
```

Even at this point the writer does not tell all, but keeps the audience in suspense awhile longer before revealing that a man working on the farm died in a fall. The old lady had to sell the farm to pay the court's judgment against her.

These facts might have been transmitted to the audience in an obvious, clumsy way. As Mosel did it, however, the viewer would scarcely be aware that exposition was taking place, so eagerly did he desire the knowledge. By making an audience want knowledge, a dramatist infuses the facts with added interest and significance and gives the process of exposition an excitement of its own.

SPECIAL DIALOGUE PROBLEMS

Thus far we have been considering the problems of creating effective dialogue that arise in the writing of almost all dramatic scripts. There are some other problems, however, that may or may not develop depending on the nature of the play.

GAINING AUTHENTIC FLAVOR

When characters represent specific occupations, come from a certain well-defined region, or live in a time period different from the present, their speech must reflect these conditions. For example, it is not enough that a physician speak like the usual well-educated person—at least not while he is discussing a case with another physician—and even in talking with patients, physicians are likely to use their own characteristic terms. In their language the average man's stiff neck becomes a myositis or torticollis, indigestion becomes gastritis, and nearsightedness becomes myopia. Terms like these should be inserted into the dialogue of a physician to give his speech an authentic ring. It is not necessary for the audience to know the meaning of all the words so long as the basic meaning of the sentence is clear.

How are you to know the special terms you should use? The best solution is to depend on your own personal experience. Even readers who are not familiar with print shops can sense in Paddy Chayefsky's play "Printer's Measure" the authentic language of the printer. It is not surprising to discover that Chayefsky actually worked in a print shop as a young man. Restricting your writing entirely to what you know personally, however, would impose an impractical limitation on your work. You cannot have personal contact with everything even in the contemporary world and when you write a play set in another century, you must obviously learn what terms to use through something other than direct personal experience.

There is a synthetic method for gaining authenticity which can be an acceptable substitute for actual experience. First of all, make up as large a list as you can of the special terms identified with the particular occupation, region, or time period you have in mind. The best way to create this list is to get in touch with the type of people you are writing about. If your script includes a Texan, talk to one if possible, noting his pet expressions. You may hear him say, "howdy," "sure enough," "I'm fixin' to get ready," or "I might could do that." If you are writing about truck drivers, prepare a description of the situations figuring in your script. Then interview some truck drivers to find out the terms they use in referring to these situations. Supplement these interviews with visits to highway restaurants they patronize. Keep your ears open, particularly for the unusual phrases that will add color and authentic flavor to your script.

If personal contacts are impossible, the next best source of terms is reading. If you can, find stories and plays involving Texans and truck drivers and check the dialogue carefully for typical expressions. You should end with a usable list of terms. As far as plays of another period are concerned, reading must be your principal means of discovering the language that will infuse your script with the atmosphere of the past. The best sources are works written during the period, with contemporary books about the period a good secondary source. Robert Sherwood in preparing to write *Abe Lincoln in Illinois* studied English grammars of the nineteenth century and read such works as *Huckleberry Finn* and *Pickwick Papers* in search of expressions that would give a period flavor to his dialogue. If you are writing about the Elizabethan age, examine the plays of Shakespeare, Christopher Marlowe, and John Webster as well as other literature of the period. Maxwell Anderson's modern plays *Mary of Scotland* and *Elizabeth and Essex* can also serve as guides to diction and usage. A partial list of the terms and expressions you will find in these sources follows:

"Take heed," "fain," "by the Queen's grace," "mayhap," "good my lord," "good morrow," "set against," "I commend me," "beyond all measure," "I grant you," "In good conscience," "divers," "lest," "unseemly," "nay," "knave," "avail," "stand forth," "constrain," "ere."

With a list of appropriate terms you are now ready to write your dialogue. By scattering expressions distinctive of a particular occupation, region, or period through your lines, you can create the language of a real-life Texan, the words of an authentic truck driver, or the rich verbiage of a genuine Elizabethan. If you can, have someone who knows the subject through personal experience check your dialogue with special attention to usage. If you carelessly permit a southerner to address a single person as "you-all," a representative of that region will quickly correct your error.

WRITING DIALECT

The main problem in writing dialect is a form of the one we have just considered—namely, that of finding the terms and style that will give the desired authentic flavor to a character's speeches. The needed information can be acquired in the ways we have just mentioned— through personal acquaintance with the dialect, by contacting those who use it, or by referring to books or plays in which it appears. Having gained a knowledge of the dialect, the writer must then decide how to indicate it in the script. Most people, whose untutored ears hear the peculiarities of dialect as mispronunciations of conventional English sounds, are likely to try to indicate the distortions in the spelling of the word. The dropping of the "g" in such a word as "fixin" and the indication of elisions, as in "many o' them be takin' t' th' water," may direct an actor toward the desired pronunciation, but spelling as an aid to dialect production does have serious limitations. The difficulty is that many sounds occurring in other languages cannot be symbolized by an English letter. No letter stands for the vowel sound the Irish use in the word "might," for the Scotsman's glottal stop, or for the consonant sound in the German's "ach." For this reason gross misspellings of a word may hinder an actor from producing a dialect rather than helping him. Usually, you must depend on the actor to know how the words should be pronounced.

In most cases, rather than attempting to suggest the pronunciation of individual words, the writer should concentrate on reflecting in his lines the basic rhythm and sentence structure characteristic of the speaker's native language. The Irish, for example, tend to reverse the usual sequence of subject and predicate and then add a further inimitable touch by beginning the sentence with "it." An Irishman might say, for instance: "It's a bit of a cold I have." An actor can scarcely avoid putting an Irish flavor into that line no matter how he pronounces the words.[4]

WRITING TAG LINES

Most of you are familiar with the expression "curtain line" as it is used in the theatre to denote the line just before the fall of the curtain that sums up, succinctly and with special impact, the meaning of what has been happening. In television this type of line, which occurs at the ends of acts and scenes, is usually referred to as a tag line. Composing effective tag lines is of the utmost importance, yet it is difficult to lay down specific rules for doing so. Tag lines should pack a special punch, they should distil the meaning of a scene into its essence. One of the most gifted television writers is Rod Serling, winner two years in a row of the Emmy award for the best dramatic script of the year. One of his many talents is his ability to write tag lines. Let us examine his drama "Noon on Doomsday" to find some examples.

You will recall that this script tells the story of the acquittal by a small town jury of a local hoodlum who, because of his prejudice, has senselessly killed an old man. A New York reporter Lanier is shocked to discover that the town, rather than trying to hide its shame, is actually celebrating. He even finds the old man's daughter dry-eyed. In the scene at the end of Act I, the reporter calls for tears; he berates the laughter he hears, the happy faces, the confetti, the flowing beer. He wants to see some sadness, some regret. Finally the girl breaks down and sobs. In the tag line to the act Serling sums up the reporter's reaction in a simple, yet moving line.

```
(VERY, VERY SOFTLY)   Yeah.   Yeah, that's

all I wanted to hear, Felicia.   Just that.
```

The second act ends with a scene between Frank Grinstead, a former state supreme court justice, and his son Rod, who defended the murderer. The son warns his father to stay away from the gathering scheduled for the next day to celebrate the acquittal. He tells him that if he tries

[4] Helpful information on dialect construction can be found in two books co-authored by Lewis Herman and Marguerite Shalett Herman: *Foreign Dialects: A Manual for Actors, Directors, and Writers* (New York: Theatre Arts Books, 1943) and *American Dialects: A Manual for Actors, Directors, and Writers* (New York: Theatre Arts Books, 1947).

to act the conscience of the people, he'll be tarred and feathered and run out of town on a pole. Then he adds threateningly:

```
I think I'd be right along with them,

helping them!... Do you think you could live

through something like that?
```

The Justice's answer, the final line of the act, is a poignant summing up of his feelings:

```
If I saw you helping them I wouldn't much

want to.
```

In the third act, the actions of the reporter, the justice, and the murderer himself bring the townspeople to some comprehension of what they have done. They finally leave the murderer alone in the town square, no longer a hero but a lonely and deserted man. He shouts his despair with a panic-stricken: "I'm sorry! I'm sorry!" The only other person left, an old man, sums up in the final line of the play the basic meaning of the script:

```
We all are, Johnny.  We're all sorry.  But

much too late.
```

These tag lines in their terseness, their richness of meaning, and their emotional power are excellent examples of what a tag line should be.

WRITING DIALOGUE FOR SCENES OF HIGH EMOTION

Situations involving high emotion confront the writer with two basic problems: (1) People in highly emotional states frequently do not say very much. (2) When they do, the words they utter are often not the kind that can be used on the air. One solution is to substitute facial expressions and bodily movements for words. Tad Mosel's play "The Out-of-Towners," the story of a married man and a spinster who meet at a convention, provides an example. A series of brief but innocuous contacts is climaxed when the two finally slip into each other's arms. Mosel, in describing this scene, writes as follows: "It is one of those extended moments for which no dialogue can be written, but it must grow in warmth and tenderness and coming-togetherness."[5]

[5] Tad Mosel, "The Out-of-Towners," in *Television Plays for Writers*, edited by A. S. Burack (Boston: The Writer, Inc., 1957), pp. 237–238.

Scenes involving angry outbursts are particularly difficult to write. What is the writer to do when realism seems to demand the use of expressions that are outlawed by broadcasting taboos? It helps to remember that the language of anger in a script need not match the expressive power of real life to attain the same impact. A "damn" or "hell," which are now permitted if the drama demands them, can jolt with as much force as a considerably stronger phrase in another context.

Another solution is to find language that is not actually profane but seems to be. Norman Corwin's script "Old Salt" achieves this illusion perfectly. Such phrases as "ye scurvy dog," "curses throttle ye," "ye pusillanimous pantaloon," "ye muscle-bound, black-hearted limpard," "ye besotted gobthrasher," "ye lickerous, gluttonous weed-smeller," carry the irresistible impact of profanity without containing a single profane word. You have to be sensitive, however, to the impressions that may result from substitutes for forbidden words. Expressions like "gleeps" or "holy barracuda" may be satisfactory for a "spoof" such as *Batman* but they are far too limp for use in a serious drama. "Oh, Jehoshaphat" has the same drawback. Such an expletive will elicit laughter rather than the emotional response you seek.

DESCRIBING THE EXPRESSION OF LINES

Beginning writers, convinced that their lines must be read in one certain way to gain the optimum effect, frequently fall into the habit of indicating the precise manner for speaking each line. Thus we see each sentence preceded by an adverb: "flatly," "sadly," "angrily," and so on. Such description is necessary only when the content of the line does not indicate how it should be read. If the lines are well written, this need should rarely exist. A justifiable use is the description used to qualify the reading of an ironic line, which carries a meaning completely opposite to the usual meaning of the words. For example:

JANE

Did you have a good time at the party?

ANN

(IRONICALLY) Great! Simply great!

With this description, the actress knows that she must convey to the audience that the time she had at the party was exactly the opposite of great.

There are other situations in which instructions to the actor can help to refine the meaning intended by the writer. But the writer who finds himself qualifying every line should begin to wonder whether it is not the dialogue itself that needs some attention. A constant obbligato of "coldly's," "sadly's," and "warmly's" may be an open advertisement of dialogue deficiencies.

NARRATION

Narration was an important element in much radio drama, but with the coming of the television form its use receded sharply. No longer was it necessary to describe what was happening for a listener who could not see—the main reason for employing narration in radio. Still it does have occasional uses even in television, and in this section we review the contributions it can make, the types of narration, and some rules for using it.

THE FUNCTIONS OF NARRATION

The main advantage of narration is that it conveys information to an audience more economically than dialogue. By employing it for exposition, the writer can use dialogue mainly to dramatize the highpoints of his play.

PROVIDING EXPOSITION.   Narration can accomplish exposition in two main ways. First of all, it can look backward to give the information about the past that is essential to understanding the present. The opening passage of Paddy Chayefsky's TV play "Printer's Measure" provides an example of retrospective narration.

NARRATOR

In 1939 when I was seventeen years old, I

went to work in a print shop in West Twenty-

sixth Street in New York...

The narration continues as the television cameras reveal the setting and the characters of the play.

Narration can also carry a story forward with great speed and efficiency. Again Chayefsky's "Printer's Measure" furnishes an example. In a few terse lines of narration he propels his story ahead and at the same time crystallizes the basic conflict of the script.

> NARRATOR
>
> And so the linotype machine was brought
>
> into the shop, and a linotypist was hired--
>
> and Mr. Healy declared war on both of them.
>
> First he challenged the machine to a race...

ACHIEVING REINFORCEMENT.   Occasionally narration may describe what is taking place even though the viewer can see for himself what is happening. This reinforcement provides information or an interpretation that enhances the audience's understanding and appreciation of the scene. As before we turn to Chayefsky's "Printer's Measure," for an example.

> NARRATOR
>
> Or else he would suddenly be seized with a
>
> paroxysm of coughing...(MR. HEALY IN REAR
>
> OF THE SHOP SUDDENLY BEING SEIZED BY PAROXYSM
>
> OF COUGHING)...which he claimed was due to
>
> lead fumes that were filling the shop...
>
> (MR. HEALY HACKING AWAY)...and he would look
>
> around at the rest of us, amazed that we
>
> were immune to it all...

PRESENTING COMMENT.   Narration can be a vehicle for presenting the writer's comment on the action directly to the audience, a privilege that is denied him if he tells his story exclusively in dialogue. Comments and observations may help to enrich the meaning of a drama, but they need to be kept under restraint, for gratuitous and unnecessary comment may dull rather than sharpen the impact. Generally speaking, the drama should be permitted to speak for itself.

GAINING A FILTERING EFFECT.   The usual objective of a dramatist is to extract from a situation the greatest emotional effect possible, and the best guarantee of maximum emotional intensity is dramatic treatment. Some events, however, may be so harrowing that complete dramatization makes them unbearable. In such cases, narration, by subduing vividness and realism and by interposing a middleman between the audience and the experience, helps to tone it down and filter its effect.

Morton Wishengrad's script "The Black Death" tells how Jews in the fourteenth century were tortured and murdered because they were suspected of causing the plague. One scene shows ignorant and terrified people suddenly turning, in their fear and hatred, on a little Jewish boy. With threats and slaps they try to make him confess that he has poisoned their well. He refuses. A priest tries to protect him. Then the threat suddenly becomes more ominous when the leader of the mob says to the priest:

```
                    MAN

     I say you lie.  Go away now.  Go away

     before we have you stoned.  What are you

     waiting for, Peter?  Bring the thumbscrews,

     I say.
```

At this point, Wishengrad suspends the dramatization. The horrible scene that follows is filtered through the narrator.

```
                    JUDAH

     He was a Jewish boy.  Agimst was his name.

     You will find it written down.  They

     tortured him only a little.  Then a little

     more.  The priest tried to interfere.  They

     stoned their priest.  He was not of my

     religion, but he was a man of God.  I

     prayed for his soul.  But the boy was only

     a boy and the flesh is very weak.
```

TYPES OF NARRATION

Narration may be spoken in the first, second, or third person. Narration, then, may be categorized in terms of the "person" in which it is presented. A second distinction in television involves the appearance or nonappearance of the narrator before the camera. Some narrators are seen as they speak whereas others are only heard as they perform in an off-camera position.

THE PERSON OF NARRATION.   The traditional type of narration is that in which a narrator, not involved in the action, tells what is happening to other people. Of the types of narration, this third-person approach is the most straightforward, the simplest, and the least "arty." Its main disadvantage is that the narrator, being a middleman who gets between the audience and the action, may weaken the dramatic impact of the story. When he breaks in, a voice from outside the story has intervened; the illusion is broken; the action is suspended and emotional intensity is inevitably lessened.

There is one kind of third-person narration that does not reach the audience by voice at all, but provides information about time intervals and settings by means of title cards. A card printed "Six Months Later" or "Moscow—1917" preceding a scene can efficiently convey information that would be awkward to insert into the scene itself.

Another form of narration, which was very popular in radio and has had some use in television, is that delivered in the first person by an individual who is involved in the action. Its main advantage in radio was that it could present information to the audience without awkwardly interrupting a dialogue scene or suspending the dramatic quality of the script. At one moment the narrator may be talking to another character in the scene; in the next he has turned to talk to the audience, but in both situations he remains in character, enduring the crises and emotions that are the focus of the action. Thus, dramatic continuity is sustained. No outsider has come between the audience and the emotion.

An extension of the first-person approach is the stream-of-consciousness technique in which the narrator not only tells the audience what is happening, but also transmits his inner thoughts and feelings. An excerpt from an Arch Oboler script "The Ugliest Man in the World" illustrates the effect:

PAUL

```
...gun in my hand gun in my hand in all my

life I never had a gun in my hand smooth

gun hard gun cold gun in my hand bullet

won't be cold warm bullet hot bullet burning

hot hot as the blood...
```

Another type of narrative presentation approaches the viewer in the second person, addressing him as "you" and inviting him to visualize himself as taking a part in the action. Second-person narration was a feature of some radio dramatic series, but it has been rarely used in television. It has the disadvantage of sounding somewhat forced and artificial, lacking the naturalness of the storytelling approach inherent in the third person or of the personal testament communicated in the first person. The second person does, however, invest a program with the quality of immediacy since it makes the use of the present tense in narration easy, and it also encourages a sense of audience participation in the events.

NARRATOR OFF- AND ON-CAMERA.   When narration is presented on television, it is usually by a narrator who does not appear on camera, at least while he is narrating. His comments are heard as an accompaniment to a scene or sequence of events. This technique is known as "voice-over" or VO narration. The *Sea Hunt* series used first-person narration in this way, presented by the leading character Mike Nelson, to explain events that were taking place on the screen and to weave the elements of the story together. He was never shown actually narrating, but he might participate in a scene that his "off-screen" voice was describing.

Voice-over narration is also used in connection with the use of a production technique known as the subjective camera. This is the approach that, in effect, places the character inside the camera. The audience sees only what he sees, and the character himself is never visible except when an arm or hand held out in front of the lens comes into view. Another way of describing the technique is to say that the camera, endowed with a voice, becomes a member of the cast. The dialogue, of course, is voiced over the scene just as the narration is. The identification with the character and action invited by this method can give the viewer an eerie sense that he is actually participating in the story.

The subjective camera may also solve a production problem. It can suggest the radical changes in the physical appearance of the character in Robert Louis Stevenson's *Dr. Jekyll and Mr. Hyde* by showing the reactions of other people to the camera and by providing an occasional glimpse of a hand that has suddenly become hairy and grotesque. By putting the imagination of the viewer to work, a more vivid result may be achieved than could be gained through the efforts of a make-up man.

The subjective camera does have serious disadvantages, however. It tends to attract attention to itself as a "gimmick" and unless it is used carefully, may confuse an audience. The events must also be told entirely in terms of what a single character sees and does, a requirement that places severe restrictions on the range of the story.

A rarely used narrative technique places the narrator on-camera and in the scene. At intervals during the story he turns directly to the audience to comment on what is happening. At these points the camera may move in to exclude the rest of the scene, or a blackout effect may be used to isolate him.

SOME RULES FOR WRITING NARRATION

When a script suddenly bursts into narration at a late stage in the action after having been confined up to that point entirely to dialogue, we can assume that the author has written himself into a corner and is using narration as an escape hatch. When this happens, even the most naïve listener becomes aware of a structural malfunction. Narration should not be used haphazardly simply because the writer finds it difficult to get certain essential information to the audience in a dramatic scene. *Make the narration an integral part of the script design.*

The choice of viewpoint has an obvious bearing on the narrative technique used by the dramatist. The omniscient viewpoint usually requires a third-person narrator unless the narrator is himself an omniscient being, in which case a first-person approach might be used. Character viewpoints are almost always related in the first person, although in unusual cases it is possible to design second- and third-person approaches that tell a story as one character sees it. The writer must be aware of the relationship between the viewpoint he needs to tell the story and the narrative method he plans to use. *Choose the narrative approach in terms of the viewpoint.*

Narration should retain the flavor of the spoken word, although it can sometimes be written in a more elevated style than is usually appropriate for dialogue, particularly when the narration is being delivered in the third person by a noncharacter voice. It must never become pretentious or cumbersome, however. And even though it may be language that has dignity, even nobility, it must always flow from the lips with naturalness and ease. *Give narration the quality of the spoken word.*

Narration by a character in the story is an extension of the dialogue of that character. It is obvious, then, that all of the rules that apply to writing his dialogue lines apply equally to writing his narration. Narration in all instances should preserve the dramatic tone of a play and enhance its over-all effect. *Write narration that fits both mood and character.*

After finishing a script, you may wonder whether you have succeeded in making your theme clear to your audience. With a narrator available, you may be tempted to use him to explain to the audience what your story is all about. It is wiser to let the story as a whole make the point, not the narration. This does not mean that a philosophical comment by the narrator at the end of the story is always out of place. But *do not use narration for an obvious pointing of the moral.*

QUESTIONS AND PROJECTS

1. Hide a microphone in a social situation and evaluate the conversation you record for its qualities as dramatic dialogue.

2. Harold Pinter, the English playwright, is noted for writing dialogue that reflects the pointlessness, repetitions, irrelevancies, and hiatuses of ordinary conversation. Study the dialogue in one of his plays (*The Birthday Party, The Caretaker,* for example) to determine whether, even though simulating conversation, it still possesses the direction and purpose of dramatic dialogue.

3. Evaluate the dialogue given to two diametrically different characters in a play in terms of content, word choice, structure, and rhythm.

4. Cite how specific information is made clear to the audience in a number of plays and rate this exposition for its naturalness and unobtrusiveness.

5. Make a list of the terms you would insert into the dialogue of each of the following characters to provide an aura of authenticity: (a) a physician, (b) an astronaut, (c) a baseball player.

6. Watch a number of TV plays and note the lines that end acts or scenes. Evaluate these tag lines for their effectiveness.

7. Check the narrative techniques used in a number of plays. Decide whether this narration was used as a crutch or as an integral and purposeful element in the script design.

9

Technical Elements and
Script Formats

Art at its best is spontaneous in origin but deliberate in preparation.
Max Eastman

The writer of television and radio programs should have some knowledge of the broadcasting media, but he does not need the special background and highly developed technical skills required of those who are involved in production—directors, cameramen, and engineers, for example. Still, he needs to know enough about his medium to take maximum advantage of the opportunities it affords him and to avoid demanding more of the technical facilities at his disposal than they can produce. He should also know how to turn his ideas into a script that can be translated accurately and efficiently into a production. What follows, then, does not cover the entire process of television, film, and radio production but considers only those elements that are of significance to the writer.

PRODUCTION METHODS

Television programs can be placed in two main categories according to the method used in producing them. One category includes all programs that are picked up with TV cameras; the other those that are recorded on film through the use of motion-picture equipment. Whether a particular script is to be produced as a TV or filmed production has important influences on the work of the writer. Within these two main methods there are also variations that control what he can include in his script, how he plans it, and the way he sets it down on paper.

TELEVISION PRODUCTION METHODS

A television program shot with TV cameras may be produced live, which means that it is transmitted while it is being produced, or it may be recorded on video tape or film for broadcasting at some future time.

LIVE TV PRODUCTION. The live production of drama is rare these days, but a number of programs in the nondramatic category are still produced this way. Among them are broadcasts of sports contests and special events, which gain most of their impact from being transmitted live, and news, sports, and weather broadcasts, which are generally done live so that they can be completely up to date. Other productions sometimes seen live are variety, audience-participation, and panel shows, interviews, and the programs of educational television stations.

The most important consideration in preparing scripts for live production is to plan for action that can continue without stopping. It must be possible for set and costume changes to be made during the broadcast of the program, and pauses cannot be introduced simply to let performers rest or move from one set to another. You would be unwise, for instance, to require an artist in a live variety show to sing immediately after he had completed an energetic dance routine. The designing of dramatic action that can progress without interruption requires great ingenuity on the part of writers, but with daytime serials now virtually the only TV drama being done live, the need for such ingenuity has almost vanished.

The restriction imposed by production in a studio is another factor affecting the writing of programs for live presentation. You are more limited in the sets you can require and the type of activity you can prescribe than when preparing a script for filmed production. Westerns and adventure dramas, which demand wide open spaces or the authenticity of real settings, can be produced practicably only on film. Television cameras have occasionally been taken out of the studio to shoot drama programs on location, but the results do not justify the difficulties. In Great Britain producers sometimes escape studio restrictions by inserting filmed episodes into studio presentations, but this method is seldom used in the United States.

RECORDED TV PRODUCTION.   Programs shot with TV cameras are now recorded mainly on video tape, a process that utilizes a magnetic system of capturing the video and audio signals. The use of this method results in a picture of such excellent quality that most people cannot distinguish a taped program from a live broadcast. Because of its superior picture quality, it was thought at one time that the video-taped program would largely replace the filmed program. This has not happened for a number of reasons: 1) the difference in the picture quality is not great enough to be crucial; 2) some stations delayed buying video-tape machines, but all had film projectors; 3) outside the United States there is a large market for television programs that can be supplied only by films since our TV technical standards differ from those of most other countries; and 4) programs on video tape suffer from the same restrictions on sets and action that characterize live TV programs.

There are two principal ways of video taping television programs. Some are produced without halting the flow of the program and are then presented on the air without editing or alteration of any kind. This method of recording is known as *live-on-tape* production. It is used to delay programs for the western areas of the United States and for other areas that do not go on daylight saving time. It also makes it possible to produce programs such as *Tonight* with Johnny Carson at a time that is more convenient for the production group than the period the program is scheduled for broadcast. Quiz and audience-participation programs are often recorded live-on-tape, as are some dramas, particularly the serials broadcast during daytime hours.

The second method of video taping involves an editing process. The editing of tape is more difficult than the editing of film, but techniques have now been developed that make the process undetectable except by the most discerning viewer. A move toward the use of movie-making techniques in producing programs in a television studio has resulted. This trend has never reached the stage where the program is broken down and recorded shot-by-shot as a film is, but a program may be recorded in sequences which are then put together by an editor. The *Andy Williams* and *Danny Kaye* variety programs have utilized this means to permit the performers to rest or to change costumes before proceeding from one sequence to another. The writer for live-on-tape production, in contrast, has the same problems of providing for continuous action as the writer for live television. One thing to remember with all recorded shows is to avoid dating them by making unnecessary references to the time of day, the weather, or even the season of the year.

There is one other method of recording a program shot with television cameras: this method utilizes a motion-picture camera which photographs the program as it appears on the tube of a television receiver. The resulting film is called a *kinescope*. Because a kinescope is markedly inferior in picture quality to a live or taped program, it is used only rarely these days. When it is used, it generally records a program that is shot without interruption, but programs may also be kinescoped in sections. A kinescope may also be produced from a video tape.

FILM PRODUCTION METHODS

The production of TV films has been influenced by both the motion-picture industry and the television industry. Most films are produced using methods that were developed in Hollywood, but a few film producers have utilized television techniques to some extent.

FILM TECHNIQUES. Most filmed programs, in contrast to television programs, are produced one shot at a time. Between shots the program comes to a halt while the director sets up the following shot and the performers prepare for their next scene. In many instances the shots are not produced in the order they appear in the drama but are made in a sequence that permits all scenes in a given set to be filmed consecutively. When you prepare scripts for this method of film production, the shot-by-shot approach must be at the forefront of your thinking. Even though you think in terms of separate shots, you must at the same time create an over-all succession of pictures that has unity and coherence.

TV TECHNIQUES IN FILM. In an effort to suggest the spontaneity of live programming, a number of attempts have been made to film a program using TV techniques. The most successful method was developed by the Desilu organization in its production of the *I Love Lucy* series. The program was not filmed in separate shots but was picked up by a number of cameras simultaneously in sequences which sometimes ran for ten minutes. Between sequences the program was stopped to set up the cameras and prepare the next action. An editor put the program together by selecting the best shots from those made by the various cameras. This method permits the production of the program before an audience to which the performers can play and which, in turn, can provide laughter for the sound track. This makes it unnecessary to add laughter later by using recordings or a laugh machine, as is done with most comedy programs.

In writing programs filmed in sequences rather than in shots, you must keep one major requirement in mind: the action should be broken into blocks that can be performed in one set for a considerable period of time. Action for the *Dick Van Dyke Show*, one of the programs that used this technique, usually took place in one of three sets—the office in which the trio of comedy writers prepared their scripts, the living room of the Rob Petrie home, or the kitchen.

PRODUCTION ELEMENTS

A television program is made up of a series of elements; some are controlled by camera placement, movement, and lens setting; other elements originate in the control room or film-processing laboratory; still others are produced by a combination of these factors or through the introduction of special devices. Since the writer expresses some of his program ideas through a manipulation of these elements, it is necessary for him to know what they are, but he does not usually need to know how they are produced. Even though a dissolve is produced in the control room in a television production and in a processing laboratory for a filmed production, the effect for the writer is the same.

CAMERA ELEMENTS

The way in which cameras are used has two important effects on what the audience sees: (1) Through camera placement and lens selection, variations in the distance and angle of the subject from the viewer may be accomplished, and these variations in turn control how much of the scene the viewer is to see. (2) The viewpoint of the audience may constantly be changed through a movement of the camera or the operation of a zoom lens.

CAMERA SHOTS. The visual unit of a television program is a shot. The terms and abbreviations for these shots vary somewhat from organization to organization and from country to country, but those that follow are the ones most commonly used.

1. *Full Shot* (*FS*). The full shot is taken at a considerable distance from a scene to acquaint the audience with the general nature of a situation before the camera closes in on a specific element. For this reason, this shot is often referred to as an establishing or orienting shot.

2. *Long Shot* (*LS*), *Medium Shot* (*MS*), *Close-up* (*CU*). The distance of a viewer from a subject is described by designating a shot as long, medium, or close-up. There are also many variations within these categories: A medium shot, for example, may be described as a medium long shot (MLS) or as a medium close-up (MCU); a close-up that shows only a portion of a face might be designated an extreme close-up (ECU) or if one wishes to add a British flavor, ECUI (extreme close-up indeed). A full shot, incidentally, would be a long shot, but not all long shots are full shots since some show only a portion of a scene.

3. *Close Shot* (*CS*). A shot midway between a medium shot and a close-up is often called a close shot. It differs from the close-up in that it does not focus on a single element in a scene but pictures two or more elements.

4. *The Number of Characters.* The number of people in a scene is indicated by using the terms *one-shot, two-shot, three-shot,* and *four-shot.* Any scene with more than four characters is designated a *group-shot.*

CAMERA ANGLES. An item often indicated by a writer is the angle from which the camera picks up the scene. Shots made with the camera shooting up into the scene or down on it are called *low-angle* and *high-angle* shots. There are also side angles, sometimes described as favoring one of the characters. Occasionally, a camera may be hung over the set to provide the audience with an *overhead* view of the action. A shot taken with a prism on the lens that tilts the picture is called a *canted* shot. A view of a character's reflection in a mirror is called a *mirror* shot. When a shot showing the face of one character over the shoulder of another is followed by one that reverses the picture to show the face of the second character over the shoulder of the first, the result is called a *reverse-angle* shot. Both shots, incidentally, are *over-the-shoulder* shots. A picture that shows one character in close-up and another behind him in medium shot or long shot is called a *combination* or *combo* shot. Sometimes the way a scene is to be shot is described in a script by referring to the way a character in the scene sees the situation. Thus we see the scene from so-and-so's *point of view*. This is usually abbreviated to POV.

CAMERA MOVEMENTS. A shot is often modified while it is on the screen by a movement of the camera as a whole or of one of its parts. There are five types of such movement.

1. *Pan.* The camera is panned by turning it to the right or left on its base in a horizontal plane to sweep the scene or to follow an element

moving across it. This movement is often used to reveal a new element in a situation.

2. *Tilt.*   The camera is tilted by moving it up or down on its base in a vertical plane to provide a sweep of the scene. Some people refer to both vertical and horizontal movements as pans. If this usage is employed, a pan may not only be to the left or right, but also up or down.

3. *Dolly.*   A dolly-in is a movement of the camera on its mount in toward a scene to decrease the field of vision and to give a closer view of the subject. A dolly-out is just the reverse. Other terms for this movement are tracking and pulling.

4. *Zoom.*   The distance from a subject may be varied through the operation of a special lens on the camera known as a zoom lens. "Zoom in or out" has the same meaning as "dolly in or out."

5. *Truck.*   A movement of the camera right or left on its mount in a line parallel to the scene or in an arc to follow a complicated movement is called a truck.

6. *Crane* or *Boom.*   The most complicated modification of a shot can be provided by the movement of a camera mounted on a crane. In addition to the movements just described, a crane camera can sweep up on a scene from a low position or down on it from above.

TRANSITION DEVICES

A number of devices are used to replace one shot on the screen with another and to help create the transitions that are so crucial in keeping the viewer oriented to the time and place of the various scenes as they follow one another.

FADE.   At the beginning of a program the picture is usually faded in from a blank screen to full-picture value. The fade-out gradually reduces the gain of the picture until it completely disappears. The fade-out, particularly a slow one, performs the same function as the curtain in the theatre, informing the audience that there is a major discontinuity in the action. Since the drama and the commercials are separate elements in a TV program, they are usually divided by fade-outs and fade-ins. A slow fade-out often indicates the end of an act, but a scene may sometimes be faded out in the middle of an act to suggest a major lapse in time.

DISSOLVE.   The fade-out of one picture combined with the fade-in of another, resulting in the blending of the two pictures for a brief period, is called a dissolve. The pace of the dissolve may vary from fast to slow depending on the needs of the script. The dissolve suggests a shorter break in the action than the fade and may, therefore, be compared in its effect to the raising and dimming of lights in a theatre which often denotes a scene change. Sometimes a dissolve is used between parallel actions taking place at the same time in different places.

A special form of dissolve is the *matched dissolve* in which one object similar or identical to another object replaces it on the screen. The TV production of Rodger's and Hammerstein's "Cinderella" used a matched dissolve to make a transition from the pumpkin in Cinderella's backyard to the magnificent coach that carried her to the ball.

CUT.   An instantaneous switch from one picture to another is called a cut. Usually, this change does not involve a transition at all but is introduced to give the audience a different view of the action. It has the same effect as the movement of a person's glance in a theatre as he shifts his gaze from one object on the stage to another. The expression *intercut* means to switch several times between two different shots. This technique is often used to show alternating close-ups of two characters in a scene. The term *cutaway* means to cut from the main action of a scene to focus the attention of the viewer on a detail. Occasionally a cut may have a transition function, as when it separates closely related parallel actions. Among the transition devices, the cut suggests the least change in the time and place of the action.

SPECIAL TRANSITION DEVICES.   A number of other devices are used to indicate a change in the time and place of a scene, particularly when the story involves a fantastic element. One such device is the *flexitron,* which causes the picture to wiggle back and forth as it disappears from the screen, a technique that is frequently used to introduce dream sequences. This result can also be gained by dripping oil down a glass placed before a lens—an effect known as an *oil dissolve*. Allied to this device is the *spiral* or *whirligig* which, spun in front of the lens, produces a weird, other-worldly effect. Sometimes transitions are accomplished by defocusing the picture and then bringing it into focus again. If the picture changes during this process, a dissolve or a fade-out and fade-in are combined with the *defocus-focus* effect. Another way of switching from one scene to another is to have a character walk up to a camera until his figure completely *blanks out* the lens. In the scene that follows either the same character or another walks away from the camera to reveal the new scene. The *whip* or *swish pan* is accomplished by panning a camera so rapidly that only a blur can be seen. This technique was often used at transitional points in *The Man from U.N.C.L.E.* series. The *wipe* pushes one picture off the screen with another in a horizontal, vertical, or diagonal movement. In this case the pictures never blend as they do in the dissolve but divide the screen until one has replaced the other.

SPECIAL DEVICES

There are a number of special devices employed in television and radio production which a writer can use to meet certain demands or to accomplish unusual effects. Some of these effects are produced in the control room or processing laboratory, others in the audio equipment, and still others through the use of special apparatus in the studio.

SUPERIMPOSITION. A dissolve that stops in the middle, leaving two pictures blended on the screen, is called a superimposition. It has the same appearance as the double exposure in photography. When produced skillfully, it can invest a scene with a ghost or show a tiny figure dancing on a piano. It also has the practical advantage of permitting titles or credits or the advertiser's phone number to be inserted over a scene. One of its disadvantages in television production is that the gain of each picture must be reduced to avoid overloading the equipment. To avoid this problem, special electronic equipment may be used to accomplish superimposition.

SHARED SCREEN. When a wipe is stopped, two pictures share the screen. This technique may be used to show both ends of a telephone conversation simultaneously, or to show, in the corner of a scene, the face of the announcer who is describing that scene.

NEGATIVE IMAGE. When polarity is switched, either in the control room or in the processing laboratory, a negative image results. It has occasional uses in stories that incorporate fantastic or abnormal elements.

LIMBO. A set that has little or no background but is identified by an object or a piece of furniture, such as a telephone booth, a desk, a sign that suggests a particular location, or a table, is known as the limbo set. It may consist merely of a dark curtain against which the action takes place. The limbo is generally used only for playing short scenes.

CAMEO. The cameo approach extends the limbo idea to an entire production. Scenes are played mostly in close-up against a dark background with just a property or a piece of furniture here and there to suggest the existence of a set. This technique is especially useful for college groups whose resources for building sets are limited.

WILD SETS. The term "wild" refers to a portion of a set that is built in a separate part of the studio to permit focusing on a particular part of the action. This set may duplicate a portion of a full set that is not accessible to the close-up camera, such as a phone or a cabinet, or it may provide something not included in the other sets. Such installations are also referred to as *detail* sets.

MODELS AND MINIATURES. A set or object that cannot be built in its normal dimensions may often be constructed in miniature. An example is a building that is to be blown up, a toy train careening over a tiny cliff, or a ship model rocking in a tub of water. Miniature construction may also be used for other reasons. Placing the normally sized actor who played the title role in *The Friendly Giant* among a group of miniature buildings made him seem to be a person of towering stature.

GRAPHICS. Photographs, drawings, paintings, and other types of graphic material frequently illustrate documentary and informational programs and may also be used in drama programs to provide titles and credits. In this latter area some writers have displayed great ingenuity. In one program about boxing, titles were painted on the backs of actors clothed in boxing trunks.

ANIMATION, PUPPETS, AND MARIONETTES. One of the most popular types of children's programs is the animated or cartoon presentation. This technique is also used frequently in producing commercials. The puppet or marionette is another common ingredient in these presentations.

REAR PROJECTION (RP). Scenes or effects that cannot be produced live in a studio or on a film set may be projected onto a screen from behind in motion-picture or still-picture form. In film usage this technique is referred to as a *process shot*. An actor photographed in front of a screen on which a picture of the White House is projected seems to be in Washington even though he has never left Hollywood. A motion picture of passing countryside, projected onto the screen behind a car standing motionless in a studio, makes the car appear to be speeding down the road. Films may also be combined in the laboratory to accomplish similar effects.

THE FILTER. An instrument that removes certain frequencies from the voices, sounds, or music being broadcast and thus endows them with a peculiar quality is known as a filter. Installed in the control panel, it may take out a range of high or low frequencies or a combination of both. The filter may be used in two basic ways: to represent a natural effect, such as a voice heard on a telephone, or to accomplish a symbolic or supernatural effect, such as the voice of conscience or the voice of a being from another world. It may also be used to communicate the thoughts of a character.

THE REVERBERATION DEVICE. Another commonly used instrument is a device that adds a reverberation or echo effect to sounds or speech. The addition of reverberation can create the sound that occurs naturally in a coal mine or barn and it can achieve such fantastic effects as the voice of a giant or the music of the spheres. On occasion, the filter and reverberation instrument are used together to produce unusual effects. Both the filter and the reverberation device should be used with moderation for both add what would ordinarily be thought of as an undesirable element to the broadcast signal. Consistency and clarity in their use are also important.

SONOVOX. A device that permits such sounds as train whistles, wind noises, or music to be articulated into intelligible speech is known as the sonovox. It is seldom employed in dramatic programs but has had considerable use in the production of commercials.

SPEECH

The responsibility of the writer with respect to speech has been discussed in the chapter on Dialogue and Narration. In that chapter reference was made to narration spoken by a person who does not appear on the screen, the *voice-over* technique. In the same way dialogue may be spoken by characters who do not appear on the screen. The symbol used to identify this technique is OS, which is variously considered to mean *off-stage, off-screen,* or *over-shot.* The exact opposite of this effect is the character seen on the screen speaking the words directly. Ordinarily this method would not be identified in any special way but in commercials, where there is often a swift interchange between voice-over and direct speech, the terms *direct-voice* (DV) or *lip-sync* may be used to avoid confusion.

SOUND EFFECTS

Most of the sound effects in television are not produced separately as they are in radio but are heard because of action that takes place in the scene. Thus, a character opening a door in a set automatically produces the necessary noise. Once in a while sound effects may be produced independently of the action to suggest the existence of an object that does not actually appear on the screen. The noise of an automobile driving up helps a viewer to visualize the vehicle even though he never sees it. The off-stage sound of a puffing steam engine can help an audience to sense the existence of an old-fashioned railroad station. The roar of an explosion, accompanied by the sight of debris floating down on the visible scene, can lead an audience to visualize what might be impossible to produce before its eyes. In radio drama, sound effects are far more important than they are in television, for they are the principal means of leading the audience to visualize a scene.

TYPES OF SOUND EFFECTS.   There are a number of ways in which sound effects can be described, but the best way is to classify them in terms of the specific function they perform.

1. *Action Sounds.*   Almost all sounds are created by some kind of movement and it is the function of most sounds to inform the audience that the action causing the sound, or some action associated with it, is taking place. Thus, the slam of a door signifies a character's angry exit from a scene. Action sounds may also help to reveal the mood of a character or to suggest a peculiarity about him. The tapping cane of a blind man is an example. An action sound such as the striking of a clock can give the audience a sense of time.

2. *Setting Sounds.*   Those sounds which, although produced by movement, are designed to indicate the locale of a scene rather than a specific action are known as setting or locale sounds. The chirping of crickets to suggest night and the roar of an airplane engine to establish an airport scene are examples. They often serve as a continuous background to a scene. Setting sounds may also contribute to a scene by helping to develop the mood and atmosphere of the situation.

3. *Symbolic Sounds.*   Sometimes a sound that is not realistically connected in any way with actual movement or real events can be used to suggest an idea or dramatic happening, particularly in a story of fantasy. The tinkling of glass chimes can suggest sunlight shining through a darkened window. A rising note on a slide whistle was used to suggest the lengthening of Pinocchio's nose every time he told a falsehood in a radio adaptation of his story.

WHEN TO USE SOUND EFFECTS.   Writers must beware of becoming so infatuated with sound effects that they use them beyond all reason. The first thing to realize is that a sound effect should not be used simply because it might occur in a given situation in real life because many sounds are merely incidental in a situation and have no particular meaning to communicate. Piling on sounds indiscriminately, furthermore, may introduce so many complications that the script becomes almost impossible to produce. A particular sound should be used only if one of the following questions can be answered affirmatively: (1) Does the sound help to make something clear? (2) Does the sound help to add realism and authenticity? (3) Does the sound enhance the mood or atmosphere of a scene? (4) Does the audience expect to hear the sound?

IDENTIFYING SOUND. It must be borne in mind that the source or cause of certain sounds cannot be determined simply by hearing the sound itself. The listener needs assistance in identifying these sounds through the use of one of the following techniques: 1) refer to the sound in the dialogue or narration; 2) make the sound clear through the general development of the action; 3) identify one sound by connecting it with another sound that is recognizable.

DESCRIBING SOUND EFFECTS. There are a number of rules for indicating the nature of sound effects in a script. First of all, you should describe sound requirements in a consistent way. There are two main methods of indicating sounds: one is to describe the action that produces the sounds and the other is to describe the sounds themselves. Using the first method, the action is usually labeled "biz" (business) and may appear as follows:

```
(DON AND HERB LEAVE THE CAR, CROSS THE

SIDEWALK, CLIMB THE STEPS TO THE PORCH,

AND KNOCK ON THE DOOR.)
```

It is then the director's responsibility to produce the sounds that reveal this action. Using the second method, the specific sounds are indicated as follows:

```
(CAR DOOR OPENS AND CLOSES; FOOTSTEPS ON

SIDEWALK, STEPS, AND PORCH; KNOCK ON DOOR)
```

This is the more common method of indicating sounds.

It is important to be completely clear about the sounds your script requires. This sound direction appeared in a student-written script:

```
(SOUND:   GIRL LEAVES ROOM)
```

Does this mean footsteps or door effects? To keep your script from becoming clogged with unnecessary verbiage, however, you should describe sounds as economically as possible. The use of the words "to denote" is unnecessary in

(SOUND TO DENOTE FALLING BODY)

and the direction:

(SOUND: COW KICKS OVER PAIL OF SOUR MILK)

raises the interesting question whether the splash of sour milk sounds differently from that of sweet milk. Still, any information that can help a director to produce a script should be included. This direction appeared in Archibald MacLeish's script "The States Talking":

(THE LAUGHTER FADES INTO THE SOUND OF THE SEA

AND THE SOUND OF THE SEA GRADUALLY INTO THE

SOUND OF THE WIND IN THE BARE TREES AND THE

DRY CORN. THE VOICES PAUSE, FADE OUT INTO

THE SOUND.)

This sequence may seem to contain some unnecessary words, but it does provide the director with a vivid representation of the effect the writer had in mind.

In addition to describing the sound, you should indicate, when necessary, how the sound is to be modified or handled, as MacLeish did in the above example. An important requirement is to indicate the perspective relationship of the sound. Is it heard on-mike or off-mike or does it approach or recede from the center of the action? It is also important to establish the volume relationship between the sound that establishes locale and other elements in the scene. Unually, such sounds are established at normal level at the beginning of a scene to make an audience conscious of the setting and then are reduced in volume so that the dialogue can be heard comfortably. For example:

EST. SOUND OF AUTOMOBILE THEN FADE TO B.

G. (background).

Finally, you should avoid attributing sounds to actions that make no sound, as for example:

(SOUND: THINGS BEING PICKED UP)

or

(SOUND: SNOW FALLING)

and you should also refrain from putting information other than sound descriptions under sound headings.

MUSIC

Music makes little contribution to the communication of meaning, but it can be a powerful aid in reinforcing the emotional effect of a drama. There are six different ways in which it can be used: 1) as a signature or theme for a drama series or for a particular drama in a series; 2) as a transition between scenes, acting as a curtain for the scene that is ending and as an introduction to the scene that is about to begin; 3) as a background to a scene or to a sequence of narration; 4) as part of the action itself, an example being the orchestra music in a night club setting; 5) as a *stab* or *sting* to point up critical stages in the dramatic development; 6) as a symbolic effect to suggest such ideas as a soft, spring day or the churning of angry emotions.

Music may make significant contributions to a drama but it must be used with moderation especially in radio. A television viewer may be scarcely aware of the music backgrounding a scene, even though it is effectively heightening his emotional reactions, because his attention is concentrated on what he sees. On radio, however, there is nothing for the listener to attend to except what is coming from the loudspeaker. Music behind dialogue needs to be used with particular circumspection. Too much music suggests that a writer has little faith in the dialogue he has written and is trying to gain emotional power by artificial means. Music behind narration can be used with more freedom, and it may help the audience to distinguish narration from dialogue.

The music for a television or radio drama can be described in a number of ways. One way is to indicate the function it performs in a script. Thus, music may be listed as "MUSIC: THEME," "MUSIC: TRANSITION," "MUSIC: CURTAIN," "MUSIC: FINALE." The way the music is to be produced in the program may also be described, as the following examples illustrate:

MUSIC: BACKGROUND; MUSIC: ESTABLISH THEN

TAKE DOWN; MUSIC: SNEAK IN UNDER DIALOGUE

AND THEN RAISE TO NORMAL LEVEL AS SCENE

ENDS; MUSIC: UP AND UNDER THEN SNEAK OUT;

MUSIC: FADE UP - UNDER - AND OUT.

Many of the above terms are those commonly used in scripts, but the writer is not bound by them; he can invent his own language as long as he makes his purpose clear to the director.

Generally you do not need to describe the mood and content of the music but simply write "MUSIC" and leave it to the director to find something appropriate. You may want to go further than this, however, if you are concerned about achieving a particular effect and believe that defining the music in specific terms will help to accomplish it. Thus, you may write

MUSIC: REDOLENT OF BAT-FILLED CAVERNS

or

MUSIC: MYSTERIOSO

or

MUSIC: AN EIGHTEENTH-CENTURY EFFECT.

If there is a particular number that supports your dramatic idea—"The Battle Hymn of the Republic" for a Civil War story, for instance—you may suggest it, but generally you will avoid listing familiar music because listeners may have associations with it that are in conflict with the script's purpose.

SPECIAL PROBLEMS IN RADIO DRAMA

The problems encountered by a writer of radio drama differ in few essentials from those facing writers for any of the dramatic media, but the fact that listeners cannot see what is happening introduces some unique difficulties.

PERSPECTIVE IN RADIO DRAMA.   One of the special problems a radio writer faces is to give his audience a sense of the perspective relationships existing in a scene. This means simply that the audience must have an understanding of the space in the scene and the way in which people and objects are situated in that space or move in it. The first step in establishing perspective is to visualize the space in which the scene takes place. Then you must decide which element in the scene is to have the volume emphasis. This becomes the spot where the microphone is placed, the on-mike position where the radio listener visualizes himself as the observer of the action. The next step is to determine the relationship of other elements in the scene to that central location.

These elements may be heard continuously off-mike, or their position may be varied either toward or away from the microphone.

Speeches, sounds, or music occurring in the central position are written without any perspective direction because it is presumed that any element in a script that lacks a perspective notation is to be heard on-mike. Every item that does not occur on-mike, however, must be preceded with a specific perspective direction such as

```
OFF-MIKE, FADING-OFF, FADING-ON, COMING ON,

GOING OFF, IN B.G., IN DISTANCE.
```

If a whole series of lines or effects is to be heard off-mike, you may prefer to insert a general note of instruction rather than writing "OFF-MIKE" over and over again.

Another perspective concept important to writers is that a character with the on-mike position may move without losing that position; you simply think of the microphone as moving with him. Sometimes, however, you need to shift the on-mike position from one element to another while the scene is actually taking place. This type of change is likely to cause confusion unless you take unusual pains to keep the audience oriented.

COMMUNICATING ACTION.   Because the listener cannot see what is happening in radio drama, you often face difficult problems in making activity clear. The tools already discussed must be your means of revealing the necessary information; narration can describe a situation; sound effects can help an audience to visualize activity; dialogue, deftly written, can indicate what is going on in a scene without seeming to. What you must avoid in this last instance is an obvious "look-see" quality, which makes drama sound contrived and amateurish.

In addition to employing the tools at your disposal, you can simplify your problem if you follow this rule: *Introduce only the activity that is essential to the telling of the story.* This means that you will discard most of the movement known in the theatre as "business." On stage or screen the drink pourings, the cigarette lightings, the crosses and re-crosses of the set have the valuable function of providing variation in the scene for the viewer. But on radio such activity is not only unnecessary but is also almost impossible to communicate, for a man lighting a pipe or rising to his feet makes no sounds that readily identify what he is doing. Moreover, a listener expects most of the sounds he hears on radio to be significant and he is likely to be misled when they serve only as decoration.

SCRIPT FORMATS

No one format for television and radio programs has been adopted throughout the industry, but there is agreement on the basic pattern that should be followed in putting a script on paper. Within this general pattern the various broadcasting organizations and film producers develop their individual styles. When you know the general principles, you can easily adapt to the special requirements of the organization for which you work.

THE TELEVISION FORMAT

Television production is dominated by the director. He decides what the audience is to see, supervising the composition of the shots being picked up by the various cameras and deciding which of these shots is to be on the air at any given moment. While one shot in the final program is being seen by the audience, he must make the preparations and give the orders for the next shot. For these reasons the TV writer, unlike the film writer, does not usually describe the shot to be used in picking up a particular scene. Instead he indicates merely *what* is to be seen, and the director, by choosing a certain camera pick-up, determines *how* it is to be seen. The television writer sometimes indicates the nature of a shot when it is important to the development of a story and he describes the techniques to be used at major transitional points. But he should not try to take over the creative role of the director by directing the show from his typewriter.

To provide a place for the notes the director needs to guide his direction of the program while it is on the air, television scripts are typed with the dialogue, description of sets and action, and notations regarding sound effects and music occupying only two-thirds of the page. The other third of the page is left completely blank; which side this is varies from organization to organization. The basic way in which information is typed in a television script follows the practice that developed in radio. The general rule is that all lines—whether they are spoken by actors, announcers, or narrators—appear in the script in regular typing, using upper- and lower-case letters in the conventional way. Everything else—descriptions of action or sets, instructions to actors, sound effects, and music—is typed in capital letters.

In addition to writing the body of the script, the writer is responsible for preparing a page that indicates the title of his script and lists the characters. As a further aid to the production group, he may also include a brief summary of the story, a description of each character, and a listing and description of the sets, music, and sound effects.

To illustrate the format used for live or video-taped television dramatic production, there follows an excerpt from James Costigan's script "White Gloves," produced on the *United States Steel Hour*.

ACT THREE:

FADE IN

THE KITCHEN.

FOCUS ON THE COFFEE-POT, CONTENTS BOILING,

ON THE STOVE. THE CAMERA MOVES BACK TO

REVEAL BILLY, IN PAJAMAS, YAWNING AS HE

LOWERS FIRE, POURS HIMSELF A CUP, ADDS

SUGAR. HE THEN GOES SLEEPILY INTO THE

LIVING ROOM, OPENS THE VENETIAN BLINDS

BESIDE THE DINING TABLE, BLINKS AT THE

SUNLIGHT, TURNS TO OBSERVE THE CHAOS OF THE

PREVIOUS NIGHT. FROM THE FLOOR, HE PICKS

UP ELLEN'S WIG, SMOOTHS ITS RUMPLED CLOTH

FLOWERS, PLACES IT ON THE TABLE BESIDE THE

WICKER-ENCASED CHIANTI BOTTLES. FINDING

PENCIL AND PAPER IN THE SIDEBOARD, HE

CLEARS A SPACE ON THE TABLE, SITS,

CONSIDERS, THEN BEGINS TO WRITE.

INSERT: SHOT OF NOTE-PAPERS,

HAND PRINTING MESSAGE,

"American Geophysical Co., Paul's Valley,

Oklahoma. Regret unable to accept position

due to..."

IN ANOTHER SHOT, BILLY SCRATCHES OUT A
WORD. ROCKY COMES IN FROM THE HALLWAY,
BUTTONING A SKIRT OVER A COTTON SHIRT, HER
EYES STILL HEAVY WITH SLEEP.

> ROCKY

What time is it?

> BILLY

Around nine.

> ROCKY

(PASSING NEAR THE WINDOW, SQUINTS)
There seems to be this sunlight.

> BILLY

It's going to be another scorcher.

> ROCKY

Nice day for a ride in the country.
(SHE TURNS AND LOOKS AT HIM. HE REMAINS
INTENT ON HIS PAPER)
Is there any more of that coffee?

> BILLY

On the stove. I'll get it.
(HE GOES INTO THE KITCHEN. ROCKY MOVES
NEAR ENOUGH THE TABLE TO SEE WHAT HE HAS
BEEN WRITING, THEN SITS AT A PLACE
OPPOSITE HIS. BILLY RETURNS WITH COFFEE-
POT AND CUPS, POURS ONE FOR ROCKY.
FOR A MOMENT THEY DRINK IN SILENCE. THEN,
UNABLE TO ENDURE THE GLOOM, SHE
IMPULSIVELY PLACES A NAPKIN OVER HER

```
                    HEAD AND FACE, LIFTS THE DANGLING END

                    UP TO REVEAL A CHARLES ADDAMS LEER AND

                    SAYS)

                              ROCKY

                    How about us last night?

                    (BILLY SMILES FEEBLY)

                    Not very funny, huh?

                    (HE SHAKES HIS HEAD)

                    I never was any good in a crisis.
```

FORMAT FOR SHOT-BY-SHOT FILMS

The director in filmed television does not have the same responsibility for devising shots that the director in live television production does. Rather, the writer of the script provides a blueprint for the program by indicating not only what is to be seen but also by describing the camera shots that are to record the action. The film director, of course, may decide to change a shot prescribed by a writer or he may shoot the same action from a number of viewpoints. He does not decide which of these shots is to be used, however. That is the function of the film editor who assembles the various shots into a completed program after the director has finished shooting. The "look" of a show then is the result of collaboration among the writer, director, and film editor.

In a script for this type of filmed production, the action is divided into a series of separate shots which are described with a number of factors accounted for: 1) the people in the shot and their appearance; 2) the movement that takes place; 3) the dialogue or narration; 4) the setting; 5) the distance of the camera from the subjects, and the angle from which it views the action. A film script usually begins with a fade-in designation in capital letters typed to the left just above the description of the first shot. This description, also typed in capital letters, includes the following information: the number of the shot, a designation of the scene as interior or exterior and the time as day or night, and the nature of the set. It may also list the people in the scene and type of shot.

The script then describes in more detail the set, the action, and the way the camera picks up the scene. The dialogue, with the names of the characters set above the lines, is also included. The writer of film scripts does not differentiate other material from actor's and narrator's lines by using capitals, as the television writer does, but uses capitals to identify the beginning of a new shot, for character names, and to indicate camera shots. If the shot ends with a dissolve or fade, the direction is set to the right in caps just below the last item of the shot. If no transition effect is indicated, it is assumed that it is a cut. The next item in capital letters details the nature of the following shot, but lists only those elements that differentiate it from the preceding shot. In an hour show there may be more than 200 separate shots listed and described in the script. Film scripts also include title pages which list the characters, sets, music, and sound effects. Some pages from a script of a program for *The Fugitive* series, "May God Have Mercy" written by Don Brinkley, illustrate this type of format. The entire script was analyzed in the chapter on Inventing the Plot.

125   INT. CORRIDOR - NIGHT - THE GUARD

  leaning against the wall, ruffling through a

  magazine. He hears GLORIA'S VOICE o.s., muffled

  and indistinct, with SOUNDS of kicking and

  hammering at the closet door. Unsure at first,

  he listens...then opens the door, sees Toby

  o.s., unconscious on the floor.

126   CLOSE SHOT - AT DARKROOM DOOR

  on the sign:

X-RAY DARK ROOM

No Admittance

The door is unlocked, it opens cautiously.

Kimble looks around, slips into the corridor.

Seeing that the Guard has gone inside, he dashes

for the firedoor at the far end of the corridor.

TRUCK WITH HIM. As he pushes it open:

     OBERHANSLY'S VOICE (o.s.)

   Reynolds -- !

He looks, startled.

127   HIS P.O.V. - DOWN THE CORRIDOR

Miss Oberhansly has stepped off the elevator.
She shouts at him.

                    OBERHANSLY (continuing)
          What're you doing -- ??

128   ANGLE - FAVORING KIMBLE

He pushes the heavy door open, vanishes down the
stairway.

129   INT.   X-RAY ROOM - NIGHT - THE GUARD

unlocks the closet door, releases Gloria.   She's
almost in hysterics.

                    GLORIA
          He...he grabbed me!   He might've
          <u>killed</u> me!

The door from the corridor opens.   Oberhansly
enters.

                    OBERHANSLY
          What's happening in here?

                    GLORIA
                    (points to Toby, still unconscious)
          Look!   Look what he did!

The guard draws his gun, rushes out.

FORMAT FOR SCENE-BY-SCENE FILMS

The responsibility of a writer of a filmed show produced in scenes rather than in shots is very similar to that of the writer for live television. He indicates what is to be seen but he does not indicate the nature of camera shots since shots from different angles and positions are being filmed simultaneously. Except for the fact that the script occupies the whole page instead of two-thirds, it is similar in appearance to the format used for live television. The dialogue, for example, is the only material typed in regular upper- and lower-case letters; everything else— descriptions of sets and action, character names, sounds, directions to actors—appear in capital letters. A scene from a script for the Emmy Award winning *Dick Van Dyke Show,* "Where Did I Come From?" written by Carl Reiner, illustrates the format. This script is divided into nine scenes, which constitute the shooting segments for the show. The pages in the script occupied by each of these scenes plus an identifying letter (A, B, C, etc.) are listed on the title page. Each of these scenes begins with the designation INT (to indicate interior), a listing of the place, and either DAY or NIGHT. Other details are then incorporated into the script as the action progresses.

```
INT.   LIVING ROOM - NIGHT


ROB READING PAPER, LAURA SEWING.   RITCH ON THE FLOOR

LOOKING THROUGH A PHOTO ALBUM.   HE IS SILENT FOR AWHILE

                        RITCH

            Daddy?

                         ROB

            (ABSENTMINDEDLY)  Yes, Ritch?

                        RITCH

            Where did I come from?

                         ROB

HE PUTS PAPER DOWN

                Uh, what did you say, Ritch?

                        RITCH

                I said, where did I come from?
```

                         ROB

Oh, that's what I thought you said ... Um,

honey, did you hear what Ritch asked?

                         LAURA

I heard, darling.

                         RITCH

Where did I, Daddy?

                         ROB

Well ... it's a pretty complicated thing,

son ... I don't know if we have the time

to go into it right now.

                         RITCH

When will you have the time?

                         ROB

Well, I don't know ... Darling, when will

we have the time?

                         LAURA

(CHECKS WATCH) Well, I think we have the

time right now. Ritch doesn't have to go

to bed for another half hour or so.

                         ROB

Oh, are you sure you're not too sleepy,

son?

                         RITCH

No, I wanno hear where I came from.

ROB

Um, yes ... now let's see ... um ... first
of all ... uh ... where do you think you
came from?

RITCH

The same place Freddie Helper came from --
New Jersey.

ROB

No, you came from New York. Don't you
remember that?

RITCH

I forgot ... but I remember about the
laundry truck.

LAURA

The laundry truck! How do you know about
the laundry truck?

RITCH

Daddy told me.

ROB

Well, how do you like that? I must have
told him about that when he was four years
old ... I didn't think he'd remember that.

RITCH

I remember, Daddy. You said the laundry
man brought me.

LAURA

Is that what modern daddies tell their
children about the facts of life?

                ROB

(SMILES) I think you got the story a
little mixed up, son.

                RITCH

(KNEELS BY ROB) Tell me the story, Daddy.
About the laundry truck.

                ROB

Well, the laundry truck only comes into
the story the day you were born.

                RITCH

Yeah, that's the story I want to hear ...
about the day I was born.

                ROB

Well, it was quite an exciting twenty-four
hours.

                RITCH

Were you there, Mommy?

                LAURA

(LAUGHS) Yes, I was there, Ritch.

                RITCH

Good.

                ROB

Mommy and I went to sleep that night
expecting that you might arrive in the
middle of the night. Mommy and I were
both lying in bed reading ... both
wondering when you would be born.

OIL DISSOLVE TO FLASHBACK:

RADIO SCRIPT FORMAT

The objective in typing a radio script is to make instantly clear the nature of all the elements and their relationships. Radio dramas receive relatively short periods of rehearsal and there is no time for the director, cast, and crew to puzzle out weird or original hieroglyphics. There should be a clear differentiation between the material in the script that is to be spoken into the microphone and that which is not. This can be accomplished in a number of ways: (1) Type all material to be spoken in regular upper and lower case letters in the usual way. Type all material that is not spoken in capital letters; this includes character names, directions for reading lines, other descriptive material, music, and sound effects. (2) Put parentheses around any element inserted into a line that is not part of the line itself; this includes directions for reading the line and music and sound effects notations. (3) Underline music and sound effects descriptions and indent them beyond the point where the dialogue or narration begins. (4) Place parentheses around descriptions of music to distinguish the music from sound effects.

It is essential that radio scripts be double spaced, for nothing invites an actor's misreading so much as the closely bunched letters on a single-spaced page. To facilitate the process of rehearsal, you should also use some system of numbering lines or cues so that a director can quickly indicate a spot in a script that needs attention.

The concluding scene from Milton Geiger's "One Special for Doc" illustrates the format. In the action prior to this scene a young man, disappointed in love, has come to Doc's drugstore seeking to buy poison. Doc, pointing out that the poison may not end everything after all but may only burn his stomach with the result that he may have to subsist on warm milk and buttered toast for the rest of his life, has persuaded the young man to join him at the local eatery where he has ordered him a hamburger.

```
101  HANK:     (FADING ON)  Here komm hamburk wit-

               greeled hunnion!

102            SOUND:  DISHES SLAM DOWN ON COUNTER

103  HANK:     Anda wan spashul for Doc!  Haw, haw,

               haw...

104            SOUND:  SLIDE OF DISHES...AND FADE OUT ON

               HANK LAUGHING
```

105 HARSHAW: (WITH STRANGE MELANCHOLY, SLOWLY) One

special for Doc. Days without end.

One special for Doc.

106 ALLEN: (WITH DAWNING AMAZEMENT AND COMPREHENSION)

One-special-for-Doc! You! Warm milk...

and buttered toast. Warm milk...

107 HARSHAW: (IN SAME SAD VOICE) You see? Do you

understand now?

108 ALLEN: (DAZED) I...I see! For life. Warm

milk...and buttered toast.

109 HARSHAW: And gruel. Don't forget the gruel.

110 ALLEN: (AGITATED) I...I...don't think...I

want my sandwich. I'm going, Doc. I've

got to go. Sorry...Doc...

111 HARSHAW: Yes, boy. Go. Go back to her...to

Julie...She needs you and wants you as

badly as you need and want her. Wait for

her if you must. She'll wait too. But

go back.

112 ALLEN: I'm going. You bet I am! So long.

I'll be seeing you.

113 HARSHAW: (SOFTLY) Good night.

114 ALLEN: (HESITATING) Thanks. And...I'm sorry

about...you know. Awful sorry.

115 HARSHAW: It's all right kid. Good night.

116 ALLEN: (FADING OFF) Good night. And thanks.

117 HARSHAW: (CALLING AFTER HIM) And give her my love.

118   SOUND: (OFF MIKE) DOOR SLAMS HARD

119 HARSHAW: (SIGHING) Crazy kids. Lucky he came to

me. I guess I handled <u>that</u> prescription

all right. (CHUCKLES SOFTLY, THEN SHOUTS)

Hey, Hank!

121 HANK: (OFF MIKE) Commink, Boss!

122 HARSHAW: (SHOUTING) Hank! Let's see some food.

I'll have a steak an inch thick, with mush

-rooms and fried potatoes. And a gallon

of tough coffee. And for heaven's sake,

take this awful-looking stuff out of my

sight, will ya!

123   (MUSIC: CURTAIN)

In addition to the formats described in this chapter there are special typing arrangements for radio and television commercials, continuities, and documentary programs. These formats are illustrated in the chapters dealing with those subjects.

QUESTIONS AND PROJECTS

1. Plan sequences for filmed TV programs that involve the use of the following devices and techniques:
   a) FS, LS, MS, CU, CS.
   b) various angles—low, high, overhead, canted, reverse; combo shot.
   c) various camera movements—pan, tilt, dolly or zoom, truck, and crane.
   d) special devices—flexitron or oil dissolve, whirligig, defocus, blank out, whip pan, wipe, super, shared screen, negative images, process.

2. Plan TV sequences that end with the basic TV transition effects—fade, dissolve, cut.

3. Design radio or TV sequences that call for the use of the special auditory devices—filter, reverberation chamber, and sonovox.

4. Design radio sequences that utilize the three basic classes of sound effects—action, setting, and symbolic.

5. Listen to a number of TV plays with special attention to the use of music. Analyze this use and decide whether it contributed to the dramatic experience.

6. Design a court room scene in a radio drama. Decide on the center for the scene (judge, jury, attorneys' locations, witness chair, spectators). Move participants to and away from this center. Switch the center during the course of the scene (from the witness chair to a spectator, for example).

10

Adaptations

The adapter may do anything which truthfully translates the import, the flavor, and the purpose of the original in its fullest possible integrity.   Max Wylie

Thus far we have been considering the writing of the original drama, the script in which the plot and characters are created by the radio or television writer. A great many broadcast dramas, however, are based on novels, short stories, stage plays, and movies. The use of existing works can be explained, first, because it helps to satisfy television's need for programs and, second, because the adaptation of well-known material carries a built-in guarantee of audience appeal. Preparing scripts founded on other works often confronts the writer with unusual challenges.

SCRIPTS BASED ON OTHER WORKS

A number of different terms are used to denote scripts that have their origin in whole or in part in material written by others. The choice of term depends on the strictness with which the writer of the broadcast version adheres to the original work.

THE ADAPTATION

The greatest degree of faithfulness to the original author's work is implied in the term *adaptation*. Perhaps the best way to describe the adapter's obligation is to say that he should try to write his script just as the original writer would have written it had he been working in the new medium. His obligation is similar to that of the translator, who must convey the ideas and feelings expressed in one language with as little change as possible. Certain changes are necessary, however; some are inevitable because of the nature of television and radio, some because the new medium requires a different approach if the spirit and flavor of the original are to be preserved. In fact, an adapter who attempts too literal a translation of another's work, who fails to make the changes demanded by the differences in the media, is falling as far short of meeting his obligations to the original author as the adapter who makes capricious or unnecessary changes. The adapter, then, has two main responsibilities: in converting material written for another medium into radio or television form, he must retain as far as possible the impact and qualities of the original, and at the same time he must make the changes called for by the demands of the new medium. He must, in other words, be as faithful to the original as the new medium permits him to be.

OTHER SCRIPTS BASED ON PREVIOUSLY WRITTEN MATERIAL

In some instances a dramatist may not seek complete faithfulness to the original work in his broadcast version but makes changes that are dictated by his own ideas and invention. Such a script should not be called an adaptation. The term to be used depends on the degree to which the new version has departed from the old. A script that derives a major share of its inspiration from the original work is usually described as being *based on* that work. The expression *freely adapted* is also used in the same way. When the original material merely provides a springboard for the dramatist's imagination, the term *suggested by* provides the most appropriate description. The script in its final form may bear little relationship to the work that inspired it. A case in point is Paddy Chayefsky's first TV play, "Holiday Song," which had its origin in a short *Reader's Digest* article, "It Happened on the Brooklyn Subway." When the hour drama was complete, only remnants of the article were left; the play's characters, plot, and theme were created almost entirely by Chayefsky.

The Reginald Rose play "An Almanac of Liberty" began with the idea of adapting the book of the same name by Supreme Court Justice William O. Douglas. Rose soon realized that the vast scope of the book, which includes a description of an incident in man's fight for liberty that took place on each day of the year, made a literal translation of the work impossible. The script he finally wrote retained only the title and the general spirit of the book. Everything else he created. Rose correctly labeled his script a play *suggested by* the Douglas work rather than an adaptation of it.

When a writer bases a script on previously written material, he should have a clear understanding of the kind of conversion he is making. If he professes to be writing an adaptation, he must recognize and carry out his responsibility to the original author. Much of the disappointment audiences sometimes experience with movie versions of well-known books lies in the failure of the movie to be faithful to the original. If these versions are labeled adaptations, audiences have a right to complain when the characters and plot seen on the screen seem scarcely recognizable. On the other hand, if his script is merely "based on" or "suggested by" the work of another writer, he is free to make the changes that his imagination may dictate. As long as the end product provides a satisfactory dramatic experience, there should be no quibbling about the liberties taken.

The rest of this chapter will deal with the principles and techniques that apply in writing adaptations. The writing of the freer versions involves the use of methods employed in writing original plays, which were described in previous chapters.

THE ADAPTER'S CHALLENGE

The question of whether it is easier or more difficult to write adaptations than it is to compose originals has received conflicting answers. In his book *The Radio Play*, Martin Maloney of Northwestern University said that "students should adapt before they try to write original plays."[1] In direct contrast, Roger Busfield Jr. of Michigan State University said in his book *The Playwright's Art* that "adaptation is for the advanced playwright" and added that "it is strange that so many playwriting courses in colleges and universities introduce the students to adaptation as a means of getting them started in dramatic writing."[2]

The conclusion that writing the adaptation is the easier task rests

---

[1] Martin Maloney, *The Radio Play* (Evanston: The Student Book Exchange, 1949), p. 10.

[2] Roger Busfield Jr., *The Playwright's Art* (New York: Harper & Row, Publishers, 1958), p. 203.

on the fact that the adapter needs to do little actual creating. The characters, setting, plot, and theme are already in existence; his job is merely to take another person's ideas and remold them into a new form. The conclusion that writing the adaptation is the more difficult challenge stems from the fact that the adapter is bound both by the original work and by the demands of the new medium. The writer of the original play can always modify his story to fit the requirements of his medium. The adapter who wishes to remain true to his material, in contrast, must meet the requirements of the new medium without materially changing what the original author created.

Whether it is more difficult to write an original or an adaptation would seem to depend on the nature of the material to be adapted. Stage presentations are relatively easy to adapt because they are composed of drama's basic ingredient—dialogue. A good way for a beginner to test his mastery of the broadcasting medium is to try his hand at adapting a one-act play. Making radio or television sense out of a long novel or an introspective short story, on the other hand, might be too much for even an experienced writer.

Another way to answer the question is to say that neither the original nor the adaptation is necessarily easier or more difficult than the other, but that each makes different kinds of demands on the writer. The writer of original dramas must have the creativity needed to conceive characters and invent plots. The adapter of works into broadcasting form, more than anything else, must possess ingenuity and a fundamental knowledge of the medium. The aspiring writer should certainly try his hand at adapting. The challenge it involves may help the beginner to find himself as a writer and should lead to an expansion and development of his skills.

CHANGES MADE BY ADAPTERS

Even though the adapter's aim is to deliver the work to the air audience with the impact inherent in the original, he will discover that he spends most of his time making changes in it. It is true that portions of the original can sometimes be carried over intact—a narrative section or a portion of dialogue, for example—but in most cases he will have to shorten it, lengthen it, translate it from one form into another, or alter it in some other way.

SHORTENING THE MATERIAL

Of all the changes an adapter must make, the most common one is to compress the material he finds in the original work. A characteristic of dramatization is that it takes more time to depict a given incident than any other literary form—occasionally as much time as that same incident takes in real life. This means that a drama cannot cover nearly so much material as a short story of the same length. In a single paragraph, the story writer may cover centuries of time, refer to events calling for a multitude of sets, or describe scenes involving thousands of characters.

Another reason why an adapter must sometimes shorten material is that the original work is longer than his finished script can be. The TV dramatist is rarely allotted more than two hours, and even this long a period is the exception. A program is much more likely to be an hour or half an hour in length. From this time, of course, must be subtracted the minutes necessary for opening and closing frameworks, credits, and commercial. Adapters for a TV series *Best of Broadway* were forced to boil down a three-act play into less than forty-five minutes of actual playing time. Those who attempt the adaptation of full-length novels face similar problems of condensation. Complicating this problem is the fact that, in addition to being brief, time periods are also completely rigid. An adaptation for television must be designed to fit a particular time period to the exact second no matter how much this restriction may damage the story.

ELIMINATING SCENES.   Removing an entire scene from a story is one obvious way of shortening it. This technique is used in preparing a feature film for TV projection when the film runs longer than the time period allotted to the program. In the same way a writer doing an adaptation looks for scenes that can be removed from the original work without materially damaging the story. Generally, however, adapting must extend beyond this mere cutting of scenes into a process that involves revision of the entire work.

ELIMINATING PART OF THE PLOT.   A full-length play or novel that develops one or more subplots in addition to developing the main plot of the story can often be shortened by eliminating the subplots. Ibsen's play *A Doll's House* deals primarily with the relationship between Nora and her husband Torvald, but it also includes a subplot involving Dr. Rank. This subplot adds much to the over-all effect of this play, but it can be removed without seriously affecting the telling of the main story. It is usually better to eliminate a subplot than to try to squeeze both it and the main plot into a relatively brief period. In removing a subplot, you must be careful that you perform a clean operation. To avoid confusing the audience, you must avoid any references to incidents that took place as part of the material you have omitted.

ELIMINATING OR FUSING CHARACTERS.   When subplots are cut, characters are often cut also. In the suggested adaptation of *A Doll's House,* the character of Dr. Rank does not even appear. Even when plot material is not actually eliminated, it is often possible to cut characters or to make one character do the work of two or three. This fusing of characters works particularly well in translating Shakespearean plays into broadcast versions since several minor Shakespearean characters often perform essentially the same function. A reduction in the number of characters also simplifies the audience's problems of keeping track of the people in the play.

If the original is a book of an encyclopedic nature, such as a *David Copperfield* or an *Anthony Adverse,* you may be reduced to covering only one incident. Or perhaps you can cover a series of incidents that illuminate one of the themes in the book. One adaptation of the Dicken's work, for example, concentrated only on the love life of David Copperfield. From all of the myriad incidents in the book *Pinocchio,* a fifteen-minute radio adaptation treated only those that bore on the little puppet's experiences in learning to tell the truth.

In deciding what to keep and what to discard, a major consideration should be what the audience will expect to hear. Is there an incident in the story that is especially famous? Have certain characters won a particular place in the public's heart? The adapter who eliminates such scenes or characters from his script is inviting public disapproval.

Finally, you should consider the special demands of the new medium. Are there scenes in the story that will dramatize particularly well? If you are writing for radio, you should look for those situations that can be readily translated into sound symbols. If your medium is television, you must take into account the number of sets your script will legitimately require.

CONDENSING SCENES.   In many instances, the substance of a given scene may be needed to maintain story coherence, but all the details given in the original work need not be included. A great deal of compression can be accomplished by pruning action and exposition that do not make an essential contribution to the story.

TRANSLATING THE MATERIAL

The conversion of material written in one literary form into a form suitable for a broadcast presentation is known as translation. Most adaptations require this type of change at one point or other.

TRANSLATION INTO DIALOGUE.   A writer who adapts stories or books into dramatic form finds that he must often turn material that appears in the original work as narration or description into dialogue. Washington Irving's "The Legend of Sleepy Hollow" contains not one single dialogue exchange, and in the whole piece there are only two spoken lines, both uttered by people who are alone at the time. Turning this story into a drama requires virtually complete translation. Some of Irving's words may be used for narration, but the bulk of the drama—the dialogue—must be entirely created by the adapter. The challenge facing him is to invest these new words with the same gay spirit and whimsical flavor that characterize Irving's story. The necessity for writing new material in the manner of the old has been appropriately described by George Wells, writer of more than 400 adaptations. He said of the adapter:

> *If the original is by James Hilton, he must strive to write in the style of Mr. Hilton. If it is a work by Conrad, he may have to dress in sea boots and oilskins. His quill must laugh with Mark Twain and chuckle with Sir James Barrie; it must be dipped in bitterness for Eugene O'Neill and in sentiment for Dickens.*[3]

Another challenge is to write dialogue that will transmit the information contained in narration and yet avoid constructing lines that are top-heavy with exposition. This is a danger because narration tends to be expository in nature to begin with, and it often contains more information than can possibly be inserted into a dialogue translation. Since the adapter cannot include all of it, he must discriminate carefully between what is essential and what is not. He must then carry this essential information over into the new form, incorporating it in such a way that the resulting dialogue sounds natural and lifelike.

TRANSLATION INTO NARRATION.   One way of condensing three-act plays or movies consisting primarily of dialogue is to communicate the essence of some of this dialogue by summarizing the points it makes in narration. The scenes thus treated, of course, should not portray the key events of the story. The emotional impact of important scenes needs to be preserved intact by presenting them in their original dramatic form.

TRANSLATION INTO SOUND EFFECTS AND MUSIC.   Sound effects and music have their principal use in radio adaptations, but they also have a place in television. The major function of music is to emphasize effects that are accomplished primarily through other means, for rarely does music communicate meaning directly.

TRANSLATION INTO SETS, COSTUMES, BUSINESS, AND ACTION.   One of the advantages of television is that visual means can sometimes be used

[3] George Wells, "Radio's Strangest Bird," *Off Mike,* edited by Jerome Lawrence (New York: Duell, Sloan & Pearce, 1944), p. 89.

to depict in an instant what a writer of fiction may have taken pages and pages to convey. In most cases the need for converting a storyteller's description into visual elements is completely evident, but because the visual can communicate meaning so clearly and so economically, the adapter should also be alert to employ visual devices where their use may not be so obviously indicated.

MODIFYING THE MATERIAL IN OTHER WAYS

Anyone who writes for radio and television finds that he must respond to certain demands inherent in the broadcast medium. The fact that he is adapting the work of someone else does not excuse him from satisfying these peculiar requirements.

THE TABOOS OF BROADCASTING.   An adapter often finds that the taboos of broadcasting are stricter than those applying to the medium for which the original work was written. He cannot ignore those taboos simply because he is writing an adaptation. Sometimes this situation dictates changes that are necessary for no other reason.

The adapter who converted Terence Rattigan's *O Mistress Mine* into a broadcast version found it necessary to make clear that the man and woman at the center of the action had been safely married from the beginning, thus completely nullifying the point made by the play's title, which he retained anyway. It should be added that, despite this modification, the play remained a diverting piece of entertainment. The translation of Garson Kanin's *Born Yesterday* into a television production was marked by more daring, but the network officials later regretted their impulsiveness. Outraged protests from the audience indicated that in this play about a kept woman certain lines should not have been carried intact into the TV version. It was concluded also that Mary Martin should not have been cast in the leading role. Thousands of people in the TV audience who knew her as the lovable and innocent Peter Pan objected vigorously to her playing anyone with the casual morals of a Billie Dawn. This experience emphasized the peculiar problems that sometimes face those who work in broadcasting.

The effect of a somewhat different kind of restriction is exemplified by the television adaptation of the well-known fairy tale "Hansel and Gretel." As told by the Brothers Grimm, it was the cruel stepmother who lured the brother and sister into the forest, hoping that they would perish. The adapter Yasha Frank felt that he could not thus villify stepmothers, so in his version it was the witch and her assistants who did the luring.

THE VIVIDNESS OF DRAMA.   The fact that an event depicted in a drama strikes an audience with greater emotional power than the same event treated in a story sometimes calls for certain modifications. The TV adaptation of "Hansel and Gretel" again provides an example. The original story ended when the witch was pushed into the oven by her intended victim Hansel. The adapter felt that to permit her to remain in the oven and be cooked into extinction conjured up a picture too horrible for young children to endure. He, therefore, showed the witch peeking out of the oven unharmed, and he even suggested that her searing experience would reform her rather than destroy her.

One of literature's most spine-chilling stories is Lord Dunsany's "Two Bottles of Relish," which tells how a murderer disposed of his victim's body by cannibalism. The producer of a network mystery series refused to present an adaptation of this story because he thought the key event was too revolting for dramatization. Yet without the cannibalism, nothing would be left of the plot. The verdict on this story is not clear-cut, however, for a local station, WHN in New York, did present an adaptation written by Edward Goldberger. Alfred Hitchcock recognized that some stories suitable for printing in a book are not suitable for presentation on television. Some years ago he published a collection of stories that producers of his TV series had decided were too shocking or too grotesque to do on television.[4]

THE NEED FOR GETTING ATTENTION IMMEDIATELY.   Alexander Woolcott once said that he would give a novelist thirty pages to catch his interest. We might allow a short-story writer thirty sentences. But the television writer cannot enjoy even this indulgence. His limit is nearer thirty seconds. The necessity for catching audience attention instantly may demand certain re-arrangements of the material to be adapted. If the original writer has begun his story slowly, it may be necessary for the adapter to move an exciting scene forward in the action and then introduce the necessary exposition after audience interest has been awakened. He might also consider the use of a teaser, although this technique, as we have noted previously, is an artificial one.

THE NEED FOR LANGUAGE THAT SPEAKS WELL.   Even where dialogue exists in the original work, some modifications may be necessary before it is suitable for dramatic presentation. What may read well on the printed page often creaks and limps when it is put into the mouths of actors. Consider the following passage from Poe's story "Marella,"

[4] Alfred Hitchcock, *12 Stories They Wouldn't Let Me Do on TV* (New York: Dell Publishing Co., Inc., 1957).

which appears just as Poe wrote it, except that character designations have been added

<pre>
                    MARELLA

        I am dying, yet shall I live.

                    HUSBAND

        Marella!

                    MARELLA

        I repeat that I am dying but within me is

        a pledge of that affection--ah, how little!

        --which thou didst feel for me, Marella.

        And when my spirit departs shall the child

        live--thy child and mine, Marella's. But

        thy days shall be days of sorrow--that

        sorrow which is the most lasting of ·

        impressions, as the cypress is the most

        enduring of trees.

                    HUSBAND

        Marella! Marella! How knowest this?
</pre>

Unless an attempt is made to capture completely the archaic style of the writing, it is obvious that the language of this passage needs modernization. It is the only dialogue action in the story, by the way, so in deciding whether to modify it, the adapter must consider that he will have to create all the other lines himself.

Sometimes dialogue need not be rewritten but may have to be distributed in a different way. Writers of books and short stories often give their characters long, uninterrupted speeches. If naturalness and a real-life quality are to be achieved, these speeches must be broken up to secure more frequent interchange among the characters. The descriptive sections of stories, particularly of the older ones, also frequently need modernization before they can be given to a radio or TV narrator.

Deciding whether to modify existing dialogue or narrative passages is one of the most difficult decisions confronting you as an adapter. You must ask yourself whether the changes you make to update the language or to make it more appropriate for speaking will destroy essential qualities of style and flavor. You should also be alert to recognize material that can be carried over without change into the new version. Some of the material in Poe's stories, for example, needs to be modified and some does not. Much of the dialogue in "The Cask of Amontillado" is marked by a crispness and direction that makes it ideal just as it is for inclusion in a television or radio version. And it would be difficult for an adapter to compose better narration than that already existing in "The Tell-Tale Heart."

RADIO'S LACK OF THE VISUAL. The writer of radio adaptations frequently encounters unusual problems because he must make action clear to an audience that can see nothing. He is most likely to overlook this responsibility when he is converting for radio presentation, stage, movie, or television plays in which portions of the dialogue are clear only because the audience can see what is happening. In such a case the adapter must put into the dialogue the facts the listener needs to understand the scene. The problem is to provide this information without being obvious about it. Radio dialogue must give eyes to the listener but it must do so unobtrusively.

LENGTHENING THE MATERIAL

The adapter rarely has to lengthen the material he is treating, but there are instances when some expansion may be necessary. This is particularly true when he happens to be adapting a Bible story. Many are so pithily told that only their bare outlines exist in the original version. Often the adapter must invent surrounding incidents, and even characters, in order to give the story enough body for dramatic presentation. He must be careful, of course, to introduce innovations in keeping with the general spirit of the story to insure that the original material and his new creation merge into a meaningful, uniform entity.

An adapter may have to add new scenes for other reasons. Sometimes it is necessary to introduce information that does not appear in the original version. Poe's story "The Cask of Amontillado" concentrates on an act of revenge, but the author found it unnecessary to explain what motivated it. Most dramatizers of this story find they must fill in this detail. Or it may happen that an incident merely referred to in the original must be dramatized completely in the broadcast version to attain equal effectiveness. Cutting material from a script may demand the creation of a new scene to serve as a bridge between the two sections of the story. To provide transitions made necessary by cuts, adapters of Shakespearean plays are sometimes faced with the awesome responsibility of constructing lines that will be indistinguishable in style and quality from those of the great Elizabethan.

When you are writing a strict adaptation, however, you should not add material or make other changes simply because you think you can improve the story. Your obligation is to reflect as well as you can the original author's work. If you set out to improve matters, you may blunt what was distinctive in the original version. A student doing an adaptaton of de Maupassant's classic story "The Necklace" decided that the writer had slighted the events that took place after the supposed diamond necklace had been lost. He therefore invented a conflict between the man and wife precipitated by their misfortune, and he spent most of his time in developing that conflict. The script bore little relationship to the original story. De Maupassant's ironic twist at the end, the whole point of the story, was de-emphasized to the verge of extinction.

STEPS IN ADAPTATION

When you set out to adapt some other person's work into a radio or television script, you will be wise to follow a well-organized procedure instead of attacking the problem on a hit-or-miss basis. Only in that way can you be assured of a satisfactory result.

CHOOSING MATERIAL FOR ADAPTATION

You make your first critical decision when you decide on the material you plan to adapt. You should realize that some stories can be told satisfactorily only in the medium of their original creation. When they are separated from that medium by the process of adaptation, the quality that made them distinctive is lost. If you choose material of this type, you will be defeated before you begin. "The Pit and the Pendulum" of Edgar Allan Poe is an example of such a work. Most of this story deals with the thoughts and experiences of one man alone in a dungeon as he endures tortures of mind and body directed at him by hidden persecutors. The adapter might consider stream-of-consciousness narration as a means of revealing this material, but with no one else in the scene until the very last moment, even this technique would be strained into ridiculousness. The lack of motivation for dialogue, however, is not the only problem facing the adapter. The hero is never named and the nature of his offense, which led to his condemnation by the Inquisition, is not revealed. At the end of the story General LaSalle dashes to the rescue with not even a hint earlier that he might be on his way.

When one reads the story, he is not aware of these problems. By keeping our attention focused on the reeking pit, on the razor-sharp pendulum, and on the red-hot walls moving in to destroy their victim, Poe achieved a unity of impression that makes nothing else seem to matter. The dramatic form, perhaps unfortunately, does not provide an opportunity for concentration of this intensity. Audiences like leading characters to be named; when a man is condemned they want to know what he has done; and drama usually requires man-to-man relationships during some part of the story.

Writers who have attempted adaptations of this tale have been forced to fill in the gaps that Poe left. One adapter, in addition to naming the prisoner and defining his offense as firing on a church, even gave him a wife. He managed to motivate dialogue by having the prisoner imagine during periods of delirium that he was talking either with his wife or with his inquisitors. Considered simply as a drama without reference to Poe's story, this script was satisfactory. In adding the details the story needed to become a drama, however, the adapter dispersed the single, unique effect that Poe had created. (Not all of Poe's stories, incidentally, present these difficulties. Effective broadcast versions of such tales as "The Black Cat," "The Fall of the House of Usher," "The Tell-Tale Heart" and "The Cask of Amontillado" have been presented.)

A number of other stories have confronted adapters with insurmountable difficulties. Ambrose Bierce's "An Occurrence at Owl Creek Bridge" and Frank Stockton's "The Lady or the Tiger," like Poe's stories, seem to lose their special flavor when converted into dramatic form, as unsuccessful television versions have demonstrated. Ernest Hemingway's "The Killers" in its short-story form delivers a jolting impact, but adapters, forced to add details the original writer left unsaid, lose this effect. Neither the movie or television version was the story that Hemingway wrote. George Pierce Baker commented on the problem of turning Robert Louis Stevenson's story "The Sire de Maletroit's Door" into a one-act play. He pointed out that the storyteller could make us believe that in a twelve-hour period the heroine completely lost her liking for one man and fell madly in love with another whom she had just met, but presented in a drama such swift emotional changes become ridiculous and unbelievable.[5]

As a beginner, you would do well to turn to less challenging material than these stories. It is obvious that you should avoid trying to adapt any material whose basic effect depends largely on the medium in which it was originally presented. It is better to learn the craft of adaptation first with material that is easily translatable into the broadcast medium;

[5] George Pierce Baker, *Dramatic Technique* (Boston: Houghton Mifflin Company, 1919), p. 10.

only when you have mastered the basic techniques of the craft, should you attack problems that have thus far defeated even the most inventive minds.

SECURING THE RIGHTS

After choosing the subject matter for adaptation, you must consider next the question of who owns the original material. If it has been published, it has probably received a statutory copyright under the provisions of the Copyright Act. Under the present law, a statutory copyright is granted for a period of twenty-eight years and may be renewed for another twenty-eight years, making fifty-six years the maximum period for which material can be protected by statutory copyright in the United States. In 1962 the Congress amended the Copyright Act to extend all existing copyrights, and further revisions of the Act are in prospect. It is essential, therefore, that you acquaint yourself with the copyright conditions existing at the time you plan to do an adaptation.

Another form of copyright that comes into existence whenever a writer creates original material is common-law copyright, which protects material that has not been published. This type of copyright has no time limit, remaining in force until the material has been published. As soon as publication takes place, however, the material must be protected by a statutory copyright or it enters the public domain and becomes everybody's property. (The courts have held that the production and broadcasting of a script does *not* constitute publication. A writer may, therefore, permit his script to be broadcast without losing his common-law rights in the material.)

You may use freely only works that are in the public domain. You must secure permission to adapt any material protected by common-law or statutory copyright and you must reach an agreement with the holder of the rights regarding the conditions under which that use is to take place. If you fail to get permission to adapt material owned by someone else, you may get some writing experience from your effort, but you are likely to end up with nothing else except a possible law suit.

If the adapter is to be paid for his script, the principal problem to be decided is the division of the script fee between the adapter and the writer of the original material. You must also settle whether the original writer is to have the privilege of approving the final script. Some writers are more cautious than others about turning their works over to an adapter for transference into another medium. Wilbur Daniel Steele, the short-story writer, contacted by a Stanford University student regarding the adaptation of one of his short stories, stated that his terms were fifty per cent of the writer's fee. He made no request that he be permitted to approve, or even to see, the finished script. Other writers, in contrast, will not permit anyone to tamper with their works under any conditions.

STUDYING THE MATERIAL

If you are to deliver to a radio or television audience the sense and feeling of another person's creation, it is obvious that you must become as familiar with it as if you had created it yourself. You must understand every character in the story; you must know what his values are; you must recognize the motivations that drive him; you must have a thorough understanding of the plot structure and the relationship between the main and subplots; you must have a clear conception of the story's theme, for it will be your responsibility to project that theme in your adaptation.

PLANNING AND WRITING THE ADAPTATION

The next step is to decide what material in the original can be included in your adaptation. Wise selection is the principal key to the adapter's success. You must then determine what changes are needed to convert this material into a version that can be broadcast and prepare to create whatever new sequences may be required to bridge the gaps your choices have left. When these decisions have been made, they should be incorporated into a plan that can guide the writing of the script. This plan can be similar in design to the one used in writing any dramatic script.

EVALUATING THE RESULT

When you have written your first draft, you must evaluate it carefully to determine whether you have been faithful to the first author's intent. Even when you have adhered as strictly as you can to the original material, you may feel that you have failed to capture the full impact generated by the original material, or you will sense that there is a somewhat different quality to this effect when the story is presented in the new medium. If you have used all of your craftsmanship to prepare a faithful adaptation, you should accept this deterioration philosophically. It is sometimes an inevitable product of the process of adaptation itself. In some instances, you cannot make the changes that an adaptation requires without doing some damage to the story. A half-hour adaptation obviously cannot communicate the depth of experience inherent in a three-act play. And it may be, as has been noted, that the original story and medium are so inextricably linked that to separate one from the other inevitably filters the effect.

There are occasions, however, when just the opposite of this result takes place. It turns out that the new medium transmits the story more effectively than the original medium did. Thus, without intending to, you produce a greater work of art than the original writer produced.

QUESTIONS AND PROJECTS

1. Which in your opinion is the more difficult writing challenge: to adapt a difficult story for radio or television presentation or to create an original script?

2. James Michener has written two novels of an encyclopedic nature, *Hawaii* and *The Source*. Prepare a script plan for an hour radio or TV adaptation of one of these novels.

3. Stories in the *Bible* are often fragmentary or are told with extreme compactness. Select a Bible story told in a few verses and prepare a plan for a half-hour radio or TV adaptation of it.

4. Write a half-hour radio or TV version of Shakespeare's *Macbeth* that tells the basic story clearly without the use of a narrator.

5. Study Conrad Aiken's story of childhood insanity, "Silent Snow, Secret Snow." Decide whether this story could be successfully converted into a radio or television drama, and if so, explain how you would adapt, it.

6. Study the latest copyright laws passed by Congress and report to the class how they affect the work of the adapter.

11

Types of Drama

Certain dank gardens cry aloud for murder; certain old houses demand to be haunted; certain coasts are set apart for shipwreck.
Robert Louis Stevenson

The techniques for writing drama considered thus far are those employed by a writer who is entirely free to create characters and plots of his own. Such complete freedom is rare these days, however. The series he writes for may demand a certain type of content or feature leading characters created by someone else. Even the basic plot developments may be dictated by a program formula. The writer's freedom may also be limited by the way in which the story appears: techniques for writing serials differ somewhat from those used in writing dramas that are completed in one program period.

In addition to a command of· basic writing techniques, the dramatist needs to understand and respond to the unique challenges inherent in each of these different situations. In this chapter we review the ways in which dramatic programs are arranged for presentation on television and consider some major program types classified according to content. The emphasis is on the unique demands these various forms and content make on the writer.

PROGRAM ARRANGEMENTS

The program series that presents separate and distinct dramas each week is known as an *anthology*. The titles of such series are broad enough to encompass material differing widely in content and style. The pure anthology places no restriction on the writer except one of creating a drama that will fit into the allotted time period. Often, however, producers introduce a common element into each program which imposes some degree of uniformity. This element may be the appearance of the same host, or of the same actor portraying different roles each week; it may be concentration on a similar type of content: a number of anthologies have specialized in the adaptation of motion pictures or stage plays; Alfred Hitchcock specialized in tales of crime and horror; Rod Serling in the *Twilight Zone* focused on fantasy.

The appearance of the same host on each program places no restrictions on the writer's freedom to create, but the introduction of other common elements establishes boundaries that circumscribe invention. As the characteristics of each program become more concrete and uniform, there comes a point when the program can no longer be considered an anthology but becomes a series in which each program is written according to a set prescription.

The anthology, once one of television's most popular forms, has now been largely supplanted by the *series* drama, which features the same leading characters in separate and complete stories every week. The appearance of the same characters also ensures that each program will deal with the same type of content; thus, there are series that focus on the problems of lawyers, doctors, nurses, comedy writers, detectives, Western heroes, and mothers and fathers. In some instances the nature of the content and the plotting formula become exceptionally rigid. The TV series *Gilligan's Island* dealt entirely with the adventures of a group of people who found themselves cut off from the rest of the world on a tropical island. Most episodes in *The Fugitive* were based on the attempt of the leading character, a man convicted of murdering his wife, to avoid being captured. The main advantage of the series over the anthology is that it presents characters who have already engaged the audience's sympathy and attention and it guarantees a certain type of program content.

The creative challenge of the series writer is both easier and more. difficult than that of the anthology writer. It is easier in that the leading characters have already been created; the general content is decided; there may be a plotting formula to follow. It is more difficult in that the series writer must accommodate himself to the particular demands that give the series its identity and its individuality. Only within that framework is he free to invent new ideas. Producing ideas that meet series requirements and yet provide the freshness and diversity necessary to maintain interest may be a more taxing challenge than that facing the writer who is free to choose any dramatic material he wishes.

A third way for arranging broadcast drama is in *serial* form. The most common type is one that continues a story without ever bringing it to an end; there are distinct episodes in the everlasting saga, but one episode does not conclude until the next is well under way. Another type of serial follows a story through a number of sequences, but definitely brings one story to a conclusion before a new one is begun. Each story may feature the same characters, or it may involve entirely new characters each time, with a continuing host serving as a connecting link. Programs that ordinarily present a complete story each week occasionally present a story in several parts spread through a number of weeks.

Serials have been broadcast at all hours of the day, but the most common is the type known as the soap opera, presented during the daytime for an audience mainly composed of women. Not only is the form of these programs distinctive but the content is also marked by special characteristics. The discussion of this type will therefore be deferred until later in the chapter when we examine the soap opera in both form and content.

WESTERN, ADVENTURE, AND CRIME DRAMAS

Westerns, adventure stories, spy tales, crime and detective stories have ranked high in audience popularity ever since the beginning of drama on the air, and today they still provide television audiences with a large share of their entertainment. Dramas in these categories differ in a number of ways, but they also share many common characteristics and for that reason confront the writer with similar problems.

THE WESTERN

The Western drama reached its first television flowering in the late 1950s when home screens were deluged with horses, guns, and tall heroes in cowboy costume. The flood has since receded but a number of popular series have continued on the air for many years, and the creation of a new series at regular intervals makes the Western one of the standard offerings on the television screen.

THE CLASSIC WESTERN.   One of the youngest and most vital of the world's mythologies is the classic Western, which was developed by the motion-picture industry on a foundation laid down by the dime novels and wild-West shows of the late nineteenth century. The idealized stories it tells have little relation to life as it really existed in the old West. The leading character is a transcendent figure, like the Lone Ranger, who, representing the forces of good, rides into town to meet and vanquish the forces of evil before disappearing into the mists on the trail, to be seen no more. The motives of the villain whose machinations make his exploits necessary are often as cloudy as those of the hero, but one thing is clear; he is all bad and the hero is all good. Contrasts of white and black are characteristic of the classic Western; the grayness that distinguishes ordinary humanity is alien to the form. Other stock characters of the classic Western are the derelict professional—the lawyer, doctor, or minister—who betrays the creed of his profession except perhaps for one glorious, soul-restoring moment; the effete easterner who, disdaining the use of violence, is often humiliated or killed; the anemic good girl who is generally the school marm; and the bad girl who works in the saloon. The climactic moment of the Western is the final confrontation between the hero and the villain, which often takes place on a street deserted by the rest of the townspeople, who cower in fear behind doors and windows.

The viewer who tunes in these dramas is often motivated by a desire to escape the drudgery of everyday life by identifying himself with a character larger than life who solves problems by direct action. There is a certain appealing purity of response in a man-to-man fight or the crack of a six-shooter. The assurance that the good will be rewarded and the bad will be punished, moreover, provides a security similar to that generated by the primitive morality play or folk tale.

THE "ADULT" WESTERN.   Western drama that diverges in certain important respects from a ritualistic framework of chase and confrontation, although retaining many of the familiar ingredients, has come to be known as the "adult" Western. It reveals a West somewhat closer to what it really was, where virtue did not always triumph and the problems were not solved by the simple application of heroic violence. Characterization is more important in this form; the figures in the drama often take time to consider and discuss the situation; the hero is sometimes torn by doubt and indecision, he experiences fear, and he is not always victorious.

The TV series *Gunsmoke* is a good example of the "adult" Western. Its producers avoided many of the old clichés, but they were also influenced by some traditions of the classic form. Even though the Marshall sometimes failed, he was still an authentic hero. He was like the conventional Western hero also in that he experienced no deep romantic involvement. Some of the villains exhibited minor tendencies toward rightdoing, but many were as black and unredeemed as the worst of the unshaven bad men who people the classic Westerns. The character of "Doc," too, seemed inspired by that stock figure of the traditional form, the derelict professional, although "Doc" was by no means a derelict and in the practice of medicine he remained a professional. Kitty seemed to have her inspiration in the saloon girl of classic form. She was not bad, however, although one might speculate regarding the nature of the business she operated at the Long Branch Saloon. In placing most of the action in the Marshall's office, the street of the town, and the saloon, *Gunsmoke* exemplified the circumscription of setting characteristic of the classic Western.

OTHER ADVENTURE DRAMA

Many other adventure series, featuring neither cowboys nor horses, exhibit the features common to the Western drama. A good example is the syndicated TV series *Sea Hunt*. Its hero, Mike Nelson, used scuba diving equipment rather than a horse to reach each week's rendevous with destiny, and the arena of combat was the ocean depths rather than a village street, but the basic characters and stories were indistinguishable from those of the classic Western. Mike Nelson, like the Western hero, was a man of uncertain background who was strong, resolute, and decisive. The stories usually included a typical chase sequence involving one diver pursuing another through murky ocean depths against a sinister obbligato of bubbling noises ending in a hand-to-hand struggle between the diver hero and diver villain, which the hero won because of his superior skill and strength.

Other adventure series with similar characteristics may be set in old England where Robin Hood is the hero, in a combat zone of World War II where the exploits of an infantry sergeant or a flying colonel are featured, or in an early America peopled by such heroes as Daniel Boone or a Davy Crockett. The middle 1960s saw a burgeoning of the spy drama, whose heroes like those of the Western were masters of violence and whose villians were as sinister and as faceless as any unshaven bushwhacker who waylaid the hero in a Western draw.

THE CRIME DRAMA

The adventure drama in which the commission of a crime is the principal plot ingredient has always had an important place in broadcast schedules. There are a number of variations of the crime formula. At one pole is the drama that depends for its effect primarily on crime itself: it attracts those who find excitement in the spectacle of violence, a group that includes most people. At the other pole is the story in which crime is merely incidental to the development of an intellectual game which provides the viewer with a chance to match his wits against those of a detective in solving a mystery. Between these two extremes, the aspects of puzzle and violence undergo all degrees of variation.

THE CLASSIC DETECTIVE STORY.   Edgar Allan Poe originated the type of story that confronts readers with a perplexing crime which a brilliant detective solves with a series of breathtaking deductions. This tradition was carried on by the English writer A. Conan Doyle in the creation of Sherlock Holmes, the name that has become synonomous with "The Great Detective" throughout the world. The classic detective story has been immensely popular in book and short story form, but it has been a relatively rare item on television. One reason is that drama demands emotional values and the story that turns on the solving of an ingenious puzzle is largely an intellectual exercise. Furthermore, a listener is handicapped because he cannot stop and ponder the clues the way the reader of a book can, but must continually attend to what is happening to avoid being left far behind.

Despite the disadvantages, one TV series *Perry Mason*, which was based on the detective novels of Erle Stanley Gardner, did place some emphasis on deductive processes. It is true, that the chief attraction was the climactic courtroom scene in which Perry Mason confounded the district attorney by unmasking the real and previously unsuspected culprit, but the ingeniously plotted puzzle confronting Mason in each story and the skill with which the writers contrived a solution that would surprise the audience also contributed to the success of this series.

POLICE DETECTIVE STORIES.   The story based on an actual or fictional police investigation is another form of crime drama frequently presented on television. The principal emphasis in these dramas is on the dogged and laborious investigations carried out in solving crimes. This places the policeman at the opposite end of the spectrum from detectives in the Sherlock Holmes tradition, eccentric men who depend mainly on intuition and deductive powers to achieve solutions. The classic detective story, moreover, is almost always concerned with murder, for any lesser violence cannot justify the attention of the great detective, but dramatized police cases cover the gamut of crime.

THE PRIVATE-EYE DETECTIVE STORY.   A crime drama that falls somewhere between the classic detective story and the out-and-out adventure story is the drama dealing with the crime-solving activities of a private detective. Part of the attraction for the viewer lies in following the deductive process as the detective ferrets out clues and tracks down the criminal. Unlike the classic detectives, however, the private eye of television carries out his investigations under the constant threat of personal danger. It is the promise of violence and adventure that undoubtedly attracts many viewers to this type of program.

COMEDY-DETECTIVE DRAMAS.   In the 1930s a movie version of Dashiell Hammett's novel *The Thin Man* was produced. It was so successful that there followed a number of other movies based loosely on the same characters, how loosely is indicated by the fact that the term "thin man," which had referred to the victim of the crime in the first movie, became in the rest of them a reference to the detective Nick Charles. This series of movies established a type of crime drama in which the commission and detection of a crime serves mainly as a framework for comedy. *The Thin Man* itself was converted into a TV version which retained those characteristics.

SPECIAL WRITING TECHNIQUES

Most dramas in the Western, adventure, and crime category involve a struggle to attain a goal. They noticeably lack the reflection and deliberation characteristic of the decision-centered drama. Pursuit is a central element in many of these dramas and the narrative line is brisk and simple. The key to the writer's success is his ability to devise exciting action and to maintain nerve-wracking suspense.

PLOTTING WESTERN AND ADVENTURE DRAMAS.   A series of constantly alternating advances and reversals is the basic plotting pattern of the Western and adventure drama. The highest points are reached when the hero seems to be caught without a chance of escape and then through the exercise of great ingenuity or strength manages to evade the trap. An episode in *The Man from U.N.C.L.E.* series provides an example. The hero, representing a secret organization dedicated to preserving world peace, is surrounded in a farmyard by evil conspirators. He manages to slip into a silo unseen, but he hears his enemies climbing the ladder to reach him. The smooth circle of the silo offers no hiding place; there seems to be no escape from the trap. Then his eyes settle on the wheat that fills the silo. By the time his enemies reach the top he is completely hidden in it, and they leave without finding him.

PLOTTING CRIME AND DETECTIVE STORIES.   When a crime in a drama serves merely to generate excitement and adventure, the method of plotting is the same as that used in other types of adventure stories. The plotting of crime stories in which the emphasis is on the steps leading to the solution of a crime is quite another matter, however. Most detective stories of this type are unique in that they are plotted backwards. You must begin by figuring out the circumstances of the crime. This involves deciding who is to be killed, who is to do the killing, how the murder is to be committed, and the place it occurs. Of particular importance at this time is devising a distinctive idea or "gimmick" which will give the story some degree of individuality. This special idea may be an unusual method of committing the crime. A story on the *Alfred Hitchcock* series, for example, featured a frozen leg of lamb as the murder weapon. The woman who used it to do away with her husband then proceeded to cook and share it with the policeman who came to investigate the crime. Other special ideas may involve an original way of concealing the body, a unique method of escape by the culprit, a point of law turned either to the detective's or to the criminal's advantage, a surprising motive, or an unusual or particularly ingenious method of solving the crime.

Your next task is to develop the process through which detection takes place. The elements in this process are: 1) to confront the detective with the crime; 2) to produce the information he needs to solve it; 3) to arrive at a solution; and 4) to provide whatever final explanation may be necessary.

One of the strongest traditions of the classic detective story is that the audience must be stunned with surprise when the identity of the criminal is finally revealed. One technique for surprising the audience is to select as the culprit the "most unlikely person," the individual who, in the light of all reason and expectation, could not possibly have committed the crime. In some stories the detective has turned out to be the criminal and in one novel the narrator telling the story was finally revealed to be the guilty party.

A modification of the "most unlikely person" approach is to throw intense suspicion on one or two leading characters and then reveal the criminal to be a character not previously suspected—a technique used consistently in the *Perry Mason* series. The audience knew, of course, that Mason's client, usually a young and beautiful woman, was bound to be innocent, because the program's formula did not permit Perry Mason to defend a guilty person. The suspense lay in trying to guess which of the other characters would turn out to be the murderer. This series was also successful in engendering suspense at the beginning of the program by permitting the audience to speculate which person, among a number of characters, would turn out to be the victim of the crime.

Ingenious use of the technique of gradual revelation is the principal means of achieving surprise in telling a detective story. You must lead the viewers step by step to the solution of the crime, but you must not permit them full knowledge of the final solution until the last fact is conveyed. The best detective stories are those in which this final revelation causes all the other facts to fall into place, thus making the solution completely understandable without further explanation.

One problem a writer faces is to play fair with the audience by revealing the clues the detective finds without at the same time killing surprise by telegraphing the solution to the crime. There are a number of ways of including clues without indicating their significance: 1) divide the clue from its application to the story by a period of time, thus disguising the connection between the two; 2) include an important clue among a number of other casual incidents which belong in the story but have no particular relevance to the solution of the crime; 3) deflect the audience's attention from a clue by following its presentation immediately with exciting action; and 4) present an item of information that actually has no relevance at the point it is introduced but becomes meaningful only when the detective connects it to the crime.

To lay a trail of fake clues would not be fair to your audience but fairness does not require that every single clue must be as available to the audience as it is to the detective, although purists might insist that this should be so. In almost all detective stories the detective sees certain things the audience is not permitted to see, or if the audience is permitted a glimpse, the detective certainly has the better view.

Some detective story writers make little attempt to surprise their audience but concentrate instead on the process of detection. Suspicion may be thrown equally on a number of suspects, one of whom is eventually disclosed to be the murderer. The audience may even be invited at the beginning of the story to observe the crime and the criminal; in such instances all interest lies in the work of the detective, and whatever surprise is produced must relate to his ingenuity in tracking down the culprit.

PLAUSIBILITY IN PLOTTING.   We have noted before that a drama must meet the test of plausibility, but viewers do not demand absolute reasonableness, and in the field of adventure and crime it seems they are willing to make the greatest concessions of all. Most of the episodes of the *Perry Mason* series ended with the lawyer forcing a confession from the real criminal in the courtroom. That these criminals, who to that point had acted with complete coolness and calculation, would collapse into a confession merely because Perry Mason pointed the finger of suspicion at them was beyond belief. Yet the audience was willing to accept these confessions because in the one-hour time period of the program they provided the only means through which Perry Mason could conclude the case on a triumphant note. In the school of adventure drama exemplified by the James Bond stories, wildly implausible characters and events are tolerated because they provide an audience with fun and excitement. It the episode from *The Man from U.N.C.L.E.* referred to previously, the audience was asked to believe that it might be possible for a man to hide by immersing himself in a silo full of wheat without suffocating.

The viewer is not only more willing to accept implausibility in adventure stories, but he is also less aware that credulity is being strained simply because he does not have time to think about what might be possible under a given set of circumstances. Excitement and action come in such copious amounts that discernment is blunted and logical analysis is crowded out.

CHARACTERIZATION.   Most adventure and crime dramas are melodramas in which the emphasis is on action rather than on the delineation of character. Usually, in fact, the writer plots the adventures first and then creates the characters needed to carry out the plot. If any of the characters has distinctiveness and individuality, it is the hero, the person whose strength, courage, ingenuity, or intuition overcomes the difficulties or solves the problem. Yet even his characterization is often a narrow one, being presented only in those elements that are specifically connected with the plot elements of the story. Perry Mason, for example, was not developed as a complete person. The audience was permitted no insight into his character beyond those qualities directly related to his role as a detective and lawyer.

THE FANTASY

The fantasy is not as prevalent on television as the adventure story, but there have been a number of series of this type and a few of them have been distinguished additions to the broadcasting scene. In the middle 1960s there was a sudden outpouring of this kind of program. The writer venturing into this field needs to understand, first of all, what a fantasy is.

A DEFINITION OF FANTASY

One main characteristic distinguishes the fantasy from other types of drama: it is a drama of events that, measured by natural law and available knowledge, could not actually take place. Other dramas, in contrast, portray events that could occur even though they have not. Note that a drama is not a fantasy simply because it exists in the imagination of the writer, for all drama is to some degree imaginative. Fantasy, moreover, is not drama that is merely highly improbable. A drama is a fantasy only if it portrays events or phenomena that could not possibly have happened. It is on this basis that any drama taking place at some future time is usually considered to be a fantasy.

A drama should not be classed as a fantasy, either, simply because it provokes horror or revulsion. The *Alfred Hitchcock* series sometimes produced dramas that were truly fantastic, but it also presented others mistakenly classed as fantasies because of the horror they induced. There was one, for example, called "The Speciality of the House" which hinted that certain guests at a restaurant sometimes turned up as the main dish for future guests. The vision it aroused was certainly repellent, but it was not a fantasy; the events could have happened.

TYPES OF FANTASIES

The analysis that follows classifies fantasies according to their content. Not every fantasy ever written will fit into one of the categories, for some are so singular that they defy classification, nor should the groups be looked on as being mutually exclusive.

MYTHS, MAGIC, AND MONSTERS.   The largest class of fantasies includes those stories that involve some application of sheer magic. Their diversity is great, presenting characters that range from the frightening monster created by *Frankenstein* to the entrancing little puppet *Pinocchio*, and involving moods varying from the chilling horror of a *Dracula* to the inimitable drolleries of an *Alice's Adventures in Wonderland*. *The Friendly Giant*, a favorite of child listeners to educational television stations, is a modern equivalent of the ogre who inhabited the imaginations of medieval storytellers, except that the motives and actions of *The Friendly Giant* are benign and helpful instead of being malevolent and destructive. Many of the cartoons occupying the TV hours designed for children are magical in nature in that they endow animals with human speech and culture and provide characters with a capacity for instant healing after the most catastrophic assault and battery.

THE SUPERNATURAL.   The line between stories of magic and stories of the supernatural is not a very sharp one since events in both groups defy the laws of nature. Generally, however, the supernatural designation refers to that large group of legends usually known as ghost stories and to tales involving such a phenomenon as telepathy, which extends psychological power beyond the limits usually recognized by scientists.

THE WORLD OF THE FUTURE.   The writers of many fantasies have imagined the world as it might exist in some future period. Some of these works were written not merely to amuse their readers but also to establish philosophical points about modern life and culture. Aldous Huxley's *Brave New World,* in picturing a future people dominated by the machine, created a biting satire on contemporary society; George Orwell in *1984* dramatically delineated the effect of dictatorship; and William Golding in portraying the reversion to animal savagery of a group of boys in *Lord of the Flies* underscored the weaknesses of mankind in general.

MOVEMENTS IN TIME.   The conjecture that periods of time do not exist consecutively but concurrently is the foundation for stories in which an individual travels from one level of time to another. This idea has provided the plotting framework for innumerable stories of fantasy.

OTHER WORLDS.   A principal element in much fantasy fiction of the present day is the voyage by humans to other worlds in the universe or the arrival on the earth of beings from outer space. Some of these stories fall legitimately within the fantasy category, but many of them utilize a fantasy element merely to trigger a tale of adventure. The story of a spaceman threatened by a monster on Mars is not much different in its basic characteristics from one that portrays a Western hero being stalked by a bad man in a sombrero.

SCIENCE FICTION.   A popular form of fantasy is one in which the writer projects future developments that could arise from the application of natural laws already established. Sometimes actual scientific discoveries have been foreshadowed by stories of this type. The atomic submarine of our day was described in many of its details by Jules Verne in his fantasy *Twenty Thousand Leagues Under the Sea,* written in the nineteenth century.

BORDERLINE FANTASIES.   Some stories rest on the borderline between fantasy and other types of drama. An example is the story that creates a world of the past about which we know almost nothing as William Golding did in *The Inheritors,* which detailed the problems and frustrations of the Neanderthal. Another borderline fantasy is one in which the writer leaves the audience to decide whether the events are evidences of powers that surmount natural laws or are subject to rational explana-

tions. A good example is Henry James' *The Turn of the Screw* (dramatized for the stage and movies as *The Innocents*). From one point of
view this story may be accepted as a powerful tale of ghosts and therefore a fantasy; from another the events may be explained as delusions
affecting its chief characters, an interpretation that makes this story
not a fantasy at all but a tragic story of disordered minds.

A story revolving around an event that seems to be clearly fantastic
in nature, but which turns out in the end to have a rational explanation
is also a borderline fantasy. A story portraying ghosts who turn out
to be illusions contrived by natural means is an example. Another example was a drama presented on the *Twilight Zone*. It told of space ex-
plorers, shot from the earth in a rocket vehicle, who landed on a planet
they could not identify. Most of the program portrayed their exploration
of the strange land into which they had been catapulted. In the end
it was revealed that their space vehicle had actually returned to earth.
The weird landscape in which they had landed was that of the Nevada
desert.

PLOTTING THE FANTASY

A number of general approaches may be used in plotting the fantasy;
it may be goal-centered or decision-centered or it may be the type of
plot designed to reveal the explanation of some mysterious event or
strange phenomenon. Since the quality that distinguishes the fantasy
from other types of stories is the existence of an assumption that defies
accepted natural law or existing conditions, it follows that the unique
problems inherent in plotting the fantasy are connected with the manipulation of this fantastic premise.

THE FANTASTIC PREMISE.   The writer, first of all, needs to have a clear
idea of just what his nature-defying premise is. Secondly, he should
make certain that this premise plays a key role in the development
of the story. A story in which a fantastic assumption is merely incidental
would be a strange concoction indeed.

To exemplify the role of the fantastic premise in plotting, let us review
Eric Knight's short story "The Flying Yorkshireman" as it was dramatized by Charles Jackson. The chief characters are Sam and Mully Small,
who are on vacation in the United States from their home in Yorkshire,
England. The fantastic premise in this story is Sam's idea that if one
has faith enough he can fly. The story, using the plotting structure
of the goal-centered play, portrays Sam's varying degrees of success
and failure in accomplishing this feat.

He first achieves actual flight in his room at night when his wife is asleep, but this adventure has a disappointing ending when he falls clumsily to the floor and wakens her. The next day he flies again when he leaps over a fence seven feet high to catch a dog which has escaped from a friend. Shortly thereafter he jumps fifteen feet and begins to attract attention as an athlete. Then in a most amusing scene he reveals to his wife that he is not really jumping but flying. One of the inimitable touches of this scene is that she takes the revelation with complete composure, noting only the utilitarian aspects of flying—that it can be helpful in washing windows and removing cobwebs from the ceiling.

Next a reporter is let in on the secret and he immediately scents the commercial possibilities inherent in exhibiting Sam's amazing talent. A successful demonstration for the press leads to a public showing at Madison Square Garden. Prior to the exhibition, however, Sam is interviewed by an ominous stranger who persuades Sam that people will be unable to accept his amazing feat as actually taking place but will rationalize it as auto suggestion or mass hypnotism. Their disbelief, the stranger says, may make it difficult for Sam to fly. Naturally, when Sam tries to fly in Madison Square Garden, he is unable to get off the ground.

The next day Sam, in disgust at himself and with a sudden burst of faith, flies through the door and alights on top of the highest skyscraper in Manhattan. There he stays despite the disturbance he causes among the excited citizenry and the consequent requests from the authorities to remove himself. Finally his faithful wife Mully climbs to his side and after a touching exchange of protestations of love for each other, Sam takes her by the hand and together they fly, not down to the streets of New York, but back across the Atlantic to their home in Yorkshire. Sam's goal has been triumphantly achieved. Not only has he flown but his faith has made it possible for Mully to fly too.

This plot, in addition to being motivated mainly by the fantastic premise, as a fantasy should be, is marked by two other desirable qualities: it presents a single fantastic assumption and the idea is a simple one. Fantasies do not need to be complicated to be effective. One of the best remembered of the radio fantasies written by Arch Oboler told how a woman gradually turned into a cat. That was all there was to the story and that was all that was needed to chill its millions of listeners.

The writer of a fantasy should also strive to realize the full potentialities inherent in his fantastic premise. The idea that a certain individual had the power to destroy his enemies merely by shouting, "Drop dead!" at them was the starting point for a radio fantasy. This idea alone was not enough for a completely developed drama, however. Fortunately the writer was equal to the task of inventing the twist he needed to

bring his story to a satisfactory conclusion. As the play ended, the character visited a canyon in the far west and in exultation at his ascendency
over mankind he screamed to the heavens, "Drop dead! Drop dead!"
Alas, the words were reflected from the canyon walls and their author
was killed by the malign power of his own echo.

Finally, it is important for the writer to determine whether his fantastic
premise can actually generate the complications necessary to produce
a satisfactory plot. To create a being, for example, who has the power
to do anything is to remove most of the potentialities for suspense and
excitement from a play. The writers of *Superman* sometimes faced this
problem.

BELIEVABILITY AND FANTASY.   To raise the question of believability
with a type of writing that is essentially unbelievable may seem ridiculous, but it is a fact that plausibility is just as important in the fantasy
as it is in any other form of drama. What happens is that the writer
and the audience strike a bargain: for the purposes of the drama the
viewers agree to accept the fantastic premise, but in all other respects
they demand that the writer's depiction of events and characters be
convincing and believable. He is even contained by the limits imposed
by his fantastic premise. If he contrives events that cannot be supported
by the assumption of nonreality he has led his audience to accept, he
exceeds the bounds of believability. There is a good illustration of this
point in "The Flying Yorkshireman." When Sam flies to the top of a
high New York building and perches there, his wife climbs up the outside of the building to beg him to come down. Believing that she could
really make the fearful climb stretches our credulity just a little. Then
Sam and Mully fly off together, but this does not bother us at all, for
it is simply an extension of the fantastic premise that Sam can fly, which
the audience has agreed to accept.

IDEAS FOR FANTASIES.   A device for developing plotting ideas, which
is especially well suited to creating fantasies, is to ask the question,
"What if?" In the case of the fantasy, of course, the "what if?" is directly
related to a fantastic premise. "What if?" questions that could lead to
fantasies are the following: What if the world's population continues
increasing at the present rate? What if scientists actually conquer aging?
What if we succeed in contriving machines to do all of our work? What
if a person goes back in time and kills his grandfather?

Sometimes the fantasies motivated by these questions are not merely
simple responses to a "what if?" but evolve into extended imaginative
creations. The dilemma created by the character who goes back in time
to change a historical occurrence has been solved by some writers

through the creation of parallel courses of human events which go down the centuries side by side, a conception that testifies to the richness of the writer's imagination. Ray Bradbury in "Mars Is Heaven," postulated the existence of beings on Mars who were able to assume the appearance and recall the past of the dead relatives of invading earthlings. When they had led these earthlings into believing that they had found the heaven of their relatives and thus lulled them into abandoning their usual security measures, the Martians returned to their original ominous forms and destroyed the invaders. This elaborate product of the imagination may easily have been set in motion by the simple query: What if heaven is located on one of the other planets?

BIOGRAPHICAL AND HISTORICAL DRAMA

Drama that deals with real people and with real events has not occupied an important place in American broadcasting, but there have been some significant ventures in this field. It is of special interest to those broadcasters whose purposes are primarily educational and it may provide unusual and challenging programming for commercial stations and networks. It should be pointed out that our concern here is with the type of drama purporting to convey what really happened, not the drama in which a real event or a historical personage serves merely as a trigger for the writer's imagination. What results from this latter process is historical or biographical fiction, which is written in much the same way as any work in which the dramatist creates his own plot and characters.

The writing of strict biography and history demands special abilities and techniques. Fertility of imagination may not be essential, but some degree of inventiveness is required. To this must be added the skill to find the facts, the discernment to select the significant and dramatic from the material available, and the power to translate these facts into strong, arresting drama.

THE TASK OF RESEARCH

If the writer of biographical or historical drama is to portray true events, he must develop techniques for finding out what really happened. There are often serious obstacles to discovering the necessary facts. Sometimes the historical record is a sparse one; we know for sure only a few isolated facts about the life of William Shakespeare, for instance. Speculation and inference must fill in the rest of his story. Even when a great deal is known about a person, there may be gaps in the record which keep us from knowing why or how a subject acted in a particular situation. The missing facts may be of critical importance in determining whether we approve or disapprove of him.

A second obstacle to discovering the truth is the existence of conflicting information. What are you to do in such a situation? One step is to separate interpretations and opinions from statements of facts. When the facts themselves are in conflict, your only recourse is to use your best judgment to decide which of the various versions is most likely to be correct. In deciding you might ask some of the following questions: What is the general reputation of a given authority for accuracy? Were his feelings toward the subject, whether friendly or hostile, likely to warp his presentation? Did he have a thesis to support which might cause him to twist the record? Was he really in a position to know what went on? Which version is most consistent with what you already know about your subject's character or the times in which the incident occurred?

A third obstacle for the television writer who must turn out scripts in short order, is lack of time. He cannot spend five years researching and writing as Catherine Drinker Bowen did in composing her biography of John Adams. Consequently he must depend for much of his information on biographies and histories written by others. He should not entirely ignore primary materials, however, for they can give him a feeling for the time and an understanding of the people which goes deeper than the mere surface acquaintance provided by another's biography or history. Letters and diaries, moreover, in recording the choice of words, pet expressions, and idiosyncrasies of a subject can be a valuable guide to the writing of dialogue. Secondary sources, in short, contain information for the main development of the script; primary sources can provide the flavor that gives it the pulse of life.

A fourth obstacle to finding the truth is to begin research with a preconceived notion of what that truth is. In such a situation you are likely to grasp eagerly at those facts supporting your ideas and discount those conflicting with them. The biographer or historian must be ready to see his pet theories dashed by the facts. The first necessity in research is an open mind. The theme, plot, and characterization of a biographical or historical drama should emerge from the material rather than be imposed on it.

Obstacles there may be, but it is clear that the person who aspires to write what is true must carry out a diligent and organized program of research. He must assemble as much information as he can in the time he has, more than he can possibly use, for only then does he have the opportunity to select the material that will give the maximum point and purpose to his script. He must have the imagination and energy to follow leads. He must keep a special lookout for material that is particularly appropriate for presentation in the dramatic form. This becomes largely a task of finding those revealing details that will convert a remote and abstract figure of the past into a living, breathing human being.

A good example of such a detail is one that Barbara Tuchman said she used in writing about William Howard Taft, our most corpulent of presidents. Taft, on recovering from an illness, sent a telegram to his friend Elihu Root saying that he had been out riding and was feeling fine, to which Root promptly wired back, "How is the horse feeling?" Allan Sloane's script about H. L. Mencken provides another example. Sloane closed this script, "Bring on the Angels," with a quotation from Mencken which underscored his uniqueness as a person and his humanity. Said Mencken: "If after I depart this vale, you ever remember me and have thought to please my ghost, forgive some sinner— and wink at a homely girl."

WRITING THE DRAMA

In addition to presenting the facts about a person or event, the writer of biographical or historical drama must create a play that has the attributes necessary for all successful drama—the capacity to catch and sustain attention, vivid characters, a well-constructed plot, and the power to arouse emotions. Sometimes the things one must do to write a good play seem to conflict with the requirement of reflecting people and events as they really existed. Let us examine this problem.

REFLECTING THE TRUTH.   Having discovered the truth about a person or event, the writer's next task is to reflect that truth in his script. One obstacle he faces is that he cannot escape inventing some of the material he presents. Dialogue is a good example. There is usually no way of knowing precisely what historical characters actually said during a given episode and yet if the dramatist is not granted the privilege of devising words to clothe a situation, there can be no drama. He must rely on invention also when there are gaps in the information he needs to complete his dramatization, for he cannot, like the writer of a book, step outside the story for a moment to make the honest admission to his readers that he simply does not know what happened in this particular instance. Always, of course, his invention should be consistent with what is known. The dialogue he devises should communicate the import of the situation as it actually took place and should be in keeping with the style and character of the people speaking. He should also refrain from using his imagination too much or what he writes can no longer be properly described as biography or history.

An attempt to convert a narrative into a rattling good story may also warp the truth. Curious instances, unusual anecdotes, and striking detail may make a drama exciting and interesting but they may also create a misleading version of the events. Another cause of distortion is the desire of the biographer to shield from public view a side of a contemporary subject that may be shocking or unpleasant. When we simply ignore what is discordant, we are on the road to creating fiction.

SELECTING MATERIAL.   Considering that broadcast periods are relatively short and that dramatic treatment takes more time than any other type of treatment, the writer must select certain facts for presentation and ignore the rest. This is true even of the writer of a book, whose means for communicating information is so much more efficient than the playwright's. Even if a writer could present everything about a subject, he would not do so, for selection and emphasis are part of his function as an artist. His obligation is to select the material which, after imaginative arrangement, will provide his work with unity and meaning and invest it with dramatic power. On the other hand, he must be sure that in doing so he does not put edges on a historical character who in real life did not have those edges.

The process of selection is illustrated by "Bring on the Angels," Allan Sloane's play about H. L. Mencken, presented at the time of that famous writer's death. With a multitude of events confronting him, Sloane had to decide what he could present in a half hour that would be of any significance. He chose to focus on a few years in Mencken's youth when he began his career as a newspaper reporter. He suggested the sweep of an entire life, however, by opening his script just before Mencken's death, going back in retrospect to the earlier years, and returning finally to the death scene. Even those earlier years could not be covered in their entirety in a single program, of course. Sloane gained further focus by concentrating on the events that demonstrated the beginnings of Mencken's iconoclastic irreverance for the traditional and conventional.

Another way a dramatist often exercises selection is to choose only one story for dramatization from many that illustrate the same characteristic. The life of a generous man may be full of incidents reflecting his generosity. One of these incidents, dramatized fully, stands for all the others which cannot be covered.

THEME.   A biographical or historical script may or may not have a readily identifiable theme. Sometimes the mere telling of the facts about a significant person or event provides sufficient substance in itself. At other times, the story may make not one but a number of statements about the human condition. In fact, the writer may realize that the material he has discovered leads him irresistibly toward a theme; to ignore or muffle a message that clamors to be revealed would be to deprive a script of much of its strength and meaning.

The process of selection is an important factor in the establishment of a theme. By retaining certain facts and leaving out others, the dramatist may find that he is inevitably formulating an underlying idea for his work. If this idea is a defensible one, it is quite proper that he carry out his selection with the object of establishing it, provided, of course, that he does not distort facts or suppress information which would refute it. A strong thesis may add to the power of a script by enhancing its unity and significance.

A good example of a historical script that focused on more than one underlying idea was the television adaptation by George Roy Hill and John Whedon of Walter Lord's book on the sinking of the *Titanic, A Night to Remember*. The principal point made by the script was that fate had played a major role in bringing about a tragedy which cost more than 1500 lives. This theme was summarized in the concluding narration of the script.

NARRATOR

If the <u>Titanic</u> had heeded any of the six

iceberg messages...if the night had been

rough or moonlit...if she had hit the ice-

berg fifteen seconds later...if her water-

tight bulkheads had been one deck higher...

if she had carried enough boats...if the

<u>Californian</u> had only heeded and come. Had

any of these "ifs" turned out right, every

life might have been saved. But they all

went against her. And never again has man

been quite so confident. An age had come

to an end.

In addition to this main theme, some subsidiary points were established. One was the unbelievable carelessness of the *Titanic's* officers in running the ship. No lifeboat drill was ever held and the officers airily dismissed radio warnings about the presence of icebergs, permitting the ship to continue on its course at twenty-two knots. Another idea effectively projected by this dramatization was the insidious way in which tragedy approached. Many lost their lives simply because they refused to believe that the unsinkable *Titanic* could actually sink, preferring its apparent stability to the instability of a flimsy lifeboat. Finally, this dramatization reflected the discrimination that operated against the poor people who were passengers aboard the ship. When the *Titanic* finally went down, it carried with it fifty-four children, all but one of whom were steerage passengers. The story of the *Titanic's* sinking is a powerful and dramatic one in itself, but the selection exercised by the writers of this adaptation to establish thematic ideas added immeasurably to the power of the television version.

A dramatist may discover in his material a theme that contradicts the usual public impression of a person or the accepted version of a well-known event. If he can support such a theme, it may invest his work with unusual interest. More often his work will reflect a theme that most people are inclined to accept, but which may actually be more questionable than a controversial one. A good example is the theme exemplified by many motion-picture biographies—that persistence will win out against all obstacles. Such a theme is misleading because it invests complex developments with too much simplicity and transforms quite different events into indistinguishable versions of the same type of success story.

PLOTTING.   The procedures that have been described for plotting all dramas can be applied to biographical and historical dramas. Many of them can be made to turn on the struggle for a goal or the making of a decision. In some cases neither of these approaches fits and a unique plotting formula must be discovered which will fit the material. This is particularly true of the historical drama in which the event rather than the person dominates. In the drama of the *Titanic,* for example, there was no key character around whom the story could revolve. The focus was on the sinking itself, and the individual stories of various people were tangential to this central event.

MAINTAINING INTEREST.   One problem you face in dealing with a well-known person or event is that the audience already knows how the story came out. Developing suspense under such circumstances is virtually impossible, but there are other techniques for arousing and maintaining the interest of the audience. One of these techniques is to take full advantage of the fact that you are dealing in truth. The line in the opening format of the *Dragnet* series—"What you are about to see is true. The names have been changed to protect the innocent."—was a powerful arrester of interest. The writers of the television version of *A Night to Remember* used the same device. In the opening moments of this script a narrator speaks to the audience as follows: "What you will see actually took place. It is as accurate as man can reconstruct that night. This is not fiction. It is fact."

Another way of stimulating interest is to develop expectancy through the use of the technique of foreshadowing. The audience may know most of what happened, but its interest in seeing it happen can be sharpened through this means. The technique of gradual revelation, used in combination with foreshadowing, can reinforce the effect. In an early part of the TV version of *A Night to Remember* the audience is told that the *Titanic* has lifeboats for only a fraction of its passengers and crew. Later this information is made more specific: there is room in the lifeboats for only one-third of the ship's complement. The existence of icebergs in the path of the *Titanic* is referred to in the first minutes of the drama. The crew and passengers ignore the warnings, but the viewers do not. They know what happened later and they shiver with expectancy. The process that led to the sinking of the *Titanic* is handled with consummate skill, again through the use of gradual revelation. Not until late in the script, for example, does the designer of the ship admit that the gash in the side is so long that the ship must inevitably sink. Up to this point even the sophisticated viewer could in his imagination entertain some hope. The skill of the writers has provided him with the feeling of living through those moments on the *Titanic* as they might have been experienced by someone who was actually on board.

CHARACTERIZATION. If a biographical drama fails to bring its chief character vividly to life, it fails almost completely. The task for the writer is primarily one of character revelation. The character exists. His task is to discover the character and then transmit his vision to an audience.

Characterization for the writer of historical drama is not quite so crucial, for his emphasis is likely to be on the events rather than on the people. Providing these events with an adequate exposition may actually take most of the time he has at his disposal. If he can, however, he should try to present historical figures who are more than mere stereotypes. Vivid characters revealed in depth can invest the cold facts of history with warmth and humanity.

THE DAYTIME SERIAL

One of the most enduring forms of broadcast drama is the daytime serial, often called soap opera because so many of its sponsors are soap makers. Established on radio in the early 1930s, it soon became the most important element in morning and afternoon programming. Just before World War II more than half a hundred serials were being broadcast daily. Television eventually drove the radio serial from the air, as it did almost all radio drama, but by the time the last of them disappeared in the early 1960s, the TV version of this form was occupying as important a place in daytime schedules as had its radio counterpart.

The serial has survived in the face of the most withering attack ever launched against a form of broadcasting. The programs and the people who view them have been denounced by critics, psychologists, and sociologists. Even those responsible for serials have occasionally joined the chorus of rebukers. One of the most sarcastic comments came from Max Wylie, a former writer of serials, who in his book *Radio and Television Writing*, described them as a "gloomy, watery, wailing, histrionic procession of Virtue, Irresolution, and Just-Plain-Bilge."[1] Viewers of soap operas have been so derided that many who habitually listen do so shamefacedly or in secret, unwilling to admit their addiction even to their closest friends.

Although the general attitude of those who write about soap operas is a disapproving one, there has in the welter of denunciation been an occasional complimentary remark. The critic Gilbert Seldes, although he was appalled by their content, nevertheless described the flexibility of form developed by the serials as radio's single notable contribution to the art of fiction.[2] Marya Mannes, in an otherwise scathing article, remarked on the ingenuity of the plotting and the fine ear for natural dialogue displayed by their writers.[3] At one time a soap opera *Against the Storm* even received a Peabody award, which is given for excellence in broadcasting.

The criticism leveled against daytime serials is not irrelevant to the writer who works in this field, but it is not the function of this book to determine the soap opera's status as an art form or to discuss its social implications. Our concern is with the peculiar characteristics of the soap opera and the special techniques employed in writing it. The prototype for today's TV serial is the form developed in radio. Viewers who remember those radio days will note that the ubiquitous organ, whose surging notes opened a scene and signaled its conclusion, has been retained. In some respects, however, the TV form has established conventions quite different from its radio predecessor. We now examine

---

[1] Max Wylie, *Radio and Television Writing* (New York: Holt, Rinehart and Winston, Inc.), 1950, p. 289.

[2] Gilbert Seldes, *The Great Audience* (New York: The Viking Press, Inc., 1951), p. 116.

[3] Marya Mannes, "Massive Detergence," The Reporter, Vol. 25 (July 6, 1961), p. 41.

the TV daytime serial with particular attention to the characteristics that distinguish it from other forms of drama. Much of what is said can also be applied to the writing of serials broadcast in the evening.

THE VIEWING SITUATION

One circumstance that requires special consideration by the writer is the fact that no one can view every episode of a serial. Even the most ardent devotees of a given program must occasionally miss seeing it. The viewers of nighttime serials are also not able to watch every episode in a story. This contrasts with the usual situation in which a specific drama is viewed in its entirety from beginning to end. Serials must be written so that the members of the audience can follow the story despite the gaps in their viewing. That writers of the now-departed radio serials were successful in preserving continuity was evidenced by the experience of a neighbor of mine who listened to a succession of daytime serials only once a week on Fridays when she did her ironing, and yet maintained that she could follow each story and keep track of the characters without difficulty.

In addition to missing an episode here and there, a regular viewer may miss a substantial number of episodes consecutively because of vacations. She expects to pick up the story on her return without undue loss of orientation. Even the viewing of a given episode, taking place as it does during the working day, is likely to be interrupted by household emergencies. The writer must also remember that a housewife's domestic chores may keep her from watching the screen constantly; he must make it possible for her to keep track of what is happening through what she hears.

THE SERIAL IDEA.   The first response to the peculiarities of the viewing situation can be said to be the serial idea itself—the telling of a story that, in defiance of the Aristotelian dictum, has no beginning, no middle, and no end, but goes on and on forever. This characteristic is particularly effective in luring back to the program the listener who may have been absent for a considerable period of time, for she will quickly recognize the characters and their same old problems, even though the specific complications may have changed. It is this change in the nature of the complications that provides whatever independent stories there are in the structure of the serial. A dilemma of some type provides the core around which each sequence is unified; the over-all story maintains its never-ending character, however, because one problem is never completely resolved until another descends.

CONSTANT TENSION. With previous listeners pulled back to the program by the nature of the serial form itself, the task of the writer is to generate an immediate renewal of interest. This need leads to another characteristic quality of the daytime serial—the maintenance of tension at a constant fever pitch. There must be "perpetual emotion," as someone has said. Conventional dramas have their flow and ebb; excitement rises to the climax but is dispersed with a resolution which permits the audience to relax. The writer of the serial cannot afford any lulls in the action. A listener who tuned in to find the heroine free from jeopardy and at peace might find no reason to continue listening. Broadcasters have discovered that domestic happiness is fatal to the daytime serial. The writer must never be deflected from his primary task of creating anxiety and suffering.

In focusing on trouble to produce emotional responses the serial is not different from other dramatic forms, but it is different in that the adversity in which it engulfs its characters is constant and consistently agonizing. The people of soap operas are catapulted almost without a break from one predicament to another. The troubles do not necessarily come singly either. On *Search for Tomorrow*, for instance, a leading character being tried for the murder of his wife was confronted simultaneously with the news that he was to be the father of a child by a young, unmarried woman.

The continuous emphasis on misfortune in the soap serial means that the kind of life it portrays—although ostensibly that of normal, everyday people—is characterized by wide variations from the norm. The stories are replete with intrigue, vicious gossip, marital infidelity, crime, financial chicanery, and catastrophic diseases. Amnesia, temporary blindness, strange attacks of paralysis, and tropical fevers abound. Almost no one ever gets the common cold or comes down with something as mundane as the "flu." Another rare experience endured by few people in real life is to be accused of and stand trial for murder. Such an event is commonplace in the lives of soap-opera characters. When the story moves from the home out into the community, it is usually into a hospital or courtroom.

Another way in which tension is maintained is an avoidance of the lightening effect of humor. There were some notable radio exceptions to this rule—serials which specialized in humorous situations—but when I listened to most of the TV soap operas available in the mid-West during a week, I found no single shred of wit or humor.

THE REPETITIOUSNESS OF SERIALS. The lack of continuous listening forces on writers the necessity of repeating elements of the story over and over again so that a viewer who has missed an episode or two may be immediately informed of the current situation. One device is to repeat a given revelation in a number of different scenes, a technique that not only helps to orient the occasional viewer but also wrings the last ounce of dramatic effect from each disclosure. The incident in the serial *Search for Tomorrow*, referred to previously, provides a good example. The revelation in point was that a young girl had become pregnant by a man who was on trial for the murder of his wife. In the first scene the girl revealed this fact to her mother; in another the mother passed the information along to her husband; then the father relayed the story to the lawyer of the accused man (with whom the father apparently still sympathized); finally, the lawyer informed the accused man. These four scenes, spread through a number of days, communicated an item of important information to new or intermittent viewers, and each scene had a dramatic effect of its own.

This repetitiousness, although it is necessary, does give the serial what is perhaps its most distinctive characteristic—an incredible slowness of movement. It is the dragging tempo of life itself rather than the foreshortened pace of drama. As Gilbert Seldes said, the serial is "the only dramatic art form in which nothing ever happens between the acts."[4] It is filled with scenes that seem to change the situation without actually moving it ahead.

Another device for orienting intermittent listeners is the expository scene which is more frequent in the soap opera than in any other type of drama. This is particularly true of the TV serial, which has dispensed with the announcer of radio, who used to sum up the current situation before each day's episode began. The information a listener needs must now be inserted in the dialogue of the opening scenes. Thus, in serials there is a constant discussion of the situation, a continual retracing of the past. Often the motivation for such a scene is an invitation to have a cup of coffee. Serial characters drink gallons of it; it is the fluid that lubricates the plotting machinery. A serial character who disliked the beverage would be definitely abnormal. One character, it is said, once refused a cup of coffee and then, aghast, asked, "Is there something wrong with me?"

THE CHARACTERS OF SERIALS

The most striking feature of characterization in the daytime serial is the predominance of strong women and weak men, a tradition that began in radio. Women who make up most of the audience are apparently flattered by the spectacle of a dominant female grappling successfully with problems largely created by the frailties of an unstable male.

[4] Gilbert Seldes, *The Great Audience*, p. 115.

James Thurber, in reviewing the nature of serials, said that the women who solve problems in soap operas must be "flawless projections of the housewife's ideal woman."[5]

The characters in TV serials are similar to those in radio also in that they do not remain mere dramatic creations for their listeners but assume the form of real people. The solitude in which listening to most daytime serials takes place is one factor contributing to this effect. The characters become company for those who are alone, being accepted almost as neighbors who come to visit for awhile. Thus, many habitual listeners talk about the people of the soap serials as if they really existed. When they get married or have babies, some listeners, for whom the distinction between dramatic creations and real-life characters has become blurred, flood the networks with gifts and letters of congratulation.

Television has not repeated the radio stereotypes in every respect, however. In radio the sympathetic characters were all virtuous people to whom the maintenance of chastity was the ultimate goal. This state of affairs was implicit in even the minor symbols of decadence. No good women in a radio serial ever smoked; the use of cigarettes, in fact, was a certain indication of innate vileness of character. The use of liquor was similarly proscribed. In TV nice people occasionally consume both cigarettes and liquor, and even the woman who has a child out of wedlock is not necessarily condemned.

PLOTTING THE SERIAL

There are a number of steps in the plotting of a daytime serial. The writer must first plan the over-all sweep of events making up his story. Then he must design the sequences, extending over a number of weeks, that center on particular dilemmas. Finally, he must devise and write each day's episode.

DESIGNING SEQUENCES. Plotting is a more complicated task for the writer of TV serials than it was for the writer of the average radio serial. Most radio serials revolved around one leading character, whose current predicament provided the focus for a given plotting sequence. The line memorization and extensive rehearsal required in television make it impossible to center the serial on a focal character, even though some actors ease the labor by using cueing devices. The single character soap opera titles of radio—such as *Ma Perkins*—have therefore given way to the umbrella-like appellations of television—*Edge of Night, The Secret Storm, As the World Turns*—which permit the treatment of any

[5] James Thurber, "Soapland," *The Beast in Me and Other Animals* (New York: Harcourt, Brace & World, Inc., 1948), p. 211

type of subject matter the writer chooses to consider and the inclusion of an unlimited number of principal characters.

With the multiplication of characters has come a multiplication of entanglements: each character has his own particular problem and at the same time he encroaches on the problems of others. The writer carries several different stories along at the same time, concentrating first on one and then on another. The existence of a number of stories which develop simultaneously provides a natural means of maintaining suspense. Just as tension rises to a boiling point, the writer can leave one group of characters and while the audience continues to worry about them, turn to the problems of a second group.

A summary of the character relationships and plotting line of *Love of Life*, as I noted them during a two-week period with some assistance from a regular viewer, provides a good example of the complexities characteristic of the TV soap opera. During this time the serial carried on the stories of four different family groups, who were either related or impinged on one another in some way. The first group was made up of the Porter family. Mrs. Porter's main problem was to earn the affection of a daughter whom she had brought back into her home after putting her out for adoption as a baby. Another aspect of this problem was the difficulty of gaining community acceptance for the girl because of delinquent tendencies which had developed in her during the years she had been abandoned.

The Latimer family composed the second group. The major problem of the father Rick was to maintain custody of a son, whose mother, Rick's divorced wife, was in a mental institution. This problem was complicated because his second wife Julie was an alcoholic and because his connection with a gambling house had blemished his reputation.

The third family group included Bruce and Vanessa Sterling. Bruce was the father of the woman in the mental institution and was therefore the grandfather of Rick Latimer's child, a relationship that made his involvement in the Latimer story a natural one. He also had other problems. His wife Vanessa had left him intending to marry a doctor and then had returned to him. He had been paralyzed at one time and at another had lost his post as the headmaster of a school. He entered the Porter's life because his son Allan was interested in one of their daughters.

The fourth family was composed of Vivian and Henry Carlson. Vivian was the grandmother of the woman in the mental institution and was therefore the great-grandmother of Rick Latimer's child; her main efforts during this sequence were devoted to winning the custody of this child even to the extent of planting a nurse as a spy in the Latimer household. A previous complication in Vivian's life was the fact that her daughter

Gay had had an illegitimate child. Vivian Carlson entered the Porter story when she refused to invite Mrs. Porter's daughter to a charity event of which she was chairman and thus blocked Mrs. Porter's efforts to gain social acceptance for her daughter.

Condensed in this way, and this summary by no means includes all of the plotting developments, the story of *Love of Life* seems incredibly intricate, but you may be sure that its five million regular listeners understand all of its convolutions down to their finest nuances.

PLANNING THE EPISODES.   Having designed the basic stories, the final task of the writer is to parcel them out, first, in the weekly portion of five episodes, then in the daily episodes, and lastly in the four- or five-minute portions that come between the commercials. Each of these sequences must end on a point of strain so that the interest of the viewer will be carried through the interruption. The greatest suspense must be generated on Friday to sustain interest through the weekend; this means that as the serial proceeds through the week, there is a gradual heightening of tension until the high point is reached on Friday. Within this pattern, tension is brought up at the end of each episode and again at the end of each scene, but the peaks are lower, of course, than those developed at the end of the week. To develop these peaks the writer must become an expert in the construction of tag lines—those lines that in a statement or a question crystallize viewers' interest and suspense and intensify their desire to see the next development. The construction of sequences for the nighttime serials follows a similar pattern.

QUESTIONS AND PROJECTS

1. Review the Western and adventure dramas now on the air:
   a) decide whether the Westerns fit into the "classic" or "adult" mold.
   b) create categories for the other adventure dramas.

2. Try to invent a key idea around which the plot of a detective story could turn. This idea might involve an unusual method of committing a crime or of concealing the body, a unique method of escape, a point of law put to unusual use, a surprising motive, or an ingenious way of solving the crime.

3. Analyze a detective drama or story to determine what clues were made available to the audience and how the solution was gradually revealed through the story's course.

4. Analyze the current TV fantasies and classify them in the following categories: a) myths, magic, monsters; b) the supernatural; c) world of the future; d) movements in time; e) other worlds; f) science fiction. State the fantastic premise of each program.

5. Create the foundation for a fantasy by developing a fantastic premise through asking the question: What if?

6. In your opinion how far may the dramatist writing historical or biographical plays go in inventing material to fill out the dramatic situation?

7. Develop a biographical or historical theme you would like to establish and plan a script that will communicate it to an audience.

8. Watch a daytime serial for a week at the beginning of the term and define the dilemmas of the characters. Return to the serial at the end of the term and define the plot movement that has taken place.

9. Devise an idea for a half-hour daytime serial. Plot one week's episodes in detail and develop an outline of the action for thirteen weeks. Prepare a complete script plan for one episode.

12

Documentaries, News, and Features

The documentary idea, after all, demands no more than that the affairs of our time shall be brought to the screen in any fashion which strikes the imagination and makes observation a little richer than it was. John Grierson

Some of the sharpest contrasts in American radio and television exist in the area of informational programming. One type of program that specializes in facts—the newscast—is among the most common in broadcasting and includes virtually everybody among its listeners. Another type—the documentary—is one of the rarest offerings on commercial stations and usually attracts only a minority audience. Between the two in frequency are the short talks broadcast on such series as CBS's *Dimension*, ABC's *Flair*, and NBC's *Emphasis*, which appear regularly in network radio schedules.

THE DOCUMENTARY

The term "documentary" is used by broadcasters in both a narrow and a broad sense. Interpreted narrowly it refers only to those informational programs that deal with a current social problem and aim at one or more of the following objectives: 1) to provide socially useful information; 2) to persuade the audience to take remedial action; 3) or to inspire or uplift. Another attribute of this type of documentary is a strong emotional quality. A. William Bluem in his book *Documentary in American Television,* said that the documentarist sets forth "not simply to register events and circumstances, but to find the most moving examples of them." In this regard the documentary can be said to be dramatic. It is dramatic also in that it adds an artistic purpose to journalistic and sociological aims. John Grierson, who first developed the documentary approach in making films, said that his objective was to deal with the actual in a creative way.

The term "documentary" is also used more broadly to refer to any program that sets out to explore a subject rather than merely to entertain. In this sense a program that simply dispenses information about historical or biographical subjects without reference to current social issues would be considered a documentary. Even broadcasts that are primarily cultural rather than controversial in nature—programs on such subjects as Michelangelo, Shakespeare, and the Louvre—are often put in the documentary category. In this section we consider all types of documentaries since the writing techniques used in creating them are fundamentally the same.

The documentary form has attracted writers for two main reasons. It gives them a chance, first of all, to use the broadcasting media to explore the significant issues of life rather than expending their resources on what may be frivolous and ephemeral. Second, it provides opportunities for experimentation and the exercise of one's ingenuity not often possible in such formula-obsessed fields as drama and comedy. Because the expected audience is small to begin with, the writer can afford to use venturesome new techniques which may disenchant some listeners, whereas the writer of entertainment scripts, committed to attracting millions, may fear to try the innovation that will lose even one of them. Thus, entertainment writing follows the well-worn trail of what has been tried and found safe; documentary writing can explore new paths of subject and technique.

DOCUMENTARY PRODUCTION METHODS

In the production of documentary programs the writing process often merges so completely with the production process that one is indistinguishable from the other. Only rarely does a script represent everything appearing on the program; the rest is inherent in the tapes or films that make up a major share of the program. This does not mean that a writing function cannot be identified, however. The producer who shoots a piece of film in the field and the editor who cuts it are carrying out a writing function. In this section, therefore, we shall be thinking not only of the writer who creates a documentary at his typewriter but also of those who work in the field or at the editing table. In some instances all these functions are carried out by the same person.

STUDIO-PRODUCED PROGRAMS.   Documentaries produced in radio, television, or film studios from completely written scripts were common just after World War II, but they have been largely replaced by programs made up of tapes or films recorded in the location where the events being portrayed actually took place.

EXISTING FILM AND TAPE.   Many TV documentaries are made up in whole or in part from film obtained from government archives, newsreel vaults, or other sources. In the same way, radio documentaries sometimes make use of existing tapes. Programs with a historical focus are the ones most likely to use this type of material. An example is CBS's *Twentieth Century* series, which often reviewed episodes in World War II through the medium of films made during that war. Programs dealing with the lives of historical figures, such as Winston Churchill and Franklin Roosevelt, are also compiled largely from existing film, much of it produced originally for newsreels.

SPECIALLY PRODUCED FILM OR TAPE.   Another major ingredient in TV and radio documentaries is film or tape produced specifically for the program. Many documentaries are composed entirely of material made to order in this way. People who were eye witnesses to great events may be brought before a camera or microphone to record their comments. In some instances a camera or tape recorder is taken into the field to picture scenes or to capture people in a situation acting just as they would were no recording being made. The term *actuality* is often used to designate this type of documentary. To permit natural responses in the situation even though the artificial element of a camera has been introduced, producers developed the *cinéma vérité* technique, which makes the cameraman a part of a given situation for a relatively long period of time and requires that he use his camera as unobtrusively as possible.

STILL PICTURES.   Some notable TV documentaries have utilized a succession of still pictures as the primary visual element. Biographies of Abraham Lincoln and Mark Twain have been presented in this way.

Still pictures have also been employed as a secondary element in a number of programs. Van Gogh's paintings were effectively used to tell part of that great artist's story.

RESEARCH FOR THE DOCUMENTARY

Since the writer of an informational program deals in facts, he must develop a technique for discovering them. If the budget for the program is low, as it is likely to be at an ETV or local commercial station, he must carry out research entirely on his own. If he is writing a network documentary, which may have a budget of $100,000, he has the assistance of skilled researchers who take over the primary task of digging out information. Even then, he cannot entirely escape research responsibility, for he must immerse himself sufficiently in the subject to develop a point of view and determine what he needs to know.

There are two stages to most research efforts. One is a general phase in which you explore your subject to establish the dimensions of the program and define the areas needing further investigation. The second is a phase in which you seek answers to specific questions that arise during the period of general research. This type of research may go on all through the preparation of the program, for a writer often discovers after he has started his script that he needs further information before he can continue writing. General reading is the main tool in the exploratory phase of research. Interviews with experts take place in the second phase when you have decided just what you want since people who qualify as authorities do not usually have time to submit to rambling fishing expeditions.

Finding films for television documentaries is another important research task. It is usually carried out by film specialists. Sometimes a subject is chosen for consideration because it is known that good films on that subject are available.

ORGANIZING THE DOCUMENTARY

The documentary, in either dispensing information or engaging in persuasion, has purposes similar to those of speeches, articles, pamphlets, and textbooks. It follows that a documentary is organized like a speech or article rather than like a drama, which aims to tell a story. The first step in writing the documentary is to arrange the material into a logical pattern which shows the relationship among the various facts and ideas. The outline that results from this effort determines the underlying structure of ideas to be presented, but it does not necessarily indicate the order in which they are to appear. That is the function of the script plan, which is prepared next. It adds the ingredient of showmanship to the presentation and thus makes it as attractive as possible.

Many people find the making of an outline tedious and difficult work and are tempted to skip this part of the process. To do so may be a grievous mistake. Neglect at this point can lead to a program that at best may be fuzzy and at worst may be completely formless. The main ideas may remain unclear and unestablished or they may not come to light at all, for a writer often perceives the points he wishes to make while he is going through the process of organization. An outline, furthermore, helps to avoid overstressing or understressing supporting points and it is a guide toward including those ideas essential to the achievement of the program's objectives. At the same time it leads to the exclusion of irrelevancies and thus helps to insure that the program will move directly to its objectives.

The organizational plan of a documentary should have several qualities—simplicity, unity, logical connection, and clarity. A major step toward creating a plan with these qualities is to make sure that the script is dominated by one overriding thought to which all the other ideas in the program are related. These supporting ideas in turn should be arranged to show their relationship to the main thought and to one another.

DEVELOPING THE IDEAS.   Your first step in organization is to determine the basic purpose of your script. It should center on one of the following objectives: 1) to inform your audience; 2) to convince people to accept a new idea or to develop a new opinion or attitude; 3) to reinforce an existing attitude or opinion; and 4) to actuate the audience to carry out a specific course of action. A given program may accomplish more than one of these objectives, but if it is well organized, it will be primarily aimed at accomplishing one of them.

The next step is to develop a preliminary statement of the central idea of the program. The nature of the central idea is implicit in its name: it is a one-sentence expression of the main point you want your program to communicate. This statement may also include the basic purpose of the program. Thus a central idea might be expressed as follows: to convince the audience that capital punishment is wrong.

The reason you should consider your statement of the central idea to be tentative is that as you develop the supporting points, you may discover that you need to modify the central idea. One of your supporting points may take you in an unanticipated direction. Your most likely step then is to revise the supporting point so that it directly reinforces the central idea. But it may happen that the supporting point suggests a more promising general approach than the one you originally envisioned and you therefore revise your central idea.

The final step in organization is to set the central idea, the main supporting points, and the subsupporting points down in outline form to make their relationships perfectly clear. A satisfactory outline is not something that springs immediately into being. A long, arduous process of expressing points, examining them critically, and then reworking them may be necessary before your outline is completely clear and consistent.

A good first step in creating an outline is to write down the ideas of the program in a list without giving any particular thought to order or arrangement. Then examine this list with these questions in mind: What seem to be the main ideas of the program? What are the subordinate points? What is clearly the supporting material? The responses to these questions will guide you in setting down the outline. There are certain patterns of organization that naturally suit certain subjects. You may find that your material fits into one of the following patterns: 1) a chronological order; 2) a space order; 3) an order that adopts an existing classification, as, for example, the effect of a certain problem on various age groups—the young, the middle-aged, the old; 4) a cause and effect order; 5) a problem-solution order. If none of these patterns is suitable, you must find your points in the topic itself. To establish an organizational plan in which the relationships among the ideas are clearly defined, you should observe the following rules:

1. Write the outline in complete sentences. Incomplete sentences or single words mask muddy thinking and fail to reveal that some ideas which seem to be related are not really related at all.

2. Make certain that the ideas of the program are set down in such a way as to reveal their true relationships. Use a consistent set of symbols to reveal which ideas are the main points, which are subordinate, and which are equal to one another or coordinate.

3. Restrict the number of main points to a reasonable number. Most programs should have no fewer than two main points and no more than five.

4. Be sure that your outline does not omit an essential step in the development of your main idea. You should also make certain that you have enough supporting material to establish your main points adequately.

5. Avoid the use of compound or multiple-idea sentences. There should be only one simple sentence after each symbol in the outline.

6. Express points as positive statements not as questions. When a point is introduced in the actual program it may be worded as a question, but questions in outlines may hide fuzzy thinking or faulty structure.

TESTING THE RELATIONSHIP OF IDEAS.   When you have completed your outline, you should examine it carefully to make sure that it expresses logical relationships. If the program is designed to persuade an audience to accept an idea or to carry out some action, a simple test can check the relationship between the main and subordinate ideas. See whether one of the following words "for," "because," or "in that" can be used as a natural link between the main idea and its supporting point. The following outline provides an example.

I. Capital punishment should be abolished.
    A. It is morally wrong.
    B. It does not deter crime.
    C. It makes judicial mistakes irretrievable.

These words can occasionally be used to test the organization of programs designed to inform, but not in all cases. Sometimes the only way to test an informational outline is to apply common sense. Ask yourself whether the supporting points constitute reasonable divisions of the main point—as for example:

I. The process of driving involves three steps.
    A. The car must be started.
    B. The car must be driven in traffic.
    C. The car must be parked.

The words—"for," "in that," "because"—fit to a degree between the main and supporting points, but they do not help very much in evaluating the outline. Common-sense analysis, however, suggests that A, B, and C are logical and complete divisions of I.

When you actually write the script, you may not follow the order of points in your outline. A supporting point may come first, for example, followed by the principle it establishes. But the process of testing just described guarantees the existence of logical relationships among the ideas of your program thus insuring a sound structure no matter what form your script plan may take.

THE SCRIPT PLAN

After you have organized your material, your next step is to devise a plan that will guide the writing and production of the documentary.

Your aim is to embellish the outline, which in itself is too bald and unadorned to hold an audience, with devices that will engage attention, insure clarity, and produce an emotional effect.

THE CONTROLLING FRAMEWORK.   Your first step in planning is to decide the controlling idea or approach that will dominate the writing and production of the script. These ideas are so many and so varied that it is impossible to catalogue them all, but a few examples may stimulate your thinking.

One of the most ingenious frameworks ever conceived was that used for the CBS series *You Are There*. The idea was to present historical happenings as if they were taking place at the moment of the program, employing the technique of the special events broadcast. CBS commentators, whose voices and faces were familiar to the audience as newsmen, described such occurrences as the fall of Pompeii and the execution of Mary, Queen of Scots as if they were actually present as witnesses, and they further developed an atmosphere of immediacy by interviewing the leading participants in these events.

Another approach to a documentary is to put it into dramatic form. The purpose of this type of drama differentiates it from other forms of drama based on facts. The documentary writer's fundamental aim is to present information or to influence behavior and the drama is merely an instrument for accomplishing these purposes. The aim of the writer of biographical or historical drama, on the other hand, is to provide entertainment and the material he uses for this purpose just happens to be the events of history or happenings in real people's lives.

A program about mental illness produced by CBS provides an example of the dramatic approach. It was postulated that a writer assigned to travel about the country to study the problem of mental illness and the means being used to treat it himself had a wife who was a victim of this ailment. This device added reality and emotional power to the program, for as the narrator listened to a physician describe the symptoms of mental illness, he evaluated them in terms of his own wife's behavior, and as he visited various types of mental hospitals, he could envision her as a patient. The listeners' interest was engaged by the drama of a man wrestling with a difficult problem, and at the same time they absorbed the facts the producers aimed to communicate.

The presentation of documentary material as drama is most easily accomplished in a studio, but the dramatic approach may be used with other production methods also. An example was a *CBS Reports* program made up of existing and specially shot film about Dr. Tom Dooley, the physician who gained fame for his efforts to bring modern medical practice to the natives of Laos. In this case the program centered on Dr. Dooley's personal battle with disease. Entitled "Biography of a Cancer," the story provided an ideal structure for a drama with a line of action rising toward a climax, which was resolved with the young doctor's tragic and untimely death.

Sometimes a framework will be suggested by the material itself. Lou Hazam, assigned to do a program on budgeting, decided that the problem of budgeting has three aspects: the burden of debts accumulated in the past; the problem of paying current expenses; the necessity of planning for future expenses. As a frame for his program, he established a budgeting clinic with specialists who counseled clients with money problems in these three areas—the past, the present, and the future. Another program by Hazam, which dealt with the problems of adolescents, used songs played by a juke box as a means of focusing on each problem. One episode dealt with a music-loving boy whose mother could not bear to hear him practice. The juke box song initiating this episode was "Momma Don't Allow No Music Played Around Here!"

A number of stations have dealt with public issues by presenting excerpts from debates in the houses of Congress as they are recorded in the *Congressional Record*. A quiz format has even been used as a means of leading into the discussion of a serious question. The commonest format of all combines a narrator, who carries the main burden of providing information, with scenes on film or dramatized in a studio which support or illustrate what the narrator is saying.

An issue which often arises in planning a documentary is whether one can tamper with what actually took place in order to enhance the effect of the program. The purists argue that any interference with the natural situation or staging of any kind is improper. This is an extreme attitude, however. Too much embellishment may distort the truth, but material presented completely in the raw may not make any point at all. Most people would agree that it is legitimate to improve the build of a program by presenting events in a somewhat different order from the one in which they actually took place if this does not affect the basic integrity of the program. The presentation need not be unimpeachably real so long as it does not violate essential truth.

THE IMPORTANCE OF A PLAN.   With so many documentaries now made up primarily of film shot in the field, a well-designed production plan has become more necessary than ever. The *CBS Reports* program on the plight of migrant workers entitled "Harvest of Shame" provides an example of a plan's importance. Research for the program indicated that migrant workers as they travel from one job to another around the country are not treated even as well as farm animals. To support this point, film was first shot of workers as they journeyed a full day without being given any rest. Then film was shot of farm animals in transport being given respites for water and exercise every four hours. These two episodes, shown one after the other on the program, constituted graphic evidence of the condition the producers aimed to expose. The capturing of this material was possible because a plan existed before shooting began.

It is especially important to devise a program plan before interviewing takes place, for only by knowing the general nature and direction of the program can you be sure of conducting interviews that will produce usable material. Those watching the NBC *White Paper* on the miscarriage of justice, entitled "Oswald and the Law," could tell that the producers had developed the main ideas of the program before the interviewing began. Their research indicated that the conviction of innocent men could be attributed to six main causes: 1) coerced confessions; 2) faulty eye-witness identification; 3) rigged trials; 4) the suppression by police or prosecution of evidence favorable to the accused; 5) the buying of evidence from underworld figures by state officials; and 6) lack of financial resources by many defendents.

Four authorities in the field of law and its enforcement were interviewed on film for this program—the dean of a law school, a leading defense lawyer, a judge who had been a police commissioner, and a prosecuting attorney. By asking all these authorities to comment on these same six causes, the producer was able to develop a series of interviews that explored the main ideas of the program in a unified and coherent manner.

The preproduction plan should not be so firm that it cannot be revised, however. One reason for flexibility is that shooting in the field comprises part of the research for the program. New ideas may develop from this activity or existing ideas may acquire new emphases. Furthermore, you always hope for the lucky accident or unlooked for development that will add excitement or an unexpected angle to the program. Even when you are using existing film or tape, you may not be entirely sure what your points will be until you have surveyed the material.

WRITING THE DOCUMENTARY SCRIPT

The actual writing of a script may be a major or minor job depending on the nature of the program. If it is composed mainly of film shot in the field or of interviews with authorities, little work at the typewriter will be required. The creative work is done mainly by the production team. Other techniques require complete scripts. But whatever the approach, the writer of documentaries faces many of the challenges that confront the writer of dramas.

GAINING ATTENTION.   The attention step is a particularly crucial one, for the mere promise of information held out by a documentary is not a powerful attraction in itself for most people. How can you gain attention under such circumstances? One step is to depict the subject of the program in the most powerful terms you can devise. You must make it vital and meaningful to the average listener. You must surround it with an aura of excitement. You must create suspense by leading your audience to wonder about possible solutions.

The teaser technique is frequently used in documentaries to focus the attention of the audience on the problem. This teaser may be a brief dramatic scene, an exciting sequence excerpted from the body of the program, or a statement by a person whose name and face are attention getting in and of themselves. This last technique was used effectively by the writer of an *ABC Scope* program on heart attacks. The program opened with a portion of an interview with Peter Sellers, a motion-picture actor who many people would remember had recently suffered a near-fatal heart attack. Sellers said little at this point, but the audience was lured with the promise that he would describe his experiences later in the program. As a further hook to interest, the audience was told that the Duke of Windsor would also appear on the program to describe an operation on an artery that saved his life.

Celebrities are not the only ones who can gain attention, however. Sometimes the so-called "little people" can do it too, if they are presented in the right way. The NBC *White Paper* on the miscarriage of justice caught attention effectively by opening with a man who told the audience in a simple yet poignant way that he had spent sixteen years in prison for a crime he did not commit.

INTRODUCING CONFLICT.   The documentary form does not provide as obvious an opportunity to use conflict for holding attention as the drama does, but the alert writer can often make use of conflict to build interest in his program. One method is to alternate interviews with people who hold clashing opinions on a subject. Another is to provide face-to-face confrontation between opponents. This method permits the development of the highest degree of conflict, but it is not so easy to control as the conflict that arises from interviews recorded separately.

INTRODUCING EMOTIONAL VALUES.   The principal means of arousing emotional response to a documentary is to present the issues as they affect individuals. A writer who is content merely to make general statements is likely to leave his audience uninvolved. A good example of the emotional power that comes from converting a general event into personal terms was seen in an NBC documentary, "The Congo—Victim of Independence." One of the tragic events referred to in the program was the massacre that took place in Stanleyville. Instead of just telling about it, the producers depicted it through the eyes of a survivor whose wife had been killed in the violence. He was pictured walking down the street where the massacre had taken place while his voice, recorded over the scene, told of the horrible events as he saw them again in memory. It was a pathetic and memorable moment. Another result of independence was an enormous economic loss suffered by white settlers and natives alike. The producers made this loss personal by focusing on the experiences of a Belgian land owner whose plantation had been destroyed. What made the treatment so touching was not merely the reflection of the Belgian's own losses, but his obvious compassion for the natives who had suffered more than he.

NARRATION.   Chief among the tools a writer of documentaries needs is a mastery of the art of writing narration, for it is the rare documentary, indeed, that does not employ narration in some form or other. Its chief function in most instances is to reinforce what is presented by filmed or taped segments, or dramatic scenes. Narration in this instance is written after the editing process is completed, for only then can the writer know what material needs narrative support.

Narration can reinforce the effect of a program in a number of ways. It can clarify the meaning of the tapes and pictures. The identification of people in a scene is an example of such clarification. In providing explanation the writer must walk the narrow line that divides saying too little from saying too much. Unnecessary narration may clutter a documentary, but too little may leave a viewer unsure of what is going on.

Narration may also provide an interpretation which enriches the contribution of a taped or filmed excerpt. It can serve also to make a transition from one idea in the documentary to another. A viewer needs to be told regularly where he has been, where he is now, and where he is going to be taken. Narration is also an effective tool for presenting the basic ideas of a script, for defining its attitudes, and for summarizing its conclusions. Finally, narration may enhance the emotional effect of a scene or taped insert with a vivid sentence or an appropriate quotation.

A brief excerpt from the opening of a documentary in the CBS series, *Twentieth Century* illustrates the effect of well-written narration. This program, "The Age of Anxiety—Part I," written by James Benjamin, dealt with mental illness.

CRONKITE: (On Screen)

This is our story as The Prudential

Insurance Company of America presents THE

TWENTIETH CENTURY.

(MAIN TITLE)

(COMMERCIAL)

CRONKITE: (Narration)

Capitol   Topeka, Kansas, is many things...Capital

city of the state..."home" to some hundred

and twenty four thousand Americans...And,

to certain other hundreds, it means "haven"

and "hope."

VA Hospital   The huge Veterans Administration Hospital,

(14)   the Topeka State Hospital, some 21

institutions are the "havens" -- for the

hundreds of <u>mentally ill</u> who come here.

The Menninger Foundation, which supervises

their treatment, symbolizes the "hope" --

that they like thousands before them will

<u>recover</u>. Within its new Children's Hos-

pital...in the private hospital for adults,

as well as in the outpatient services, the

Menninger Foundation's aim is not only <u>to</u>

<u>treat</u>...<u>but to teach those who will treat</u>

...to teach that patients are <u>salvage-</u>

<u>able</u> -- patients such as these young men

playing touch football on the grounds.

Bars and walls are gone. <u>Optimism</u> now

```
holds patients until they are ready to
leave.  And the world inside the hospi-
tal has become a waystation to the world
outside.
```

THE NEWSCAST

Entire books have been devoted to the craft of writing news; obviously it is impossible in a few pages to cover the subject in detail, but it is hoped that the main characteristics of the newscast will be made clear, particularly as they differ from those of the documentary and the feature talk. The purpose of a newscast is to report what is happening *now* in the community, in the nation, and in the world. It does not seek to interpret the significance of events; that is the function of news analyses, editorials, and documentaries. The minimum requirement for obtaining the information needed for a newscast is service from at least one of the press associations—the Associated Press or United Press International—which transmit their dispatches by teletype. A large station or network generally utilizes a second press association service, a local, national, and international reporting staff of its own, a still picture source, service from a national news film or video tape company, and a camera unit.

SELECTING NEWS STORIES

The first task in preparing a newscast is to select the stories to be included, for even a fifteen-minute radio newscast cannot present all the dispatches that flow through a teletype machine, and a television newscast, which must incorporate films, can cover even less. Two criteria should control the selection of news items. (1) Select those stories that are of the greatest *significance* to your audience. (2) Select those stories that are of the greatest *interest* to your audience. Any story involving the security of the United States concerns every citizen. Such a story would have a prominent place on a newscast because of its importance. The story of a local crime may not be particularly significant, but because it involves people in the community, it is of great interest to the local audience.

Sometimes factors other than those of significance and interest do influence the selection process. One is the availability of film for a TV newscast. In an effort to keep the program as visual as possible, the newscaster may be tempted to use a story simply because there is film to illustrate it rather than because it meets the tests just described. If this film deals with such predictable and unexciting occasions as the opening of a bridge or the inauguration of a public official and neglects the significant events of the day, the program may lose its quality of immediacy and degenerate into a meaningless newsreel. Films of interviews with people who have been involved in the real news events of the day are more vital and interesting. They also reflect the real problems of the community, which all responsible radio and television stations should cover in their news broadcasts.

A second factor that influences the selection of items is the relationship of local newscasts to network newscasts. A network can cover the major national and international events better than a local station. For this reason the writer of a local newscast airing in the early evening just before or after a network news show gives his major attention to the local scene. When writing for a late evening local newscast with a network news program nowhere near, he can cover stories strictly in terms of their news merit whether they be national, international, or local.

A third factor influencing selection is that most major news stories take place during the day and are reported soon after they happen on newscasts scheduled from ten until six o'clock. The writer of a late night or early morning newscast must realize that most of the stories on the teletype happened hours before and have already appeared on previous news programs. In this situation, how can he keep his program from sounding like a rehash? One approach is to search diligently for a new development in a major story to try to update the story, as the news man terms it. Another is to ignore the existence of the previous newcasts, or assume that his listeners did not hear them, and report the news as if it had just happened.

ORGANIZING THE NEWSCAST

A newscast made up of many diverse items cannot be organized like a program that revolves around just one theme, but it should have some order and arrangement. The first decision is to choose your opening story. Usually this will be the biggest story of the day, big either because of its significance or because of its interest to the audience. Another criterion for making this choice is to consider what the audience is most anxious to hear. An important news story may be developing—an international crisis, for example, or a local kidnapping. People turning to the news expect, first of all, to hear the latest development in a big story that is already in the news.

After choosing the first story, you must decide next how to arrange the other items in the news. The importance of stories affects the order of items not only at the beginning but down through the newscast. Generally, the newscaster deals with the most important news first. There is danger, however, that by putting all of the exciting items at the beginning he will lose his audience for the rest of the show and cause unhappiness for a sponsor who is just as anxious that listeners hear his last commercial as his first. Because most people are eager to know what the weather is going to be like, newscasters hold their audiences by delaying the weather forecast until the end. As a further incentive to listening all the way through, human-interest stories and sports news frequently wind up a broadcast.

The nature of the news on a given day may decide what plan of organization is most appropriate. A common pattern is to divide the news into local, national, and international events. If the opening news item deals with a local event, other local events might be considered before the national and international news is covered. Some newscasters use a geographical plan, moving in order from one world capital to another. One of the best procedures is to present the news in terms of certain major topics, which may change from day to day according to what is happening in the world. The advantage of this plan is that it is flexible and is best adapted to showing relationships among the various news items. A topical arrangement might present news under such headings as: political developments, labor happenings, world trouble spots, weather on the rampage. Another important criterion in the ordering of items on a program is the need for balance and variety in the visual aspects of a TV newscast.

Achieving a sequence that permits transitions from one item to another may dictate the placement of some stories. Two items concerning the same person should be put together because there is a natural linkage between them and one identification of the person will suffice for both items. Stories with other types of common elements should be presented in sequence to make transitions possible. A newscaster who has been considering international strife might move to a labor dispute with the line, "There was conflict of another type on the labor scene." Such transitions help to link items, but they should not be used if they tend to imply relationships that do not actually exist. A forced or overly clever transition is worse than none at all. Often the best transition is one that simply says, "on the local scene," or "on the Washington front." But the best way to help the listener make transitions is to arrange the news dispatches into groups of related items.

Some newscasters make transitions through the use of the dateline technique, which calls for preceding each item with the place of its origin. This technique may work for the short newscasts, but in longer ones the repetition of place names becomes monotonous and mechanical.

Moreover, this device makes for a disjointed program in which the single news items appear to bear no relationship to one another. Incidentally, you should be careful not to put a story of a tragedy right next to one with comedy overtones or the transition problem will become difficult.

WORDING THE NEWSCAST

The wire services prepare summaries, which can be torn off the machine and read in their entirety without editing or alteration, expressly designed to fill fifteen- and five-minute periods. This "rip-and-read" policy, however, places two major limitations on a station's news service. It precludes the use of news originating in the local community unless that news is of sufficient importance to justify its inclusion on a national or state wire, and it prevents the station from developing a news service with an individual style and flavor. For these reasons many stations do not present press dispatches as they come from the wire but use them merely as a source of news information. The actual newscasts are constructed and written by their own newscasters or editors. Let us now consider some of the qualities that distinguish good news writing.

GENERAL QUALITIES. Should there be a difference between material that is written to be heard and material that is written to be read? The operators of the Associated Press apparently think so, for they write the news in one version for newspaper use and in another version for their radio and television clients. Others argue that good writing is good writing no matter how it is to be received. Without attempting to settle this question, we can note that much of what is written in newspapers is unsuitable for broadcasting on radio and television. The main reason for this is the attempt by the newspaper writer to get all of the salient facts into the first two or three paragraphs of his story so that it can be cut to fit the page without denying the reader any important information. Trying to provide answers to the "who, what, why, where, and how" of a story at the very beginning calls for long, complicated constructions which result in what is called an "inverted pyramid." This pattern is considered by many to be bad style even for newspapers, and it is certainly inappropriate for the radio and television newscast.

Allan Jackson, the CBS newscaster, has lectured frequently to college students on the craft of news writing. His advice is to "keep it tight, terse, simple—and make it flow." The need for directness and simplicity becomes apparent when one reflects that the newscaster has only a few sentences to tell a story to which a newspaper writer may devote several paragraphs. The listener, furthermore, must understand the story the first time through; he has no chance to go back over the material the way a newspaper reader can. For this reason avoid inversions, long modifying phrases, and involved constructions. Short sentences should predominate. Generally, take the normal route from subject to verb and keep them close together. Sentences do not necessarily have to be complete. Lowell Thomas often used a headline approach—"New Floods in India"—to make a transition from one item to the next. Use easy-to-understand words instead of fancy and complex ones. Remember that verbs are more important in a newscast than adjectives, but when adjectives are used, there should be no doubt about the subject they modify. Be alert to the articulation problems that certain phrases may involve. Allan Jackson cited "the Joint Chief's Chairman" and "the earth's first space" as phrases that might trip even the most fluent newscaster.

Imbue the newscast with an atmosphere of excitement, for it deals, after all, with events that often have a critical influence on the lives of everyone. This does not mean that the treatment should be sensational or shocking, but it should be forceful and active. The passive voice has little place in a newscast. Make each story sound as if it has just happened and particularly avoid dating stories unnecessarily. When dealing with a story that is already in the news, start with a fresh angle or new lead before reviewing what is already known by most listeners.

SPECIAL PROBLEMS. A number of special problems face the writer of news copy.

1. Since news often involves controversial matters, it is easy to let one's particular bias color the presentation. The hallmark of the straight newscast is objectivity. You must be certain that you report the facts accurately without letting that report be warped by your personal opinions.

2. You must guard against making judgments not warranted by the facts. To refer to an accused man as a killer or thief before the courts have decided his guilt or innocence is to be guilty of prejudgment and possible libel which can lead to damage suits. To report that an individual has jumped from a ten-story building is to say that he has committed suicide. This judgment may not be justified by what is known at the time of the newscast. To say that he fell is to imply an accidental death, which again the facts may not establish. The word "plunged" tells what happened without making a judgment.

3. Because a newscast is heard rather than read, you must be especially careful that the order of words does not create misunderstandings. Make sure that the antecedents of pronouns are completely clear. Guard against misleading the audience with qualifying phrases. The best procedure is to place the qualifying phrase or clause ahead of the item it modifies. The danger of doing the reverse can be illustrated by the

following example. "Iraq's Chief of State, the Iraqian counterpart of Lyndon Johnson, died today." A person half-listening to the broadcast might gather that the President of the United States had died.

4. Identifying quoted material often presents difficulties for a newscaster. The awkward "quote . . . unquote" technique is rarely used today. The more direct "Senator Fulbright said" is better form. If the quotation is a long one, it is wise to introduce "Senator Fulbright went on" in the middle and to remind the audience at the end that Senator Fulbright made the statement. The important point is to make sure that the audience differentiates the quoted material from the rest of the newscast, particularly if the quotation is controversial or opinionated. To be sure that there are no misunderstandings, identify the source before you give the quotation.

5. The television newscaster has the special problem of relating his copy to silent filmed material. If there is a direct relationship between what he is saying and what is on the screen, he is said to have written *to* the film. This is what he is doing when he identifies the people in the film or discusses the action directly. In other cases, however, the writer lets the film speak for itself while he covers another phase of the story. This is called writing *away* from the film. In writing this copy, the writer must also decide whether the film tells the basic news story or merely reinforces it.

6. A commonly used technique to arouse interest is to begin the newscast with a series of headlines. The purpose is to arouse interest in the story without revealing the story itself. If the headlines tell too much, the audience will have its curiosity satisfied before the program is well under way. Thus, the headline "Chief of Staff resigns with blast at the President" contains too many details. "Turnover at the Pentagon" will hold the listener to find out what is going on.

A SAMPLE NEWSCAST

The following radio newscast was presented by Allan Jackson for the CBS West Coast audience on a Saturday evening. In describing his approach to it, Mr. Jackson pointed out that the story about Sukarno's apparent fall from power in Indonesia had come in and been reported almost ten hours before and there had been no new information since. Feeling the story was too important to be dropped altogether, he gave it a touch of freshness by making the lack of further information newsworthy in itself before reviewing the details that most people already knew. Note that Mr. Jackson connects items with a transitional word or phrase when there is a direct relationship between items, but he does not force a transition unsupported by the material. Instead he merely moves briskly to the next story without preamble. The final story illustrates the practice followed by many newscasters of ending with a story that has a definite "human interest" value. This newscast, which shows the punctuation used in the air script, exemplifies the crispness and economy in writing style that Mr. Jackson advocates in his lectures.

JACKSON

The Chinese nationalist island of Formosa

was rocked by an earthquake during the

afternoon -- Several houses were knocked

down in Taipeh - and eleven persons were

injured -- but apparently no major damage

was inflicted.

On the diplomatic front, the Chinese

Nationalists were rocked in Paris this

morning -- when they were unceremoniously

evicted from the building that used to be

their embassy - before the French recognized

the Chinese communists two years ago. The

French maintain that the remaining

Nationalist delegation to UNESCO has no

diplomatic status -- and that the building

belongs to the Chinese communists. The

communists promptly announced that they'll

move right in.

President Johnson received an un-

expected vote of confidence from a major-

ity of the nation's governors attending a

White House briefing on Viet Nam. Several

Republicans were among those voting for

the resolution -- in fact, the resolution
-- to support and endorse administration
policies in Viet Nam wholeheartedly - was
offered by Ohio's Republican governor James
Rhodes.

There were other subjects covered at
the White House conference -- such as
federal-state relationships...but Viet Nam
was the key subject -- and President Johnson said that higher spending for the war
may force a bigger deficit than expected.

Vice-president Humphrey -- in a
telephone speech to a New York students'
meeting -- said - we are fighting in Viet
Nam -- not to impose a government or way
of life on the people of Viet Nam -- but
to assure that they will be able to decide
their own future...and to show that aggres-
sion cannot be an acceptable means of settling international disputes -- or realizing
national objectives.

More news in a moment - after a word
from Chevrolet.

(COMMERCIAL)

JACKSON

There has been no indication from
Indonesia yet -- whether American corre-
spondents are to be allowed to reenter the

country -- now that Sukarno has signed
over all his presidential powers to the
Army. On the surface, at least, Sukarno
remains president in name only -- and
according to some reports, is restricted
to his palace...but diplomatic observers
in Washington disagree over just what has
happened -- whether it's a coup -- a power
shift -- or only a temporary political
maneuver by Sukarno...until the army re-
stores civilian order.

The White House confirmed during the day
that our diplomats are engaged in intensive
consultation with allied governments - on
French president De Gaulle's threat to
pull out of the integrated NATO command.
Our ambassador to Paris -- Charles Bohlen -
flew home to consult on the problem...and
a House foreign affairs subcommittee --
which had planned to hold hearings on the
future of NATO later in the year - has
moved up those hearings to the latter part
of this month - because of De Gaulle's
action.

Word came out of Cuba today that a
former U.S. Air Force captain -- and a
longtime Cuban resident - has been sentenced
to thirty years in prison on charges of

spying for the U.S. Central Intelligence
Agency. He's Kirby Lunt of Santa Fe, New
Mexico. Neither his trial nor his sentence
was announced publicly in Havana. Our
government was informed by the Swiss embassy -- which represents American interests
in Cuba.

A thirty-seven year old FBI agent of
Seattle - George Foster - is in good condition after a frightening ordeal during the
night -- when he was buried - in his crum-
pled car - by a massive snowslide - about
ten miles east of Snoqualmie Pass in Washington. He spent eight hours in that en-
tombment -- before snow-plows finally --
reached the level of his car. Foster is
in good condition in a hospital in
Snoqualmie this evening -- and, answering
reporters' questions -- said -- "You bet I
prayed."

That's the news -- now a word from
Chevrolet.

(COMMERCIAL)

NEWS TELEVISION FORMAT

One of the main objectives in preparing copy for a television newscast
is to show the relationship between what is seen and what is heard.
To accomplish this purpose, most stations and networks set up the copy
in two columns with video information on the left and the newscaster's
copy on the right. Specific details of format vary from place to place,

but the one that follows illustrates the basic arrangement. To save space the announcer's copy has been summarized.

Video	Audio
RP--MAP--SOUTH VIET NAM JONES ON CAMERA	Jones: There was new action in South Viet Nam as American forces struck an enemy base forty miles south west of Saigon.
ROLL CUE: SAIGON FILM SIL: 4 SEC. SOF: 25 SEC.	Jones: Our special correspondent in that area interviewed a marine captain who took part in action in that sector two days ago.
OUT CUE: This is your special correspondent in Viet Nam reporting from Saigon.	
JONES ON CAMERA	Jones: (Air raids over Viet Nam)
TELOP 1 DESTROYED BRIDGE	Jones: The Pentagon has just released this picture of a bridge destroyed by our planes in Communist territory.

```
JONES ON CAMERA                Jones: As the action con-

                                      tinues in Viet Nam,

                                      questions about our

                                      involvement continue

                                      in the United States.

FULBRIGHT:                     Jones: The Foreign Relations

   STILL IN STUDIO                    Committee headed by

                                      Senator Fulbright

                                      went on with its

                                      hearings on Viet

                                      Nam.

JONES ON CAMERA
```

This format illustrates the use of a number of symbols frequently used in setting up a television newscast. RP (rear projection) means that a picture is projected on the screen behind the newscaster as he continues talking into the camera. The term ROLL CUE indicates that point in the announcer's copy at which the director signals the projectionist to roll the film. This cue is necessary because film takes from three to four seconds to reach the speed needed for proper projection. This particular film is silent (SIL) for the first four seconds. The announcer voices his comment over this part of the film, then ceases as the sound recorded on the film (SOF) takes over. The OUT CUE indicates the last words of the correspondent recorded on the film. As these words end, the announcer in the studio resumes his presentation. TELOP refers to a still picture that is brought into the program by an opaque projector located in the projection room. The STILL IN STUDIO is a picture on an easel which is picked up by one of the TV cameras in the studio.

FEATURE TALKS

With the exception of political speeches and sermons, which originate outside the broadcasting industry, it is customary to think of the straight talk as a program form that disappeared from the American broadcasting scene a long time ago. The short feature talk that deals with some news development or human-interest story still survives, however, and is, indeed, an important factor on network radio. Subjects include the leading news story of the day, a sidelight on the news, fashion notes, comments on human behavior, a profile of a celebrity or personality in the news, a report from Europe, or an essay on human frailty. Local broadcasts that often include talks are programs for women, farm reports, how-to-do-it sessions, and human-interest features often made up mainly of audience-contributed anecdotes which illuminate the foibles of mankind. A type of broadcast talk that has become more common as educational television stations have spread around the country is the lecture, illustrated with visuals, delivered as part of a series which approximates a college course in its organization and subject matter.

WRITING THE FEATURE TALK

The problem of preparing a talk for broadcasting differs little in its basic essentials from the problem of preparing a talk for any public-speaking situation. The writer assigned such a task can therefore do no better than to refer to a text on public speaking for guidance in composition. Because there are a number of excellent books dealing with this subject, only a few salient points will be covered here.

A sound structural plan is as important for a talk as it is for a documentary. The principles of organization discussed earlier in this chapter apply to the writing of any feature program that concentrates on a single theme or subject. The general purpose and the central idea should be clearly defined in your mind before you begin writing, and you should also have prepared a relevant and logical succession of supporting points.

The beginning and ending of a broadcast feature are particularly important, the beginning because the deftness with which you snare audience attention may decide whether you are to have any listeners at all, and the ending because it leaves the audience with a last impression which will either ensure memorability or guarantee that what you have written will soon be forgotten.

Experience has shown that material with certain qualities has a high potentiality for maintaining interest. Among the elements that will help to hold your audience are the following: the introduction of the striking, the novel, or the unusual; references to the familiar; ideas in opposition which produce conflict; consideration of what is vitally important to the audience; the use of techniques that arouse suspense and curiosity; the inclusion of specific material such as examples, testimony, statistics, comparisons, and contrasts which make abstract ideas concrete. You should try to lead your audience to visualize what you are describing through the use of strong imagery. Make experiences come to life. Write so that the talk transmits a feeling of movement with ideas rising from point to point until a climax is reached. This development will communicate a sense of activity which is attention holding.

The language of a broadcast talk must take into account the fact that the audience is composed of isolated people who cannot experience the social facilitation operating in a group assembled in one auditorium. Even though millions may be listening, you are writing, not for a mass audience, but for a single person sitting at his ease in a home setting. This means that you should employ the direct, informal style characteristic of conversation. Clarity is important, too, for your audience cannot ask you to repeat, or request clarification of a complex thought. Of particular importance in attaining clearness is the use of "signpost" language which establishes connections between your ideas and points the way in which your thought is moving.

SAMPLE FEATURES

A regular feature of the CBS evening newscasts, anchored on television by Walter Cronkite and on radio by Douglas Edwards, is a brief commentary written and presented by Eric Sevareid. Most often these talks are designed to clarify the issues in a situation currently in the news; sometimes they concentrate on the less important happenings that illuminate the foibles of mankind; occasionally, they reflect the deep emotions aroused by certain events. Clarity of thought, incisive wit, and grace of expression mark Mr. Sevareid's writing. An excellent example of his art is the memorial he presented on the day of the funerals for the three astronauts who were killed while practicing for the first Apollo space mission. With quiet eloquence he reflected the feelings of a nation saddened as it had not been since the death of President Kennedy by the tragedy of young men struck down at the height of their powers.

ERIC SEVAREID

(Talk broadcast on CBS NEWS)

        Grissom and White and Chaffee - mortals who

    aspired to the moon and eternal space -

    were returned to the earth today from which

    they came and to which we all belong.

    They had lived life more intensely in a

    very few years than most of us do in our

lifetimes, and they shall be remembered far
longer. They were among the men who wield
a cutting edge of history and by this sword
they died.

Grissom and Chaffee were buried near the
grave of Lt. Thomas Selfridge, the first
American military pilot to be killed in an
airplane crash nearly 60 years ago. Then,
the air above the ground was as unfamiliar
as the space above the air. The men who
go first are accounted heroes and rightly
so, whatever the age, whatever the new
element and horizon. Space, said the late
President Kennedy, is our new ocean and we
must sail upon it. It was truly the hazards of the unknown oceans and territories
that took the lives of earlier heroes, like
Magellan or Captain Cook, men who went
first and were killed by inhabitants of the
Pacific.

It was not precisely the unknown hazards
of space that killed our astronauts; it
was the hazards of fallible man's calcu-
lations. It was not a technical failure;
all technical failures are human failures.
It was the familiar, never totally escap-
able failure of the human brain to cope
with the complexities it has arranged. A

slight miscalculation, a single slip, then

a spark, a flame, and the end of three

remarkable products of those infinitely

more complex mysteries, genetic in-

heritance and environment, the processes

that occasionally produce personalities

like Grissom and White and Chaffee - men

who are brave but not brash, proud but not

self-conscious, thoughtful but not brooding,

men of a health, a wholeness we all aspire

to but so few attain. We are told they

will be replaced. This only means that

other such men will take their places.

The three cannot be replaced. There never

was a replaceable human being.

In many instances feature talks are presented as separate programs in such series as CBS's *Dimension,* ABC's *Flair,* or NBC's *Emphasis.* Frank McGee appeared regularly on *Emphasis* in a series called "Second Thoughts." As with the Sevareid talks, the range of subjects covered by Mr. McGee was wide and his purposes varied. Sometimes he aimed to convey information, at others he pled a cause or sought to inspire, but in many instances he aimed merely to amuse, as in this example. But whatever his subject or purpose, his touch was light and conversational and his tone personal—the hallmarks of the feature talk.

FRANK McGEE, "Second Thoughts"

"Leg-watching"

(As broadcast on Emphasis, NBC)

I always thought that a girl's legs

were meant to be looked at purely for

pleasure. There is nothing like the sight

of a trim ankle or a finely-wrought calf to
sweeten the life of a male burdened down
by thoughts of death and taxes. This fall,
legs should be in evidence more than ever.
Reports from Paris state that skirts will
be higher--four inches higher. I don't
know how many American women will go along
with that piece of fashion legislation,

but some will, and every male eye on the
street will be glued on them.

Until now, leg-looking was a pretty
uncomplicated joy. But along comes K. P.
Saxena, who identifies himself as a psy-
chologist in Bombay, India. Mr. Saxena,
who doesn't care much about the beauty
part, has made a character-revealing study
of the female leg and is interested in the
psychological aspects of ankle and calf.
I believe Mr. Saxena's study was primarily
aimed at women. Yet I suspect that a great
many men will hang on his words as clues
to the character of the women whose legs
they watch and sometimes admire.

Here is what Mr. Saxena said recently
on the subject of women and their legs.
If women twist their legs around each other,
they are imaginative and artistic. In fact,
these women are very interested in music.

If women stretch out their legs with one
foot resting on the other, they are self-
confident. But Mr. Saxena issues a warning:
These confident gals have violent tempers.
Shall I go on? Of course! Now, if women
cross their legs, with the top leg bal-
ancing lightly, they are schemers. If they
hold their legs parallel, knees together
and feet in line, they are perfect --
almost too good to be true.

On the other hand, if women sit with
their knees squeezed tightly together while
their feet are spread far apart, they are
cold, self-centered egotists. And if they
keep their knees and toes together and their
heels apart, they are shy and lack assurance.

After digesting this information, I
offer, somewhat in retaliation, McGee's
Guide to Men's Legs, or footwork for the
secretary to ponder. I think that a man's
legs reveal just as much character as a
woman's, if not more. And they do this
even if they aren't looked at quite as often
or appreciated quite as much.

According to McGee's Guide, to be
published full length soon, if a man drums
his toes on the inner sole of his shoes,
he is impatient, demanding and hard to

please. So secretaries applying for a job
would be wise to remove the boss's shoes
before making up their minds. If the boss's
toes drum, watch out. However, if they are
relaxed, and the boss puts his knees together to form a lap on which you could
sit, he is obviously kind, considerate and
warmhearted. I think even Mr. Saxena would
agree with me on that. Naturally, he might
also be married. It is hard to tell a
married man from looking at his legs except
for scars the legs may carry. And those
are hard to see because most men wear
trousers which are not getting any higher
this year or next.

I have more observations on the psychology of men's legs to offer. But these
are all in McGee's Guide, to be published
in both hardcover and soft-cover versions
which can be mailed to you in an argyle
wrapper.

Frank McGee, NBC News, New York.

QUESTIONS AND PROJECTS

1. View a documentary on TV and prepare a structural outline of the content. Evaluate this outline for unity, emphasis, and coherence.

2. Create five subjects that might be given documentary treatment on radio or television. Develop a schedule of interviews for one of these subjects, making sure that the resulting filmed interviews will provide satisfactory material for the program.

3. Observe a number of documentaries with special attention to:
   a) attention-getting devices.
   b) methods of defining and clarifying the subject of the program.

4. Prepare a five-minute newscast using the stories from your daily newspaper. Describe your pattern of organization (topical; geographical; local, national, international) and briefly outline one other pattern you might have used.

5. In a number of newscasts evaluate:
   a) the headlines (do they tell too much? do they arouse interest?)
   b) the transitions (are they forced or natural?)

6. Select subjects for feature talks that fit into the following categories:
   a) philosophical; b) informational or educational; c) entertainment;
   d) news interpretation.

13

Children's Programs

Programs for children should be childlike but not childish. Shari
Lewis

Young boys and girls are among the most avid consumers of television
programs; surveys repeatedly indicate that the average elementary school
child spends some twenty hours a week with his eyes glued to a TV
screen, almost as much time as he spends in school. The effect of taking
this much time for one activity and the influence the programs may
have on children is a subject of much public concern. Television has
been attacked on a number of counts, among them that it is a passive
experience which lures children from more fruitful activities; that it
warps values by presenting a distorted picture of people and events;
and that it causes emotional damage which may even lead to juvenile
delinquency. Television is criticized also because its tremendous potentialities are primarily dedicated to attaining commercial purposes instead
of being used to enlarge the child's vision of the world.

Much of the agitation, it is true, is aroused not by programs written
especially for children but by programs meant for adults that children
view. This only deepens the responsibility of the writer for children.

He need not accept all of the objections as valid, but he must at least be alert to the practices that some people have found questionable. He also needs some understanding of childhood itself and a knowledge of the program content and writing techniques best adapted to meeting the child's unique needs.

THE NATURE OF CHILDHOOD

In answering the question—What is a child?—it is certainly too naïve to say that a child is simply a little adult. On the other hand, many of the attributes that characterize adult life exist in embryo in the child.

LIMITED EXPERIENCE

Some of the differences between adults and children are obvious to everyone. A young child clearly lacks the large reservoir of experience that is characteristic of an adult. One consequence of direct concern to the writer is the limited vocabulary of a child. Another is that he cannot discern relationships which may be perfectly clear to an older person. He tends to see items in an experience as separate and unconnected and he may have special problems in understanding time sequences. He is primarily aware of the present and his own existence in it and it is difficult for him to conceive of a world of which he was not a part. The concept of future time is even more difficult for him to comprehend. His lack of sophistication also causes him to assign roles to people as he is familiar with them in real life, and violations of these concepts may create confusion. Stories that portray children carrying out heroic actions may perplex him, for he sees a child as a relatively powerless person who is dependent on others for his well being.

SEEING LIFE IN SIMPLE TERMS

A second major difference between an adult and a child is that a child sees the world in essentially simple terms instead of in the complex terms of an adult. The child does not comprehend the shades and nuances of character which are actually true to life; rather he sees people in absolute colors as being good or bad and he understands only the most obvious of motives. He also tends to see events literally. A very young child does not realize that happenings in a fantasy are only "make-believe;" he accepts them as true. Millions of children for a period in their lives actually believe in that most fantastic of creatures

Santa Claus. A child seeing a man shot in a movie may believe that a man really had to be shot to make the scene. Some children even think that the characters in a television program are little people who live and sleep in the set behind the screen.

REPETITIONS

A third major difference between adults and children is that children enjoy repetitions of the same experience much more than adults do. Most children delight in hearing the same story read over and over again in exactly the same way and complain bitterly if the reader varies his technique in the slightest. A child may watch as if fascinated a television cartoon that he has already seen many times before. He hears without objection the constant reiteration of a long theme song like that used on every episode of the *Mickey Mouse Club*.

DIFFERENCES IN CHILDREN

Thus far we have been thinking of children as if they were all cast from the same mold. Actually, the differences between boys and girls of one age and those of another, and the differences even among children of the same age group, may be as profound as the differences that distinguish adults from children. The writer of scripts for children must take these differences into account. It is impossible, of course, to adapt to all of the individuals who may be in his audience, but he should have a good idea of the general age level toward which he is aiming. Fortunately he does not have to worry too much about whether his listeners are boys or girls, for important differences in their interests and needs do not develop until adolescence.

EARLY CHILDHOOD.   One generalization which seems obvious is that the younger a child is, the more limited is his fund of experience, but this is not the only variable. Another factor that distinguishes children of different ages is the relationship of the child to the world outside. The child of preschool age sees himself as the focus of the universe and in a completely self-centered way relates what is happening entirely to his own needs and concerns. One of the main ways in which he discovers himself is through his responses to others, and of these responses the most common is imitation. The writer can never afford to disregard the imitativeness of childhood.

As a child matures, his interest in himself is gradually supplemented by an interest in the world outside. An important step in this process takes place when the child first goes to school, and people outside his immediate family begin to assume an important role in his life. He feels a strong need to associate with people of his own age and becomes interested in sports, both as a participant and as an observer. The world around him begins to attract his attention, a matter of critical significance to the writer, for at this stage the child develops intense curiosity about what things are, how they work, and where they come from.

LATER CHILDHOOD.   The interest of the older child continues to range out from his immediate environment, both in time and space, and he becomes curious about events in the past and even about worlds that may exist among the stars. Stories of foreign lands and facts about them attract children of this age and they also become interested in the lives of great men and women. A child of nine distinguishes clearly between the real and the fantastic, and although he may still indulge in "make-believe" thinking, he knows that he is only pretending.

As children enter the adolescent period, they discover the world of popular music as it is heard on radio and for many the earplug of the transistor receiver seems to become a substitute for the infant's pacifier. The writer of children's scripts, however, need not be concerned about this age since audience surveys show that adolescents are not interested in programs written specifically for them but view almost exclusively programs designed for general audiences and adults.

ADULT VALUES IN THE CHILD

It is important for the writer of children's scripts to appreciate the differences that distinguish his audience from the one of adults, but it is just as important to recognize their great similarities. Children and adults turn to a television program for much the same reason—to escape the humdrum routine of their everyday existence. They want to be taken into a world outside the one that immediately surrounds them, to feel the excitement of rousing adventure, to savor the stimulation of new knowledge, to experience the emotional arousal that effective drama can accomplish. The vicarious enjoyment in the forbidden which helps to explain the great popularity of crime drama among adults is also a factor in children's listening. One of the appeals of clown programs for young children is that the clown can do things the child is not permitted to do: he can mumble and stumble, drop things, and make a mess of himself and his surroundings.

Delight in comedy is another common characteristic of both children and adults. Everyone, whatever his age, likes to laugh and have fun. Most people also enjoy actual participation in a program; the adult who shouts out the answers to quiz questions before the guests on the program can respond is having an experience somewhat similar to that of the preschool children who claps and sings along with the *Romper Room* lady.

THE CONTENT OF CHILDREN'S PROGRAMS

A helpful guide for the person who aspires to write for children is to note what broadcasters have done for children in the past and what they are doing today. It should be recognized, however, that such an examination cannot provide final answers to all the questions. Some programs represent clear adaptations to the special needs and characteristics of children, but the suitability of other practices is hotly debated. One problem is that concern for the child runs head on into commercial considerations; unfortunately, some programs considered most undesirable for the child are also the most likely to attract him.

BASIC SUBJECT MATTER

The Television Information Office at one time surveyed the television stations of the nation to discover what programs they produced for at-home viewing by children between the ages of four and twelve. The results of this survey, published in the book *For the Young Viewer*, provide a good index to the range of subjects covered by various children's programs.

EXPLORATION.   Many TV programs appeal directly to the child's urge to explore—to find out about himself, his neighborhood, and the world. It is significant that four children's programs produced by national networks all suggest this purpose in their titles—NBC's *Exploring* and *First Look*, ABC's *Discovery*, and NET's *What's New?*—and many locally produced programs have a similar focus. The range of programs produced under this heading is a wide one. Travel to other lands and visits to such places in the community as zoos, museums, hospitals, public buildings, state fairs, and factories may be featured, but exploration is not limited merely to places. Programs explore the past to make the child acquainted with historical personages and events; they introduce him to the discoveries of science; they take him into the world of the theatre; they tell him about sports; some simply help him to examine ideas and traditions.

ORIENTATION.   Having found out about the world through exploration, the child now needs help in making his adjustment to it. A number of programs aim to orient the child by teaching him what he can expect from the world and what is expected from him in return. Many such programs therefore deal with manners, morals, and health practices. They help to augment what is taught in the home, to reinforce the ethical teachings of the schools, and to deepen the effect of religious upbringing.

DOING. The purpose of some programs is to stimulate children to engage in worthwhile activity. In a sense such programs reverse the direction of exploratory programs; instead of taking the child outside his home to visit other places and peoples, they bring talented people into the home to lead the child into rewarding activities. Children may be taught to improve skills they have already developed such as maintaining proper posture or spelling, or they may be introduced to new skills such as painting, folk dancing, making puppets, training pets, or carving soap.

STORYTELLING. A large number of children's programs, perhaps the largest number of all, are designed to tell a story. These programs may range from those employing very simple formats to those engaging in a complete dramatic presentation.

MULTIPURPOSE. A number of programs are not limited to one type of content but fuse several elements into a program that seeks a variety of goals. This is particularly true of the longer programs. Because the child's attention span is short, his interest might drift away if one type of material is continued for too long a time. Therefore a typical program of this type might present a short film about another land (exploration); have a brief discussion on a topic such as: "how do you act if you don't get the Christmas gifts you expected?" (orientation); teach the proper way to swing a baseball bat (doing); and close with a cartoon story (storytelling). One problem in such programs is maintaining unity. A colorful personality helps, but a theme to which all of the elements in the program can be related is the best unifying device.

THE PROBLEM OF VIOLENCE

One of the perennial controversies in television revolves around the question whether the violence so common in programs is harmful to children. The writer of plays for children cannot escape this problem merely by excluding violence from his work, for to do so would eliminate an element intrinsic to the dramatic form. The question is how much violence is permissible and what kind? Two extended studies of the effect of television on children, one directed by Wilbur Schramm in the United States and the other by Hilde Himmelweit in Great Britain, arrived at substantially the same answers to this question. Their findings provide a reasonable and workable guide for the writer.

1. Stylized or ritual violence, such as that occurring in cartoons or Western dramas, usually does not frighten children. Shooting seems not to be disturbing except to very young children because the bullet cannot be seen, but the use of knives can be frightening because the child can see the weapon and its effect and he may vicariously feel the wound.

2. Violence that takes place in an unfamiliar setting is less likely to be frightening than violence that can be imagined as happening in the child's own home or street. The sight of a dark room or a stormy night or a glimpse of a face peering in at a window may terrify a child because it brings back the fears he feels in his own dark bedroom.

3. The magnitude of a disaster is less important to a child than the prospect of hurt to someone with whom he identifies or feels attachment. The threat of injury or death to children or to a beloved animal such as *Lassie* or *Flipper* is particularly agitating. In line with this finding, the Canadian Broadcasting Corporation refused to use an episode of *Flipper* that showed the porpoise being attacked by sharks.

4. Black and white characters are less likely to arouse fears than the complex characters we designate as gray. A child feels more secure when he can immediately tell the "good guys" from the "bad guys." A character who seems to have both good and bad qualities may confuse a child even if he does not disturb him.

5. A program in a series that follows a rigidly established pattern is less likely to be frightening than an individual show even though the series drama may contain a great deal of violence. Because the child is familiar with the conventions of the series, he has the security of knowing the pattern of events and can have confidence in the final supremacy of the hero-figure.

6. The knowledge that events are make-believe rather than real reduces fear. As has been mentioned, this distinction is more difficult to maintain with younger than it is with older children; the age of a child is therefore an important factor. A small boy listening to a radio adaptation of Oscar Wilde's "The Selfish Giant" burst into tears when the giant finally died because he was too young to discount what he heard and reacted to it as if it were real. The tendency of young children to become totally absorbed by what they see and hear means that they should not be exposed to situations that are highly emotional or violent or in which tension is prolonged for too long a time. Heavy music, dead silence, ticking clocks, or sudden noises may make a scene intolerable to children. Graphic portrayals of torture are likely to be especially

disturbing. Shrieks of agony or other evidences of pain should be avoided.

In an earlier chapter it was pointed out that writers may be assigned the task of adapting material that is usually thought of as being for children even though it contains violent scenes and characters. The classic children's story "Rumpelstiltskin" as told by the Brothers Grimm, features one of the most unsavory characters in literature: a king who threatens to kill a young girl unless she can produce gold and who decides to marry her only when she has satisfied his avariciousness. Other tales, among them some included in the *Arabian Nights,* are even more bloodthirsty. It is well to remember that many of these stories were not written originally for children at all but for adults. Turning them into TV offerings suitable for children, particularly when we remember that dramatic treatment intensifies the effect of violence, often requires some modification of the original characters and plots.

OTHER UNDESIRABLE CONTENT

Violence in children's shows has been the most common target of criticism, but it is not the only one. In an unusual exercise in self-examination, the National Broadcasting Company at one time organized a Children's Program Review Committee and then published its criticism even though many of the complaints applied to shows then being carried by NBC. On the basis of the committee's report, NBC established the following standards:

1. Do not portray as acceptable action that would be forbidden at home and which might have a bad effect on the relationships between children and parents.

2. Avoid bad grammar and poor pronunciation except when they are given a clear character identification.

3. Eliminate overdone and destructive slapstick and such crudities as calling on performers to play the trombone with a mouth filled with watermelon.

4. Refrain from an overemphasis on money and exhorbitant rewards for successes that are simply the result of chance.

5. Be careful that the information included on programs is accurate and expressed in terms the child can understand. Misguided enlightenment can be worse than none at all.

A reference to children's programming is included in the TV code of the National Association of Broadcasters. It contains the conventional strictures against undue emphasis on violence and sex and warns against making crime attractive, demanding that the criminal meet with inevitable retribution. There is another type of content to be avoided also, not because it is harmful to children but because it does not interest them. That subject is romance. Children realize that men and women fall in love and get married, but the subtler meanings of the emotion are beyond their understanding and interest. Anyone who has heard a group of children at a Saturday movie matinee groan when a love scene starts will appreciate the soundness of this suggestion.

INCLUDING POSITIVE VALUES

Most people considering children's programs tend to think first about what to avoid, but it is just as important to consider what to include. There are a number of suggestions in the documents we have reviewed. The NAB code emphasizes the importance of affording opportunities for cultural growth and promoting "commonly accepted moral, social, and ethical ideals characteristic of American life." It also demands that programs "reflect respect for parents, for honorable behavior, and for the constituted authorities of the American community." The NBC committee report criticized the lack of balance in children's programs and suggested more of the following: how-to-do-it shows, field trips to interesting, instructive places, music, greater contact with people and customs of other countries, hobby material, simple story telling, child-animal series, and adventure stories other than Westerns.

One of the best descriptions of positive values in children's programs was prepared by Dr. Fred Rainsberry while he was Supervisor of School Broadcasts and Youth Programming for the Canadian Broadcasting Corporation. The main points of that policy statement were as follows:

1. Because children's programs play a part in determining the artistic taste and social attitude of adults of the future they should: (a.) Communicate traditional and essential values. (b.) Include vital material that will add to the child's stature as an experiencing person. (c.) Help the child to develop a sense of social responsibility.

2. Programs should exploit the child's urge to imitate, the type of imitation that will have a significant creative and developmental effect.

3. Programs should preserve the creative and spontaneous urge to self-expression, an urge that can be ruined by dull and tasteless programming.

4. Programs must be based on an understanding of current trends in culture.

At one time the CBC produced its own version of the American puppet show *Howdy Doody*. The way in which this program differed from its American counterpart illustrated some of the CBC's policies with respect to children's programs. In comparison to the American, the Canadian *Howdy Doody* was slower-paced and less noisy; it substituted nature films for segments of old movies; it made the lead a disciplined person rather than a blatant exhibitionist; it included more music; it eliminated tension; it substituted whimsy for frenzy.

One word of warning is necessary with respect to the execution of high-minded principles such as those of the CBC. In endeavoring to include concrete values in his scripts, the writer may fall into the distressing error of moralizing. This is no more palatable to children than it is to adults. As we have noted before, a child tunes in a television set to seek entertainment, relaxation, excitement, and release from humdrum living. Moral and educational values must be achieved incidentally to the major goal of entertaining the child.

Akin to the mistake of moralizing is that most pernicious of faults— writing down to children. Patronizing a child is the worst mistake a writer can make. Obviously you have to write in terms of the child's understanding, but you should nevertheless communicate your own sense of enjoyment in the subject. A supercilious attitude will be quickly detected and deeply resented.

SPECIFIC WRITING TECHNIQUES

Writing a children's script does not require radical new approaches or techniques which differ basically from those already covered. The methods of gaining and holding attention described in Chapter 6, for example, apply as much to children's scripts as they do to programs meant for a general audience. The unique nature of children and the responsibility of the broadcaster for contributing to their proper growth and development do call, however, for some adaptations in the usual techniques.

THE STRUCTURE OF THE PROGRAM

Many children's programs, particularly those aimed at the youngest age group, are built around the telling of a story. In television a number of visual techniques can be used to illustrate the event: the narrator drawing pictures while he talks; still pictures; animation; puppets; and actors appearing in silhouette or in dramatic scenes. The radio narration may feature only a storyteller, or it may add such devices as music at transition points; sound effects; actors to read voices; a proxy listener to ask questions of the narrator; and dramatic scenes. Many stories for children are completely dramatized, of course. Other programs of a nonfiction type employ a wide variety of visual and sound effects to achieve their purposes.

In developing a program series, maintain a simple and coherent program structure which follows a consistent pattern from week to week so that the children know what to expect. If the program is dramatic, keep the story line as direct as possible by developing a few scenes completely rather than by writing a staccato succession of short scenes. Start the main story promptly and provide enough action and excitement to hold attention, for suspense and urgency are as important as they are in adult drama.

Present as few major characters as possible to avoid complicating the child's problem of keeping track of people. Introduce them early and keep them consistent. You should be careful in naming your characters. One common mistake is choosing a bizarre name such as Nicodemus Nimbletoes which carries little meaning to a child. A funny character name can be an asset to a program but only if it is funny to the child.

Since the attention span of children is shorter than that of adults, you should vary the content and pace as much as possible and avoid encompassing too much information in one broadcast. Generally, you should keep in mind the youngest children toward which you are aiming your program and try to make it meaningful and interesting to them. This does not mean that children will not enjoy programs meant for another group; it has been discovered that some children, particularly the brighter ones, like the challenge of viewing programs meant for older children.

RELATING TO THE CHILD'S EXPERIENCE

The child's limited fund of experience and his lack of sophistication require a number of adaptations. It is obvious that the language used in a children's program should be simpler and more direct than that used for adults. One important requirement is a careful attention to vocabulary. This does not mean that you should use only words the child already knows, for to do so would nullify the contribution that broadcasts can make to the growth of a child's vocabulary, but you should introduce new words so that their meaning becomes clear from the context. For young children, nouns, verbs, and pronouns are the most important parts of sentences, and adverbs and adjectives should be used sparingly. Keep grammatical structure simple, particularly for the very young child. Avoid dialects if possible, for they are not easily understood.

A child's craving to find out about the world around him provides you with an automatic hold on his attention, but you can quickly lose it if you present new material in such a way that bewilderment rather than enlightenment results. Introduce fresh ideas in the environment of the familiar. Furthermore, the problems you treat should be ones that are related to the real or easily imagined experiences of the children.

Because children have difficulty with the concept of time, you must be especially careful when time concepts are involved. Programs should proceed chronologically if possible, for a child expects a story to move forward. If it moves backward, he is likely to be confused, which means that the flashback technique should be used sparingly if at all. For the same reason avoid extreme shifts in time and space and be sure that transitions are simple and clear.

QUESTIONS AND PROJECTS

1. Consider how the interests and capacities of children in the four-to-eight age group differ from those in the nine-to-twelve age group. Then suggest two subjects or stories particularly adapted to the needs of each group.

2. What is your personal response to the often-heard criticism that television purveys too much violence, especially for children?

3. Watch a TV program designed for children with special attention to vocabulary. Decide whether the language is simple enough for a child to follow the program yet sufficiently challenging to expand his vocabulary.

4. The familiar stories "Bluebeard" and "The Emperor's New Clothes" present difficulties of different types for the writer who proposes to adapt them into dramas for children. Read these stories, decide what the problems are, and indicate how you would deal with them in adaptations.

5. Suggest subjects for children's programs in each of the following content categories: exploration, orientation, doing, storytelling, and multipurpose.

14

Comedy

Television is a medium of entertainment which permits millions of people to listen to the same joke at the same time and yet remain lonesome. T. S. Eliot

Programs in which comedy is a major ingredient have been important in broadcasting since the early 1930s. For many years in succession during the period of radio's dominance, ten of the first fifteen programs in audience popularity were comedy programs. Comedy has continued to hold its place in the television era as one of the most important elements in the broadcasting bill of fare; in the middle 1960s more than a third of network TV shows featured comedy. Turning out the scripts for all of these programs provides rich rewards for those who can respond to the special demands such writing imposes. Laying down principles for achieving success as a comedy writer, however, involves unusual difficulties.

Laughter, to begin with, is an intensely personal experience. What is funny to one person may not be funny to another person at all. As Jean Kerr, the playwright and humorous essayist, put it, "In many ways what makes you laugh is as private as what makes you cry."

E. B. White put his finger on a second problem when he said, "Humor can be dissected as a frog can, but the thing dies in the process and the innards are discouraging to any but the pure scientific mind." Explaining the point in a joke does kill the fun, and yet we cannot understand its mechanism unless we take it apart to see how it works. The analyses that follow may spoil a number of jokes for you even though they have made millions laugh, and it could even dampen the fun in future jokes.

A third problem is that many jokes are funny in the context in which they are heard, but when they are repeated outside of that situation, they lose their mirth-provoking power. You undoubtedly have had the chastening experience of describing to your friends what seemed to be a hilarious incident at the time it happened only to have them greet your story with nothing more than frowns or puzzled looks. A comedy program develops its own atmosphere of fun in which even a poor joke may seem funnier than it really is.

Finally, we should recognize that analyzing humor, although it is an intriguing exercise in itself, may contribute little to an individual's ability to write comedy programs. The possession of natural talent is more important to the person who turns out comedy scripts than it is to the writer of any other kind of material. To make an audience laugh, your view of events and people must be eccentric. What others see as round you must see as a little out of round. Many people who turn out comedy, in fact, cannot seem to help being funny. When I asked Phyllis Diller for permission to use a line from one of her comedy routines, she wrote an amusing letter which included a funny story explaining how that particular line had come into existence. To my request to Henry Morgan for United States and world rights for the use of some of his material, the comedian replied, "You may also use it on the nearby planets." Instruction cannot give you a comic sense, but if you possess it, an understanding of what makes people laugh may help you to sharpen its edge and realize its full potentialities.

THE ROOTS OF LAUGHTER

A number of people have tried to devise a theory that would explain the motivation for all laughter. The theories differ to some extent, but each one identifies elements found in situations that make people laugh. It seems reasonable to assume that a comedy writer who inserts these elements into his script will succeed in producing laughter, provided the presentation is effective and the atmosphere is congenial to humor.

Let us review these elements and illustrate them by references to jokes and comedy situations.

TRIUMPH

An element that can be discerned in many comedy situations is a condition of triumph; we laugh to express the feeling of superiority or elation accompanying it. The particular kind of triumph we experience may be one of several varieties.

TRIUMPH IN A FIGHT. The most primitive type of laughter is that which issues from the throat of a person who has been victorious in a duel. Besides expressing his feeling of joy, it helps him to dissipate the energy and strain he had mobilized in preparation for the battle. The loser in the struggle accomplishes the demobilization of his resources in just the opposite way; he weeps. Albert Rapp in his book *The Origins of Wit and Humor* expressed the belief that all laughter can be traced back to this primitive roar of triumph. He described laughter as an essentially hostile reaction which is born out of man's hatred and aggressiveness. If there were no hostility in mankind, he argued, there would be no laughter and no need for it.

VICARIOUS TRIUMPH. Few people actually engage in personal combat these days, but there is still a great deal of laughter motivated by feelings of triumph because we participate vicariously in the success of the victor. Those who see the struggle directly identify themselves with one of the participants, usually the winner, and they laugh in unison with him. It is not even necessary to see the actual conflict, for evidence of a struggle substitutes for the scene as a whole and triggers a laugh reaction. That is why the possessor of a black eye, the obvious loser in a struggle, is almost universally greeted with giggles. Other manifestations of defeat call for the same reaction. We titter when someone trips and stumbles because these actions recall the moment in a fight when the defeated one is beaten to the ground. If the person who stumbles is stuffy or dignified, we laugh even harder, for the sharp contrast between his dignity and his discomfiture enlarges our feeling of superiority.

Generally, of course, we laugh only at the minor mishaps of others but greet those afflicted by major misfortunes with sympathy and help. Thus we laugh at a man when he falls down, but we stop laughing if he fails to get up. It seems clear, however, that this sympathetic reaction is a thin veneer on a more primitive response. Young children often laugh uproariously at other people's misfortunes, and their idea of a joke is to inflict pain or embarrassment on some other person. The sight of a disabled or misshapen person may send them into gales of merriment because they have not yet learned that such an outburst is improper. Reactions of this type are not limited to children, however. In China, witnesses to floggings and even to executions have been seen convulsed with laughter. The literature of our own Western civilization contains many examples of laughter provoked by the damaged, the battered, the deformed, and the crippled. Laughter at physical misfortune, as an expression of vicarious triumph, appears to be elemental in mankind.

TRIUMPH THROUGH WORDS.   A struggle does not necessarily involve physical combat but may be fought with words alone, particularly in a civilized situation. A clever person with a rapier thrust of wit may achieve a triumph as complete as that of the caveman who batters his adversary to the ground with a club. Once, for example, an old lady was greeted by an insolent young man as follows:

"Good morning, Mother of Asses."

"Good morning, my son," she replied.

We can imagine that she went down the road shaking with laughter at her triumph in this duel of wits.

Just as a symbol of triumph in physical combat can make us laugh, so can a reminder of a triumph achieved wholly on a verbal plane. The element most likely to induce laughter, of course, is the verbal thrust that demolishes the adversary. It follows that much humor is based entirely on derision. Percy Hammond, the drama critic, ended a comment on a musical revue with these words: "I have knocked everything except the chorus girls' knees and nature anticipated me there." That is pure, undiluted ridicule. Moreover, it is savage. The important place of derision in comedy can be observed in the routines of many of the comedians who present monologues. Phyllis Diller's comment that her husband Fang "lost so much blood after cutting himself shaving that his eyes cleared up" is an example of sheer venom. The "stand up" comedian Alan King employs material of the same type. In a retort attributed to Groucho Marx, "I never forget a face, but I'll make an exception in your case," the attempt to belittle is obvious.

Many times in a contest a blunder by the loser tilts the scales against him. Mistakes made by other people therefore remind us of triumph, and the superiority feeling that follows is a frequent cause of laughter. If the person committing the error is one we look on as our better, our laughter is even louder. One television announcer, for example, took a puff from a sponsor's cigarette, smiled with rapture, and said, "M'm. . .m that's real coffee." The viewers who heard that boner undoubtedly howled with greater glee than they would normally have had anyone else made the mistake because the announcer whose usual sureness of delivery contrasted so sharply with their own bumbling speech had fallen into this error.

TRIUMPH OF GETTING THE POINT.   A kind of triumph implicit in much comedy which is quite different from what has been discussed thus far is the feeling of superiority experienced when one sees the point of a story. This type of triumph alone seems to be an important factor in causing a laugh response to many jokes. It is one of the reasons we laugh at puns—if we do. Richard Sheridan when asked to explain the difference between a man and woman replied, "Madame, I cannot conceive." The feat of discerning Sheridan's double meaning gives us a feeling of satisfaction and we laugh.

The importance of letting the listener get the point on his own is emphasized by what happens when we explain a story to a person who has failed to get the joke. Having been denied the feeling of triumph that comes from seeing the point himself, the listener almost never laughs. This fact has two lessons for the comedy writer. First, he must make adroit use of the technique of implication. The skillful writer does not tell viewers directly that Jack Benny is stingy and penurious. Instead, he lets them see that the phone Benny has invited his guests to use in his home is actually a pay telephone. Or he has Benny accosted by an armed robber. "Your money or your life," mutters the robber. There is a long pause. "Well?" asks the robber. "I'm thinking it over," says Benny. The second rule for the writer is that he must avoid following his punch line with an explanation, trusting his listeners to get the point on their own.

TRIUMPH OVER RESTRAINT.   The gratification we experience when we conquer a repression is still another form of triumph that causes laughter. That is why employees at a company picnic laugh so uproariously when someone, under the special rules that come into being for such an occasion, makes fun of the boss. For the same reason college students howl with glee at even the feeblest joke on their professor. And Protestants listen to jokes about their ministers and Catholics to jokes about their priests with particular relish.

The greatest triumph over repression comes, however, when a joke contains a sexual implication, for such a reference breaks through the most rigid taboos that society can muster. For this reason humor with sexual overtones is likely to elicit the loudest outburst of all. In fact, sexual references alone, unsupported by any other humorous element, often seem sufficient in themselves to make many people laugh. The type of triumph involved in breaking this taboo can also reinforce the effect of jokes that are funny for other reasons. Richard Sheridan's pun about the difference between men and women gains impact because it nudges into the area of the forbidden.

The restrictions surrounding radio and television make it necessary for such references to be exceedingly deft and indirect if the broadcaster is to elude censorship, but he is not entirely denied the power to arouse the laughter that is inherent in prohibited topics. The forbidden cannot be explicit in the script but must be aroused only in the listener's mind by a process of suggestion or the use of an implied double-meaning. The broadcaster can then argue that he should not be blamed if the listener chooses the wrong meaning. Bob Hope and Johnny Carson are comedians who usually maneuver successfully down the narrow line separating what goes too far from what goes just far enough to break pleasantly through some of society's sterner restraints.

INCONGRUITY

A second major ingredient in many laugh-provoking situations is an incongruity. We tend to laugh at the approximation of two elements that do not naturally belong together. Another way of stating this point is to say that we laugh at the incompatible, the absurd, the outlandish, and the grotesque. Even a mere contrast may make us laugh. The fact that Stan Laurel was thin and Oliver Hardy was fat enhanced the humor of their comedies.

EXAMPLES OF INCONGRUITY. The power of incongruous language to arouse laughter is illustrated by one of the most famous cartoons ever printed in the *New Yorker* magazine. It showed a mother trying to persuade her child to eat his food. "It's broccoli, dear," she says. "I say it's spinach," replies the youngster, "and I say to hell with it."[1] Incongruous language of another type makes us laugh at the children in Charles Schulz's comic strip *Peanuts*. The complexity of their language style and the ideas they express reveal a sophistication and maturity quite out of keeping with their age. Incongruity of language plus some surprise also explains the humor in Ring Lardner's story about a boy and his father: "Are you lost, Daddy?" "Shut up," he explained.

The capacity of incongruity to provoke laughter is illustrated by the effect one gains merely by jumbling words. A good example is the so-called spoonerism, named after a certain Reverend Spooner, who was often guilty of interchanging the syllables of words. At the end of a

[1] Caption for a Carl Rose drawing; reprinted by permission; Copr. © 1928, 1956, The New Yorker Magazine, Inc.

wedding service, he is reputed to have said, "It is kisstomary to cuss the bride." Reverend Spooner was not the only victim of this type of error. Mel Allen introducing a show sponsored by a tobacco company said blithely, "It's smipe poking time, gentlemen," and Ben Grauer closed a program with the statement, "We are deepful grately for your being here." Jimmy Durante has consistently employed gross mispronunciation as a comedy technique and Maxie Rosenbloom, the former boxer, has been equally successful in making people laugh simply by misusing words, as he did in the statement, "This caps the Kleenex." The most celebrated practitioner of this technique, of course, was Richard Sheridan who in *The Rivals* created Mrs. Malaprop, a character whose very name has come to symbolize the humorous misuse of words.

SHEER ABSURDITY.   Incongruity carried to its farthest extreme becomes sheer absurdity, which also has marked power to make people laugh. Stephen Leacock's famous line that the young man "flung himself upon his horse and rode madly off in all directions" illustrates the laugh-provoking capacity of utter nonsense. The delightful inconsistency of Samuel Goldwyn in discussing the naming of a motion-picture character brings a smile to our lips. "Let's not call the hero Joe," said Sam. "Every Tom, Dick, and Harry is called Joe." The arrant nonsense of a motto said to be hanging on a TV comedian's wall, "Death is nature's way of telling us to slow down," may make us laugh, and then again it may not.

Sheer absurdity was at the heart of a TV monologue so hilarious that it was a significant element in advancing the career of the comedian who delivered it, George Gobel. It seemed that the hubcaps from George's car had been stolen and George called his insurance company for payment. "Was the car locked at the time, Mr. Gobel?" asked the insurance adjuster. "Yes," replied Gobel, "but this particular time I very carelessly neglected to take the hubcaps off and put 'em in the car before I locked it . . . It's all my fault. It's just one of them silly, stupid, unfortunate incidents."[2]

INCONGRUITY THROUGH EXAGGERATION.   A common technique for introducing incongruity into a situation is to exaggerate it. This is supposed to be a peculiarly American form of humor, but its use is not limited to this country. When the English writer Noel Coward sent a picture of the Venus de Milo to one of his friends and said, "This is what will happen to you if you don't stop biting your nails," he was employing this technique. The French writer Rabelais was also a master of exaggeration. It is true, however, that America has had outstanding practi-

[2] Quoted in Steve Allen, *The Funny Men* (New York: Simon and Schuster, Inc., 1956), p. 176. (Material written by Harry Winkler).

tioners of the art. Mark Twain in his "Jumping Frog of Calaveras County" employed exaggeration for humorous effect. So did the writers of the *Paul Bunyan* stories. Sid Caesar, the television comedian, often extends a simple act into outlandish exaggeration. When he ties a shoelace, the lace is not restricted merely to the shoe but in pantomime ends up wrapped around his leg and thigh. As a doctor he does not merely tap the patient's chest, but his shoulder, his arm, his hand, an even the floor. Then he ends up by saying, "Your trouble is termites."

Many people who recall the *Jack Benny* program remember the vault in which he kept his money. It was a masterpiece of exaggeration. Located deep beneath his home, it was approached through a long tunnel, barricaded at regular intervals with heavy metal doors, and reinforced with chains. The sound of these doors being opened one by one as Jack Benny approached his vault is one of the memorable recollections of radio. But the stroke of genius in this routine was the creation of the guard Ed, who spent his life in the abyss below, guarding Benny's money. If the audience had not laughed before, it could always be depended on to explode when lonely Ed asked plaintively, "How are things on the outside?"

INCONGRUITY THROUGH UNDERSTATEMENT. A direct opposite of the technique of exaggeration is the introduction of incongruity by understating a situation or under-reacting to it. This technique is supposed to be English in its origin, and it is true that some English writers, particularly P. G. Wodehouse, are unusually skilled in employing it, but Americans have also used understatement with telling effect. When Mark Twain said, "The reports of my death are grossly exaggerated," he was employing understatement and in the passage that follows the humor arises almost entirely from Mark Twain's deliberate inadequacy in expressing the terror he experienced in escaping from a dangerous situation.

I went away from there. I do not say that I went away in any sort of a hurry, but I simply went—that is sufficient. I went out at the window, and I carried the sash along with me. I did not need the sash, but it was handier to take it than it was to leave it, and so I took it.

A small-town newspaper once carried the following news item. "A traveler would have missed the noon train yesterday, had he not stepped on a peach pit at the head of the depot stairs." Understatement is the primary reason for the humor of this statement, but it also contains other laugh-producing factors—the use of indirection which permits the listener the triumph of fashioning the image of what happened in his own mind and the vision of a person falling ignominiously down a flight of steps, suggesting triumph in a fight.

The technique of under-reacting to a situation is akin in its effect to that of understatement. The comedians of the silent-film era were notable for their use of it. One of Buster Keaton's characteristic techniques was to keep a stony, fixed expression on his face no matter what indignities or perils were being visited upon him. Another favorite comedy device of the movies was to stand unresisting while someone committed mayhem upon one's person.

SURPRISE

A third element found in many laugh-provoking situations is surprise. Often it is combined with other laugh-provoking elements. Incongruity gains at least part of its effect, for example, because it is unexpected. There are also other ways in which the comedian may surprise his audience and earn a laugh.

SUBSTITUTING ONE MEANING FOR ANOTHER.   In many instances we laugh at a joke because we are led to expect one meaning and are given another. The main reason we chuckle at puns is that the sense of a word is suddenly switched, as in the following example: "Two old maids went for a tramp in the woods. The tramp got away." Other factors support the comedy effect, of course: it skirts the edge of the forbidden and presents two people in a ludicrous situation. The laugh-provoking power of derision frequently reinforces the surprise element in puns, particularly those employed by critics. A music reviewer once wrote, "A quartet played Brahms last night. Brahms lost." One of the most famous pieces of dramatic criticism ever written was composed by Eugene Field when he said of a Shakespearean performer, "He played the King as though he were in constant fear that someone was going to play the ace."

Switching a listener suddenly from one meaning to another may not require what is usually thought of as a pun, however, as the following joke illustrates. "My whole freshmen year I wore brown and white shoes," a college student recalled. "Actually they were impractical because the white one kept getting dirty." Note that the comedy effect of the switch in meaning is reinforced by the essential absurdity of the picture it presents. Surprise plus derision gave the following criticism of a dramatic performer its snap. "She ran the gamut of emotions from A to B." Lord Byron employed the same technique of turning what seemed to be a compliment into scathing disparagement when he wrote, "Southey will be read after Dante and Homer are forgotten—but not until then."

A variation of the surprise approach is the technique of interpreting literally what most people tend to take figuratively. Told that "Schools and parents ought to get closer together," a father replied, "I certainly agree because then I wouldn't have so far to walk to PTA meetings." Children often amuse us in the same way, but their assumption of the literal meaning is unintentional, being simply a reflection of their lack of sophistication. Sometimes in their innocence they also surprise us by carrying an expression from one situation in which it belongs over to another situation in which it does not. A little boy, for example, who had heard his mother say, "I would have finished the washing but I ran out of soap," said: "I would have finished my dinner but I ran out of stomach."

NO MEANING AT ALL. A second basic technique of surprise is to lead a listener to expect a meaning and then leave him with no meaning at all. The philosopher Immanuel Kant described this technique as "the sudden transformation of strained expectation into nothing." We laugh because our train of logical thought is suddenly derailed. The sheer absurdity with which we are usually left is further stimulus to laughter. When Stephen Leacock wrote "The legendary Bulbecks were a fabulous race, half man, half horse, half bird," he seemed momentarily to be conveying sense and then the whole structure collapsed into nonsense. The horse in Groucho Marx's statement, "I'd horsewhip you if I had a horse," seems to have a certain logical significance until we recognize that it is a complete irrelevancy. Peter de Vries is another who makes skillful use of the technique that jolts our thought processes. "Top soil in Connecticut is far from dirt cheap," a character in one of his books remarks. Another says, "Anybody who goes to a psychiatrist ought to have his head examined." James Thurber's reply to a woman who told him his books were funnier in French, "Oh, yes, I lose something in the original," is a prime example of the thought that suddenly twists around on us and deceives our expectation.

The so-called "Irish bull" is another example of humor arising from ideas whose logical inconsistencies and contradictory statements leave the listener with no meaning at all. The following "bulls" illustrate the mirth-provoking potentialities of a single idea straining to go in opposite directions at the same time. An Irish parishioner chided one of his fellows for not attending services with these words: "If you'd been in church this morning and saw how few were there, you would have been ashamed to have been absent." A distracted father on a trip with his child said to his whining offspring; "The next time I take you anywhere I'll leave you home." Then there are the words of the Irish architect: "Where will you find any modern building that has lasted as long as the old ones?"

COMBINING THE TECHNIQUES

As we have seen, most laugh-provoking situations contain an element of triumph, of incongruity, or of surprise and many of them, it is clear, contain more than one of these elements. The multiplication of the comedy elements in a situation often multiplies its power to induce mirth, as is illustrated by a line from a Fred Allen script: "Next Sunday the Reverend Dr. Jones will preach on 'Skiing on the Sabbath' or 'Are our Young Women Backsliding on Their Week-ends!'" This line, first of all, arouses a ludicrous picture in the listener's mind. Some degree of surprise or reversal also develops as the listener perceives that the last line has a double meaning. In addition, there are two elements of triumph: one is the satisfaction that arises from divining the play on words involved in the two puns, and the second is victory over repression inherent in the implied reference to a portion of the human anatomy whose mention is usually taboo.

The humor of this Fred Allen line is primarily dependent on two puns, and while we are on the subject it may be well to consider for a moment the place of the pun in humor. Puns have been called the lowest form of humor, but this can be interpreted to mean, not that they are beneath contempt, but that they are the foundation on which a great deal of humor is built. We have seen that they are a principal tool for achieving surprise in a joke, for the pun by its very nature leads the listener in one direction and then suddenly switches him into another. Many writers have been addicted to their use, Shakespeare among them. Mercutio in *Romeo and Juliet* even after he had been stabbed could not resist a pun, saying, "Ask for me tomorrow and you shall find me a grave man." Yet the questions persist. Are puns worthy of the perpetrator? Are puns really funny? Do they deserve to be greeted with laughs or with groans?

The answer seems to be that some puns are funny and some are not. The funny ones are those that help communicate a richness of meaning and effect, such as those in the Fred Allen line just quoted. The unfunny ones are those that involve only a play on words but nothing much more than that. The jokes, "One Turk meeting another one said, 'I don't remember your name, but your fez is familiar'," or the definition of a music lover as a stereotype are thin and unsatisfying. They deserve to be greeted with groans, rather than laughter.

Another characteristic of the funny pun is that it has the quality of spontaneity. It seems to spring naturally from the situation. The labored, artificial pun produced by dint of great effort and careful prearrangement is usually not very funny. "A radio announcer has small hands because he needs wee paws for station identification" is an example of a forced pun. Jean Kerr put what she says is the only pun she ever contrived in this category. It involved a remark made to a monsignor who had been waiting for many years to become a bishop, "Long time, no See."

A funny pun, finally, is one in which the double meaning darts into the mind of the listener instantly. The sudden flash of the unexpected is an essential element. If one must ponder before he sees the joke, he is likely not to laugh. Thus the pun "One man's Mede is another man's Persian," although immensely clever, is so complex that it may not make us laugh. The same comment applies to the triple pun in the story about the three Texas boys who called their ranch "Focus" because it was where the sons raise meat (sun's rays meet). Ogden Nash's wit in the following lines from *The Private Dining Room* may be almost too dazzling to generate spontaneous mirth:

I am a conscientious man, when I throw rocks at sea birds I leave no tern unstoned,

I am a meticulous man, and when I portray baboons I leave no stern untoned.

CREATING COMEDY MATERIAL

The task of creating a comedy program is one of the most onerous that can face a writer, particularly when he must manufacture a new script every week. Generations of comedy writers have testified to the anguish this effort entails. To guide you as you face the difficult challenge of amusing an audience, the major factors that make people laugh have been described. The successful incorporation of elements of triumph, incongruity, or surprise into comedy material, however, requires some additional knowledge of comedy programs and the mechanics of script writing.

TYPES OF COMEDY PROGRAMS

One major group of comedy scripts motivates laughter by placing funny characters in funny situations, and in this group the most common type is the comedy drama, or situation comedy, as it is often called. Being dramas, in addition to making audiences laugh, they must be written to meet the criteria that apply to any type of drama. The writer must create characters and a plot, try to build suspense, enlist audience sympathy for his characters, make those characters believable insofar as he can within the confines of his comedy idea, construct a story that immediately engages the attention of his viewers, carry them forward on a rising plane of interest to a climax, and provide a sound and satisfying resolution.

Another type of comedy script presents characters in a situation but does not develop the situation into a complete plot with a beginning, a middle, and an end. Programs in the *Jack Benny* series, for example, often revolved around the fact that Jack was buying gifts for his friends, was going to New York to make a personal appearance, or was visiting Yosemite on a skiing holiday. Many times the idea for comedy on variety shows is inspired by incidents in the lives of the guests, and the framework for the script is often the actual process of putting on the show. A third type of character-comedy script features a series of sketches in which the leading comedian plays a variety of roles. Examples are Red Skelton's impersonation of such characters as Cauliflower McPhugg and Clem Kadiddlehopper, and the Reggie Van Gleason III and Joe the Bartender sketches of the *Jackie Gleason* show.

Another major type of comedy depends for its humor not on character, but on the construction of a series of gags or jokes. The best examples of such material are the monologues delivered at the beginning of their shows by comedians like Bob Hope and Jackie Gleason. Much of the material used by "stand-up" comedians, such as Alan King and Phyllis Diller, also falls into the gag category. Fred Allen was primarily a gag comedian. In his scripts there was no development of a continuing situation and little if any building of character, although the jokes might be grouped around some kind of theme.

TEAM WRITING

One condition that distinguishes the writing of comedy from the writing of most other types of scripts is that in most instances the material is created by teams rather than by a single person. The *Jack Benny* programs were turned out by four writers, and Bob Hope regularly employs seven writers to prepare material not only for his television programs but also for his appearances before service men, at dinners, and at benefits. The reason for the team approach seems to be that creating material that will make people laugh is difficult for a person sitting all by himself at a typewriter. The presence of other minds is required to create an atmosphere congenial to the invention of jokes, and a writer needs to bounce comedy ideas at other people to test their effectiveness. Their reactions in turn trigger new comedy inventions, and thus a script is slowly built, one joke inspiring another. Many writers shuttle regularly from one team to another with the result that a given person often has credits for a long string of different comedy series.

THE WRITING ROUTINE

The production of a comedy script through team effort requires that the conception of the idea and the writing of the script follow some type of organized pattern. Specific practices differ from group to group, of course, but the pattern usually includes three well-defined steps of planning, writing, and revision.

CONCEIVING THE SHOW IDEA. The construction of a script begins with a conference, which usually includes both the comedian and his writers, to determine the general premise of the show and the content of individual scenes or sketches. The success of the final script depends greatly on whether this premise is one that naturally produces comic moments. If it does not, the writing that follows may be hard, slugging work. Comedy-dramas in addition to a premise for each individual show, are often governed by a prevailing idea that unifies the series as a whole. A good example is the *Beverly Hillbillies*, a series that focused on the basic incongruity of mixing hillbillies with the glamor and sophistication of the Hollywood scene.

The context of family life juxtaposed with the activities of a comedy writing team provided the setting for the *Dick Van Dyke* show from week to week, within which the writers created premises for the individual shows. Many of these premises constitute excellent examples of comedy ideas. In one program the fun grew from the fact that Rob Petrie (the role played by Dick Van Dyke) had a brother whose personality while he was awake was utterly different from what it was when he was a sleepwalker. In another show it was established that Rob's wife Laura had an obsessive desire to open packages even when they were not addressed to her. The climax came when she opened a package containing a rubber life raft, which promptly inflated and filled the living room. The premise of a third show was that Laura, as a master of judo, was better able to protect herself than her husband Rob, who was capable only of conventional measures of self defense. A fourth show began with the revelation that a nude picture of Laura was on display at a local art gallery. (It developed that a painter commissioned to do a portrait of Laura had used his imagination to paint her nude even though she sat for him fully clothed.) The script focused, of course, on Rob's desperate efforts to get that picture out of the art gallery. All of these basic ideas were excellent choices for comedy dramas, for inherent within them were multiple laugh-producing possibilities.

WRITING THE SCRIPT.   After the controlling idea of the show is decided, the next step is to write the actual script. This may be done by the team in group sessions, or individual writers may be assigned to do parts of the script independently. Whichever method is followed, maximum use must be made of the writer's wit and inventive powers. Sherwood Schwartz, at one time a writer for Bob Hope and the creator of *Gilligan's Island,* described one technique for setting these creative powers into motion. The process begins with the invention of a straight line which the writer then tries to follow with a funny rejoinder. Thus: "My apartment is so small that. . ." "My aunt is so fat that. . ." "My uncle is so tight that. . ." Schwartz cited as a successful termination of this procedure: "The traffic was so slow coming home from the football game that I had to leave the car twice to make payments."[3]

The demand for material is so prodigious, however, (the *Jack Benny* radio program required thirty-five new jokes every week) that writers cannot usually produce the necessary material by depending exclusively on their own resources. One measure is to establish a file of jokes. David Freedman, who wrote the *Eddie Cantor* show for many years, is reputed to have collected more than 400,000 jokes. These jokes cannot be used, however, in their original form since they would be recognized by many people as old jokes. To disguise them a process called "switching" is used. This means appropriating the basic point of the joke but casting it in another context. Consider this joke, which Stephen Leacock recorded in his book on *Humor.*

A Scotchman's wife was dying. Calling her husband to the bedside, she said, "John, I know you dinna like Aunt Janet but you'll let her ride with you in the carriage to the funeral?"

The husband, much moved, answered, "I'll do it for you, Maggie, but it'll spoil my day!"

This story has had innumerable descendents, among them the story about the golfer who requested permission to play through the foursome ahead of him; otherwise, he explained, he would miss his wife's funeral.

The old riddle—"What is black and white and red all over?"—also has a switch. The answer is no longer—"a newspaper," but—"an embarrassed zebra." As a further example of switching, consider the strong resemblance of a joke originated by Goodman Ace to a routine that appeared on the *Jack Benny* program. Goodman Ace said that when he read in the *Reader's Digest* that cigarettes were bad for him, he

---

[3] Sherwood Schwartz, "How to Write a Joke," *Off Mike,* edited by Jerome Lawrence (New York: Duell, Sloan & Pearce, 1944), p. 15.

gave up reading the *Reader's Digest*. Jack Benny planned to give his guitar player Frank Remley a bottle of bourbon for Christmas but was blocked by an order from Remley's doctor forbidding him to drink liquor. Therefore Jack had decided to give him something else he thought he'd like—the name of a new doctor.

Many switches have been worked on the joke that is often looked on as the prototype of all jokes: "Who was that lady I saw you with last night? That was no lady, that was my wife." There is the musician's version. "Was that an oboe I saw you playing last night? That was no oboe, that was my fife"; the kitchen version: "Was that a ladle I saw you using last night? That was no ladle that was my knife." The magician's version: "Who was that lady I saw you saw last night? That was no lady, that was my half-sister." And then there is this shortened version. "Who was that lady I saw you out wit last night?"

Another technique for producing material is to fall back on the use of topics that through the years have evoked laughter because they have inherent in them some basic element of humor. For generations comedians have been making up successful jokes about such subjects as mothers-in-law, marriage, women's hats, old maids, spinach. In the New York area a reference to Brooklyn makes people smile, in Detroit it is Hamtramck, and on the west coast, Pismo Beach. Another common practice is to build jokes around events in the news, popular sayings, current advertising slogans, song titles, and the like. A joke often gains impact from the mere fact that it is topical. Sid Caesar appearing in a family sketch on the *Ed Sullivan* show revealed that he had just bought a copy of "Sex and the Single Baby" for his new-born child. The sheer absurdity of this remark and its tinge of the taboo gave it some laugh-making potentialities, but it drew its major effect from its reference to a book and movie that were then making news, *Sex and the Single Girl*. Another category of topics are those relating to characters: Bob Hope's nose, Jack Benny's stinginess, Bing Crosby's wealth.

Related to the use of character topics is the development of "running gags" or jokes that are repeated either through a program or through an entire series. Examples are Jack Benny's vault, a closet on the *Fibber McGee and Molly* show that at regular intervals spewed its contents all over the living room to the accompaniment of a long drawn-out sound effects, and the hostility of Morey Amsterdam to the bald-headed producer on the *Dick Van Dyke* show. Running gags used with moderation can be of help in building a show but they can easily be overdone. In the 1930s a radio show featured a comedian named Jack Pearl as the world's greatest liar Baron Munchausen. Invariably when one of his exaggerations was questioned, the Baron replied, "Vas you dere,

Sharlie?" This line, funny at first, soon lost its humor through overuse, and the show shortly disappeared from the air. Eddie Cantor was a wiser comedian. He had developed a quacking sound which he used regularly in his radio show. When he made a personal appearance in a theatre, the audience as one man quacked at him when he stepped on the stage. He resolved never to use the device again.

REVISING THE SCRIPT. After a draft of the script has been written, the final step is to evaluate the results in a final conference. This is the point when poor jokes are eliminated or improved, new jokes are added, and the whole show is sharpened and polished. A good example of what happens in these conferences took place during the preparation of a script for the *Henry Morgan* series. One of the features of the show was a take-off on Drew Pearson's radio program, which featured predictions of things to come. In the original version the commentator was introduced as "Drew Morgan, a man whose predictions have proved eighty-five per cent accurate." This was followed by the statement, "I predict my predictions will be predictions fourteen per cent of the time." In the final version both of these statements had been replaced by: "Here is Drew Morgan, a man whose predictions have proved one hundred per cent accurate fourteen per cent of the time." A nonjoke and a poor joke had been combined to produce one fairly good joke.

EVALUATING COMEDY MATERIAL

The forms of comedy are so diverse and the art of humor so complex that distinguishing the qualities characteristic of effective comedy writing is a difficult task. The humorous story, for example, which bubbles along through a string of incongruities and absurdities without reaching any particular point, is quite different from the story or situation that has nothing funny in it until a punch line snaps the audience into laughter. Although the long, elaborate nonsense story is occasionally heard in a broadcast, television usually features comedy that depends on a punch line or gag for its effect. The questions that follow are those to be applied in evaluating this kind of material.

BASIC ELEMENTS

Does the comedy material manifest one or more of the elements that constitute the roots of all laughter? A sketch that fails to reflect some element of triumph, incongruity, or surprise is not likely to amuse. If it reflects all three of them, it is almost certain to be funny. Sometimes writers create material that masquerades as humor but which falls flat because it contains none of these elements or contains an element that is too feeble in its effect. Merely using a word in two different ways, for example, does not necessarily create a joke, as the following sequence indicates.

HE

I really like roast beef and potatoes best.

SHE

Why don't you try something different oc-

casionally--broiled quail, for instance.

HE

I quail at the thought.

Switching the meaning of the word "quail" in this exchange incorporates very little surprise and suggests no incongruity or triumph. It is not a joke. We may smile but only because the speaker has shown a little ingenuity and not because he has appealed to our comic sense. On the other hand, consider this example:

SHE

Do you like bathing beauties?

HE

I don't know. I never bathed any.

This is a joke because the switch in the meaning of the word involves a major element of surprise. The surprise, moreover, is accompanied by the suggestion of an idea that is usually suppressed, thus adding an element of triumph.

ARRANGEMENT

Is the material arranged in a way that will secure the maximum possible effect? A joke is a delicate entity which a clumsy arrangement can easily damage. One thing that broadcast writers must be particularly careful about is to put the point of the story at the very end of the last line of the exchange or part of the story may be covered by laughter that is triggered too soon. This point can be illustrated by rewriting an episode from a *Jack Benny* program which took place while Jack and Mary Livingstone were sitting beside a swimming pool. As originally written the dialogue went like this:

<pre>
                    JACK

      It's a little embarrassing to say the

      least, but your bathing suit is a bit snug

      and skimpy.

                    MARY

      If you don't like it, go in and take it off.
</pre>

Consider what would happen if Mary's line had been written as follows.

<pre>
                    MARY

      Go in and take it off if you don't like it.
</pre>

This version might still get a laugh but it would likely be a bit muffled and indecisive. The point has come too soon to permit a clean reaction.

Giving the point away before the audience has had a chance to build up any expectation is another type of error. There is a story about a man who came to see a doctor because he was tired and rundown.

<pre>
                    DOCTOR

      There's really nothing the matter with you.

      All you need is a little relaxation. Why

      don't you take the night off and go to see

      Bob Hope?

                    MAN

      But I am Bob Hope.
</pre>

Consider what would happen if you told the audience before this dialogue exchange that the man who came into the doctor's office was Bob Hope. All other elements would remain the same but you would ruin the joke by depriving the audience of the opportunity to be surprised.

ECONOMY

Have you presented the material with the maximum economy? Unnecessary words can clutter a story so much that its effect will be seriously damaged. Simple, direct language which focuses on the key ideas is the ideal to be sought. This does not mean that condensation cannot be overdone. Some stories gain much of their effect from the repetition of certain key phrases or ideas. To eliminate this repetition might blunt most of the joke's point.

NATURALNESS

Do your jokes spring from the situation as if there were an inevitability about them, as if they were happening in spite of themselves, so to speak? Nothing is more inimical to the production of laughter than a labored, contrived effect. As we have noted before, one reason we often groan at puns rather than laugh at them is their air of ponderous contrivance. Yet a writer cannot gain the qualities of effortlessness and spontaneity in comedy writing without much hard work. That is the paradox. Intense labor is needed to arrive at an unlabored effect.

CLARITY

Is your material completely clear? In no other form of writing is complete understanding by the audience so essential to arriving at the ultimate effect. There will be no laughter at all if people do not understand.

SUDDENNESS

Can your audience see what you mean instantly? Suddenness is an essential attribute of comic writing. A joke that has to be explained is no joke at all. It is just as damaging if the listener has to take time to figure out the point for himself. The following joke provides an example: An actor named Ishmael found this note from his agent in his mail box: "Don't call me, Ishmael, I'll call you." The average person would probably take too long to recognize the relationship between this line and the first sentence of *Moby Dick* to permit a comic effect. When he finally sees the connection, he might feel a quiet satisfaction at his erudition, but laughter can only be provoked by the flash of triumph that comes from instant recognition. As Max Eastman said in his *Enjoyment of Laughter,* "Jokes have to happen suddenly in order to happen at all."

APPROPRIATENESS

Is your comedy writing appropriate to the situation? This question has a number of possible applications. If you are writing for a specific comedian, you must write material that fits his style. The gags of a Bob Hope, for example, all seem to have been invented by the same mind so consistent in style are they, and yet through the years many different writers have produced them. If the comedy vehicle is drama, the humor must be appropriate to the characters and the situation. It is true that we allow comedy writers a little more leeway in this regard than we do the writer of serious drama, but complete irrelevancy is undesirable, and the best jokes are those inspired by the character or the situation. This point was illustrated occasionally by the *Dick Van Dyke* show, which, because it featured characters who were actually comedy writers producing material for a comedy show, could sometimes present the jokes that developed from this effort, jokes told for their own sake, in other words. Yet this comedy was never as funny as that arising from the story itself.

There are a number of other ways in which the quality of appropriateness can be interpreted. The material obviously must be appropriate to broadcasting. It may be funny if it skirts the edges of what is usually suppressed, but if it goes too far it may shock rather than amuse. The joke: "He attended a wedding at which the bride was pregnant—so the guests threw puffed rice" would be appropriate in a night club but not in a television show. The writer must have an extraordinary sensitivity to what falls within the bounds of good taste and acceptability and what exceeds it. Comedy in many instances deals with the unpleasant but this unpleasantness must be handled playfully. If it causes real pain there will be no comedy. Knowing what subjects he can handle, realizing the difference between going far enough to create a laugh but refraining from going too far is what divides a good writer from a crass and ineffective one.

QUESTIONS AND PROJECTS

1. Analyze the jokes and situations in a comedy show for the elements of triumph, incongruity, and surprise.

2. View a number of situation comedies and state the premise for each show in one sentence. Decide whether these premises were fruitful sources of comedy values.

3. Write the funniest gag line you can think of for each of the following straight lines: (a) "My brother is so lazy that. . . ; (b) My uncle is so rich that. . . ; (c) My aunt is such a hypochondriac that. . . .

4. Write three switches on each of the following jokes:
   a) One man told another that he played chess with his dog every night. "You mean to say your dog plays chess," said the first man, "Why that's wonderful." "What's so wonderful?" replied the first man, "I beat him regularly two out of three."
   b) A woman came to a psychiatrist because her husband had developed the delusion that he was a jet airplane. "Have him come in to see me tomorrow," said the psychiatrist. "He can't make it tomorrow," said the woman. "He has to appear in court for flying low over Newark."

5. Write a three-minute monologue for a stand-up comedian.

15

Commercials

Nothing except the Mint can make money without advertising.
Thomas Babington Macaulay.

Some approach the writing of commercials with certain reservations. A few regard it as mere hack work, controlled entirely by the sordid demands of business. Program writers with this opinion should remember that since commercials provide the main support of American broadcasting, the eventual survival of programming depends on their effectiveness. They may be routine sometimes, a fault from which other types of writing are not immune, but often they are marked by a high degree of craftsmanship—even artistry in some instances. What really counts, however, is whether commercials move products. Artistry is beside the point. Applying esthetic standards to the process of selling soup or cereals is irrelevant.

A second reservation arises from the view of some people that the writers of commercials are part of a malign conspiracy dedicated to manipulating people into buying products by exploiting their weaknesses. It cannot be denied that advertisers do tend to deal in threats, promises, and certainties. To promise that those who buy a product will be blessed with instant happiness is part of a standard advertising appeal. The ethics of such approaches is a proper subject for evaluation but it is beyond the scope of this book. The person contemplating a career as a copywriter is interested in knowing how commercials are designed and written. That is our focus. Those who plan to write commercials will become acquainted with selling techniques that have proved effective. Those who are the target of advertising campaigns, and that includes all of us, may learn some ways by which we are persuaded to buy.

The writer of commercials may be the employee of a local radio or television station, who for a relatively modest stipend, turns out a whole series of commercials every week, writing for as many as fifty different clients at one time. He may be the person who secures the client in the first place, gathers the information for the commercial, writes it, and he may even be the announcer who delivers it on the air. The employee of a national advertising agency, in addition to being more highly paid than the local station writer, usually concentrates his efforts on extolling the virtues of relatively few products. Even at that he does not work alone; the preparation of commercials in a large advertising agency is a team operation in which the initial writer's work is reviewed and revised until every sentence and effect is finely honed.

TYPES OF COMMERCIALS

There are a number of ways in which radio and television commercials can be classified. They vary in length, for example, running as little as two seconds or lasting for many minutes, but most are from eight seconds to one minute in length; some are written in one-minute lengths that can be cut without rewriting to twenty- or thirty-second versions.

THE ADVERTISING ARRANGEMENT

Advertising on radio and television is presented in a number of different arrangements which are designated by special terms. Except for lead-ins, most commercials are written and produced separately from the program. Usually a number of advertisers join to sponsor a program and the messages they present are known as *participating* commercials. Because time for these commercials is sold in much the same way as space in a magazine, the arrangement is known as the *magazine* format. Sometimes a company, or even two different companies, may advertise two or more products in the same commercial. When the products are related in character, purpose, or use and are advertised in a single, un-broken announcement, the result is known as an *integrated* commercial. When the products are unrelated and the commercial is divided into two clearly separate announcements, the result is known as a *piggyback* commercial. Sometimes a company may request that its commercial pe-riod be divided into two halves separated by program material. This pattern is known as the *split* commercial. When a local advertiser pays for a commercial that is cut into a program being broadcast nationally, the advertising is said to be *cooperative*.

Spot commercials are those presented by a station during the period between programs when the station identifies itself. The term also refers to commercials presented on a participating basis during programs of music or movies. A spot commercial presented by a local station to advertise a product that is sold nationally is known as a *national spot announcement*. A message presented free-of-charge on behalf of some community enterprise or interest, such as the United Fund or a campaign to eliminate fire hazards, is known as a *public service announcement*.

PRODUCTION TECHNIQUES

Another way in which commercials differ is in the techniques used to produce them. Most of the commercials presented on large stations and on networks are transcribed, filmed, or video taped. The prepon-derance of the recorded commercial can be attributed to several advan-tages it brings the advertiser: 1) it ensures uniformity in presentation; 2) it eliminates the possibility of a mistake which may distort the com-mercial message or make it seem ridiculous; and 3) it permits the use of a wide variety of production devices. Not all of the advantages are on the side of recordings, however: 1) the live presentation is much cheaper to produce than a recording or film, which may cost $50,000 or more for a single minute; 2) the live presentation can be revised to reflect changes in prices or to announce special sales; 3) the imme-diacy and spontaneity of the live presentation may help a popular per-sonality to sell the product.

A great many different techniques are used in the production of com-mercials, among them: 1) two or more voices to present sales messages; 2) interviews; 3) dramatizations; 4) music—instrumental or sung; 5) sound effects; 6) live action with the announcer in view; 7) live action with voice-over announcing; 8) electronic effects; 9) candid recordings or films; 10) still-picture sequences with voice-over narration; 11) ani-mation; 12) puppets; 13) a combination of devices.

THE SELLING APPROACH

The ultimate aim of commercials is to sell products, but there are marked differences in the way they approach this objective. Some seek immediate sales, others eventual ones, a few merely seek to develop a feeling of good will toward the advertiser. The approach may vary also from the light and subtle to the direct and obvious.

NAME AND ACTION COPY.   One of the ways in which commercials accomplish eventual sales is to imprint the name of the product on our minds through constant repetition. Seeing the product in a store, we respond to it as something we know and are thus more likely to buy it than the unadvertised product next to it on the shelf, even though we actually know nothing about the relative qualities of the two brands. Advertising designed with the primary aim of establishing the brand name, which makes almost no claims of any kind for the product itself, is known as *name* copy. The following commercial includes some material designed to make the audience want the product, but its main purpose, obviously, is to etch the name Wyler in the listener's mind.

ANNCR: Lady, I see you're buying America's best selling lemonade mix. Wyler's -- W-Y-L-E-R-S -- Wyler's.

LADY: Wyler's lemonade is marvelous.

ANNCR: Why do you insist on Wyler's?

LADY: I just love Wyler's lemonade. In fact the whole family loves all the Wyler's drink mixes.

ANNCR: Why Wyler's?

LADY: Especially the children.

ANNCR: But why Wyler's?

LADY: It's so easy ... energy-giving sugar's already in it.

ANNCR: Why Wyler's?

LADY: Just empty the green foil envelope, add water and ice ...

ANNCR: But why ...

LADY: The girls in the bridge club love the low-
        calorie lemonade.

ANNCR: But, lady, why Wyler's?

LADY: Why Wyler's?

ANNCR: Yes.

LADY: Why not?

Almost all commercials make some attempt to establish the product name, but most also employ persuasive appeals that are stronger than those in the preceding commercial. The goal is to make listeners experience a need and then to seek the advertised product as the best means of satisfying that need. Such advertising is known as *action copy*.

MESSAGE INTENSITY. The commercial designed to enhance the reputation of the sponsor rather than to convert listeners into immediate buyers of its products is called *institutional*. Banks and telephone companies and manufacturers such as steel companies, whose products are not sold directly to consumers, often make use of institutional advertising. The tone of this type of commercial is stately and dignified and it is frequently educational in nature.

A somewhat more intense approach attempts direct-selling but keeps it to a low-pressure level. The listener is appealed to as a reasonable, thinking individual by an announcer who does not exhort him to immediate action—"before it is too late!"—but speaks instead in a relaxed and well-modulated tone in language written to match. This soft-sell approach would be used by a bank that decides to go beyond the institutional message to persuade listeners to open savings accounts or to use the bank as a source of loans, or by a telephone company that wishes to convince listeners of the desirability of an extension phone.

The most intense approach attempts persuasion through high-pressure methods. The tone of such commercials is strongly emotional. The voice of the announcer is likely to be loud and high pitched and he races through the copy at break-neck speed, emphasizing points with forceful gestures. The copy is filled with admonitions to act now and is likely to resound with superlatives which emphasize the special nature of the offer and its short duration. The listener may get the feeling that the advertiser is trying to bludgeon him into buying the product. For this reason commercials of this hard-sell type are said to employ a *slug* approach.

THE HUMOROUS VS. SERIOUS APPROACH. Commercials can be distinguished further according to whether thay are humorous or serious in their approach. There is constant debate in the advertising industry regarding the selling impact of humor in a commercial. The issue will probably never be settled because people on either side can point to humorous commercials that were outstanding successes or abysmal failures. What does seem to be clear is that humor contributes certain advantages and certain disadvantages.

The major contribution of humor is that it arrests and holds attention and helps to make the commercial stand out among the multitude of its competitors. Its appeal may even get it discussed by viewers. People talked about the Piel's Beer commercials of Bob and Ray and the Chun King commercials of Stan Freburg. The Alka Seltzer commercial that associated relief of stomach distress with pictures of human abdomens in various stages of agitation accompanied by a catchy melody received notable viewer reaction. The memorability of humor makes it particularly suitable for use when the major objective is to make the viewer remember the name of the product. Another advantage of humor is that it may soften the innate hostility many feel toward commercials and thus gain a more positive attitude toward the product.

Although research indicates that the commercials we like are the most effective, it also shows that the commercials which irritate us most are next in effectiveness. A poll of television viewers, reported in 1965, showed that the most unpopular advertising campaign was the one incorporating the slogan, "Us Tareyton smokers would rather fight than switch," yet that campaign increased sales of the cigarette by almost one third. When commercials that simply repeat straight high-pressure arguments are so successful, it is not surprising that many advertisers refuse to experiment with anything so unpredictable in its effect as humor or whimsy.

Another argument against the humorous commercial is that although it may effectively snare attention on its first presentation, it probably loses its capacity to sell products more rapidly with successive renditions than the straight commercial does. Much humor depends on surprise and with repetition there is no surprise left. Yet when a filmed commercial costs many thousands of dollars, the economics of the situation dictate that it must be repeated many times.

There is also the danger that humor may obscure the basic advertising message because the machinery of joke-making takes so much time that there is little opportunity to stress important selling points. This is a major handicap when new and distinctive goods and services must be explained to the audience. Humor, then, is usually used in connection with established products to produce a switch or angle designed to arouse interest anew.

TABOOS IN COMMERCIALS

The writer of commercials is subject to the general taboos of broadcasting and in addition is governed by some restrictions that apply particularly to advertising. One problem he faces is what to do about rival products whose claims of superiority he may wish to discount. The NAB television code recommends offering products on their positive merits and prohibits disparaging references to competing products. Generally this means that competing brands are not mentioned by name, although there are exceptions to this rule. A Gillette TV commercial showed a hand pushing away other brands before picking up the Gillette package. The usual practice is to cover the competing brand's name with a "beep-beep," as was done in the Personna blade commercials, or to use a general term instead of a brand name. The manufacturer of an aspirin, in contending that his product was better than its competitors, referred not to Anacin but to the "combination of ingredients" product and not to Bufferin but to "buffered aspirin." Writers of commercials for margarine even avoided using the word "butter" in referring to their competition but instead used the term "higher-priced spread," a substitution that carried a built-in argument for the use of margarine.

A number of other restrictions appear in the television code or in the policy manuals of stations, networks, and advertisers. False or deceptive advertising is, of course, prohibited. There is a clause in the TV code requiring that "personal endorsements (testimonials) shall be genuine and reflect personal experience." In the advertising of medical products, claims that a product will effect a cure or the employment of such terms as "safe," "without risk," and "harmless" must be avoided. Furthermore, the code prohibits the use of physicians, dentists, nurses, or medical technicians in commercials either directly or by implication, and permits the use of a laboratory scene only when it is directly related to bona fide research. Some products of a personal nature cannot be advertised on radio and television at all.

The code protects the interests of children by prohibiting their exploitation either by employing them improperly in the commercial itself or by using appeals that will take advantage of their naïveté and emotional immaturity. Most of the tobacco industry follows a code that forbids advertising appeals primarily directed toward persons under twenty-one. Cigarette commercials that make health claims are also prohibited and smoking cannot be presented as a means of relieving tension or be portrayed as essential to social prominence, distinction, success, or sexual achievement. No longer, moreover, can smoking be connected with athletic success. Well-known athletes, in fact, are not used in cigarette advertising any more. Other performers must be at least twenty-five years of age before they can be pictured smoking cigarettes in commercials.

One of the more intriguing taboos relates to commercials for beer. It may be advertised on television, but the networks and most stations forbid showing the beverage actually being consumed on camera. The temperance forces in this country lost the major war for prohibition but they seem to have won this small triumph.

PLANNING THE COMMERCIAL

Your first step in planning a commercial is to gain as much knowledge of the product as possible. These are among the questions you need to ask at the beginning: What are the peculiar advantages of this product? Does it have a unique quality on which the commercial can focus? Is its major appeal its price, its quality, its convenience, or its beauty? Is it primarily an item of intrinsic value? Does it have major shortcomings which must be taken into consideration?

The place the commercial is to occupy in the over-all campaign to sell the product is also a matter of importance. Sometimes printed and broadcast advertising are integrated so completely that the same language is used in both media. Radio commercials frequently reinforce the appeals presented in television advertising. A given commercial may feaure a basic appeal that is to be repeated over again, or it may be one step in an advertising campaign that is to be developed in stages over a period of time. The following radio commercial was part of a national campaign conducted by Chevrolet through radio, television, magazines, and newspapers to emphasize the point that "Now is the time to get a number one buy on the number one car at your number one dealer's."

```
MUSIC:   QUICK INTRO - THEN, UNDER:

GROUP:   (SINGING)  There's no number like number one

                    And no time like now!

                    Now is the time to get a Number One

                    buy on the Number One car...Chevro-

                    let...At your Number One dealer's!

                    Now is the time to dri-i-i-ive a

                    great deal...
```

NOTE: ("DRIVE" IS HELD QUITE LONG, MUSICALLY)

        With Corvair...Chevy II...Chevelle

        ...or Chevrolet!

MUSIC: PUNCTUATION.

GROUP: (SINGING)   Should you wait? No, no, no!

        Hesitate? No, no, no!

        Now is the time to get a Number One

        buy on the Number One car...Chevro-

        let! At your Number One dealer's.

        Now is the time to climb into a new

        Chevrolet...today!

MUSIC: BIG STING - THEN, ALL MUSIC OUT.

GROUP: (MORE QUIETLY AND RATHER CUTELY)

        Tomorrow at the latest!

MUSIC: UP AND OUT, BIG AND FAST.

The nature of the prospective audience must also be taken into account. If the commercial is to be used in one of the popular night time network shows, no special adaptations are required, for an audience of thirty million includes all kinds of people. Some network shows do select a particular kind of audience, however: daytime programs are largely directed toward women, sporting events to men, and some programs are meant primarily for children. At the other extreme from the mass audience of network television is the small audience of an FM radio station specializing in classical music. This type of service draws the intellectual, the well-educated, the well-to-do. The products advertised on such a station and the appeals used to sell them are quite different from those employed on a big network show.

FINDING A KEY SELLING POINT

Most successful commercials are built around an exclusive attribute that sets the product apart from its competitors and gives potential consumers a specific reason for buying. In his book *Reality in Advertis-*

ing, Rosser Reeves, head of the Ted Bates agency, called this key point the "unique selling proposition." It may be a quality possessed by the product alone or it may be common to a number of competing products which no other advertiser is exploiting. Finding a key selling point around which the commercial can revolve is one of the most important steps in planning. Its importance becomes obvious when one realizes that many of the products advertised on radio and television—cigarettes, beer, bread, gasoline, toothpaste—are not really very different from their competitors.

An example of a unique quality was that claimed by the makers of Winston cigarettes, who, to negate the feeling of many people that smoke strained through a filter is bland and unsatisfying, argued that the smoke from their special "filter-blend" tobacco retained its richness and flavor through filter and all. The ungrammatical but catchy slogan "Winston tastes good like a cigarette should" reinforced this key idea and gave the cigarette a special identity which helped to make it one of the industry's largest sellers. The storyboard for a ScotTowels' TV commercial illustrates how both the video and audio portions of the commercial emphasize the key selling point that ScotTowels are heavy-weight for heavy work.

An appeal that any toothpaste maker might have used, which was pre-empted by the makers of Gleem, was the argument that their toothpaste was specially made for people "who can't brush after every meal." This slogan seemed to invest the product with a quality that met a unique need and yet it would be difficult to find a household where it did not exist. Sometimes key selling points of competing products run into one another head-on. Anacin argues that its combination of ingredients provides faster, more complete relief. Bayer counters with the claim that its product is composed only of "pure" aspirin. Zenith emphasizes the quality of its hand-crafted television sets; RCA points to printed circuits that eliminate human error. These claims, though completely antithetical, still make sales for their respective makers.

Occasionally, a clever writer can even turn an apparent shortcoming into a key selling point. Volkswagen, entering a car market in which bigness and yearly model changes were among the most desirable attributes, fearlessly advised potential buyers to "Think Small" and brandished the point that it never changed models as other car manufacturers did by showing a line of identical cars with the caption underneath: "The Volkswagen Theory of Evolution."

Centering the commercial on one compelling reason for buying a particular product does not mean that all other points in its favor should be ignored. The result of such absolute concentration might be a rather stark—and perhaps ineffective—sales appeal. Details are needed to add

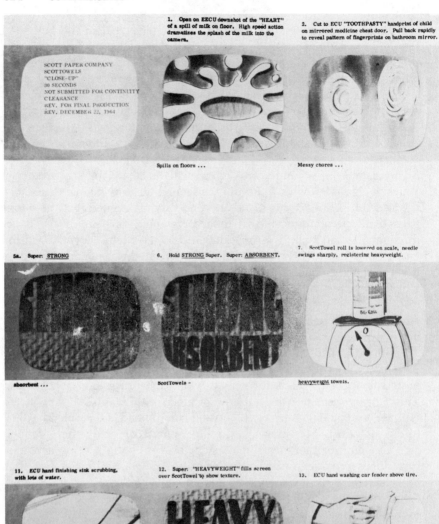

1. Open on EECU downshot of the "HEART" of a spill of milk on floor. High speed action dramatizes the splash of the milk into the camera.

2. Cut to ECU "TOOTHPASTY" handprint of child on mirrored medicine chest door. Pull back rapidly to reveal pattern of fingerprints on bathroom mirror.

SCOTT PAPER COMPANY
SCOTTOWELS
"CLOSE-UP"
30 SECONDS
NOT SUBMITTED FOR CONTINUITY
CLEARANCE
REV. FOR FINAL PRODUCTION
REV. DECEMBER 22, 1964

Spills on floors ...

Messy chores ...

5a. Super: STRONG

6. Hold STRONG Super. Super: ABSORBENT.

7. ScotTowel roll is lowered on scale, needle swings sharply, registering heavyweight.

absorbent ...

ScotTowels -

heavyweight towels.

11. ECU hand finishing sink scrubbing, with lots of water.

12. Super: "HEAVYWEIGHT" fills screen over ScotTowel to show texture.

13. ECU hand washing car fender above tire.

stay strong.

They're heavyweight

for heavy work.

A TELEVISION STORYBOARD

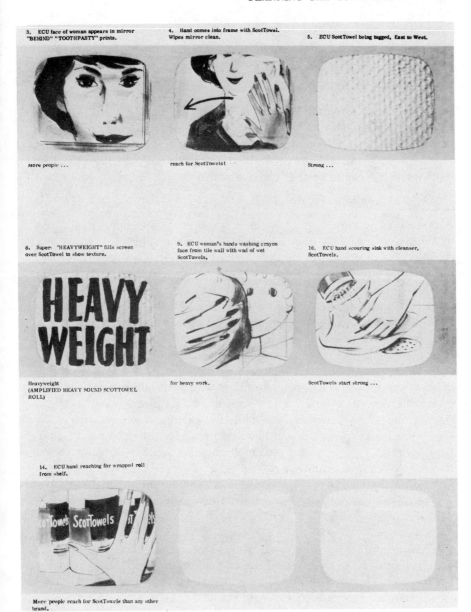

3. ECU face of woman appears in mirror "BEHIND" "TOOTHPASTY" prints.

More people ...

4. Hand comes into frame with ScotTowel. Wipes mirror clean.

reach for ScotTowels!

5. ECU ScotTowel being tugged, East to West.

Strong ...

8. Super: "HEAVYWEIGHT" fills screen over ScotTowel to show texture.

Heavyweight
(AMPLIFIED HEAVY SOUND SCOTTOWEL ROLL)

9. ECU woman's hands washing crayon face from tile wall with wad of wet ScotTowels.

for heavy work,

10. ECU hand scouring sink with cleanser, ScotTowels.

ScotTowels start strong ...

14. ECU hand reaching for wrapped roll from shelf.

More people reach for ScotTowels than any other brand.

FOR SCOTTOWELS

color, dimension, and depth. They should not, however, be permitted to obscure the basic message. The key to the process is *emphasis*.

THE PERSUASIVE STRUCTURE

Because most commercials aim at stimulating the audience to make an immediate purchase of the product, they must be strongly persuasive in nature. Successful commercial appeals usually contain four distinct steps. They do not always occur in the same order, but they need to be there if the commercial is to have a strong and complete persuasive structure.

GAINING ATTENTION. If a listener is to respond to a commercial's persuasion, you must first gain his attention, a formidable task when you consider the multitude of appeals cascading constantly from radio and television receivers. In a single year the average person is exposed to 10,000 TV commercials. That is why techniques for compelling interest loom so importantly in the construction of a commercial. Many concentrate almost entirely on devices that will make people watch or listen. Among the means used are beautiful girls, children, animals, sound effects, music, stop-action photography, which makes a cigarette pack seem to open itself or sends cigarettes marching in platoons, a succession of stills synchronized to give a comic jerky effect, hamburgers that applaud the use of a new kind of catsup, a white knight on a horse. Among the more traditional methods of gaining attention are to tie the commercial in with a recent news event, a sports happening, a prominent personality, or a holiday; to emphasize the new, novel, or the latest; to ask a rhetorical question; to make a sincerely personal approach. With so many special devices being used to gain attention these days, a single, unadorned voice may have the quality of unusualness that makes us listen.

ESTABLISHING NEED. The most crucial step in the development of an action appeal is to make the listener feel an overwhelming need for the product. The normal individual experiences a number of basic needs which commercial products can help to satisfy. These innate drives have been catalogued in a number of different ways. One authority simply listed them as self-preservation, security, sex, and status. In the classification that follows, needs are described in terms that are particularly meaningful to the writer of commercials.

1. *Self-preservation*. The desire to preserve one's life and health is one of the most powerful of all drives. A great many products are rele-

var.t to this need—among them medicines, anti-blowout tires, and safety belts.

2. *Security and Ease.*   Most people have the desire to live comfortably and well and want to feel secure against catastrophes which may threaten their particular way of life. The majority of people also seek ways of improving their lot and adding to the general joy of living. Many products contribute to satisfying these needs—among them tasty food, central heating, life insurance, and fine automobiles.

3. *Response to Others.*   Another of the powerful human urges is the desire to be accepted by others, particularly by members of the opposite sex. The advertising of numerous products is specifically directed toward satisfying this need—personal items in particular, such as deodorants and soaps. The affection one has for members of his family is also part of the response urge; thus, parents react favorably to appeals promising better things for their children.

4. *Prestige.*   An innate desire of almost everyone is the urge to be important, to count in this world. This drive is related to the desire to be accepted by other people, but it goes beyond it to the point where we want to be looked on as superior to others. Some products, such as clothes that get attention or an automobile that bespeaks wealth, help to express the ingrained snobbery characterizing most of us.

The necessity for giving time and attention to developing a need for the product varies according to its nature. There is a clearly felt need for many of the articles advertised on radio and television even before the commercial begins. The confirmed smoker's craving for cigarettes exists when he tunes in the commercial and the writer can concentrate on persuading him that a particular brand of cigarettes will best satisfy it. There are some products, however, for which the average person may not be able to visualize any need at all. Because most people do not on their own recognize the value of home insulation, the advantages of a filter on the furnace, or the benefits of a water softener, the development of a feeling of need for these products is one of the most important parts of the commercial.

Somewhere between these two examples is the product for which most people feel a need but not a strong enough one to motivate buying. A writer confronted with this situation must recognize that some desires are more powerful than others. The urge to preserve one's life, for example, is stronger in most people than the longing for status or even for response from the opposite sex. On the other hand, some people may be willing to sacrifice some of their security and ease and even their money to win the affection of another person. When the need most closely related to the product is a weak one, the writer reviews the basic human desires to see whether he can appeal to a more powerful drive even though the connection of that second need to the product may seem remote and indirect. He knows that the more urgent the drive he appeals to, the more persuasive his commercial message will be.

The advertising of soap products used by women provides a good example of this rule in operation. The desire to be clean does influence our actions to come extent, but unfortunately for the soap manufacturer, not very powerfully. Even though soap seems related most obviously to cleanliness, if the writer is to achieve maximum sales of the product, he must connect it to a much stronger need. A far more powerful drive in most women than the urge to be clean, one that dominates their lives from adolescence until they either achieve their goal or abandon it in despair, is the longing to get married. A review of the advertising of personal soap for women reveals that to be the desire on which many soap commercials focus. They promise cleanliness only incidentally. Instead, they promise beauty, but many do not stop even there; they go all the way and promise marriage. The first scene of one television commercial showed a young woman in the shadows. In the next she was washing her face with the right soap. In the last scene she was out of the shadows arrayed triumphantly in a wedding gown. The makers of deodorant soaps and mouth washes utilize the same basic appeal by suggesting that the users of their product at least will not drive away prospective mates.

Even many of the household soap commercials directed toward married women depend for their motivation primarily on appealing to the response urge. Why should a woman want to get her husband's shirt so dazzlingly white? The implication is that by doing so she will retain his respect and affection. The same appeal is inherent in the commercials for household soap. In promising users smooth, beautiful hands, they suggest that washing dishes can be a beauty treatment instead of an onerous chore.

Women, of course, are not the only targets of commercials centering on the response urge. Commercials for the men's hair dressing Brylcreem demonstrate that the use of the product automatically guarantees exciting attention from women. Commercial writers often take advantage of the affection parents have for their children. In the early 1950s the television industry, recognizing that nothing is more likely to make a parent feel guilty than the charge that he is failing to provide his children with the advantages available to other boys and girls, conducted a campaign emphasizing that children living in a home without a television set were underprivileged. This campaign was harshly criticized for its cold-blooded assault on parental emotions, but it undoubtedly motivated a great many mothers and fathers to buy TV sets. Food makers frequently try to sell their products by arousing concern for the welfare of children. One bread manufacturer presents his product not merely as a wholesome, tasty food but as an absolute essential to the development of a sound, healthy body.

SATISFYING NEED.   Once the need has been established, the next step is to convince the audience that the product not only satisfies that need, but satisfies it better than anything else on the market.

1. *Demonstrations.*   One of the best ways to convince an audience that a product will meet a need is to show it being used. Demonstration is easy on television but it is not impossible on radio. The skillful use of words and sound effects leads the radio listener to visualize the product in action. In television, however, it is the picture that sells the product. What you show in action is more important than what you say. Sound and voice are used mainly to emphasize what the pictures demonstrate. This brings up the further point that the video and the audio should be firmly linked. Nothing can so quickly disperse a commercial's effect than a series of pictures that go in one direction while an announcer goes wandering off in another.

A commercial for Band-Aids illustrates the effectiveness of making the picture the primary persuasive element in a TV commercial. The compelling reason for buying projected by this commercial was that a Band-Aid would stick to everything under any conditions. The picture that established this point was a Band-Aid firmly stuck to an egg suspended in boiling water. No supporting words were really necessary to establish the selling argument. The picture told the whole story.

The storyboard for a Marathon TV commercial also illustrates an approach in which the selling appeal was made primarily through pictures. The purpose of the commercial was to instill a desire for Christmas candles and to tell viewers that they could be obtained at their local Marathon gasoline station. This message was effectively communicated by the simple device of showing a little girl coming to a Marathon station to buy some candles.

2. *Science.*   One of the best ways of convincing people that a product will satisfy a need is to suggest that it has been developed in a scientific laboratory. A device for doing this is to give an ingredient in the product a scientific or seemingly scientific name. We are told, for example, that Dial soap has hexachlorophine. Most of us do not know what hexachlorophine is, but the word has an impressive ring to it and it suggests that scientists have been involved in developing the product. Hexachlo-

Music

Music

Music

Bright red candles...
pretty enough to be a gift..
so friendly and cheerful
at Christmastime.

Music

you can get these beautiful
Christmas candles at your
nearby Marathon station. It's
Marathon's way of saying --
Happy Holidays!

Art Director   Nicholas Schneider
Writer   Patricia W. Kemp
Producer   Nicholas Schneider
Agency   Campbell-Ewald Detroit
Advertiser   Marathon Oil Company

rophine, incidentally, is a term actually used by chemists to identify a certain substance, but if the use of a legitimate chemical term is inappropriate, advertisers often coin words with a scientific sound. We are told that Pepsodent toothpaste contains "irium," a term invented by an ingenious copywriter. The use of formulas in advertising has much the same effect as the use of chemical terms. Being informed that K-34 is an ingredient in Gillette shaving cream, we infer that scientists have been at work to improve the product. The manufacturers of Kent cigarettes utilized the scientific approach when they claimed that their filter of micronite (a term now outlawed by the cigarette code) was a product of the atomic age.

A second major means of providing scientific support for a selling argument is to submit or seem to submit the product to a scientific test. By implication, this is what the manufacturers of Ivory did when they advertised that their product was $99^{44}/_{100}$ percent pure. Only scientific testing, it was obvious, could arrive at a result so specific, and the slogan, in addition, had an attractive kind of honesty. More recently Crest toothpaste has made an outstanding sales increase by advertising the results of experiments that show its toothpaste materially reduces the number of cavities. Sometimes experiments are conducted on the air as part of the commercial. Two gloves are stained with ink. Then they are dipped before the viewers eyes, one in an ordinary cleanser, the other in the advertiser's product. One ink stain disappears, of course, while the other persists, black and resistant.

3. *Testimonials.* Another device that persuades a listener he will be satisfied with a product is the testimonial. The statement of a beautiful movie star that she uses a certain soap or shampoo carries the inescapable implication that all who do likewise will acquire her beauty and glamor. A child following the example of a famous athlete in eating a certain breakfast food sees himself attaining similar physical prowess. The virility and good looks of the baseball players who shave on television provide a subtle but powerful impetus toward purchase of the product. To the sophisticated person, of course, testimonials are suspect because it is known that many of them are purchased. Some advertisers, therefore, take pains to make clear that the statements favoring their product came from the completely unprejudiced, from satisfied users "who didn't know they were being filmed."

Advertisers also make use whenever they can of statements favoring their product that originate with seemingly objective organizations because of the extra measure of persuasion such testimonials carry. The Proctor and Gamble Company used a favorable quotation from a publication of the American Dental Association to advertise its Crest toothpaste. The Colgate-Palmolive Company then introduced a new toothpaste Cue, containing the same anti-cavity ingredient and included exactly the same quotation in its advertising.

MOTIVATING THE PURCHASE. The last step in the commercial is to provide the final impetus toward a sale. This step may be a summary of the main points followed by an admonition to "Act now—Don't delay . . . Do it today . . . Try it now." If the offer is part of a special sale, the listener may be warned, "Act now before it's too late . . . This is your last chance . . . The offer may never be repeated." If the product is not one for which there is an immediate need—it may just happen that the viewer watching an aspirin commercial does not have a headache at the particular moment—he is urged to buy immediately anyway, "for a headache may strike at any time!" Sometimes this last step involves the mention of a merchandizing scheme calculated to impel listeners to action: "See your dealer tomorrow. You may already have won a new car!" In short, the action step aims to develop the highest degree of compulsion possible. When it is over the listener's lethargy should be drained away. He should turn from the commercial with an irresistible urge to buy.

Occasionally, writers of commercials must overcome inherent negative reactions before they can persuade potential consumers to use the product. A classic example of such a negative reaction was the attitude formerly held by most people toward women who smoked cigarettes. Equally classic was the success of the tobacco industry in changing this attitude. It opened up a vast new market by conducting a subtle campaign over a great many years that managed to translate the woman smoker from a person who was looked upon as not quite nice into one who was accepted by most people as completely respectable. The manufacturers of small cigars are now using similar techniques to influence women to use their product.

The tobacco industry faced an even greater challenge with the revelation in the 1950s that there was a definite connection between cigarette smoking and various health problems—particularly lung cancer. The industry's response to this challenge was as successful as its conversion of women to smoking. It managed to convince millions of alarmed smokers, who might actually have given up the habit, that a filter placed between them and the tobacco would exclude the lethal ingredients.

Other products have also faced antagonistic reactions which copywriters have succeeded in modifying. A tea company attempted to negate the feeling that tea drinking was for "sissies" by advertising its brew as "strong and hearty." The makers of women's hair coloring preparations faced somewhat the same problem as the makers of cigarettes: dyeing one's hair was considered not quite respectable. The assault on this attitude was two-pronged. First, the idea was emphasized that changing the color of one's hair was no more momentous an act than changing one's dress. Second, for those women who still felt guilty about tampering with nature, the idea was planted that no one would know anyway. Clairol advertising carried the slogan: "Does she—or doesn't she? Hair color so natural only her hair dresser knows for sure."

Somewhat akin to the problem of negative reactions already in the listener's mind is the possibility that advertising may bring a negative reaction into being. No tobacco manufacturer, for example, would think of advertising that the filter in his cigarette provides better protection against lung cancer than other filters, even if the cigarette code would permit him to do it, because the mere arousal of such an unpleasant connotation would undoubtedly lose more sales than it would gain. The tobacco industry learned this in an earlier period when it was realized that slogans which reminded listeners of tobacco-created problems, even though they promised to protect against them, probably inhibited more sales than they promoted. So a whole series of slogans was abandoned, among them, "not a cough in a carload," "guard against throat scratch," and "no cigarette hangover." Advertising for cigarettes today emphasizes only such virtues as smoothness, flavor, and lightness and there is no hint of the harmful effects that may arise from their use. In the same way a beer maker discovered that stressing the low-calorie content of his beer had exactly the opposite effect from what he intended. It reminded people that beer is fattening.

THE PRESENTATIONAL FRAMEWORK

The final step in planning a commercial is to design the framework that will establish the key selling point and carry out the steps in the persuasive process. One of the most common formats is to design a problem-solution approach in the form of a one-minute drama. In the first part a character is presented with a problem; in the second he finds a solution—the product; and in the third he experiences a happy resolution. A commercial for Phillip's Milk of Magnesia illustrates this format. In the first scene a young lady tells her boy friend that she feels she can't enjoy the dance because her stomach is upset. In the second scene she finds Phillip's Milk of Magnesia in the medicine cabinet. In the third, now glowing and radiant, she meets her boy friend at the door. One reason the dramatic approach is used so often is that commercials must arouse emotion and drama is inherently emotional. It is one of the best means of making contact with the listener and arousing such feelings as anxiety, envy, sympathy, or anger, all or any of which may be a powerful influence in motivating him to buy a product.

The following commercial began with a problem: What is a mother to do when members of her family develop eating habits that threaten to deprive them of essential vitamins? The solution—Total—a breakfast cereal that provides one hundred percent of every vitamin required by adults.

VIDEO	AUDIO
OPEN ON MAN LAYING KITCHEN TILE. HE PLACES TILE IN POSITION AND CONTINUES TO TROWEL. HE LOOKS UP AND REACTS TO ANNOUNCER'S VOICE.	ANNOUNCER: (VO) Hey, it's lunchtime!
CUT INTO CU AS MAN CONTIN-UES TO TROWEL AND REACHES FOR ANOTHER TILE AS HE ANSWERS ANNOUNCER.	MAN: (DV) Can't stop now.
CUT TO GIRL AT DESK TYPING LETTERS. BY HER IS PAPER CONTAINER WITH STRAW AND A HARD-BOILED EGG ON WAX PAPER.	ANNOUNCER: (VO) Not many vitamins in that skimpy lunch!
MOVE INTO MCU AS SHE REACTS TO ANNOUNCER'S VOICE AND ANSWERS. SHE FLIPS TYPE-WRITER KNOB AND PLACES HAND ON STACK OF LETTERS AS SHE SPEAKS.	GIRL: (DV) I'm swamped. Gotta get these letters out.

CUT TO MOTHER IN KITCHEN SCENE AS SHE ASKS QUESTION WITH CONCERN.	WOMAN: (DV) What's a mother to do?
DISSOLVE TO BREAKFAST SCENE. MOTHER PASSES TOTAL TO DAUGHTER.	ANNOUNCER: (VO) Serve them "Total,"
CUT INTO CU AS GIRL POURS TOTAL.	the vitamin cereal, for breakfast.
DOLLY UP TO DOWN SHOT OF SAME BOWL.	The only leading cereal, hot or cold,
HOLD BOWL AND WIPE OFF STYLIZED CLOCK AROUND RIM OF BOWL.	with a whole day's vitamin supply.
PULL BACK AND IRIS IN ON BOWL MATTING OUT REST OF SCENE.	One bowl, one ounce
SUPER "100% OF EVERY MINIMUM DAILY."	gives you 100% of every minimum daily
HOLD SUPER AND ADD SUPER UNDER IT "ADULT VITAMIN REQUIREMENT NOW."	...adult vitamin re- quirement now...
HOLD SUPER AND ADD "SET BY THE UNITED STATES GOVERN- MENT."	set by the U.S. Government.

CUT TO TOTAL PACKAGE WITH	JINGLE:
BOWL OF FLAKES ON TABLE.	Enjoy "Total" every
	day.
WIPE ON STYLIZED CLOCK	Feel vitamin safe
OVER BOWL.	all day.

An experimental set-up, as we noted earlier, may provide a framework for a commercial. In one soap commercial a housewife standing in a field or flying in a balloon is asked to judge which of two washes is the whiter. The commercial reaches its climax when she chooses the clothes washed by the advertised product. In a commercial for Shell, two cars, one filled with a gasoline containing a mileage ingredient found in Shell gasoline, the other with gasoline lacking this ingredient, start out together. The car with the mileage ingredient in its gasoline passes the stalled first car, its gasoline exhausted, and travels miles farther.

Sometimes a commercial may be devoted almost entirely to sheer demonstration. This is particularly true of automobile commercials at the beginning of the model year. The mere sight of a new car flashing down a road is enough to arouse an irrepressible desire for ownership in the breasts of many motorists.

WRITING THE COMMERCIAL

Turning a plan for a commercial into final copy ready for production is an arduous process of finding the right words and pictures to communicate the message and contriving devices that will support them. In this process two qualities should be sought above all others: *memorability* and *persuasiveness*.

MAKING THE AUDIENCE REMEMBER

The principal technique for making the audience remember the product name and absorb the key selling point is to repeat it constantly. Even though repetition may irritate, there is no doubt that it is the copywriter's most effective selling tool. As noted earlier, some commercials of the name copy or reminder type do little more than engage in repetition. A television commercial for a clothing store consisted of nothing more than the store's name bouncing around the screen, breaking up, reassembling in a multitude of variations, advancing and retreating, as the letters changed, switched, and combined. The movement held the eye as the name insinuated itself into the viewer's consciousness. A radio commercial for Pal razor blades used the word "pal" over and over again not only in reference to the blade but in all of its other possible meanings and uses. A one-minute Gallo wine commercial included thirty mentions of the product name. Commercials of the action type also employ repetition to implant the key selling idea with an indelible imprint. A commercial for Lark cigarettes repeated the line, "There's nothing like a Lark," seven times in one minute.

A second major tool for attaining memorability is music, for melodies, as we all know, linger tenaciously in our minds. How often have we found ourselves humming the tune from a commercial, even though we may hate ourselves for it. Moreover, music helps to make the repetitiousness of a commercial palatable, for we are accustomed to repetitions in songs and the musical setting permits the writer to repeat the name many more times than he would be able to in straight copy without becoming ridiculous. Music for commercials may be specially composed; some of it is so well done that it has become popular on its own. Some is adapted from melodies in the public domain that through the years have demonstrated their staying power. The Motorola Company, for example, appropriated the melody of "Happy Birthday to You" to advertise its product. Contemporary composers have also permitted their best melodies to be converted to commercial use—for a fee, of course.

A third technique for making a product name and message memorable is to incorporate them in a catchy slogan. The history of advertising abounds with examples. There are the cigarette slogans "Lucky Strike means fine tobacco," and "Turn to Salem for a taste that's springtime fresh." There is the Avis message, "We're only number two. We try harder," and Dial's "Aren't you glad you use Dial? Don't you wish everybody did?" In addition to persuasive appeal, these slogans give the products identity and make them difficult to forget.

The writers of the radio commercial for the Florida Citrus Commission faced the problem of distinguishing Florida grapefruit from other grapefruit. The qualitites they stressed—low calorie content, a plentiful supply of Vitamin C, ease in serving, economy, freshness and juiciness—are common to grapefruit in general. But they gave this commercial distinction and memorability by using a lilting melody and catchy language to spotlight the weight-reducing qualities of their particular product.

MUSIC: BRIGHT UP-TEMPO RHYTHM

SINGER: How many shapes can a person take

          If a person could change shapes?

MUSIC: BRIDGE

SINGER: Slimmer shapes 'n thinner shapes

          Low calorie grapefruit trimmer shapes!

ANNCR: Well, of course we don't mean you!

MUSIC: STING

ANNCR: You buy Florida grapefruit because it tastes

          good...right!

MUSIC: STING

ANNCR: You buy Florida grapefruit because they're

          fresh and juicy and sweet...right?

MUSIC: STING

ANNCR: You buy Florida grapefruit because they perk

          up a breakfast...and they're easy to fix...

          right?

MUSIC: STING

ANNCR: And you know Florida grapefruit is loaded with

          natural Vitamin C...and kids love 'em...and

          they're economical and...right!

MUSIC: STING

ANNCR: Then would you mind telling a plump friend...

          that Florida grapefruit are very low in

          calories?

MUSIC: STING

JINGLE: How many shapes can a person take

          If a person could change shapes

MUSIC: BRIDGE

SINGER: Slimmer shapes 'n thinner shapes

          Low calorie grapefruit trimmer shapes!

A fourth device for imprinting product names and messages is to connect them with an easily remembered symbol. The black eye patch of the model who wears Hathaway shirts and the bearded face of Commander Whitehead, the man who merchandizes Schweppes products, are examples. The American Tobacco Company had great success giving black eyes to those who smoke Tareyton cigarettes, inescapable proof that they would "rather fight than switch." In the same way they tied a hat with a bite out of it to Lucky Strike filters to symbolize the slogan "Show me a filter cigarette that really delivers taste and I'll eat my hat."

WORDING THE COMMERCIAL

Your first objective in wording a commercial is to be *clear*. This is even more important than being grammatical as the American Tobacco Company demonstrated with its Winston and Tareyton slogans. Use words and phrases the audience is sure to understand and be certain that your ideas develop in logical progression. Writers sometimes use scientific or pseudoscientific terms, whose meaning is not made clear, simply to add dressing or persuasive appeal, but the main ideas should always be expressed in familiar terms. Avoid giving the impression that you are talking down to your audience. Your tone should be conversational and informal, and it should show some respect for the listener's intelligence.

In addition to being clear, it is important to choose words that are appropriate to the product. "Efficient" may be an accurate word with reference to some perfumes, but it is not an appropriate one. Your words should match the product. Often writers use double adjectives to catch the quality they are attempting to communicate. Bread is "oven-fresh," beer is "cool-brewed," grapes are "sun-ripened." Verbs are important in commercials because they are the words that suggest action.

Research into the effect of commercials shows that certain words have more selling power than others. You can enhance the impact of the commercial by sprinkling these persuasive words at intervals through your copy. David Ogilvy, the head of a major advertising agency, in his book *The Confessions of an Advertising Man* listed a number of expressions that have unique selling force, among them the following: "introducing, it's here, just arrived, new, sensational, remarkable, startling, magic, quick, easy, hurry, last chance."

Another characteristic of selling copy is that it is *concrete* and to the point. Generalizations and unsupported superlatives have little persuasive effect. Because the buyer likes to feel that he is motivated by the facts to choose one product in preference to another, commercials should provide him with specific information.

THE COMMERCIAL FORMAT

The formats used for radio and television commercials have been illustrated in the commercial scripts and storyboards included in this chapter. The radio commercial script follows the pattern employed in typing other kinds of material for radio; the TV commercial script, on the other hand, is different from both the television and filmed dramatic script in that the script is typed in two columns with video information on one side and audio information on the other. TV commercials are also frequently presented in storyboards which show a series of panels illustrating the picture content with the accompanying audio material for each panel typed below.

REVIEWING THE COPY

Once written it is important to review and revise the copy with great care. These are some of the questions you might ask yourself as you examine your work: Will I catch the attention of the audience? Have I created enough desire for the product? Do I show it in action? Have I focused on a key selling point which emphasizes that the product is different or better than its competitors? Have I provided enough information about it?

In addition to these basic points there may be minor matters needing attention. You may discover that you have unintentionally used alliteration in such a way as to make your product seem ridiculous, or your copy may contain a verbal pitfall that will trap an unwary announcer. It is also possible that an idea you have expressed may not have come out quite the way you intended. The writers of the following material probably wished they had reviewed their copy with more care: "All hats one-half off"; "When I see a lady who does her own housework and dishwashing and who has soft, pretty hands, I know she has been using her head"; "We stand behind every bed we sell"; "When clothes get dirty just throw them in our washer and let 'er rip."

It may be well to recall at this point that the one goal of a commercial writer is to sell the product he is advertising. In so doing he may be humorous, ingenious, or dramatic, but his aim is not to enthrall audiences with these qualities, but to use them in the interests of his product. He may even be artistic, but again artistry must be subordinated to the basic objective of gaining sales. It is possible that devices used to arouse interest are so attention getting in themselves that the audience will remember them rather than the sales message or the product name. In this regard I am reminded of a commercial for a car which showed a lion riding grandly in the back seat of a convertible unbeknown to the driver. The commercial ended with the gag: "Lions optional at extra cost." I remember the lion very well and I remember the joke, but, as proof of my point, I cannot remember the name of the car. This may be a case where the distinctiveness of the attention-getting device and the wit of the writer obstructed the attainment of his primary objective—selling the car. He may have been too clever for his product's good.

QUESTIONS AND PROJECTS

1. Write two commercials for the same product, one of the name or reminder type, designed to establish the product name, the other of the action type, aimed at immediate sales. Write the action commercial in both a soft-sell and a hard-sell version.

2. Write a sixty-second commercial that can be cut without rewriting to a thirty-second version.

3. Define the key selling point of a widely advertised product. Devise a new and different key selling point for this product.

4. Define the key selling points in the commercials for three competing products and decide which is the most effective.

5. What in your opinion is the place and function of humor in broadcast advertising?

6. Analyze the persuasive steps (attention, need, satisfaction and action) in three commercials and evaluate their effectiveness.

7. Find and evaluate a commercial in which a stronger need for a product was used than the more obvious and relevant need.

8. Write commercials for one product in three different presentational frameworks.

9. Make your own list of words that have a powerful persuasive appeal to potential buyers.

16

Continuities

Americans, with their millions of television and radio sets, apparently stand most in fear of a moment of silence. Giraud Chester

The main concern of this book is the writing of scripts—the material that either forms the essential substance of a program or stands as a unit in a program that includes other segments. In addition to scripts, writers in broadcasting are often called on to prepare continuities, which usually serve one of the following functions: 1) to link the various parts of a broadcast; 2) to guide performers who are presenting a show extemporaneously; 3) to provide copy for use between programs.

Most continuities are prepared by the regular staff of a station or network; often they are people whose main job is something other than writing. Producers, directors, assistant directors, production assistants, and salesmen, especially in local stations, may find themselves writing bridging or connective material. In some cases a continuity writer prepares material in partnership with the master of ceremonies of a variety or quiz show, the host of a homemakers program, the broadcaster of a sports event, or a raconteur who performs on an ad-lib basis. The writer's function in such instances is to provide notes and ideas, which the performer puts into words while he is on the air.

GENERAL CONTINUITY

Public-service programs featuring talks, interviews, or discussions usually require the writing of openings and closings. The openings should gain the attention of the listener and orient him to the nature of the material to come. Sometimes the lure of the program may be the speaker himself; he may be a renowned authority, a local leader, a person in the news, or a celebrity. Sometimes it is the subject that provides the opportunity for arousing interest. In this case a good technique is to ask an intriguing question which will be answered during the program. The orientation of the audience should be accomplished as briskly and as briefly as possible. Irrelevant and unnecessary information can dull interest and delay the program so long that listeners will switch to another station. The purpose of the closing announcement is merely to provide the listener who may have tuned in late with basic information about the program. At the minimum it should include the name of the participants and the subject of the discussion. If the program is one in a series, a reference to the next week's broadcast, written in such a way as to motivate viewers to tune in again, might also be included.

The practice of promoting future broadcasts with plugs at the end of programs or between programs is steadily growing. Particular emphasis is given to retaining the audience already tuned into the station by mentioning the program that follows. Plugs for the next day's programs or even for those coming in a week may also be included, however. Sometimes a station or a network may build an audience for a special program by using plugs that gradually build in quantity and intensity through the period of a week.

The writer of a promotional plug has a very brief time for communicating his message. What he must do in a sentence or two is to crystallize the most attractive and interest-arousing feature of the coming program. The star of the program may be the best bait. Or perhaps it is the star in a new kind of role—Jerry Lewis playing a serious part in a *Ben Casey* episode, for example. Possibly something in the program itself can arouse interest—a drama that promises an unusual twist or a documentary that provides new insights into a current problem. Perhaps even the audience before whom the program was performed can stimulate interest. In promoting a program on Bob Hope's Christmas tour, much of the material drew attention to the audience of soldiers who witnessed the comedian's antics. An added impact is provided by having the star of the program present the plug.

THE INTERVIEW

A main vehicle for presenting guests on many different types of shows is the interview. In the early days of broadcasting, it was often written out and read word for word by the host and guest, but even the most skillful readers had difficulty maintaining naturalness and spontaneity. Most interviews are now ad-libbed, but this does not mean that they go on the air without preparation. An outline of the topics to be covered is often developed before air time and the host may use notes to guide his questioning. The success of an interview depends largely on the skill of the person who asks the questions on the air, a performance function that is beyond the scope of this book. A writer may assist him, however, in research and in planning questions. The nature of the preparation depends to some extent on the kind of interview to be presented.

PERSONALITY INTERVIEW

Many interviews with figures from the entertainment or sports worlds are designed to illuminate their personality and background. The interviewer needs to know something about the guest's background so that he can direct his questions toward bringing out the information of most interest to the audience. It is important also to consider what the celebrity would like to be asked. One question a movie star or singer waits for anxiously is a query about his latest release since he is probably making the rounds of radio and television stations just to promote that picture or record. To fail to ask that key question would be a grievous error. An equally grievous mistake would be to ask a question about a subject the guest prefers not to discuss. Writers can direct interviewers to ask pertinent questions and to avoid embarrassing subjects.

Not all interviews of the personality type are with celebrities. Interviews with contestants on quiz shows or with the individuals who phone in their opinions on a controversial subject also belong in the personality category. Where there is no opportunity for previous contact with the individual, questions about name, age, marital status, occupation, children, and hobbies are about the only ones that can be asked. Where contestants are available ahead of time, a writer through some discerning research may be able to develop questions that will carry the program away from the rut of clichés.

AUTHORITY INTERVIEW

The second major type of interview is designed to bring out the special information possessed by an expert. His stature as an authority may make him a celebrity, but revealing him as a person is only an incidental element in the interview; the focus is not on him but on what he knows. A writer can be of material assistance to an interviewer in preparing this type of program.

The first matter to be considered is the interviewer's introduction of his guest. Unless the guest is already well known to the audience, the interviewer needs to establish his position as an expert, for even distinguished authorities in certain fields are often little known to a general audience. This introduction should not be long or involved, for such openings are interest killers, but should center on those points that will make the guest most intriguing to the audience. The second part of the introduction should stimulate the interest of the audience in the subject to be discussed. A question that will arouse audience curiosity followed by the promise that the question will be answered during the interview helps to attract listeners.

The second step is to plan the way in which the material is to be covered. The procedures for doing this are basically the same as those used for planning any program of a factual nature. The outline for an extemporaneous interview, however, must be more flexible than an outline for a fully scripted show. The interviewer must be left free to follow leads that may develop while the show is actually on the air to permit the whole exchange to have a natural, conversational flavor.

The final step in preparation is to design the questions the host is to ask of the authority. Again they must be considered not as absolutes but as ideas which an adept interviewer can weave into a smoothly flowing conversational pattern. In the construction of these questions certain practices should be followed.

1. Arrange the questions to maintain an even balance of interest throughout the sequence. Interviews often start with stimulating questions, but slide steadily down hill in interest value thereafter.

2. Design questions requiring comment and interpretation from the authority rather than a mere "yes" or "no."

3. On the other hand, do not ask questions so broad that answering them requires long unbroken speeches from the authority. The most natural sounding interviews feature frequent exchanges between the guest and host.

4. Construct questions that permit natural transitions from one question to another. An interview composed of an unrelated and unconnected series of questions sounds mechanical and artificial.

5. Ask only one question at a time. When two or more questions are asked together, one of them is likely to be overlooked.

MUSIC PROGRAMS

Radio stations are presenting as much music as they did before the advent of television, but the number of programs for which continuity is specially written has noticeably decreased. Most music is now recorded and announcers ad lib their introductions instead of reading them from a prepared continuity, or the music is played without any introductions at all. The result is that writers employed by radio stations in the past to turn out continuity for music programs have been supplanted by music librarians, whose function is merely to select the records to be played. There are still some music programs, however, of both the recorded and live variety for which continuity is prepared ahead of time, particularly those broadcast by educational radio stations and by special networks set up to carry the performances of major orchestras and opera companies. Continuity is also written for a scattering of TV programs that focus primarily on music.

PLANNING AND WRITING MUSIC CONTINUITIES

A writer preparing continuity for the broadcast of a group such as the New York Philharmonic Orchestra plays no role in planning the program whatsoever but is merely given a list of the selections in the order they are to be played, and is required simply to write the material that will introduce those selections. At the other extreme, the writer in some situations may be given the entire responsibility of developing a music show to be presented from recordings. In such instances he has full authority to create the theme of the show and to select the music to illustrate it.

PLANNING THE MUSIC PROGRAM.   The writer who has the responsibility for planning a music program may choose between two approaches. He may create a straight program that is developed around no particular theme or idea but aims only for some uniformity of mood or a reasonable transition from mood to mood. The other approach is to build around an idea that gives both music and continuity a definite focus. Most unifying ideas apply to programs of popular and semiclassical music, but some of them are also used to organize programs of classical music. There are any number of such ideas. The unifying element may be: 1) a mood; 2) a personality associated with certain songs; 3) a season;

4) a composer; 5) a setting, such as Broadway; 6) holidays; 7) a period in time; 8) anniversaries; 9) music of various nations; 10) music associated with historical events; 11) a topic. An interesting example of an "idea" series broadcast on a national network shortly after World War II was a fifteen-minute weekly series entitled *Something Old, Something New, Something Borrowed, Something Blue.* Each program featured four numbers representative of these ideas; the "something borrowed" was a theme from a classic that had become a popular number.

WRITING THE MUSIC PROGRAM. A writer handed a list of selections to be played on a classical music program must usually do some research to discover the facts needed to write the introductions. There are a number of standard works, such as Grove's *Dictionary of Music and Musicians,* that can provide most of the information required. In writing continuity for classical programs you should recognize that to a certain extent you are conducting a class in music appreciation since your audience is likely to include a number of people who may be receiving their first experiences with this kind of music. On the other hand, there may be others who have heard the particular selections many times before and for whom anything you write may be an old, old story. What you need to do is to strike a mean between the needs of these two types of people, writing material that will enrich the experience of the beginner without being too naïve for the sophisticated listener.

Classical music continuity may contain information of various types: 1) facts about the composer's life; 2) an anecdote that throws light on the composition of the particular number; 3) the place of the music in the world of music in general; 4) the way in which the composition was first received and how it has been accepted since; 5) the place of the number in the repertory of the orchestra performing it; 6) material about the artists performing the music.

When a concert is presented live, the continuity writer must usually write more material than will actually be used because the length of waits between numbers is somewhat uncertain and the precise time the conductor will begin the concert is not known. The writer therefore needs to prepare what almost amounts to padding, material that will be interesting if there is time for it, but which is not essential to an understanding of the program as a whole.

There is little that can be said to guide the writing of continuity for programs of semiclassical or popular music. Each program presents its own unique problems, but there are a few general principles that can serve as reference points for guiding the writing and evaluation of music continuities of all types.

1. With the music program as with any other, you should seize the

attention of the audience immediately and inform the listeners what is in store. The opening music can assist in attaining these objectives but the continuity carries the main burden.

2. Write continuity that is in harmony with the mood and nature of the music, with the performers, and with the intended audience, and maintain a consistent style throughout the program. You might write material for popular selections in a snappy, colloquial—perhaps even a slangy style—whereas the language you would employ in introductions to symphonic music would be stately and dignified.

3. Avoid the use of such trite expressions as "the orchestra will now render" or such worn-out devices as "the orchestra asks the musical question: 'Why do I love you?'."

4. Resist the temptation to be overly cute. In most instances, choose the straightforward word or approach rather than the elaborate one. It may be acceptable at times to say that a performer "tickles the ivories" or "jounces the old eighty-eights" but it is usually better to say simply that he "plays the piano."

5. Provide the information about the number that you think the audience would like to hear. If the selection is a long one, as is frequently the case on a classical music program, repeat the name of the selection at the end for the benefit of those who tuned in late.

6. Make your comments about selections pertinent and specific rather than permitting them to remain vague and generalized.

7. In most instances the music is the important element in the show, not the continuity. Your purpose should merely be to identify the music and to add to the listeners' enjoyment and understanding of it. An exception to this rule is the program that presents an idea which the music illustrates. In such cases the continuity is as important as the music.

SAMPLE CONTINUITIES

The segment that follows is from a continuity written by Patricia Matusky for a program similar to many broadcast by FM stations around the country—*Music of the Masters,* a regular offering of the University of Michigan station WUOM. In its dignity of tone and in the nature of the information it provides, this continuity is typical of those used to introduce such programs.

ANNCR: We continue MUSIC OF THE MASTERS now with

Liszt's "Faust" Symphony. The Faust

legend is probably one of the oldest, if

not most popular, in Western religious
folklore. The story of the wise, just man,
tempted by evil and either succumbing or
refusing the temptation has been the subject of countless legends, poems, and
ballads for centuries.

The basic Faust legend as known to us
today had its beginning in the puppet plays
of medieval Europe. These little dramas
were the connecting bridge between the
earlier religious morality plays and the
secular theatre which finally developed.
The early versions were a mixture of religion, comedy, philosophical meanderings and
a good deal of pagan mythology. Faust has
since then appeared in a number of versions
for the stage, and a vast number of early
Faust operas were brought out.

As one critic has said, the "Faust"
Symphony is a musical dramatization - not
a musical illustration. The first movement, entitled "Faust," is intended to
represent the longings and sufferings of
man, as reflected in the soul of Faust.
The second movement, "Margaret," represents
innocence and simplicity. The final movement, "Mephistopheles," is sneering,
cynical, and diabolical.

And now - we hear a complete performance of "A Faust Symphony" by Franz Liszt. In this recording the Choral Art Society and the New York Philharmonic are directed by Leonard Bernstein. The tenor soloist is Charles Bressler.

MUSIC: C 6515-16 Sides 1-3 "Faust Symphony" (70:55)

The next segment from a continuity prepared by Deborah Goodell for another WUOM program illustrates the use of an anecdote to arouse interest in a musical selection.

THEME: UP, TO :30, HOLD AND UNDER

ANNCR:

Welcome to MUSICA ANTIQUA...Tonight we hear keyboard music performed at the court and royal chapel of Louis XIV of France. Paul Maynard, who has been director of music at New York's St. Joseph Church since 1950 and harpsichordist of the New York Pro Musica since 1954, is the performer on both the harpsichord and the organ.

Louis XIV of France, known to his subjects as the "Sun King," to himself as "the state" and to history students as a "cause of the French Revolution," wrote in his Memoirs, "I placed various persons in different kinds of work and directed their special skills, which is perhaps, the greatest talent of princes..." Certainly

Louis XIV was blessed to an unusual degree
with this talent for selecting his ministers
...especially those who ministered to him
personally, such as valets, cooks, musicians
and other entertainers. He often took
time from his "more important occupations"
to concern himself with the music and
musicians who surrounded him. He helped
select the harpsichordists at the court
and the organists at the royal chapel.

Louis was specially fond of the organ
and seems to have had a royal affinity for
the king of instruments. In 1693, he pre-
sided over a competition to select a new
organist for the Royal Chapel at Versailles.
All the great organists in France applied.
But a young and unknown organist was chosen
when the King, asserting his position,
commented to the other judges: "I shall
be glad to know your opinion; in my own
judgment, it is the young man I never heard
of before who played best and seems to me
most worthy."

The winning contestant was Francois
Couperin, later and justly called, "Le
Grand." Paul Maynard now performs three
short and one longer work for organ by
Francois Couperin.

MUSIC: <u>C 6398, Side 2, Bds. 7-9 and 11</u>

<u>(4:05 and 7:40)   FRANCOIS COUPERIN</u>

In addition to presenting classical music, WUOM also does occasional programs of a lighter nature. The one that follows, the first in a series prepared for the National Educational Radio Network, illustrates the type of program in which the topic discussed in the continuity is as important as the music being presented.

MONEY, MACHINES AND MUSIC!

Program One

STANDARD OPEN ANNCR: Money, machines and music!...

(SOUND EFFECTS   Mechanical pianos, band organs,

AND MUSIC)   violin players...nickelodeons by

the thousands were made just

forty years ago.

(MUSIC UP THEN UNDER) They made

music and they made money; and

now they are museum pieces.

(MUSIC UP)

(MUSIC TO BG AND   As early as 1863 a player piano

OUT UNDER ANNCR)   was patented by a Frenchman

named Forneaux. But, the heyday

of the nickelodeon was in the

late teens and early twenties of

this century. In 1923, the peak

year of their manufacture, over

200,000 player pianos of all

types were produced in the

United States.

Forneaux's machine was called the Pianista. Later there were dozens of makers and literally hundreds of models with wonderful names such as: Pistonola, Auto-Grand, Air-O-Player, Dulcitone, Playotone, Vacuola and Wondertone to name just a few. One popular model was the Midget or Baby made by the Seeberg Company of Chicago. This was a 44-note coin-operated player piano with a mandolin attachment. It cost about $750 and was used in many pool rooms and cigar stores. Here from an autographed roll by James P. Johnson is "Teddy Bear Blues" as mechanically reproduced by a Seeberg Midget.

MUSIC   1:35   TEDDY BEAR BLUES

The relatively simple player piano without the mandolin attachment was used in many homes, especially farm homes. Large dance halls and amusement parks often had more involved machines.

One, sometimes called the Work-
horse, was the Seeberg model G
...Here's this ingenious gadget
with..."Paddlin' Madeline Home."

MUSIC   2:10   PADDLIN' MADELINE HOME

A third style of orchestration
made by the Seeberg Co. was the
model KT Special. This device
consisted of a 65 note piano
with mandolin attachment, 39
whistles, castanets, triangle
and tambourine. It sounds like
this playing "Toodle-Ooh" by
Fats Waller.

MUSIC   1:57   TOODLE-OOH

In 1912 Henry K. Sandell patented
one of the most intricate of all
mechanical music makers, an
electric self-playing violin. It
was manufactured by the Mills
Novelty Company as the Violano-
Virtuoso, a violin and piano in
the same case, controlled by one
specially coded roll of music.
One tune produced for this amazing
machine was..."I Wonder What's
Become of Sally?"

```
MUSIC   2:25    I WONDER WHAT'S BECOME OF SALLY?

                            Carnivals and merry-go-rounds

                            were the main customers for Band

                            Organs.  These machines produced

                            a tremendous volume of sound for

                            outdoor use.  The Band Organ we

                            will hear playing "The Drum

                            Major" was made in North

                            Tonawanda, New York

MUSIC   2:05    THE DRUM MAJOR

                            The nickelodeons we've heard

    (START BACK-TIMED       today are part of the collection

                            of Mr. Jack Wirth of Ann Arbor,

                            and this is the first in a

                            series of thirteen·programs

                            called Money, Machines and Music.

                            Next week, a conversation with

                            Jack Wirth; and more from that

                            roll of James P. Johnson played

                            on the Seeberg Midget.

    MUSIC UP                Your announcer has been Merrill

                            McClatchy.  Scripts and produc-

                            tion by Ralph Johnson.  This is

                            the University of Michigan

                            Broadcasting Service.

    MUSIC UP TO CLOSE       This is the National Educational

                            Radio Network
```

For a number of years the Bell Telephone Company has presented programs of music on television, most of which revolve around some kind of unifying idea. The following segment is from a continuity written by Will Glickman for a program that featured the music of the song and dance men of America's vaudeville stage. The host was Donald O'Connor and his special guest was Anthony Newley. The show opened with a song and dance performed by the two stars and then continued with the following:

(MUSIC: CONTINUES AS DONALD AND TONY SPEAK)

> DONALD O'CONNOR

Good evening, ladies and gentlemen.

Tonight's hour is a sentimental look at

the show-business personality called the

Song and Dance Man. Perhaps you already

guessed that by the little pasquinade

that Tony and I just did.

> TONY

Pasquinade means a brief musicalized

scene of a slightly satirical nature....

Which is pretty fancy talk for a song-and

-dance man!

> DONALD

Sorry.

> TONY

Remember, Donald, how Fred Allen describ-

ed a song-and-dance man.

> DONALD

"Half gypsy and half suitcase." And that's

the kind of fellow our show's about this

evening...!

(BILLBOARD)

 (MUSIC: SEGUE TO BELL THEME)

 (SLIDES: THE BELL TELEPHONE HOUR & THE SONG AND

   DANCE MAN)

      BRANDT   (VO)

  The Bell Telephone Hour...Presents "The

  Song and Dance Man"...

 (CUT TO CAST AS NAMED)

With Donald Voorhees and the

Bell Telephone Orchestra...

Starring --

Janet Blair...

Shani Wallis...

Nancy Dussault...

The Nicholas Brothers...

Special Guest --

Anthony Newley!...

And your host, ladies and gentlemen,

Donald O'Connor!

 (APPLAUSE)

(DONALD O'CONNOR: INTRO TO DOUBLE ACT)

 (MUSIC: UNDERSCORE)

VARIETY PROGRAMS

Local radio and television stations often produce programs which, like magazines, include a variety of material—interviews with visiting celebrities, local officials, and experts in various fields, household hints, answers to listeners' letters, contests, and other features. Writers who work with the personality who appears on the air in producing and preparing the material for the show have a number of functions. They include such duties as developing ideas for the show, finding material, creating outlines, keeping track of visitors to the city, arranging interviews, preparing questions for these interviews, deciding the order of events on the show, reading letters, doing the research necessary to answer questions, and inventing contest ideas.

A network program that mixes such elements as news, interviews, recorded music, comedy bits, and features in a presentation that continues through an entire week end is the *Monitor* program of the NBC radio network. The week-end period is divided into segments of approximately three hours, each produced by a separate team made up of a writer, host, producer, and production assistant. The three-hour segments are in turn divided into half-hour units. The opening continuity for one such sequence, broadcast during a New York subway strike, illustrates the use of human-interest material and the billboarding of the main attractions to be heard during that half hour.

NELSON: This is Monitor. I'm Barry Nelson,

           happy to be here this afternoon.

           Actually, I'm happy just to be sitting

           down. Boy, we've done a lot of walk-

           ing in New York this week! Somebody

           estimated the ground covered by the six

           million commuters to the city at about

           four miles a day per person. For the

           five working days, that's a total of

           120 million miles. At that rate, they

           could have walked to the moon and back

           240 times! Space travel the hard way!

           We'll hear about space travel the funny

           way in this half-hour, from Jose Jimenez

           as the Astronaut. And the delightful

           world-traveler Ilka Chase will tell us

           about some of her adventures. Let's

```
                    begin with "One Step Above"...Claus

                    Ogerman style.

    DISC:           ONE STEP ABOVE (CLAUS OGERMAN) (1:56)
```

On television the most common type of network variety show is the evening program offering various kinds of entertainment—music, comedy, dancing, dramatic sketches. One type is the straight vaudeville arrangement best exemplified by the *Ed Sullivan* show. Another type is the show built around a singing performer, such as Perry Como or Andy Williams, and a third type is the program in which a comedian like Bob Hope, Jackie Gleason, or Danny Kaye serves as the focus.

Shows such as these may call for anything from a simple continuity to a complete script. An example of continuity is the material read or ad libbed by Ed Sullivan between the acts of his show. His function is to introduce the entertainers and he usually does it in a straightforward, unadorned way. Sullivan is not a performer and only occasionally does he take part in the acts. Perhaps it is his willingness to make simple introductions and to keep the spotlight on the performers instead of attempting to be clever himself that helps explain his staying power on the air waves. Even though Sullivan's material is simple, it is skillfully written. He shows particular finesse in holding the audience by reviewing at intervals the exciting acts that are still ahead and by reminding viewers at the end of an act by an outstanding performer that "He will be back."

In other variety shows the material that comes between the acts frequently has comedy overtones as it places the title characters in various types of situations with the guests on the show. Andy Williams, for example, not only sings songs but participates in most of the sketches. Although these programs essay an atmosphere of spontaneity, they are carefully rehearsed and the lines are either committed to memory or are read from prompting devices. The material for these shows should properly be called a script rather than a continuity, for it does not merely link and introduce elements in the show; it is part of the show itself.

In addition to preparing continuity for variety shows, writers are often required to set up the rundown or routine sheets that indicate the events in the program, their length in minutes and seconds, and the time they are scheduled. Formats for these sheets vary. The following indicates the style used by *Monitor* for the fifteen-minute period in which the continuity quoted earlier appeared.

```
                         M O N I T O R
PROD:  VOUTSAS                    PAGE    1
WRITER:  PFIZER      Routine Sheet   DATE  JANUARY, 9
P.A.:  BUCHANAN                   TIME   2:00:00
HOST:  BARRY NELSON
```

TIME				NEMO
2:00:00	NEWSMAN:	TEASE LINE		
	BEEPER			
	BARRY:	BILLBOARD		
	NEWS			
	ET:	PONTIAC COMMERCIAL	(0:30)	
	NEWS			
2:04:45	BARRY:	CLOSING BILLBOARD		
	BEEPER			
2:05	BARRY:	LINES		
	DISC:	LAROS THEME - SINGING STRINGS RUNS 2:00 (45) DEADPOT 2:05:10		
2:07:10	BEEPER			
2:07:15	CTG:	THEME: "NITE FLIGHT" (UP & UNDER)	(0:15)	
2:07:30	BARRY:	BILLBOARD	(0:20)	
2:07:50	DISC:	ONE STEP ABOVE CLAUS OGERMAN S62/C-2 (CLEAR :05 UNDER :05	(1:56)	
2:09:45	BARRY:	INTRO TAPE	(0:20)	
2:10:05	TAPE	ILKE CHASE (BRAD CRANDALL) O:HOW ABOUT THE TITLE... C:BRAD CRANDALL FOR MONITOR.	(5:04)	
2:15:10	BARRY:	WRAP & BEACON CUE	(0:10)	
	BEEPER			
2:15:20	DISC:	BLUES IN THE NIGHT 101 STRINGS CUT 1	(1:10)	

QUIZ PROGRAMS

One of the most durable types of shows in American broadcasting is the program revolving around the asking of questions or the performance of some kind of stunt. The participants may be selected from the audience, or they may be a group of authorities, celebrities, or specially selected people such as college students. Programs of the first type are known as audience-participation shows and those in the second group are called panel shows.

The format for the first quiz shows was a simple one. People from the studio audience were asked questions; if they knew the answers, they received a small sum of money. Refinements of this pattern were not long in coming. The *Dr. I.Q.* program paid its prizes in silver dollars and arranged for announcers to ask questions of people in their seats instead of bringing them to the platform. It was this practice that developed the famous line, "I have a lady in the balcony, Doctor."

The next step was to introduce suspense by giving contestants the option of taking what they had won, or gambling that they would either double their money by answering the next question or lose everything if they failed. Suspense increased as the prizes became bigger and bigger. Conflict entered the picture too as contestants competed with one another for the prizes. A panel show such as *What's My Line?* arouses interest by letting the audience watch a group of celebrities wrestle with a question to which the viewers know the answer. As a further fillip to interest, many programs now feature celebrities who join selected members from the audience to engage in games and stunts.

One observation prompted by the history of audience-participation and panel shows is that it is difficult to find a completely original program idea. A number have been inspired by old-time parlor games. Others merely represent switches on ideas that are already on the air. A review of the development of some well-known audience-participation and panel shows demonstrates how this process works. *Information Please* featured a panel of intellectuals who answered questions on every conceivable subject. It was followed on the air by *Quiz Kids,* which featured a panel of precocious youngsters who also answered questions on every conceivable subject. A modification, the reverse of this one, was exemplified by the programs *Juvenile Jury* and *Life Begins at Eighty.* First on the scene was *Juvenile Jury,* a program that featured discussions of various personal and social problems by youngsters. *Life Begins at Eighty* dealt with personal and social problems, but involved people at the other extreme of the age spectrum. The Goodman-Todson Agency has produced a number of programs employing a panel of four celebrities which differ only in the nature of the information sought and the way in which the contest is scored.

CRITERIA FOR A SUCCESSFUL SHOW

A review of the successful panel and audience-participation shows reveals that most of them satisfy certain criteria.

SIMPLICITY. The basic ideas of successful shows are simple ones which can be explained to the contestants and to the audience in a sentence or two. Elaborate and complicated ideas usually do not work because too much time must be taken to explain them, and there is also the danger that neither the contestants nor the audience will really understand what is going on. It is particularly important that the method of scoring the results be simple and straightforward.

TITLE. Successful shows have titles that serve two functions: they focus on the basic element in the show and they can be used at intervals as a slogan or summary statement. *What's My Line?*, *To Tell the Truth*, and *People are Funny* are examples.

INVOLVEMENT BY THE AIR AUDIENCE. Most successful shows provide an opportunity for the radio and television audience to participate actively in the show. This participation can be accomplished in a number of ways. In panel shows the audience member can try to think of the answers to the questions before one of the experts does, and when he succeeds, can enjoy the satisfaction of being brighter than a recognized authority. Sometimes audience members are given the answers to the questions before the panel goes to work. In such cases they can enjoy the superior feeling one gets when watching the strivings of other people to obtain information one already knows. The suspense and conflict elements in many shows also help to involve the viewer.

SHOWS THAT FAILED. A large number of panel and audience-participation shows have had short stays on the airwaves. One of these was a program called *Don't Make Me Laugh* which featured contestants who could win prizes if they were able to listen to the jokes of a leading comedian without smiling or laughing. It was discovered that when money was at stake, most people could stay grim no matter what the comedian did. It was also a depressing experience for funny men to perform before stony-faced contestants. Another failure was called *On the Spot*, which boasted a panel that could supposedly answer any question on any subject. When listeners began to confront them with such questions as "Who is the mayor of Albuquerque?", the format broke down. These ideas probably looked good on paper, but the final test under actual broadcasting conditions revealed their defects. Panel and audience-participation shows require a rigid tryout period in a simulated radio or TV situation before they can be considered ready for the air.

WRITING THE SHOW

The creative contribution in the panel and audience-participation field lies in devising the show idea. After that the writing job becomes the relatively routine chore of making up questions or finding contestants. These tasks, of course, must be carried out skillfully if the values inherent in the basic idea of the show are to be realized. The best designs can be destroyed by careless, ineffective preparation from week to week. The actual material of the show is not prepared for word-for-word delivery but is drawn up in an outline form from which the master of ceremonies adlibs. Material in this form is referred to as a rundown of the show. The following rundown for *I've Got a Secret,* a Goodson-Todman presentation, illustrates the way the continuity is set up for the opening of the show and the first problem. The writer and producer of the individual show must find guests and devise problems for presentation to the panel from week to week.

VIDEO	AUDIO
ON CELEBRITY	CELEBRITY
	Good evening. (TALK)
	" ... and this is
	"I'VE GOT A SECRET!"
HOLD CU ONE SECOND	(APPLAUSE)
	(MUSIC IN)
(AFTER ONE PHRASE OF	(APPLAUSE OUT)
MUSIC)	
CUT TO TITLE DEVICE:	ANNOUNCER:
1. "I'VE GOT A ...	
... SECRET!"	"I'VE GOT A SECRET!
	... brought to you
	by ...
	POST CEREALS ...

VIDEO	AUDIO

CUT TO FILM: POST CEREALS
    (65-505)

> The Cereals that make breakfast a little bit better ... POST CEREALS.

CUT TO FILM: (:30)
    (68-103) (COLOR)

CUT TO TITLE DEVICE:

    1. "I'VE GOT A ...

       ... SECRET!"

> (POST CEREALS)
>
> ANNOUNCER:
> (ON CUE FROM DIRECTOR)
> Live ...
> From New York ...
> Here is "I'VE GOT A SECRET!"
> starring ...
>
>   (MUSIC -- PLAY-ON)

DISSOLVE TO STAGE

STEVE ENTERS ON CUE

> STEVE ALLEN!
>
>   (APPLAUSE)

ON STEVE

> ALLEN:
> Good evening. Welcome to another edition of "I'VE GOT A SECRET!" Now I'd like you to meet our Panel.
> First, BETSY PALMER!
> Then,   BILL CULLEN!
> Then,   BESS MYERSON!
> Then,   HENRY MORGAN!

VIDEO	AUDIO
ON STEVE ALLEN	STEVE:
	All right, Panel,
	are you ready to
	play the game?
CUT TO PANEL	(THEY ANSWER)
	Then may we have our
	first contestant,
	please?
CUT TO CONTESTANT	(CONTESTANT ENTERS)
	(APPLAUSE)
	Hello. Will you tell
	us your name and
	where you are from?
	(HE DOES)
	All right, _____
	if you will whisper
	your secret to me,
	we will reveal it at
	the same time to our
	audience at home.
SUPER SECRET	(APPLAUSE)
	And to help classify
	this secret, it con-
	cerns _____ ,
	and we'll start with
	_____
	(<u>FIRST</u> <u>SPOT</u>)
	(PLAY GAME)
	(PAY-OFF)

SPORTS AND SPECIAL EVENTS

Most of the commentary for a sports or special events broadcast is ad-libbed by an announcer who describes what he sees. In many instances, however, his on-the-spot description is complemented by background material which must be prepared ahead of time. A writer may help an announcer compile this background information. Its nature depends on the event being covered. If it is a football game, the announcer needs information about such items as the following: the competing schools, the history of the competition between them, the significance of the contest in the conference race, and the players. This information is available in publicity material which the competing schools make available to all broadcasting organizations covering the game. It contains many more facts that can possibly be used. The task of the writer is to abstract the most pertinent and interesting items and set them up so that the announcer can easily refer to them during the broadcast.

Bill Flemming, a sportscaster for the ABC television network, in preparing for a football broadcast, constructs a chart composed of squares containing statistical and background material about the players on the offensive and defensive teams of each school. He tacks the charts for each school on small boards, putting the offensive chart for a given school on one side, the defensive chart on the other. When the ball changes hands, Flemming has only to flip the two boards over to have information about the incoming players immediately available to him. Each square on the chart contains the following information: the player's number, his name, his position, his height, his weight, his year in school, other points of interest. Information about players who participated in a game broadcast by Flemming between teams of the University of Michigan and Northwestern University, illustrates the type of material appearing on the charts.

> 83 . . . Rocky Rosema . . . End . . . 6'2" . . . 214 . . . Junior
> Grand Rapids, Mich. Early Mono . . . just getting back.
> 18 . . . Rick Sygar . . . Back . . . 5'11" . . . 185 . . . Senior
> Niles, Ohio . . . Second baseman, baseball team . . . P.A.T.'s—18
> of 19, 1965, 26 of 26, 1966
> Broke leg twice as a soph.
> 19 . . . Carl Ward . . . Back . . . 5'9" . . . 178 . . . Senior
> Cincinnati, Ohio . . . Started every game since soph. year
> 48 yd. run in Rose Bowl highpoint of football career.
> 33 . . . Dave Fisher . . . F.B. . . . 5'10" . . . 210 . . . Senior
> Ketterling, Ohio . . . B+ student in Arch. and Design
> Won "golden helmet" for combined abilities in '65
> High School All-American. Total loss—12 yards in two years.

In preparing for other types of sports broadcasts, information appropriate to the particular event is prepared and charted in the same way.

Getting background material ready for a sports event, which often follows predictable lines, may be easier than preparing for a special event, whose precise development no one may be able to foretell. The launching of astronauts, for example, has often been marked by long and unexpected delays during which the announcers must continue the broadcast. It is obvious that extensive material must be ready for such eventualities. The information a writer prepares may be supplemented with special demonstrations and exhibits made ready for use in case there is a halt in the proceedings.

The event that includes a group of happenings so similar that a description of each one of them becomes ridiculous presents special problems. A parade, particularly when it features not much more than marching soldiers, puts even the most eloquent of announcers to the severest of tests. He needs background facts to leaven his running account of the event. A procession such as the Mummers Parade in Philadelphia and the Tournament of Roses Parade in Pasadena is more varied than the usual military parade, but information must still be compiled for those describing it. Let us consider some of the items a writer might assemble for announcers assigned to these events. First in order is to prepare information about the units making up the parade; in the case of bands the identity of the leader, the number of marchers, and special distinctions would be listed. Viewers watching the Purdue University Band march in the Rose Parade were told, for example, that it was the largest college band in the country and featured the largest drum in the world. Information compiled by the writer can also be used to guide the art department in making title cards to be superimposed over the various units for identification purposes.

Other notes of a miscellaneous nature add to the enjoyment of the audience. To cite some examples: TV viewers of the Mummer's Parade were told that a local bridal shop in Philadelphia had been bought out by men participating in a marching exhibit satirizing the marriage of a President's daughter; the audience to a Rose Parade found out that it was viewing the forty-sixth appearance of the Salvation Army Band but the first appearance in that parade of a Navy Band; the racing car in one float, it was made known, had actually been used in the previous Indianapolis 500-mile race; the number and nature of the flowers making up the various Rose Parade floats was included in the information provided the announcers—one float contained 500,000 individual blossoms, another 15,000 orchids, a third 28 varieties of roses. We might note that the work of writers in preparing background information for these parades is so important to the success of the broadcasts that they are identified in the credits at the end of the program.

Political events require the writer to assemble facts about the people involved, the background of the event, and its possible future consequences. In other instances the writer must try to assemble the information that will be most interesting and relevant. In preparing for any special event or sports broadcast, forethought is of the utmost importance. The writer must be certain that he has gathered enough material to permit the announcer to make a continuous running commentary. At the same time he must recognize that much of what he is at great pains to provide will probably not be used. In this respect he keeps company with the writer who prepares extensive notes for a symphony concert only to find the conductor unexpectedly raises his baton on time.

QUESTIONS AND PROJECTS

1. Find out what authorities are visiting your campus in the near future. Select one and, for the guidance of an interviewer, prepare a list of questions designed to explore the special field of that authority for a general audience.

2. Write continuity for the following with the emphases as indicated:
   a) *Brandenburg Concerto No. 3 in G. Major*—J. S. Bach (facts about the composer's life).
   b) *Ninth Symphony* . . . Beethoven (place of this music in the total work of the composer).
   c) *Concerto for Violin* . . . Bartók (place of this in the music world.)
   d) "Toreador Song" from *Carmen* . . . Bizet (the way this opera was first received by the public).
   e) *Fourth Symphony* . . . Tschaikowsky played by the Cleveland Orchestra directed by George Szell (facts on orchestra and director).

3. Decide on a theme for a half-hour music program. Then select music and write continuity that will bring out this theme.

4. Assume that you have your choice of leading show business personalities and variety acts. Design a variety show; prepare a rundown sheet; write connective continuity.

5. Watch three quiz or game shows. Describe the framework of each show as succinctly as you can and present your descriptions to the class. Do these shows meet the tests of simplicity, catchy and descriptive titles, suspense, and involvement by the air audience?

6. Assume that you have been assigned to prepare material on your football team for a broadcaster from a visiting school. Prepare information on the six players who are most likely to be involved in the action.

7. Prepare continuity to open and close the broadcast of a special event soon to take place in your community.

Bibliography

SCRIPT REFERENCES

This section lists the scripts referred to in the text that are available in published form plus other scripts and script compilations of value to writers.

Aurthur, Robert Alan, "Man on a Mountain Top," in *Best Television Plays*, Gore Vidal (ed.) (New York: Ballantine Books, Inc., 1956), pp. 109–134.

Barnouw, Eric (ed.), *Radio Drama in Action* (New York: Holt, Rinehart and Winston, Inc., 1945).

Boyd, James (ed.), *The Free Company Presents* (New York: Dodd, Mead, & Co., 1941).

Britton, Florence (ed.), *Best Television Plays 1957* (New York: Ballantine Books, Inc., 1957).

Burack, A. S. (ed.), *Television Plays for Writers* (Boston: The Writer, Inc , 1957).

Chayefsky, Paddy, *Television Plays* (New York: Simon and Schuster, Inc., 1955.

———, "The Bachelor Party," in *Television Plays*, pp. 219–259.

———, "The Big Deal," in *Television Plays,* pp. 89–126.

———, "Holiday Song," in *Television Plays,* pp. 1–35.

———, "Marty," in *Television Plays,* pp. 133–173.

———, "The Mother," in *Television Plays,* pp. 181–219.

———, "Printer's Measure," in *Television Plays,* pp. 41–81.

Corwin, Norman, *Thirteen by Corwin* (New York: Holt, Rinehart and Winston, Inc., 1942).

———, "Old Salt," in *Thirteen by Corwin,* pp. 137–163.

Costigan, James, *Little Moon of Alban and A Wind from the South* (New York: Simon and Schuster, Inc., 1959).

Coulter, Douglass (ed.), *Columbia Workshop Plays* (New York: Whittlesey House, McGraw-Hill Book Co., Inc., 1939).

Crabtree, Paul, "The Pilot," in *Best Television Plays 1957,* Florence Britton (ed.) (New York: Ballantine Books, Inc. 1957) pp. 167–194.

Dyne, Michael, "A Tongue of Silver," in *Best Television Plays 1957,* Florence Britton (ed.) (New York: Ballantine Books, Inc., 1957).

Fitelson, H. Williams (ed.), *Theatre Guild on the Air* (New York: Holt, Rinehart and Winston, Inc., 1947).

Foote, Horton, *Harrison, Texas* (New York: Harcourt, Brace & World, Inc., 1956).

———, "The Midnight Caller," in *Harrison, Texas,* pp. 153–187.

———, "The Trip to Bountiful," in *Harrison, Texas,* pp. 219–263.

———, "Three Plays (New York: Harcourt, Brace & World, Inc., 1962).

———, "A Young Lady of Property," in *Harrison, Texas,* pp. 1–41.

Geiger, Milton, "One Special for Doc." in *Plays from Radio,* A. H. Lass, Earle L. McGill, Donald Axelrod (eds.), pp. 180–189.

Gilroy, Frank D., "A Matter of Pride," In *Best Television Plays 1957,* Florence Britton (ed.) (New York: Ballantine Books, Inc., 1957), pp. 10–42.

Grafton, Samuel and Edith, "Mock Trail," in *Television Plays for Writers,* A. S. Burack (ed.) (Boston: The Writer, Inc., 1957), pp. 153–199.

Goldberger, Edwin, "Two Battles of Relish" adaptation of the story by Lord Dunsany in *100 Nonroyalty Radio Plays,* William Kozlenko (ed.) (New York: Greenburg, 1941), pp. 6–12.

Hailey, Arthur, *Close-up on Writing for Television* (New York: Doubleday & Company, Inc., 1960).

Hill, George Roy and John Whedon, "A Night to Remember," in *The Prize Plays of Television and Radio 1956* (New York: Random House, Inc., 1957) pp. 83–121.

Hitchcock, Alfred (ed.), *12 stories They Wouldn't Let Me Do on TV* (New York: Dell Publishing Co., Inc., 1957).

Knight, Eric, "The Flying Yorkshireman," adapted by Charles Jackson, in Max Wylie's *Radio Writing* (New York: Holt, Rinehart and Winston Inc., 1939), pp. 325–339.

Kozlenko, William (ed.), *100 Nonroyalty Radio Plays* (New York: Greenburg, 1941).

Lass, A. H., Earle L. McGill, and Donald Axelrod (eds.), *Plays from Radio* (Boston: Houghton Mifflin Company, 1948).

Liss, Joseph (ed.), *Radio's Best Plays* (New York: Greenburg, 1946).

MacLeish, Archibald, "The States Talking," in *The Free Company Presents,* James Boyd (ed.) (New York: Dodd Mead & Co., 1941), p. 238.

Miller, J. P., "The Rabbit Trap," in *Best Television Plays,* Gore Vidal (ed.) (New York: Ballantine Books, Inc., 1956), pp. 192–221.

Mosel, Tad, *Other Peoples Houses* (New York: Simon and Schuster, Inc., 1956).

———, "Ernie Barger is Fifty," in *Other Peoples Houses,* pp. 5–38.

———, "The Haven," in *Other Peoples Houses,* pp. 77–114.

———, "The Lawn Party," in *Other People's Houses,* pp. 117–157.

———, "My Lost Saints," in *Best Television Plays,* Gore Vidal (ed.) (New York: Ballantine Books, Inc. 1956), pp. 69–109.

———, "The Out-of-Towners," in *Television Plays for Writers,* A. S. Burack (ed.) (Boston: The Writer, 1957), pp. 199–241.

Noble, William, "Snapfinger Creek," in *Best Television Plays 1957,* Florence Britton (ed.) (New York: Ballantine Books, Inc, 1957), pp. 68–99.

Oboler, Arch, *Oboler Omnibus* (New York: Duell, Sloan & Pearce, 1945).

———, "The Ugliest Man in the World," in *Oboler Omnibus,* pp. 49–66.

The Prize Plays of Television and Radio 1956, Collected by the Writers Guild of America, (New York: Random House, Inc., 1957).

Rodman, Howard, "The Explorer," in *Best Television Plays 1957,* Florence Britton (ed.) (New York: Ballantine Book, Inc., 1957), pp. 99–167.

Rose, Reginald, *Six Television Plays* (New York: Simon and Schuster, Inc., 1956).

———, "An Almanac of Liberty," in *Six Television Plays,* pp. 161–203.

———, "Thunder on Sycamore Street," in *Six Television Plays,* pp. 57–111.

———, "Twelve Angry Men," in *Six Television Plays,* pp. 111–161.

Serling, Rod, "Noon on Doomsday," in *Television Plays for Writers,* A. S. Burack (ed.) (Boston: The Writer, Inc., 1957), pp. 307–352.

———, *Patterns* (New York: Simon and Schuster, Inc., 1957).

———, "Patterns," in *Patterns,* pp. 43–85.

———, "The Rack," in *Patterns,* pp. 91–136.

———, "Requiem for a Heavyweight," in *Patterns,* pp. 181–242.

————, "The Strike," in *Best Television Plays*, Gore Vidal (ed.) (New York: Ballantine Books, Inc., 1956), pp. 163–194.

Sloane, Allan, "Bring on the Angels,' 'in *The Prize Plays of Television and Radio 1956*, (New York: Random House, Inc., 1957), pp. 121–141.

Vidal, Gore (ed.), *Best Television Plays* (New York: Ballantine Books, Inc., 1956).

————, "Visit to a Small Planet," in *Best Television Plays*, pp. 221–248.

Williams, Tennessee, *Cat on a Hot Tin Roof* (New York: New Directions, 1955), p. 98.

Wishengrad, Morton, *The Eternal Light* (New York: Crown Publishers, 1947).

————, "The Black Death," in *The Eternal Light*, pp. 139–153.

GENERAL REFERENCES

Allen, Louise C., Andre B. Lipscomb and Joan C. Prigmore, *Radio and Television Continuity Writing* (New York: Pitman Publishing Corp., 1962).

Allen, Steve, *The Funny Men* (New York: Simon and Schuster, Inc., 1956).

Archer, William, *Play-Making* (Boston: Small, Maynard and Company, 1912).

Baker, George Pierce, *Dramatic Technique* (Boston: Houghton Mifflin Company, 1919).

Barnouw, Erik, *Handbook of Radio Writing* (Boston: D.C. Heath & Company, 1948), p. 14.

————, *The Television Writer* (New York: Hill and Wang, 1962).

Barry, Michael (ed.), *The Television Playwright* (New York: Hill and Wang, 1962).

Bluem, A. William, *Documentary in American Television* (New York: Hastings House, Publishers, Inc., 1965), p. 23.

Bowen, Catherine Drinker, "*The Writing of a Biography* (Boston: The Writer, Inc., 1950).

Brown, Donald E. and John Paul Jones, *Radio and Television News* (New York: Holt, Rinehart and Winston, Inc., 1954).

Busfield, Roger, *The Playwright's Art* (New York: Harper & Row Publishers, 1958).

CBS News, *Television News Reporting* (New York: McGraw-Hill Book Company, 1958).

Chester, Giraud, Garnet R. Garrison and Edgar E. Willis, *Television and Radio*, Third Edition (New York: Appleton-Century-Crofts, 1963).

Ciardi, John, "Robert Frost: The Way to the Poem," *Saturday Review,* Vol. 41 (April 12, 1958), p. 14.

Cowley, Malcolm, "How Writers Write," *Saturday Review,* Vol. 40 (November 30, 1957), pp. 11–13, 35–36.

Crews, Albert, *Professional Radio Writing* (Boston: Houghton Mifflin Company, 1946), p. 232.

Downer, Alan S., *The Art of the Play* (New York: Holt, Rinehart and Winston, Inc., 1955), p. 6.

Eastman, Max, *The Enjoyment of Laughter* (New York: Simon and Schuster, Inc., 1957), p. 296.

Efron, Edith, "Can a TV Writer Keep His Integrity?," *TV Guide,* Vol. 10 (April 21, 1962), pp. 8–11.

Egri, Lajos, *The Art of Dramatic Writing* (New York: Simon and Schuster, Inc., 1946), p. 94.

Field, Stanley, *Television and Radio Writing* (Boston: Houghton Mifflin Company, 1958).

For the Young Viewer, edited by Ralph Garry, F. B. Rainsberry, and Charles Winick (New York: McGraw-Hill Book Company, 1962).

Gallishaw, John, *The Only Two Ways to Write a Story* (New York: G. P. Putnam's Sons, 1928).

Greene, Robert S., *Television Writing* (New York: Harper & Row, Publishers, 1952).

Grierson, John, *Grierson on Documentary* (London: Collins, 1946).

Grove, George, *Dictionary of Music and Musicians,* Eric Blom (ed.) (New York: St. Martin's Press, Inc., 1955).

Hart, Moss, *Act One* (New York: Random House, Inc., 1959), p. 166.

Herman, Lewis, *A Practical Manual of Screen Playwriting for Theatre and Television Films* (Cleveland: World Publishing Company, 1952) .

Herman, Lewis and Marguerite Shallet Herman, *American Dialects: A Manual for Actors, Directors, and Writers* (New York: Theatre Arts Books, 1943).

——— and ——— *Foreign Dialects: A Manual for Actors, Writers, and Directors* (New York: Theatre Arts Books, 1943).

Hilliard, Robert L., *Writing for Television and Radio* (New York: Hastings House, Publishers, Inc., 1962).

Himmelweit, Hilde T. *et al., Television and the Child* (London: Oxford University Press, 1958).

Jackson, Allan, *You Have to Write, Too* (Mimeo) (New York: CBS News, 1961).

Kerr, Jean, "What Makes Me Laugh," *Saturday Evening Post,* Vol. 232 (March 19, 1960), pp. 21, 64–65, 68.

Kerr, Walter, *How Not to Write A Play* (New York: Simon and Schuster, Inc., 1955).

Lawrence, Jerome (ed.), *Off Mike* (New York: Duell, Sloan & Pearce, 1944).

Leacock, Stephen, *Humor* (New York: Dodd, Mead & Co., 1935), p. 216.

MacGowan, Kenneth, *A Primer of Playwriting* (New York: Random House, Inc., 1951).

Maloney, Martin, *The Radio Play* (Evanston: The Student Book Exchange, 1949).

Mannes, Marya, "The Captive Writer," *The Reporter*, Vol. 21 (Aug 20, 1959), p. 32.

———, "Massive Detergence," *The Reporter*, Vol. 25 (July 6, 1961), p. 42.

———, "Time for a Story," *The Reporter*, Vol. 21 (July 9, 1959), p. 34.

Maugham, Somerset, "The Vagrant Mood," *The Decline and Fall of the Detective Story* (New York: Doubleday & Company, Inc., 1953), p. 109.

Nash, Ogden, *The Private Dining Room* (Boston: Little, Brown and Company, 1953), p. 32.

Odets, Clifford, "How a Playwright Triumphs," *Harpers,* Vol. 223 (September, 1966), p. 73.

Ogilvy, David, *Confessions of an Advertising Man* (New York: Atheneum, Publishers, 1963), pp. 105–106.

Porter, Katherine Anne, "Flowering Judas," in *This is My Best,* Whit Burnett (ed.) (New York: The Dial Press, Inc., 1942), p. 539.

Prideaux, Tom, "A Boost for Rep Boom," *Life,* Vol. 58 (April 2, 1965), p. 19.

Rapp, Albert, *The Origins of Wit and Humor* (New York: E. P. Dutton & Co., Inc., 1951).

Rees, Goronowy, Review of *Woman and Thomas Harrow,* by John Marquand, *The Listener,* Vol. 61 (January 22, 1959), p. 180.

Reeves, Rosser, *Reality in Advertising* (New York: Alfred A. Knopf, Inc., 1961).

Roberts, Edward Barry, *Television Writing and Selling* (New York: The Writer, Inc., 1957).

Schramm, Wilbur, *Television in the Lives of Our Children* (Stanford, Calif.: Stanford University Press, 1961).

Schwartz, Sherwood, "How to Write a Joke" in *Off Mike,* Jerome Lawrence (ed.) (New York: Duell, Sloan & Pearce, 1944), pp. 9–23.

"The Script and the Scribe," *Television Age,* Vol. 10 (October 15, 1962), pp. 27–30.

Seldes, Gilbert, *The Great Audience* (New York: The Viking Press, Inc., 1951).

————, *Writing for Television* (New York: Doubleday & Company, Inc., 1952).

Siller, Bob, Hal Terkel, and Ted White, *Television and Radio News* (New York: The MacMillan Company, 1960).

Steinbeck, John, "Critics—From a Writer's Standpoint," *Saturday Review*, Vol. 38 (August 27, 1955), p. 20.

Swallow, Norman, *Factual Television* (New York: Hastings House, Publishers, 1966).

Swinson, Arthur, *Writing for Television Today* (London: Adam and Charles Black, 1963).

Trapnell, Coles. *Teleplay: An Introduction to Television Writing* (San Francisco: Chandler Publishing Co., 1966).

"The Theater," *Time*, Vol. 85 (April 23, 1965), p. 59.

Thurber, James, "Soapland," *The Beast in Me and Other Animals* (New York: Harcourt, Brace & World, Inc., 1948), pp. 191–260.

Tuchman, Barbara W., "History by the Ounce," *Harpers*, Vol. 231 (July, 1965), pp. 65–75.

Tynan, Kenneth, *Curtains* (New York: Atheneum Publishers, 1961), p. 101.

Van Druten, John, *Playwright at Work* (New York: Harper & Row, Publishers, 1953), p. 171.

Wainwright, Charles Anthony, *The Television Copywriter* (New York: Hastings House, Publishers, Inc., 1966).

Wells, George, "Radio's Strangest Bird," in *Off Mike*, Jerome Lawrence (ed.) (New York: Duell, Sloan & Pearce, 1944), pp. 85–96.

West, Jessamyn, "Horace Chooney, M.D.," in *The Writer's Art*, Wallace Stegner, Richard Snowcroft, and Boris Ilyin (eds.) (Boston: D. C. Heath & Company, 1950), pp. 325–343.

White, Paul W., *News on the Air* (New York: Harcourt, Brace & World, Inc., 1947).

Wilde, Percival, *The Craftsmanship of the One-Act Play* (Boston: Little, Brown and Company, 1931), p. 285.

Wylie, Max, *Radio Writing* (New York: Holt, Rinehart and Winston, Inc., 1939).

————, *Radio and Television Writing* (New York: Holt, Rinehart and Winston, Inc., 1950).

Index